UNDERSTANDING
ARGUMENTS
AN INTRODUCTION TO INFORMAL LOGIC

Second Edition

UNDERSTANDING ARGUMENTS

AN INTRODUCTION TO INFORMAL LOGIC

Second Edition

Robert J. Fogelin
Dartmouth College

HARCOURT BRACE JOVANOVICH, INC.
New York San Diego Chicago San Francisco Atlanta London Sydney Toronto

ISBN: 0-15-592858-9
Library of Congress Catalog Card Number: 81-85590

Printed in the United States of America

Illustrations by Eric G. Hieber, eh Technical Services

PREFACE

This book is about arguments. It considers arguments not in the narrow sense of quarrels or squabbles, but in the broader, logician's, sense of giving reasons in behalf of some claim. Viewing arguments in this way, we see that they are a common feature of daily life, for we are often involved in giving reasons or evaluating reasons given by others. These are not only common but important activities. Deciding what to believe, how to act, how to judge others, and the like are all, in the end, questions to be settled by weighing reasons. Traditionally, logic has been considered the most general science dealing with arguments.

For certain purposes, arguments are best studied as abstract patterns. Logic is not concerned with particular arguments—for example, your attempt to prove that the bank, not you, has made a mistake. The task of logic is to discover the fundamental principles for distinguishing good arguments from bad ones. The study of those general principles that make certain patterns of argument reasonable (or valid) and other patterns of argument unreasonable (or invalid) is called formal logic.

A different, but complementary, way of viewing an argument is to treat it as a *particular use of language:* arguing is one of the things that we do with words. This approach places stress upon arguing as a linguistic activity. Instead of studying arguments as abstract patterns, it takes them "in the rough," as they occur in actual argumentation. It raises questions of the following kind: What is the place of argument within language as a whole? In a given language (say, our own), what words or phrases are characteristic of arguments? What task or tasks are arguments supposed to perform? When an approach to arguments has this form, the study is called informal logic. As its subtitle indicates, *Understanding Arguments* is primarily a text in informal logic.

The second edition of the book has been influenced by my own teaching experiences with the first edition and by the helpful and generous comments received from other instructors. For example, somewhere between the first draft of the first edition and publication, one of the quality rules for the syllogism was lost. This omission was first pointed out to me very graciously by Linda Bell of Georgia State University. With this edition, the text as a whole has been changed in a number of substantial ways. The opening chapter has been divided into two chapters and expanded so that more emphasis could be given to Grice's theory of conversational implication. Two new sections on definitions have been added to the discussion of fallacies of clarity in Chapter 5. More significantly, two wholly new chapters have been added to Part One: Chapter 7, "Between Premise and Conclusion," and Chapter 8, "Fundamental Issues." In Chapter 7 procedures are presented for ascertaining the fundamental principles that lie, often unstated, at the bottom of a given argument. Chapter 8 applies these procedures to two important and emotionally charged areas of contemporary debate: capital punishment and the morality of abortion.

Major changes have been made in Part Two as well. Some dated material has been dropped and two new chapters have been added. Chapter 12, "Language and Contemporary Issues," presents Robin Lakoff's classic "Talking about Women." It also provides two illustrations of the way word choice influences the presentation of an argumentative position. Chapter 16, "Concerning Flim-Flam," offers two articles critical of the paranormal–UFO–astrological–Bermuda Triangle rhetoric that has captured so much of the public's imagination. Finally, in Chapter 17, which concerns philosophical arguments, I have changed the selections to A. M. Turing's "Computing Machines and Intelligence" and, in reply, Keith Gunderson's "The Imitation Game." I believe that all these changes make the material in Part Two more relevant and more accessible to students.

I am indebted to Patricia James of Kent State University and Josiah B. Gould of the State University of New York at Albany for their reviews. I also wish to thank Jacqueline Armstrong for help in proofreading galleys and Carolyn Johnson of Harcourt Brace Jovanovich and Florence Fogelin of *Plain English* for their splendid help throughout the writing of this second edition.

ROBERT J. FOGELIN

CONTENTS

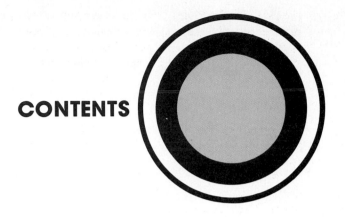

PREFACE   v

PART ONE
THE ANALYSIS OF ARGUMENT

1 THE WEB OF LANGUAGE   3
Language and Convention   4
Kinds of Conventions   6
Speech Acts   7
Performatives   9
   Promises 10/ Other Kinds of Performatives 11/ Authoritative Performatives 14/
   Argumentative Performatives 16/ Explicit Performatives 18
Statements   19
Summary   20

2 CONVERSATIONAL IMPLICATION   23
Things Left Unsaid   24
Conversational Implication   28
   Violating Conversational Rules 31

Pragmatics   33
Levels of Language   35

3   THE LANGUAGE OF ARGUMENT   37
The Basic Structure of Arguments   38
Arguments in Standard Form   40
Validity, Truth, and Soundness   40
Assuring, Hedging, and Discounting   45
      Assuring 45/   Hedging 46/   Discounting 47
Parentheticals   49
Argumentative Performatives   50
Substitutes for Arguments   50
      Slanting 51/   Slanting and Persuasive Definitions 52

4   THE ART OF CLOSE ANALYSIS   57
An Extended Example   58
      "Clerk Hire Allowance, House of Representatives" 58
Standpoints   74

5   FALLACIES OF CLARITY AND RELEVANCE   79
Clarity   80
      Vagueness 80/   Heaps and Slippery Slopes 83/   Where Do You Draw the Line? 85/
      Ambiguity   87/   Equivocation 90/   Definitions 90/   The Role of Definitions 92
Irrelevance   93
      Arguments ad Hominem 96/   Appeals to Authority 97

6   OTHER USES OF ARGUMENTS   103
Refutations   104
      That's Just Like Arguing . . . 105/   Counter-Examples 107/   Self-Sealers and
      Vacuity 113
Explanations   116
Excuses   121

7   BETWEEN PREMISE AND CONCLUSION   123
Suppressed Premises   124
You Can Draw Your Own Conclusions   132

8   FUNDAMENTAL ISSUES   137
Rock Bottom Disagreements   138
Capital Punishment   139
Abortion   144
      Weighing Factors 150

9 THE FORMAL ANALYSIS OF ARGUMENT: PART ONE 153
Validity and Formal Analysis of Argument 154
The Propositional Calculus 154
Conjunction 154/ Disjunction 159/ Negation 160/ How Truth Functional Connectives Work 160
Some Further Connectives 165
Conditionals 167
Logical Language and Everyday Language 173
Other Conditionals in Ordinary Language 176/ Summary 179

10 THE FORMAL ANALYSIS OF ARGUMENT: PART TWO 183
Categorical Propositions 184
Domain of Discourse 187
The Four Basic Propositions 188
Existential Import 189
The Classification of the Basic Propositions 191
Quality 192/ Quantity 192
The Square of Opposition 193
Contraries 193/ Contradictories 194/ Subcontraries 196/ Subalternation 197
Pragmatics and the Square of Opposition 198
The Theory of Immediate Inference 202
Conversion 202/ Obversion 205/ Contraposition 207
The Theory of the Syllogism 211
Valid and Invalid Syllogisms 213
Venn Diagrams for Syllogisms 213
Existential Import 216
Problems in Applying the Theory of the Syllogism 220
A System of Rules for Evaluating Syllogisms 221
Distribution 221/ Quality 222/ Quantity 223

PART TWO
SPECIMENS OF ARGUMENTS

11 AN ISSUE OF PUBLIC CONCERN 227
Safety in Nuclear Power Plants 228
"Incident at Brown's Ferry" (NOVA) 229

12 LANGUAGE AND CONTEMPORARY ISSUES 247
"Talking About Women," Robin T. Lakoff 248
"Protesters are 'Ugly, Stupid'," Jeffrey Hart 261
"A Record of Being Right," Ian Menzies 262

13 LEGAL REASONING   265

Analogy in Legal Reasoning   267
    "Hawkins v. McGee"   268
The Law of Torts   269
    "Palsgraf v. Long Island Railroad Co."   271
The Question of Constitutionality   277
    "Plessy v. Ferguson"   278
    "Brown v. Board of Education"   285

14 A MORAL DEBATE   289

The Question of Abortion   290
    "A Defense of Abortion," Judith Jarvis Thomson   291
    "Abortion and the Sanctity of Human Life," Baruch A.
        Brody   305

15 SCIENTIFIC ARGUMENTS   317

The Law of Buoyancy   317
    "On Floating Bodies," Archimedes   318
Conflicting Scientific Interpretations   323
    "Dialogue Concerning the Two World Systems—Ptolemaic
        and Copernican," Galileo Galilei   324
The Orgone Theory of Wilhelm Reich   332
    "The Objective Demonstration of Orgone Radiation,"
        Wilhelm Reich   332

16 CONCERNING FLIM-FLAM   339

" 'Cold Reading': How to Convince Strangers that You Know
        All About Them," Ray Hyman   340
"Critical Reading, Careful Writing, and the Bermuda Triangle,"
        Larry Kusche   354

17 PHILOSOPHICAL ARGUMENTS   359

"Computing Machinery and Intelligence," A. M. Turing   360
"The Imitation Game," Keith Gunderson   381

APPENDIX   395

"Performative Utterances," J. L. Austin   395
"Logic and Conversation," H. P. Grice   407

INDEX   425

For Eric, John, and Lars

An argument isn't just contradiction.

Can be.

No it can't. An argument is a connected series of statements intended to establish a proposition.

No it isn't.

Yes it is.

Argument Clinic,
From MONTY PYTHON'S PREVIOUS RECORD

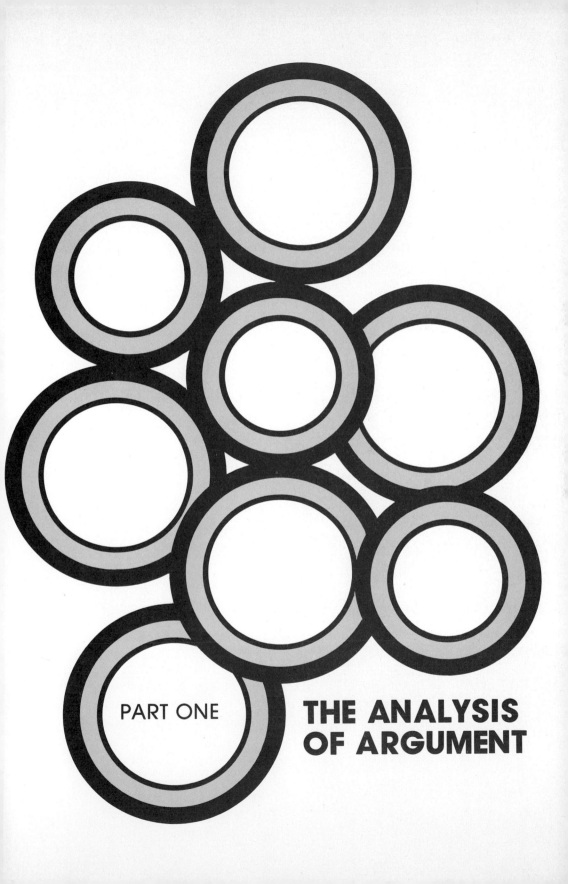

PART ONE

THE ANALYSIS OF ARGUMENT

THE WEB OF LANGUAGE  1

As an introduction to our study of informal logic, this chapter will survey the general nature of language. In doing so, it will stress two main ideas. First, language is <u>conventional</u>. Words take on their meanings within a rich system of linguistic customs. In order to understand the nature of language, we must go beyond the spoken and written symbols to the conventions that give them meaning. Second, language is <u>diverse</u>. We sometimes use it to communicate information, but we also use it to ask questions, issue orders, write poetry, keep score, and perform an almost endless number of functions. Methods will be presented here for discovering and analyzing these different uses of language.

Language and Convention

Language is conventional: it is governed by a complicated network of shared norms. Some of the conventions of language are obvious at first glance. There seems to be no reason why we, as English speakers, use the word "dog" to refer to dogs rather than to cats, trees, or anything at all. Any word might have been used to stand for anything. Beyond this, there seems to be no reason why we put words together in the way that we do. In English we put adjectives before the nouns they modify. We thus speak of a *green salad.* In French adjectives usually follow the noun, and so instead of saying *verte salade* the French say *salade verte.* The conventions of our own language are so much with us that it strikes us as odd when we discover that other languages have different conventions. A French diplomat once praised his own language because, as he said, it followed the natural order of thought. This strikes us English speakers as silly, but in seeing what is silly about it, we see that the word order in our own language is conventional as well.

It is important to realize that our language is conventional, but it is also important not to misunderstand this fact. From the idea that language is conventional, it is easy to conclude that language is *arbitrary,* so that it really doesn't matter which words we use. It takes only a little thought to see that this is not true. If I wish to communicate with others I must follow the system of conventions that others use. To put matters simply, conventions do not destroy meaning by making it arbitrary; conventions bring meaning into existence.

A misunderstanding of the conventions of language can lead to pointless disputes. Sometimes, in the middle of a discussion, someone will declare that "the whole thing is just a matter of definition." Now there are times when definitions are important and arguments turn upon them, but in general this is not true. Suppose someone has fallen off a cliff and is heading toward certain death on the rocks below. Of course, it is a matter of definition (of convention) that we use the word "death" to describe the result of the sudden stop at the end of the fall. We might have used some other word—perhaps "birth"—instead. But it certainly will not help the person who is falling to change the meaning of the word "death" in the middle of his plunge. It will do no good for him to yell out, "By death I mean birth." It will not help even if *everyone* agrees to change the meaning of the words in this way. If we all decided to adopt this new convention, we would then say, "He fell from the cliff to his birth" instead of "He fell from the cliff to his death." But speaking in this way will not change the facts. It will not, for example, make those who care for him feel better.

The upshot of this simple example is that the truth of what we say is rarely just a matter of definition. The words we use are governed by conventions, and in the process of learning our language we learn to follow these conventions in speaking. (Only later do we develop some understanding of these conventions.) We then go on to make certain claims about the world. Others can understand what we say because we follow the ordinary conventions that give meaning to our words. Whether what I have said is true or not will depend, for the most part, on how things stand in the world. For example, if a German wishes to say that snow is black, then he will use the words "Schnee ist schwartz." Other Germans will *understand* his words, but unless snow is different in Germany than every place else, they will also think that he has said something false, and may wonder how he could make such a mistake. In general, then, the truth of what we say is not merely a matter of definition or convention, and when someone uses this ploy in the middle of an argument we can usually assume that he or she is in desperate shape.

In the last sentence I have used two qualifying phrases: "in general" and "usually." To say that something holds in general, or usually, is to admit that there may be exceptions. Such a qualification is needed in this case because *sometimes* the truth of what we say is simply a matter of definition. Take a simple example. The claim that a triangle has three sides is true by definition, because a triangle is defined as "a three-sided closed plane figure." Again, if someone says that sin is wrong, he has said something that is true by definition, for a sin is defined as, among other things, "something that is wrong."

Consider a more complicated case. Suppose someone argues that the only true democracies exist in communist states. He admits that in such states there are no general elections where a large portion of the population is allowed to choose between competing parties, but he goes on to say that a genuine democracy exists only when the party in power reflects the interests of the masses. Here we might challenge the definition of a democracy that he is using and then be met by the following reply: Why should everyone in the world be bound by the capitalist definition of a democracy? Alternatively, we can accept his definition and argue that communist parties do not reflect the interests of the masses. We might then be told that no democracy is perfect, especially those in newly emerging nations. Here the only way to stop our heads from swimming is to return to common sense and reject both the definition and the facts. Historically, in a democracy the people *choose* the policies that govern them, or at least the representatives who formulate these policies. When this choice is absent, democracy does not exist. A despotism, however benevolent, is not a democracy. We should advise our opponent to be candid enough to admit that he is against a democracy and, if he is in favor of another form of government, to give it another name and defend it on its own terms. If he is misrepresenting the facts, we can say that too. In short, we need not be driven to silence by a person who distorts the meaning of words and tampers with the facts. We can simply point out that he is distorting and tampering.

Sometimes, then, it is important to ask a person to define his terms.

We should do this whenever we think that someone is distorting the meaning of words to win an argumentative point. We can also ask for a definition in order to clarify, if we think that someone is speaking in a vague and loose way. But it makes no sense to ask that *every* word be defined. This would prove an endless task and we would never get around to saying anything in particular. Beyond this, asking for definitions is often just silly. If someone says "Pass the butter," it does not usually cross our minds to ask him to define "butter."

In sum, people are able to communicate with each other because they share certain linguistic conventions. These conventions could have been very different and in this sense they are arbitrary. But it does not follow from this that the truth of what we say is also merely arbitrary. In general, the truth of what we say is settled not by an appeal to definition, but by a look at the facts. Sometimes, however, the conventions of our language are misused or even abused. Here it makes sense to call for definition in order to restore mutual understanding. It would be absurd to ask that every word be defined.

Kinds of Conventions

In the previous section we saw that a language is a system of shared conventions that allows us to communicate with one another. If we pause to look at language, we see that it contains many different kinds of conventions. We have seen that words have meanings conventionally attached to them. The word "dog" is used conventionally to talk about dogs. Proper names are also conventionally assigned, for Harry Jones could have been named Wilbur Jones. (There are, of course, social limits involved in giving meanings to words. You cannot name your son John D. Rockefeller unless you happen to be named Rockefeller. But setting aside limitations of this kind and others the assignment of meanings to words is conventional.)

Other conventions concern the way in which words can be put together to form sentences. These are often called *grammatical* rules. Using the three words "John," "hit," and "Harry," we can formulate sentences with very different meanings. For example, "John hit Harry" and "Harry hit John." We recognize that these sentences have different meanings because we understand the grammar of our language. This grammatical understanding also allows us to see that the sentence "Hit John Harry" does not mean anything at all—even though the individual words possess meaning. (Notice that "Hit John, Harry!" does mean something: it is a way of telling Harry to hit John.) Grammatical rules are very important, for they play a part in giving a meaning to a sentence as a whole. Admittedly, some of our grammatical rules play only a small role in this important task because they are largely stylistic. If I say "Hopefully he will be here tomorrow," I have uttered an ugly and ungrammatical sentence, yet I still make sense. If I violate deeper and more fundamental grammatical rules, I speak nonsense. It is worth noting, however, that some grammatical rules which seem only stylistic at first sight do make important contributions to the meaning of a sentence. The subjunctive mood is an example.

There are, then, at least two kinds of conventions that give meaning to what we say. The ones that assign meanings to individual words are commonly called *semantic* conventions. The conventions that lay down rules for combining words into meaningful wholes are called grammatical or *syntactical* conventions. The study of semantic conventions and syntactical conventions is largely the job of linguistics. Although important advances have been made in this field, every linguist will acknowledge that the amount unknown far outweighs the amount known. For this reason, linguistics is one of the most exciting fields of scientific investigation.

Later on we shall look more closely at semantic and syntactical conventions, for at times they are a source of fallacies and other confusions. In particular, we shall see how these conventions can generate *fallacies of ambiguity*. But before we examine the defects of our language, we should first appreciate that language is a powerful and subtle tool. We will next examine the wide variety of jobs that language can perform.

Speech Acts

When asked about the function of language, it is natural to reply that we use language to communicate our ideas. But this is only *one* of its uses. This becomes obvious as soon as we set aside our prejudices and take a look at the way our language actually works. Adding up a column of figures is a linguistic activity, but it does not communicate any ideas to others. When I add the figures I am not even trying to communicate anything to myself; I am trying to figure something out.

Writing a poem is a more interesting example. Sometimes poems convey factual information, and at other times they express philosophical truths. Poems also express emotions. Yet often the most important fact about a poem is that it is an artistic creation in the same way that a painting or a sculpture is an artistic creation. A poem is a linguistic artifact. We get a bad theory of poetry, and may even lessen our appreciation of poetry, if we think of a poem as a mere device for conveying the poet's thoughts and emotions to others. Consider one example:

Upon Julia's Clothes
ROBERT HERRICK

Whenas in silks my Julia goes,
Then, then, methinks, how sweetly flows
The liquefaction of her clothes.

Next when I cast mine eyes, and see
That brave vibration each way free,
O, how that glittering taketh me!

Using a modern idiom, Herrick might have said "Julia's terrific figure turns me on." This second way of speaking leaves little doubt about what Herrick thinks and how he feels about Julia. The poem, by comparison, may fail to some extent in communication, but the chief difference lies elsewhere. Herrick's emotions are, after all, fairly common. His mode of expressing them, however, produces one of the most perfect poems in the English language. A poem is not simply a news broadcast with fancy frills.

Poetry provides an example of language used for purposes other than communication, but beyond that it is a complicated linguistic phenomenon that defies easy analysis. A look at our everyday conversations produces a host of other examples of language being used for different purposes. Grammarians, for example, have divided sentences into various moods:

(1) Indicative

(2) Interrogative

(3) Imperative

(4) Expressive (and some others)

For example:

(1) He is in England now that spring is here.

(2) Is he in England now that spring is here?

(3) Go to England now that spring is here!

(4) Oh to be in England, now that spring is here!!

The first sentence states a fact; we can use it to communicate information about a person's location. If we use it in this way, what we say will be either true or false. Notice that none of the other sentences can be called either true or false.

People who insist that language is always used to communicate information might try to defend their position in the following way: In asking a question, a person communicates a desire to know something. This explanation is often just wrong. When teachers ask questions on examinations, they are not communicating the desire to know the answers; presumably they know the answers already. An attempt might be made to patch up the argument by saying that the teacher is communicating the desire to know whether the *students* know the answers to the questions. This, however, is *not* what he is asking. An examination question looks like this: "Did Lincoln rely heavily on his cabinet in formulating war policy?" not like this: "Do you know whether Lincoln relied heavily on his cabinet in formulating war policy?" It would be hard to fail an examination made up of questions of the second kind.

Someone might try other ways of showing that asking a question is really a way of communicating information, but the arguments will become more and more complicated and arbitrary. This itself is a sign that one is looking at things in the wrong way. The philosopher J. L. Austin has introduced the notion of what he called the *descriptive fallacy*,[1] the mistake of taking the simple indicative sentences used to state facts as the model for all uses of language. Stating facts is one of the important things we do with language, but it is not the only thing—nor even the only important thing—that we do with language. When pointed out, this idea may seem pretty obvious—hardly worth making a fuss over—but its consequences for the philosophy of language have been profound.

Performatives

We have already noticed that grammarians have traditionally classified sentences into different moods (indicative, interrogative, imperative, expressive, etc.) and thereby recognized that sentences can perform different jobs. This classification, though helpful, gives only a slight indication of the vast number of things done with words. Even sentences in the indicative are a mixed batch, for not every sentence in the indicative is used to state a fact. This was emphasized by Austin, who noticed that some indicatives express what he called *performatives*. Two examples, verdicts and promises, will help explain this notion.

Verdicts At the close of a hearing, the appellate judge announces: "The judgment of the superior court is affirmed." This is an important announcement for the parties involved, but it does not state a fact. One party may think that the verdict is incorrect, but he cannot say that it is false. It would make no sense for him to stand up and say, "Your honor, you are not telling the truth; you do *not* affirm the judgment of the superior court." The judge may be thought wrong to have rendered this decision, but there is no question that he has rendered it. Furthermore, and this is important, he renders the verdict by saying the words, "The judgment of the superior court is affirmed." It is this *speech act* on the part of the judge that *makes* this so.

Baseball umpires also pass verdicts. The following story is told of the old-time umpire Bill Klem. On a close play, a runner came sliding

---

[1] J. L. Austin, "Performative Utterances," in J. O. Urmson and G. J. Warnock, eds., *Philosophical Papers*, 2nd ed. (Oxford: Clarendon Press, 1970), p. 234. Reprinted in the Appendix to this book, pp. 395 ff.

into second base. For a moment Klem said nothing. When the runner asked whether he was safe or out, Klem replied, "You ain't nothin' 'til I say so." Klem was right. Whether the runner is safe or out awaits the decision of the umpire. Of course, the umpire is guided by certain complicated rules in calling a runner safe or out. If the runner is tagged before he reaches the base (and the ball is not dropped, etc.), then the umpire is *supposed* to call him out. Yet if the umpire calls him safe (and doesn't change his mind), the runner *is* safe. He becomes safe when the umpire utters the words "You're safe" (and doesn't take this back). The runner "ain't nothin' " till the umpire says so and then he is what the umpire says he is.

These two cases of verdicts show some obvious features of performatives. Although they are formulated in the indicative, they do not *describe* the situation at hand and thus cannot misdescribe it either. When the umpire makes a bad call, he does not say something that is false, even if his call is based upon a false belief—for example, that the second baseman missed the tag. Beyond this, the performative utterance brings about a change in the game. If the player is called safe, he may remain on second base; if he is called out, he is obliged to leave the field and an out is chalked up against his team.

Promises If I say to someone, "I promise to help you if you get in trouble," I place myself in a new relationship to that person. I now have an *obligation* to help him if, in fact, he does get in trouble. In many cases I would have no obligation at all had I not spoken these words. If I had said instead, "Look, if you get into trouble, don't come around asking for my help," then I would have indicated that I would take no responsibility for helping him. In contrast, the promise binds, for if I break my promise he has a *right* to blame me. Again, when I promise, I am not describing anything—not even my own intentions. I can make a promise with no intention of keeping it, although then I will have been dishonest. All the same, I will have made a promise. If I break a promise it does not help to say, "It seems that I have made a bad guess about what I was going to do." In promising, I am not just predicting what I will do; I am committing myself to doing it. The commitment comes about through uttering certain words *in certain contexts.*

The reference to *context* introduces another important theme: the effect of settings on performatives. If someone forces me to make a promise by twisting my arm nearly to the breaking point, the promise is not binding. I am under no obligation to keep this promise because it was given under duress. I haven't really promised at all. But not all performatives are void when exacted from us. In a schoolyard brawl, pounding my head on the ground, my opponent demands that I *give up.* Or, somewhat strangely, he demands that I say "Uncle." Saying "I give up" or "Uncle" is a way of surrendering or acknowledging defeat and it is a performative utterance that is typically forced out of us. Notice that if I say "I give up," I am not supposed to resume the fight when my opponent lets me up, nor—in civilized schoolyards at least—has my opponent the right to go on pummelling me. By saying "I give up," I change the relationship between us.

Other Kinds of Performatives Performative utterances are interesting first because they help to break the spell of the descriptive fallacy; they help us to see that we do a great many other important things with language besides reporting facts. Beyond this, they draw attention to a whole range of linguistic conventions which, until recent years, have largely gone unnoticed. A whole new world opens up when we ask how many kinds of performative utterances there are and what the *conventions* are that govern them. This is an area that you can explore on your own, and it's fun.

How many kinds of performative utterances are there? We can use what I shall call the *thereby test* as a rough-and-ready way of finding performative utterances. It works best for statements in the first person. Here are some examples of this test:

If I say "I promise to meet you tomorrow," I thereby promise to meet you tomorrow.

If I say "I bid five clubs," I thereby bid five clubs.

If I say "I surrender," I thereby surrender.

If I say "I apologize," I thereby apologize.

If I (as a minister) say "I pronounce you husband and wife," I thereby pronounce the couple husband and wife.

Here it seems that *saying* something amounts to *doing* it. The situation is quite different with statements of fact. If I say "I am six feet tall," I am not thereby six feet tall. If I say "Munich is the capital of Germany," Munich is not thereby the capital of Germany. (On the other hand, an absolute monarch of Germany might declare that Munich is the capital and thereby make it so.) The thereby test will turn up a great number of performative utterances, especially if we imagine ourselves playing various roles.

But now we must remind ourselves that performatives take place only in special contextual settings. We have already noticed that if a person is *forced* to say "I promise," he is not usually said to have really promised. A more obvious example is the person who "promises" to do something when talking in his sleep. Again, if a person is led to promise something on the basis of fraudulent information, he will probably not be held to the promise. (Issues of this kind arise in the Law of Contracts, for signing a contract is another example of a performative act.) Promising is an act governed by conventions, and if we want to know the nature of promising we must look to the conventions that govern it.

We can again use baseball umpiring to make some obvious points.

Suppose the *shortstop* shouted "You're out!" This would be a very odd thing for him to say, unless perhaps he were trying to confuse the runner. It would certainly annoy umpire Klem. Sometimes, then, only a certain *official* can make a performative utterance; if it is made by someone else, it has no effect. The average citizen cannot pronounce a couple husband and wife. A spectator cannot raise objections in a courtroom. A janitor cannot pronounce a patient dead on arrival at the hospital even if he can tell, as well as anyone else, that the patient is dead. The *first* thing we might ask about a particular performative, then, is whether the right to use the performative is assigned only to a particular official—for example, a judge, minister, justice of the peace, umpire, or coronor. Sometimes such a convention exists; sometimes it does not. I do not have to have an official position to make a promise or offer apologies—although there is such a thing as offering *official* apologies, which cannot be done by just anyone.

In trying to discover the conventions that govern our language, it helps to give the imagination free play and really think of lunatic examples. There is a good reason for this. Our conventions are so much with us that it often takes extreme measures to bring them to the surface. As the runner slides into second base, the base umpire shouts "Strike two!" Here the right person makes the call, but there simply is no convention for calling strikes on anyone but a batter. If an umpire speaks in this way, we might think that he is making a joke, has gone mad, or is seeking early retirement. The example brings out another important point. The umpire is in charge, but *his powers are limited by the conventions that define his role.* More strongly, his actions make sense only in terms of these conventions. An umpire can call a strike on a batter, but *there is no such thing* as calling a strike on a base runner.

Of course, most departures from convention are not this extreme, for we rarely invoke conventions that do not exist. (It can happen, though. A person may attempt to plead justifiable homicide in a court where such a plea is not allowed.) Usually our departures from convention involve only the kind of thing that Austin called *hitches* and *flaws.* In a hitch, things have not been carried out completely; a loophole has been left open. With a flaw, things are not done quite correctly. With contracts, a hitch or a flaw can make the contract *void* —that is, not legally binding. Some contracts are void if they are not properly notarized and witnessed. (But the law is complicated on these matters and is not as narrowly legalistic as many lay persons suppose.) Hitches and flaws also arise in everyday life. If someone uses the performative utterance, "I bet five dollars that the Yankees win today," I cannot remain silent and then expect to collect the bet if the Yankees lose. The bet is not completed unless I say "Done," or "You're on," or shake hands. The bet may also be off if the terms are not spelled out clearly. People do not make bets of the following kind: "I bet five dollars that the Yankees don't do too badly today." Such a bet would leave open too many possibilities for disagreement on who has won. Acceptance of the wager and spelling out its terms are among many features that form the conventional background of making a bet.

Most performative utterances also presuppose a background of accepted *facts*. It would be senseless for me to walk in and surrender myself to the police, if no one supposes that I have committed a crime. The police would not know what to make of my "surrender." They might lock me up, but for quite a different reason. Apologizing is an interesting case. I cannot apologize for something unless it is generally believed that I have done something wrong, for in apologizing I *acknowledge* that I have done something wrong. Beyond this, I am expected to feel sorry for what I have done and to have no intention of doing it again. Imagine an apology of the following kind: "I don't think I have done anything wrong, I do not feel a bit sorry for what I have done, and given half a chance I'd do it again, but I apologize." Such an apology is quite *empty*, and would not be treated as an apology at all. Apologizing is a complicated linguistic act, governed by conventions and presupposing certain facts. In order to understand this underlying structure, it is best to think of cases where an apology fails for one reason or another.

As a simple model for analyzing performative utterances, we can ask the following questions:

(1) Does a person have to have some official position in order to perform the speech act?

(2) Are there any special words or formulas associated with the speech act?

(3) What facts are presupposed in the use of the speech act?

(4) What feelings (if any) are assumed?

(5) Is any response or uptake needed to complete the speech act?

(6) More generally, what social function does this performative serve?

Answers to these questions might be: (1) In order to pronounce a couple married, one must be a minister, a justice of the peace, a ship's captain, etc. (2) In bidding five clubs, you are expected to use the words "Five clubs." (3) Surrendering to the police presupposes that you have violated some law—or at least are *thought* to have done so. (4) When you congratulate someone, you are assumed to be pleased with his or her success. (5) A bet has not been made unless someone has accepted it. (6) The institution of promise-making exists because, in order for cooperation to exist, one human being must be able to rely on another to do what he says he will do. Through making a promise, a person not only expresses an intention to do something but also accepts an *obligation* to do it. Either through a fear of criticism or a desire to be moral, this obligation will help ensure that the person will do what he says he will do. The question of social function is not always easy to answer.

So far we have noticed that a performative utterance can *do* something in the sense of bringing about a new relationship in a context. When an umpire calls a runner out, the runner's position in the game is thereby changed. When someone makes a promise, he thereby undertakes an obligation to do something. Sometimes it is important that some exact formula is used; the exact wording of a judge's verdict is often crucial. In some cases, the use of a performative utterance is the *only* way to do a certain thing. This, however, is not always true. Sometimes what I say will amount to a promise even if I do not use the words "I promise." This leads to another important feature of performative utterances. In some contexts it is not clear what I am trying to do with the words I use. It may, for example, be unclear whether I am promising that I will do something, or merely stating that in all likelihood I will do it. Here I can use the explicit formula "I promise . . ." in order to *clarify* the force of my remarks. After I say "I promise . . . ," it is no longer in doubt that I have, in fact, promised.

Authoritative Performatives The notion that performatives make our linguistic moves more *explicit* comes out also in another area of everyday life. Consider the naked imperative, "Close the door." In using this imperative I may be doing a number of things—issuing an order, making a command, making a request, offering advice, asking a favor, giving a suggestion, begging a favor. People are very sensitive about being told what to do—being bossed around—and for this reason we rarely use simple imperatives in polite conversation. We often put a "please" in front of our imperatives. More interestingly, we sometimes drop the imperative mood altogether and speak in the form of questions: "Could you close the door?" or "Do you mind closing the door?" Later on we shall see why it is often appropriate to use a question in place of an imperative, but first we can examine how performatives function in this area.

Although the name is far from perfect, we shall here speak of *authoritative performatives.* An authoritative performative clarifies the authoritative relationship between the person issuing an imperative and one who is subject to it. It is a sign of our sensitivity in this area that we have so many such performatives marking out very subtle distinctions. The most obvious example of a performative in this field is a command:

If I say "I command you to go," I thereby command you to go.

But not everyone can issue a command. I cannot command a passerby to give me change for a dollar. Commands typically involve a relationship between a *superior* and a *subordinate.* A general can issue commands. Traditionally, God has been said to issue commands. Of course, a general does not have to use the formula "I command . . ." in order to issue a command. If he shouts "Charge!" that will count as a command and those soldiers who do not charge will be disobeying his command. Yet even generals sometimes direct people's actions without commanding them to do things. Thus, sometimes explicit clarification is necessary, as in the following contrasting remarks:

> "Young man, I am not ordering you to end your investigations, I am simply giving you a piece of good advice."

> "Young man, I am not advising you to stop your investigation, I am ordering you to do so."

Obviously, these two remarks have a very different force.

In the last example, we have shifted from talking about commands to talking about orders. A superior cannot only command a subordinate to do something, he can also order him to do something. The notions are different. I can *order* a person off my land, but it would sound odd if I said that I *commanded* him to leave my land. I can order him to leave my land because I have a *right* to keep people off my land, but they are really not my subordinates. In fact, however, we rarely go around issuing orders. Instead, we *ask* people to do things. Suppose we ask someone to leave our land and he doesn't. We can imagine how the conversation might continue:

> Look, I've asked you nicely to leave my land; now I'm ordering you to leave. If you don't leave, I shall call the police and have you charged with trespassing.

That I am in a position to call the police explains, in part at least, why I am in a position to issue an order.

Asking is weaker than ordering, but there are certain things that we do not even have a right to ask. (Think of some contexts in which people say, "You have no right to ask that.") It would be very odd for me to ask someone to leave *his* land. I might *advise* someone to leave his land, perhaps because it is about to be overwhelmed by an avalanche. Weaker still, I might *suggest* that he leave his land, thereby minimizing the extent that I am butting into his business and telling him what to do. There are other examples: I can also *beg* someone to do something, and here the authoritative relationship is completely reversed.

We have thus discovered a broad spectrum of authoritative performatives present in our language. (Other languages contain such expressions as well, although the match is not always exact.) Spread out on a printed page this way, these distinctions may seem trivial, but in everyday life we respond to them, sometimes quite violently. We have all heard remarks of the following kind:

I do not mind helping you, but I won't be ordered around.

What right do *you* have to tell *me* what to do?

I think that I have had enough of your advice for one day.

Authoritative performatives provide subtle mechanisms for making adjustments in a sensitive area.

It is time to introduce some important qualifications. The force of a performative comes under many contextual influences. Performatives are highly sensitive to context. A "suggestion" uttered in a sinister tone of voice can have the force of an order—especially if the person making the suggestion is carrying a machine gun. A piece of "friendly advice" can be a threat. Social relations make an obvious difference. It matters who is speaking and to whom. Beyond this, our everyday talk often involves a subtle play upon these background conventions. This often comes out as irony and understatement. We shall come back to these devices when we examine actual arguments later on, for they often make a great deal of difference. For the moment, we will set these features of language aside in order not to consider too many things at once. There is still more to say about performatives.

Argumentative Performatives The performatives we have examined thus far concern either interpersonal relations or the relationships between persons and institutions. We can now look at a different kind of performative, which Austin called *expositives*.[2] We will call them *argumentative performatives*. Here are some examples, using the *thereby test:*

If I say, "I deny the charge," I thereby deny the charge.

If I say, "I claim he's lying," I thereby claim he is lying.

If I say, "I concede the point," I thereby concede the point.

If I say, "I allow such and such," I thereby allow such and such.

If I say, "I conclude that such and such," I thereby conclude that such and such.

If I say, "I stipulate that such and such," I thereby stipulate that such and such.

These performatives are obviously concerned with arguments. In particular, they are used to *make moves* in arguments. Furthermore, they are not statements about arguments, since they are not even statements. If the lawyer finishes his speech to the jury by saying, "I conclude that the

---

[2] J. L. Austin, *How to Do Things with Words* (New York: Oxford University Press, 1965), pp. 160 ff.

evidence merits acquittal," it makes no sense for someone to say, "No you don't!" We may disagree that the evidence merits acquittal and go on to challenge this, but we cannot disagree that the lawyer has drawn this conclusion.

There are other argumentative moves that are not expressed as performatives. I can challenge someone's claim by saying "I doubt that," but "I doubt that" does *not* express a performative. This is shown by applying the thereby test. If I say "I doubt that" I do not thereby doubt it. Whether I doubt something or not is a fact about me. There are some interesting intermediate cases that change with contexts. Sometimes if I say that I agree I do not *thereby* agree, for again, whether I agree or not is typically considered a fact about me. But in other contexts, saying that I agree amounts to entering into or making an agreement. Here the utterance is performative. Usually "I agree to . . ." is a performative, whereas "I agree that . . ." is not. In a court of law, however, saying "I agree that . . ." is often performative. It is one way of stipulating facts that will not be contested, and by it I waive my right to contest certain facts later on.

Why does our language contain argumentative performatives? What useful purpose do they serve? We have already noticed that argumentative performatives allow us to make moves *in* an argument. By saying "I conclude . . . ," I draw a conclusion. By saying "I acknowledge what has been said," I thereby acknowledge what has been said. Yet our language provides other means for making argumentative moves. We can mark a conclusion by using a word like "therefore." I can say something like this: "It has been shown that my client was in Detroit on the night in question, therefore he could not have committed this crime." Here I draw a conclusion without using the phrase "I conclude." Again, I can disagree with someone by saying "That's not so" or by saying the opposite of what he has said. In fact, we can imagine a society where arguments are carried out *without* the use of argumentative performatives. They would simply use words like "therefore" instead of phrases like "I conclude."

So the question remains: Why do we have argumentative performatives at all? Part of the answer is that argumentative performatives make our argumentative moves explicit. If I want to make it perfectly clear that I am concluding something, I can signal this by saying "I conclude. . . ." I will probably reserve this expression for the *final* conclusion, thus leaving little doubt what the argument is intended to show. At other times during an argument it is important not only to disagree but also to make it clear that we are disagreeing. In this way we point explicitly to the part of our opponent's argument we wish to reject. We usually reserve argumentative performatives for the *important* parts of opposing arguments.

Performatives also allow *subtle* moves to be made in the course of an argument. Sometimes an arguer will say, "I grant the point for the sake of argument" (thereby granting the point for the sake of argument). This is a powerful move if it can be carried off, for nothing is better than refuting an opponent on his own grounds. This device also contains an escape hatch, for if our efforts go badly, we can still challenge the statement previously granted just for the sake of argument. Somewhat differently, we can say, "I reserve comment" (thereby reserving comment). Here we neither reject a claim nor accept it (even for the sake of argument); we let it pass until we see what is made of it. This is a useful tactical device. If we are arguing from a strong position, it is a good idea to keep the line of the argument clean. By reserving comment we can avoid being drawn into irrelevant discussions that will cloud the issue. At other times we do not know what we want to say in response to a particular point or we are not quite sure what the person is going to make of it. Reserving comment is a way of not sticking our necks out prematurely. Argumentative performatives are, then, powerful and subtle tools for making moves in an argument.

Explicit Performatives To give the discussion more order, I shall single out one kind of performative for special consideration. Austin called them *explicit performatives*. Explicit performatives are always in the first person, present tense, and they satisfy the thereby test *exactly:*

If I say, "I promise. . . ," I thereby promise. . . .

If I say, "I resign," I thereby resign.

The form of this test is itself useful. The verb that appears first inside the quotation marks and then outside of them identifies a kind of speech act—here, *promising* and *resigning*. We assume that all the background conditions are in order, and where necessary we play the role of the required official. I cannot marry couples, yet assuming the role of a minister I can still use the thereby test:

If I say, "I pronounce you husband and wife," I thereby pronounce you husband and wife.

In contrast to these last examples, the umpire does not utter an *explicit* performative when he says, "You're out." Assuming the role of an umpire, I apply the thereby test in this way:

If I say, "You're out," you are thereby out.

The expression "You're out" passes the thereby test; but it is not in the first person, and no verb appears that will serve as the name for the speech act. In contrast, "I call you out," though a bit odd sounding, is an explicit performative. We turn to explicit performatives because they serve an important theoretical purpose: they are a useful tool in discovering different kinds of speech acts.[3]

Statements

Since we have dwelled on the fact that language is used for a great many purposes besides asserting something that is either true or false, we can now discuss this use of language without suggesting that it is the sole use or even the most important use of language. When we use language to assert something that is either true or false, we are making a *statement*. It is in saying something that is either true or false that statements differ from imperatives, questions, performatives, exclamations, and other uses of language.

First we should notice that there is a whole family of activities included in "saying something that is either true or false." *Describing* is one such activity, and it has special features of its own. I can describe a building by giving a list of its most important features. Descriptions are not only true or false, but good or bad, rough or accurate, detailed or sketchy, etc. These special terms used in criticizing a description give us a good idea of the nature of this kind of speech act.

Another use of a statement is to give an *example:*

Seven is a prime number.

Here I do not start with the number seven and go on to describe it, for I could have picked some other number, say, three, as my example.

We can get a feel for the many functions performed by statements by noticing that they can be used to answer different kinds of questions. Here are some examples:

Describing:

What is the sparrow like?

---

[3] This definition of explicit performatives is not perfect. It lets in things we want to exclude. Here is one curious example:

If I say, "I speak English," I thereby speak English.

Although it is hard to get clear about this, *speaking English* does not seem to be a speech act in the same way that making a promise is. They are not on the same *level*. We will come back to the idea of levels in a moment. At this point we face a choice that comes up in every investigation. We can make our definition of an explicit performative more precise and thus pile up complications, or we can keep our definition simple and put up with some bad results. Where to strike the balance between simplicity and accuracy is always a difficult problem that must be settled by practical considerations. For our present purposes, clarity and simplicity seem most important, so we shall accept a definition of an explicit performative that we know is not quite right.

He's a little bird who owned a golden arrow and killed cock robin with it.

Ascribing:

Who killed cock robin?

The sparrow killed cock robin.

Giving an example:

Give me an example of a murderer.

The sparrow who killed cock robin.

Classifying:

What crime did the sparrow commit?

The sparrow committed first-degree murder.

If you think of more questions, you will uncover more speech acts that make a statement. Statements are, then, a whole family of speech acts.[4]

Summary

It may be helpful to summarize the terms introduced in this discussion:

A *speech act* is a use of language to make a significant move within a language game.

Performatives are one important kind of speech act—roughly, they are speech acts in which the saying of something constitutes the doing of it.

Explicit performatives are performatives of a special kind: they are in the first person (non-continuous) present and they meet the thereby test. (In saying "I ø," I thereby ø.) Explicit performatives are often used to make the nature of a speech act clear. For this reason they can serve as a guide in discovering different kinds of speech acts.

Thus, as the following chart indicates, explicit performatives are a subclass of performatives, and performatives themselves are one kind of speech act.

---

[4] This issue is explored in detail in J. L. Austin, "How to Talk: Some Simple Ways," in Urmson and Warnock, *Philosophical Papers*, pp. 134–53.

Speech Acts

Examples: 1. It's about five feet high.
2. Get out!
3. The gun was behind the radio.

Performatives

Examples: 4. Four clubs.
5. Helen.

Explicit Performatives

Examples: 1'. I estimate that it is about five feet high.
2'. I urge you to get out.
3'. I swear that the gun was behind the radio.
4'. I bid four clubs.
5'. I pick Helen.

Notice that the explicit performatives 1' through 5' make clear the nature of the speech acts expressed in sentences 1 through 5. Sentence 3', for example, indicates that the information in sentence 3 is being sworn to rather than being put forward, say, as a mere guess.

Exercise 1: Using a good-sized college dictionary as your source, use the thereby test to discover ten verbs that can be used to formulate explicit performatives.

Exercise 2: Consider the following performative utterances:
   (a) "I give you permission to leave."
   (b) "I claim this land in the name of Queen Victoria."
   (c) "I confer upon you the degree of Bachelor of Arts with all the rights and privileges appertaining thereto."

For each example, answer the six basic questions about performatives given on page 13. It is important to start with the most obvious facts and then trace things out in detail.

Exercise 3: Repeat Exercise 2 for five performative utterances you have discovered in doing Exercise 1.

Exercise 4: Speech acts that are superficially similar often reveal important differences when examined in detail. To see this, give a speech act analysis of the following performatives and then point out any underlying differences that distinguish them:

    (a) "I quit."

    (b) "I resign."

    (c) "I surrender."

CONVERSATIONAL IMPLICATION

2

This chapter will discuss the pragmatic rules that govern our use of language and the conversational implications that this system of rules makes possible. Language is primarily an instrument for achieving practical results—for getting things done. When we use language to convey information, for example, a set of practical or pragmatic rules relevant to this purpose helps us to do so in an efficient way. This system of background rules, first explored systematically by H. P. Grice, also allows us to convey information without actually stating it. The phenomenon of conversational implication will be explored here in detail. The chapter will conclude with a summary of the various levels of language and the systems of rules governing them.

Things Left Unsaid

> A: What did you think of Jay's performance as Hamlet?
>
> B: Well, he certainly knew all his lines.

Anyone overhearing this conversation would assume that B does not think well of Jay's performance. B seems to be engaged in a verbal practice known as damning with faint praise. By examining this interesting phenomenon closely, we can explore a system of important rules that governs our use of language.

To begin with, getting all the lines right while acting Shakespeare's *Hamlet* is no small achievement—the role has a lot of them. Yet we do not usually praise actors for remembering their lines, for this is the least they are expected to do. On the other hand, we usually criticize actors who forget their lines. One thing that B's remark indicates is that there is criticism that cannot be leveled against Jay: he forgot his lines. How does an acknowledgment of this positive feature take on the negative force of criticism? The answer is not hard to find. A has asked B to give a *general* evaluation of Jay's performance. To do this fairly, B must take into account all of the positive features of Jay's performance and balance them against the negative features. Now if the only positive comment that B makes in behalf of the performance is that Jay remembered all of his lines, this plainly suggests that there is nothing else good to say about it, or at least nothing of importance. If that is so, Jay's performance must have been pretty rotten.

This simple example illustrates a number of important points. First, although the significance or import of a remark is obviously related to its literal meaning, import is not usually determined by literal meaning alone. Second, understanding the import or significance of a remark usually requires understanding the purpose of the conversational exchange in which the remark occurs. The purpose of the exchange between A and B was to have B give a general assessment of Jay's performance. We all have some idea of the qualities that make up a good performance, for example, the ability to portray a character in a realistic and compelling manner. We assume that B took these possible qualities into account and, moreover, that they formed the central part of his evaluation of Jay's performance. His failure to mention these matters explicitly suggests that he could find nothing good to say about them. This silence on features of Jay's performance, features that B should have mentioned if he thought well of them, plainly indicates that he did not think well of them.

Now if we change the conversational setting, B's remark can have a wholly different import even though its literal meaning is unchanged. Suppose that Jay is a very gifted, but flamboyant, young actor. He is difficult to direct and often takes liberties with the script. In fact, there are those who have suggested that he is too lazy or too arrogant to memorize all his lines. Given this background B's remark takes on a wholly new significance; it no longer amounts to damning with faint praise. Rather, its point is to defend Jay. Thus the example illustrates another important point: that understanding the import or significance of a remark often depends upon knowing the *beliefs* shared by those involved in the conversation.

In sum, the significance or import of a remark will usually depend upon at least three factors: (1) the character and content of the speech act, (2) the common purpose of those involved in the conversational exchange, and (3) the shared beliefs and understandings the participants bring to the conversational setting. Later in this work (in Chapter 7) we will show the importance of making these common beliefs or unstated assumptions explicit. In this chapter we will concentrate upon understanding the significance of a remark in terms of the goal it is intended to achieve.

We have seen that language can be used in a great variety of ways. In saying something we may be making a promise, offering advice, handing down a verdict, making a statement, etc. Even the activity of making a statement covers a variety of cases—describing and classifying, for example. Here we have spoken of different kinds of *speech acts*. We can next notice that the very same speech act can be used to achieve different *purposes* in different contexts. Consider some of the reasons that we make statements: in a court of law, we make a statement to get something on the record (for example, "My name is Irving Trombley and I live in Littleton, New Hampshire."). We make statements to exhibit or show off our knowledge ("That is a piece of Late Ming porcelain."). We make statements just to keep a conversation going ("It's rather chilly for this time of year."). We make statements to remind people of things they already know ("Your uncle has money to spare."). Finally, we use statements to convey information.

Without forgetting that the notion of a statement covers a variety of speech acts that can be used to achieve a variety of purposes, we can look for a moment at cases where statements are used for the purpose of conveying information. This activity is governed by a set of rules or conventions that have been explored by the philosopher Paul Grice.[1]

Grice first speaks of a very general principle that he calls the Cooperative Principle (CP):

> Make your conversational contribution such as is required, at the stage at which it occurs, by the accepted purpose or direction of the talk exchange in which you are engaged.

[1] H. P. Grice, "Logic and Conversation," in Donald Davidson and Gilbert Harman, eds., *The Logic of Grammar* (Encino, California: Dickenson Publishing Company, 1975), p. 67. Reprinted in the Appendix to this book, pp. 407 ff.

This, of course, is *very* general. It considers a standard case where conversation is a cooperative venture—that is, where all parties have some common goal in talking to each other. (A witness being cross-examined does not accept this principle.) The principle states, quite simply, that in such a context, what we say should contribute toward achieving this goal. This general principle gets more content when we examine other principles that fall under it. One such principle is the rule of *Quantity* or the rule of *Strength*. Grice states it in these words:

(1) Make your contribution as informative as is required (for the current purposes of the exchange).

and possibly

(2) Do not make your contribution more informative than is required.

Here is an application of this rule: A person comes rushing up to you and asks, "Where is a fire extinguisher?" You know that there is a fire extinguisher five floors away in the basement, and you also know that there is a fire extinguisher just down the hall. Suppose you say that there is a fire extinguisher in the basement. Here you have said something that is *true*, but you have violated the rule of Quantity. You have held back an important piece of information that, under the rule of Quantity, you should have produced. A violation of the second version of the rule would look like this: Starting with the basement, you say where a fire extinguisher is located on each floor.

There is another cluster of rules that Grice calls rules of *Quality*. In general:

Try to make your contribution one that is true. More specifically:

(1) Do not say what you believe to be false.

(2) Do not say that for which you lack adequate evidence.

In a cooperative activity, you are expected not to tell lies. Beyond this, you are expected not to talk off the top of your head either. When we make a statement, we can be challenged in the following ways:

Do you really believe that?

Why do you believe that?

How do you know that?

Are you sure?

That a person has the right to ask such questions shows that statement making is governed by this rule of *Quality*. (In a court of law, we are expected to tell the truth, the whole truth, and nothing but the truth.

The demand for the *truth* and *nothing but the truth* reflects the rule of Quality; the demand for the *whole truth* reflects the rule of Quantity.)

The next rule is called the rule of *Relevance*. Simply stated, it says: Be relevant! Though easy to state, the rule is not easy to explain, because relevance itself is a difficult notion. It is, however, easy to illustrate. If someone asks me where he can find a fire extinguisher, I might reply, among other things, that there is a fire alarm box just down the hall. Though not a direct answer to his question, it is obviously relevant to this person's concerns. Perhaps a violation of the second version of the rule of Quantity, i.e., giving too much information, should be treated as a violation of the rule of Relevance. But the clear-cut violations of this principle are stronger than this. They involve *changing the subject.* Interruptions are typically violations of the rule of Relevance.

Another rule concerns the *Manner* of our conversation. We are expected to be clear. Under this general rule come various special rules:

(1) Avoid obscurity of expression.

(2) Avoid ambiguity.

(3) Be brief.

(4) Be orderly.

In obvious ways, all these rules contribute to the business of conveying information.

There are probably many other rules that should govern our conversations. *Be polite!* might be one of them. *Be charitable!* is another. That is, we should put the best construction on what others say and our replies should reflect this. We should avoid quibbling and unnecessary challenges. There are also rules that govern linguistic performance. Speak clearly, loudly enough to be heard, in a language the other person understands, etc. For the most part, however, we will not worry about them.

If we look at basic rules we notice that they sometimes overlap. The rule against offering too much information, as we have seen, could be treated as part of the Relevance rule. The rule against speaking ambiguously could be treated as a rule governing the linguistic rather than the speech act, and so on. More important, these rules sometimes clash, or at least push us in different directions. The rule of Quantity encourages us to give as much information as possible, but this is constrained by the rule of Quality, which restricts our claims to things we believe to be true and can back with good reasons. The demands of the rule of Quantity can also conflict with the demand for brevity. Again, in order to be brief, we must sometimes simplify and even falsify, and this can come into conflict with the Quality rule that we have good reasons to support the truth of what we have said. An ongoing conversation is a constant series of adjustments to this background system of rules.

Conversational Implication[2]

We have seen that speech acts are governed by a system of conventions. These conventions vary according to the kind of speech act in question. We have just seen, for example, that statement-making is governed by conventions concerning quantity, quality, relevance, and manner. Of course, when people make statements they do not always follow these conventions. People withhold information, they lie, they talk off the tops of their heads, they wander off the subject, they talk vaguely and obscurely. Yet in a normal setting where people are cooperating toward a shared goal, they conform quite closely to these rules. If, on the whole, people did not do this, we could not have the linguistic practices we do. If we thought, for example, that people very often lied (even about the most trivial matters), the business of communicating would be badly damaged.

But not only do we follow these conventions, we also (1) realize that we are following them, and (2) expect others to assume that we are following them. These points are obvious. If I say that there is a fire extinguisher down the hall, I realize that I am supposed to believe what I say. This explains why it would be odd to say this: "There is a fire extinguisher down the hall, but I do not believe it." This statement, after all, could be true. I might not believe that there is a fire extinguisher down the hall, and there might actually be one there (one, perhaps, that I never noticed). Even so, I am not supposed to state that there is a fire extinguisher down the hall unless I believe it. The person I speak to is *entitled* to assume that I believe it. He too understands these conventions, and, unless he doubts my integrity, he *expects* that I will follow them.

Here, we have to be careful. If I am a pathological liar and my listener knows this, he may doubt that I believe what I say. He has a right to criticize me for abusing linguistic conventions, but since he knows that I lie he is not trapped into believing that I am, in fact, following them. Yet in normal cooperative situations people make assumptions like these:

People follow conventions.

People realize that they are following conventions.

People realize that others assume that they are following conventions.

---

[2] The notion of conversational implication was also developed by Paul Grice. What follows borrows heavily from his discussion, but there are some important modifications as well. These differences become obvious by comparing this section with his essay, "Logic and Conversation," which is reprinted in the Appendix of this text. Most of the changes are simplifications rather than attempted improvements on his original work.

This leads to the following important result: *In a standard cooperative context, the performance of a speech act conversationally implies that all the conventions governing that speech act are satisfied.*

A series of examples will bring home this obvious point:

Stating:

A person states that there is a fire extinguisher in the lobby.

This conversationally implies:

(1) That this is the nearest or most accessible fire extinguisher.

(2) That the speaker believes this to be true.

(3) That the speaker has good reason for believing this, and is not merely guessing.

(4) That this information is relevant to the listener's interests.

(5) That the remark is intelligible to the listener.

Bequeathing:

A person states in a will that he bequeaths his Stutz Bearcat to a nephew.

Among other things, this conversationally implies:

(1) That he owns the Stutz Bearcat.

(2) That he is not about to sell it.

(3) That he believes that the nephew has some interest in receiving it.

(4) That he is sane.

Such conversational implications are carried by all of the speech acts we have examined, for all speech acts are governed by conventions, and in performing a speech act we conversationally imply that these conventions are satisfied.

It is important to realize that conversational implication is a pervasive feature of human discourse. It is not something we employ only occasionally for special effect. In fact, virtually every conversation relies upon these implications, and most conversations would fall apart if those involved in them refused to go beyond literal meaning to take into account the implications of what is being said. In the following conversation B is literal-minded in just this way:

A: Do you know what time it is?

B: Not without looking at my watch.

B has answered A's question, but it is hard to imagine that A received the information he was looking for. Presumably he wanted to know what time it was, not merely whether B, at this very moment, knew the time. Finding B rather obtuse, A tries again:

A: Can you tell me what time it is?

B: Oh yes, I have only to look at my watch.

Undaunted, A gives it another try:

A: Will you tell me what time it is?

B: I suppose I will as soon as you ask me.

Finally:

A: What time is it?

B: Two o'clock.

Notice that in each of these exchanges B gives a direct and accurate answer to A's question, yet, in all but the last answer, he does not provide what A wants. Here we might say that B is taking A's question too literally, but we might better say that the problem is that B is doing nothing *more* than taking A's remarks literally. In a conversational exchange, we expect others to take our remarks in the light of the obvious purpose we have in making them. We expect them to share our commonsense understanding of why people ask questions. People often want to be told the time, but only rarely, for example, when they are trying to synchronize their activities, do they care whether others know what time it is. In his replies, B is totally oblivious to the point of A's questions and, like a computer in a science-fiction movie, gives nothing more than the literally correct answer to the question he has been asked.

Broadly speaking, conversational implication takes place because our discourse is governed by a system of shared rules or conventions. The relationship between what is said and the rules governing the saying of it can be exploited in two directions:

(1) From speech act to rule

(2) From rule to speech act

When I say something, I conversationally imply that all the rules for saying that sort of thing have been satisfied. Thus, when I assert something, I conversationally imply (given the rule of Quality) that I believe what I am asserting. At times, the real point of asserting something is to make our beliefs known. By saying that a certain candidate will win the election I thereby express my belief on the matter and, perhaps, indicate my loyalty to that candidate. Or I can promise something primarily to indicate my strong resolve to do it. The implication holds because one of the conditions for the proper use of the expression "I promise . . ." is that I am strongly resolved to do whatever I promise. The acceptance of this condition explains in part such odd remarks as "I promise to give you a good beating if you ever do that again." Such a remark is not really a promise, but its point is clear. In each of these cases, the point in making the remark is to imply the content of some rule that must hold if the remark is being made correctly.

Proceeding in the other direction—that is, from some rule—we sometimes say things in order to indicate that an important condition for employing some further speech act has been satisfied. The most obvious case is saying something that gives good grounds (that is, that satisfies the rule of Quality) for saying something else. For example, "It is past noon and I'm starving" conversationally implies the statement it justifies: "It is time for lunch." Likewise, if someone says to his young children "Why, that movie is X rated," his remark conversationally implies that they cannot see it.

Violating Conversational Rules We can next look at a set of conversational implications that attracted Grice's attention. Sometimes our speech acts *seem* to violate certain conventions. On the assumption that the conversation is good-willed and cooperative, the listener will then attempt to make sense of this in a way that overcomes this appearance. Here is one of Grice's examples:

A: Where does C live?

B: Somewhere in Southern France.

If A is interested in visiting C, then B's reply is not adequate and thus seems to violate the rule of Quantity. We can explain this departure on the assumption that B does not know exactly where C lives and would thus violate the rule of Quality if he said anything more specific. In this case, B's reply conversationally implies that he does not know exactly where C lives.

In a more extreme case, a person may even flout one of these conventions—that is, obviously violate it. Here is Grice's example and his explanation of it:[3]

[3] Grice, "Logic and Conversation," pp. 71 ff. (p. 407 in this book).

> A is writing a testimonial about a pupil who is a candidate for a philosophy job, and the letter reads as follows: "Dear Sir, Mr. X's command of English is excellent, and his attendance at tutorials has been regular, Yours, etc." (Gloss: A cannot be opting out, since if he wished to be uncooperative, why write at all? He cannot be unable, through ignorance, to say more, since the man is his pupil; moreover, he knows that more information is wanted. He must, therefore, be wishing to impart information he is reluctant to write down. This supposition is only tenable on the assumption that he thinks that Mr. X is no good at philosophy. This, then, is what he is implicating.)

This is another case of damning with faint praise.

We can intentionally violate the rule of Relevance by pointedly changing the subject. Grice again:

> At a genteel tea party A says "Mrs. X is an old bag." There is a moment of appalled silence, then B says "The weather has been quite delightful this summer, hasn't it?"

The conversational implication here needs no explanation. We can also violate the demand for brevity and thereby *not* say something that could be said briefly. Here is one final example from Grice:

> Miss X produced a series of sounds which corresponded closely with the score of 'Home Sweet Home.'

By not saying simply that Miss X *sang* "Home Sweet Home," the speaker indicates, through a conversational implication, that he is not willing to call what she did singing.

Examples of this kind can be produced indefinitely. Rhetorical devices depend upon conversational implications. Overstatement and understatement are obvious examples, and so is irony. If I say something so blatantly false that my listener assumes I cannot possibly mean it, he concludes by a conversational implication that I mean the opposite. Many jokes depend on conversational implications to set up the punch line. The buildup points in one direction, and then the standard implications are reversed at the end. The more we examine phenomena of this kind, the more we become impressed with the richness of the conventions that underly the language we speak. Furthermore, we do not simply *follow* these conventions, we manipulate them, play with them, and play off them. Here the tired metaphor of the iceberg has its place. The explicitly spoken language is merely the tip—the visible surface—of a vast underlying structure.

Exercise 1: Given a normal conversational setting, what might be the conversational implications of the following remarks:
    a) It's getting a little chilly in here.
    b) I've known George Bush since he was a boy.

c) Well, Lloyd has done it again.
d) This dessert is very filling.
e) I got here before she did.
f) There are planes leaving every day for Russia (Said to a student radical).
g) Does anyone else here like anchovies on his pizza?

Exercise 2: During the 1980 presidential campaign, Jimmy Carter made the following statement in Atlanta, Georgia:

You've seen in this campaign the stirring of hate and the rebirth of code words like "states' rights" . . . racism has no place in this country.

In response, George Bush, the Republican vice-presidential nominee, said that he was "appalled at the ugly, mean little remark Jimmy Carter made last night." Beyond the literal statement, what are the obvious conversational implications of Carter's statement? Do they amount, as Bush seems to think, to accusing the two principal Republican candidates of racism?

Pragmatics

To sum up: We have laid down the following principle: *In a standard cooperative context the performance of a speech act conversationally implies that all the conventions governing that speech act are satisfied.* We have also pointed out that people sometimes deliberately flout conventions for special effects. Overstatement, understatement, and irony are examples of this. Without a standard background of conventions which most people follow most of the time, these special devices would not work. In the correct sense of this phrase, these exceptions *prove* the rule.

Grice himself talks mainly about the use of statements to convey information, but he is careful to note that his principles have a much wider application. To illustrate this, consider the activity of offering advice. All of Grice's rules, with only minor changes, apply again:

Quantity:

(1) We should not hold back relevant advice.

(2) We should not be excessive in giving advice.

Quality:

(1) We should believe that our advice will be useful to the other person.

(2) We should have good reasons for the advice we offer.

Relevance:

(1) Obviously, our advice should be relevant to the person's concerns.

Manner:

(1) Our advice should be clear, brief, orderly, etc.

In obvious ways, these rules further the activity of advising. It is also obvious that advising will carry conversational implications in virtue of these background rules. Once more, a speech act of advising carries the conversational implication that all these rules are satisfied. I can also explicitly flout these rules to achieve a special effect. I can advise someone to go jump in the lake.

So far, so good. But the idea of conversational implication is unclear in an important respect and so needs clarification. In particular, we have not distinguished between *speech act conventions* and what I shall call *pragmatic conventions.* When a speech act convention is not satisfied, the speech act does not come off—it is void. A bid made under duress is not a bid at all, for it is one of the conventions governing this speech act that the bid be made (more or less) freely. In the same way, I cannot bequeath a watch I do not own, or appoint someone to an office when I lack the authority to make such appointments.

We can contrast these failures (where the speech act is void) with failures to satisfy Grice's conversational rules. If, for example, I make a statement carrying less information than the context demands, I have, nonetheless, *made a statement.* Again, if, violating the rule of Quality, I say something that I believe to be false, I have, once more, made a statement. In short, violating these Gricean conversational rules does not vitiate or destroy the speech act in the same way that violating a speech act rule does. If we think for a moment, we can see why this is so. All of Grice's principles were specifications of the Cooperative Principle—generally speaking, the rule that we should make contributions that further the *goal* of a particular linguistic exchange. This principle concerns the outcome of a speech act, the end to be achieved, or its purposes. It concerns the practical outcome of the activity or, as philosophers say, its *pragmatic* significance.

These reflections suggest that we should distinguish between speech acts and what I shall call *pragmatic* acts. Sometimes this distinction is reflected in the words we use to describe a linguistic performance. For example:

I warned him of the danger.

I alerted him to the danger.

In the first case I describe the kind of speech act I performed; the effect upon the other person is left open. He may, for example, have ignored my warning. In the second case I indicated the effect my speech act had upon him: I alerted him. Here is another example:

I advised him to leave.

I persuaded him to leave.

Again the second, but not the first, utterance includes a reference to the effects of my speech act.

Here again we can use the thereby test to bring out the difference we have in mind. If I say "I advise you to leave," I thereby advise you to leave. On the other hand, if I say "I persuade you to leave," I do not thereby persuade you to leave, indeed, the remark hardly makes sense. "Advise," then, is a speech act verb whereas "persuade" is not. Since persuading concerns the effect of a speech act, we shall say that it concerns the pragmatic act. (The test does not seem to work quite as well for "warn" and "alert." Undoubtedly, if I say "I warn you," I thereby warn you; but only some speakers of English use "alert" in this way. In their usage, the verb "alert" sometimes refers to a speech act—the act of alerting—and sometimes to a pragmatic act—the act of making someone alert.)

But now a problem arises. Speech acts have all sorts of effects. By describing my trip to Europe I may bore someone out of his mind. This may even be my intention, because I want him to go home. I can also engage someone in conversation so that I distract his attention while I pick his pocket. There is obviously no end to the kinds of effects that speech acts can have. In order to place some limits on this discussion, we must speak about the *standard* goals that are achieved by different kinds of speech acts. A standard goal—but not the only goal—of making a statement is to convey information. Grice's maxims specify rules that help us to achieve this standard goal. The standard goal—though again not the only goal—of issuing an order is to get someone to do something. Rules similar to those developed by Grice for statements hold here as well. Rules or conventions that serve to help us achieve standard goals we shall call *pragmatic rules* or *pragmatic conventions*. Grice's rules are pragmatic conventions that pertain specifically to the efficient exchange of information. Although we have not pursued the matter in detail, it is clear that parallel pragmatic rules govern all uses of language, not only those involved in information exchange. Grice, of course, did not invent these rules; he found them at work in our everyday language. He called our attention to things that, in a way, we knew all along.

Levels of Language

We can now return to the idea that language contains rules or conventions operating at various levels. We can summarize the discussion as follows:

Linguistic Acts and Linguistic Conventions
(saying something meaningful in a particular language)

Speech Acts and Speech Act Conventions
(doing certain kinds of things with words)

Pragmatic Acts and Pragmatic Conventions
(achieving a certain standard result by performing a speech act)

This is oversimplified, but it gives at least a rough idea of the levels of convention that govern our language.[4] To take a simple example, if I say, "I'll see you tomorrow," first of all, I have performed a *linguistic act:* I have uttered a meaningful expression in the English language. I have also referred to certain things in the world—myself and some other person—and indicated some relationship between them. The character of the *speech act* will depend upon context. I may, for example, merely be making a statement of fact. If I expect to see someone's tightrope act tomorrow, I might tell him this. It is more likely, however, that I use this sentence to express an intention. As we know, the pragmatic act (which concerns the effect of the speech act) depends heavily on the kind of speech act used and the context in which it is used. Perhaps the remark "I will see you tomorrow" is intended merely as a piece of information or as a reminder that may prove useful if we have need for further dealings with each other. My remark can also have the force of a threat; perhaps its point or purpose is to scare you silly so that you will cough up the money I am trying to extort from you. You are expected to respond to the conversational implication of my words. Indeed, conversational implication is often the heart of the matter.

Exercise 3: Certain verbs pertain to the character of the linguistic act, others to the speech act, and still others to the pragmatic act. For example, "Harry mumbled" describes his linguistic act; "Harry promised" describes his speech act; and "Harry infuriated everyone" describes one of his pragmatic acts. Using the thereby test, particularly to distinguish speech acts from pragmatic acts, decide whether each of the verbs below concerns a linguistic act, a speech act, or a pragmatic act.

inform	advise	shout
misspell	soothe	claim
convince	whisper	amuse
pledge	enlighten	abbreviate
confuse	conclude	dissolve
frighten	challenge	astonish

[4] It corresponds to Austin's distinctions between locutionary, illocutionary, and perlocutionary acts. See *How to Do Things with Words*, pp. 94 ff.

THE LANGUAGE OF ARGUMENT

Using the general discussion of Chapters 1 and 2 as background, this chapter will examine the use of language to formulate arguments. It will provide methods for analyzing genuine arguments in all their richness and complexity. The first stage in analyzing an argument is the discovery of its basic structure. One must determine which words, phrases, and special constructions indicate the premises and conclusion. The second stage is the study of techniques used to strengthen an argument. These include guarding (or hedging) premises so that they are less subject to criticism, offering assurances concerning debatable claims, and discounting possible criticisms in advance. Finally, the chapter will consider various substitutes for arguments, devices that give the appearance of being arguments without actually offering reasons for the claims that are made.

In the first two chapters we saw that language is used for a great many purposes beyond making statements, or saying things that are either true or false. When we make a promise or make a bet, we are not stating a fact. Turning now to arguments, we see that they, like promises and bets, are not used to make statements. Although an argument is (typically) constructed from statements, the argument itself, taken as a whole, is not a statement. A single example will illustrate this:

Socrates is older than Plato; Plato is older than Aristotle; therefore, Socrates is older than Aristotle.

Taken as a whole, this sentence does not express anything that is either true or false.

This does not mean that we have no way of rejecting a bad argument. Here is an example of a bad argument:

Socrates is older than Plato, therefore Plato is older than Socrates.

(This argument is so bad that it is hard to imagine anyone actually using it, but bad arguments often serve as good examples.) What would we say to a person who produced such an argument? In ordinary words, we would say that his conclusion does not *follow from* what he has said. The basic point is that we never call arguments true or false. If you are tempted to do so, you are off on the wrong track. Statements are true or false; arguments are not.

The Basic Structure of Arguments

Arguments are not statements, yet they are constructed out of statements. Now let's ask a very simple question: What *words* turn a batch of statements into an argument? Suppose we start with a simple list of statements:

Socrates is mortal.

All men are mortal.

Socrates is a man.

This is not an argument, but we can turn it into an argument by the use of the single word "therefore":

Socrates is mortal.

All men are mortal.

Therefore Socrates is a man.

We now have an argument—again, a bad argument, since the conclusion does not follow from the reasons offered in its behalf, but it is an argument nonetheless. It should be obvious how the word "therefore" works: it signals that the statement following it is a *conclusion* and that the statement (or statements) that come before it are the *reasons* offered in support of the conclusion. Here is another way of turning the list into an argument:

Socrates is mortal,

since all men are mortal

and Socrates is a man.

This produces a new argument—this time, a good argument, for the conclusion does follow from the reasons offered in its behalf. "Since" operates *roughly* in the opposite way from "therefore." The word "since" indicates that the statement or statements that follow it are reasons and that the statement (if any) that comes before it is the conclusion. There is a variation, however, where the conclusion is tacked onto the end of a since-sentence:

Since all men are mortal and Socrates is a man,
Socrates is mortal.

"Since" flags reasons; the remaining connected statement is then taken to be the conclusion, whether it appears at the beginning or at the end of the sentence.

Here is a partial list of connecting terms that introduce an argumentative structure into language by marking out reasons for a conclusion:

accordingly	thus	since
for	hence	then
because	so	therefore

We shall call all these terms *warranting connectives.* In various ways, they all present one or more statements as the warrant or backing for some other statement.

Sometimes a single sentence will contain more than one of these warranting connectives. Here is an example:

Since all men are mortal, Socrates is mortal,
for Socrates is a man.

Both the words "since" and "for" signal the appearance of a reason: the conclusion itself appears in the *middle* of the sentence. This is an interesting example. Together with the other examples, it drives home the point that a conclusion can appear anywhere in a sentence formulating an argument: at the beginning, in the middle, or at the end. Our ability to locate the conclusion of an argument depends upon our understanding of warranting connectives.

Arguments in Standard Form

It will be helpful to have a standard way of writing out arguments: For centuries, logicians have used the following scheme:

All men are mortal.

Socrates is a man.

∴ Socrates is mortal.

The reasons are listed above the line; the conclusion is placed below the line; and the symbol "∴" is read "therefore." Logicians refer to the reasons stated above the line as *premises*. (For now we will not worry about the order of the premises.) This notion of a *standard form* is useful because it helps us to see that the same argument can be expressed in different ways. For example, it is not hard to see that the following two sentences express the same argument, i.e., the argument stated in standard form above:

Socrates is mortal, since all men are mortal and Socrates is a man.

All men are mortal, so Socrates is mortal, since he is a man.

By putting arguments in standard form, it becomes easier to compare them and to test their validity.

Validity, Truth, and Soundness

To have an argument at all, some statement must be marked out as a conclusion and other statements must be marked out as reasons or premises for this conclusion. Of course, merely connecting sentences together with words like "since" or "therefore" will not always produce a good or acceptable argument. As we have already noticed, an argument is no good if the conclusion does not follow from the premises. When the conclusion does follow from the premises, logicians say that the argument is *valid*. Validity is a central notion in logic and it is important to understand it clearly.

Validity is a technical notion, but it matches the commonsense idea of one thing following from another. Later on in this book we shall examine the idea of validity with some care; for now, we will rely upon the commonsense understanding of it. But we must be careful not to confuse *validity* with *truth*. Arguments are valid or invalid, but, as we have already seen, they are never either true or false. We can bring out this difference by noticing that an argument can be valid even though all the statements it contains are false:

All fishes have wings.

Whales are fishes.
_____

∴ Whales have wings.

It is not hard to see that the conclusion does *follow from* the premises, for, if fishes had wings and whales were fishes, then whales would have wings. Here is another example:

All fishes have lungs.

Whales are fishes.
_____

∴ Whales have lungs.

Again we have a valid argument since the conclusion does follow from the premises, yet this time the premises are both false and the conclusion is true.

Although the notions of truth and validity are different, there is one important relationship between them. Something false never follows from something true. More technically, there are no valid arguments that start from true premises and lead to a false conclusion. This too should square with your commonsense ideas about reasoning. If you reason correctly, you should not be led from truth into error. Until we discuss the notion of validity more carefully later on, in Chapter 9, we will rely upon common sense in seeing whether a conclusion validly follows from a set of premises. Unless the argument is very complicated or tricky in some way, most people are quite good at this.

It should already be clear that an argument can be valid but still unacceptable. A valid argument with false premises will be rejected just because the premises are false. Obviously, you cannot prove something by offering a premise that is false. We thus make *two* demands upon an argument that is offered as a proof:

(1) The argument must be *valid.*

(2) The premises must be *true.*

When an argument meets both of these demands, it is said to be *sound.* If it fails to meet either one, the argument is said to be *unsound.* Thus an argument is *unsound* if it is invalid; it is also unsound if *at least one* of its premises is false:

	Premises True	At Least One False Premise
Valid	Sound	Unsound
Invalid	Unsound	Unsound

The goal of a proof is a sound argument, not just a valid argument.

Exercise 1: Relying on your natural sense of what follows from various statements and upon your commonsense knowledge of the world, analyze the following arguments, indicating:

  a) Whether the premises are true or false.
  b) Whether the argument is valid or invalid.
  c) Whether the argument is sound or unsound.

Examples:

Munich is in Germany or Austria.	True
Munich is not in Austria.	True
∴ Munich is in Germany.	True

The argument is both valid and sound.

Munich is in France or Austria.	False
Munich is not in France.	True
∴ Munich is in Austria.	False

The argument is valid, but not sound.

1. General Motors has plants in America and Europe.

   ∴ General Motors has plants in America.

2. The Giants will win the pennant.

   ∴ Either the Giants or the Reds will win the pennant.

3. If the Giants win the pennant, then the Dodgers will not.

   ∴ If the Dodgers win the pennant, the Giants will not.

4. Canada is bigger than Spain.
   Spain is bigger than Portugal.

   ∴ Canada is bigger than Portugal.

5. If the Giants win the pennant, the Dodgers will not.
   The Giants will not win the pennant.
   _____

   ∴ The Dodgers will win the pennant.

6. Nobody is completely lacking in a sense of humor.
   _____

   ∴ General Grant was not completely lacking in a sense of humor.

7. Nobody completely lacks a sense of humor.
   Grant completely lacked a sense of humor.
   _____

   ∴ Grant was nobody.

8. Anyone religious believes in God.
   Some Buddhists do not believe in God.
   _____

   ∴ Some Buddhists are not religious.

9. Anyone religious believes in God.
   Some Buddhists believe in God.
   _____

   ∴ Some Buddhists believe in God.

10. Greeks come from the Mediterranean area.
    _____

    ∴ Rich Greeks come from the Mediterranean area.

Exercise 2:

    (1) All squares are rectangles.
    (2) All squares are triangles.
    (3) All squares have four sides.
    (4) All squares have three sides.
    (5) All triangles have four sides.
    (6) All rectangles have four sides.
    (7) All triangles have three sides.
    (8) All triangles have two sides.
    (9) All squares have two sides.
    (10) All rectangles are squares.

Using the above statements, construct arguments with two premises and
a conclusion such that:
    (a) The argument is valid, but all statements are false.
    (b) The argument is valid, the premises false, and the conclusion
        true.
    (c) The argument is invalid, but all the premises are true and so is
        the conclusion.

(d) The argument is valid, one premise true, one premise false, and the conclusion is true.

(e) The argument is valid, one premise true, one premise false, and the conclusion is false.

Exercise 3: Why can't you construct an argument that is valid having true premises and a false conclusion?

Now that you are accustomed to analyzing arguments in terms of their validity and soundness, you may be struck by the fact that everyday talk is not this elaborate. We seem to be drawing more distinctions than are found in everyday life. There is a reason for this that is connected with what we called the rule of Quantity in Chapter 2. Recall that if we call an argument *unsound,* we can have two criticisms in mind: that the argument is invalid *or* that one of the premises is false. We have no right to call the argument unsound if we cannot show one of these two things. If we do have this additional information, the rule of Quantity demands that we bring it forth. If we think the argument is unsound because it is invalid, we should make the stronger claim that it is invalid. If we think that the argument is unsound because one of the premises is false, we should come right out and say that one of the premises is false. For this reason, we do not often say that an argument is unsound or no good and let the matter stand there. We actually point out what is wrong with the argument, since this makes the criticism more pointed and informative. Again, we rarely stop with saying that an argument is valid, for when arguments are used to prove something, validity is not enough. A proof should be *sound* as well as valid. Simply saying that an argument is valid leaves open an important question: Are the premises true? Thus our *summary* judgments of arguments tend to maximize information.

(1) In accepting an argument, we say that it is sound rather than merely valid.

(2) In rejecting an argument, we say that it is invalid or has a false premise, rather than just saying that it is unsound.

In this way, we avoid saying less than we are in a position to say. *Sound* is stronger than *valid,* and *invalid* and *false* are stronger than *unsound.*

It is important to note facts of this kind as we go along in order to see the connection between logical theory and everyday argumentation. Our everyday talk is governed by a variety of principles at the same time, and what we actually say is the result of all these principles working simultaneously. Thus, though our arguments are guided by logical principles, to see them clearly we must look through a very tangled thicket.

Assuring, Hedging, and Discounting

The notion of soundness draws our attention to the importance of having true premises in our arguments. We cannot justify or explain something by citing things that are themselves false. This, however, presents a problem in argumentation. In order to justify one statement, I cite some others in their behalf. The question naturally arises why you should accept these new statements. Shouldn't I present an argument for them as well? If I do this, the problem comes up again: in proving the premises, I will just introduce further premises that are also in need of proof, and so on indefinitely. It now looks as if every argument will be infinitely long.

The answer to this ancient problem depends upon an obvious fact. The activity of arguing or presenting proofs depends upon a shared set of beliefs and upon a certain amount of trust. When I present reasons, I try to cite these shared beliefs—things that will not be challenged. Beyond this, I expect people to believe me when I cite information that only I possess. But there are limits to this. People do lie, and the range of shared beliefs is not firmly fixed. This presents a practical problem. How can I present my reasons in a way that does not produce just another demand for an argument? Here we use three main techniques:

(1) Assuring: indicating that we have back-up reasons without actually stating them.

(2) Hedging: weakening our claims so that they are less subject to attack.

(3) Discounting: anticipating criticisms and rejecting them.

In this way we build a defensive perimeter around our premises.

Assuring When will we want to give assurances about some statement we have made? If we state something that we know everyone believes, assurances are not necessary. For that matter, if everyone believes something, we may not even state it at all; we let others "fill in" this step in the argument. We offer assurances when we think that someone *might* challenge what we say. In giving assurances we sometimes cite authorities:

Doctors agree . . .

Recent studies have shown . . .

It has been established that . . .

I can assure you that . . .

An unimpeachable source close to the White House says . . .

Here we do not actually cite reasons; we merely indicate that they can be produced on demand. In a context of trust, this is often sufficient.

On the other hand, we as critics should view assuring remarks with some suspicion. Following the rule of Relevance, we should expect a person to give assurances only when he has a good reason to do so. Yet in point of fact, assuring remarks often mark the *weakest* parts of the argument, not the strongest parts. If someone says "I hardly need argue that . . . ," it is often useful to ask why he has gone to the trouble of saying it. In particular, when we distrust an argument—as we sometimes do—this is precisely the place to look for weakness. You should develop a keen eye for phrases of the following kind:

It's certain that . . .

Everyone agrees that . . .

Of course, no one will deny that . . .

It is just common sense that . . .

There is no question that . . .

If these phrases are used, they are used for some reason. Sometimes the reason is a good one; sometimes, however, it is a bad one. In honest argumentation, they save time and simplify discussion. In a dishonest argument, they are used to paper over cracks.[1]

Hedging *Hedging* represents a different strategy for protecting premises from attack. We reduce our claim to something less strong. Thus instead of saying *all*, we say *most*. Instead of saying something straight out, we use a qualifying phrase like "it is almost certain that," "it is very likely that," etc. Law school professors like the phrase "it is arguable that. . . ." This is wonderfully noncommittal, for it really doesn't indicate how strong the argument is, yet it does get the statement into the argument.

Broadly speaking, there are two ways of hedging what we have said:

(1) Weakening the extent of what has been said: retreating from "all" to "most," from "most" to "some," etc.

(2) Using probability phrases like "it is likely that," "virtually certain that," etc.

[1] This topic will be discussed more fully in Chapter 5.

If we weaken a claim sufficiently, we can make it completely immune to criticism. What can be said against a remark of the following kind: "There is some small chance that perhaps a few politicians are honest on at least some occasions." You would have to have a *very* low opinion of politicians to deny this statement. On the other hand, if we weaken our premises in this way to avoid criticism, we must pay a price. The premise no longer gives strong support to the conclusion. The general strategy is this: We should weaken our premises sufficiently to avoid criticism, but not weaken them so much that they no longer provide strong evidence for the conclusion. Balancing these two facts is one of the most important strategies in constructing and criticizing arguments.

Just as it was useful to zero in on *assuring* terms, it is useful to keep track of *hedging* terms. Hedging terms are easily corrupted. They can be used to insinuate things that cannot be stated explicitly into a conversation. Consider the effect of the following remark: "Perhaps the Secretary of State has not been candid with the Congress." This doesn't actually *say* that the Secretary has been less than candid with the Congress, but it suggests it. Furthermore, it suggests it in a way that is hard to combat. A more subtle device for corrupting hedging terms is to introduce a statement in a guarded form and then go on to speak as if it were not guarded at all. After a while, the word "perhaps" disappears.

> Perhaps the Secretary of State has not been candid with the Congress. Of course, he has a right to his own views and I am sure that he is acting honestly. All the same, this is a democracy where officials, even in the Administration, are accountable to Congress.

Discounting The general pattern of discounting is to cite a possible criticism in order to reject it or counter it. Notice how different the following statements sound:

> The ring is beautiful, but expensive.

> The ring is expensive, but beautiful.

Both statements express the very same facts—that the ring is beautiful and that the ring is expensive. Yet they operate in different ways. We might use the first as a reason for *not* buying the ring; we can use the second as a reason *for* buying it. The first sentence acknowledges that the ring is beautiful, but overrides this by pointing out that it is expensive. In reverse fashion, the second statement acknowledges that the ring is expensive, but overrides this by pointing out that it is beautiful. The word "but" discounts the statement that comes before it in favor of the statement that follows it.

"Although" is also a discounting connective, but it operates in reverse fashion from the word "but." We can see this using the same example:

Although the ring is expensive, it is beautiful.

Although the ring is beautiful, it is expensive.

Here the statement following the word "although" is discounted in favor of the connected statement. A partial list of terms that function as discounting connectives includes the following conjunctions:

although	nonetheless
but	still
however	yet
nevertheless	though

Exercise 4: Give examples of statements using the discounting connectives above, and then indicate which statement is discounted when two are conjoined by each connective.

The clearest cases of discounting occur when we are dealing with facts that point in different directions: that the ring is beautiful is a reason for buying it, that it is expensive is a reason for not buying it. We discount the fact that goes against the position we wish to take. Discounting is, however, often more subtle than this. We sometimes use discounting to block certain conversational implications of what we have said. This comes out in examples of the following kind:

Jones is an aggressive player, but he is not dirty.

The situation is difficult, but not hopeless.

The Democrats have the upper hand in Congress, but only for the time being.

A truce has been declared, but who knows for how long?

Take just the last example. The claim that a truce has been declared naturally suggests that peace has been restored. The but-clause cancels out this suggestion. The nuances of discounting terms can be very subtle, and a correct analysis is not always easy. All the same, the role of discounting terms is often very important in capturing the force of an argument. These terms anticipate criticisms, control conversational implications, and, in general, point to structures within an argument that are not actually stated. Once more, it is often useful to ask yourself why a term occurs in an argument—what would the argument be like without it?

Parentheticals

The philosopher J. O. Urmson has noticed the importance of parenthetical expressions in our language.[2] Sometimes parenthetical remarks are just asides—we put things in parentheses because of the rule of Relevance—but sometimes they play an important role in adjusting our remarks to the background rules that govern them. They allow us to comment on what we are saying at the very same time that we are saying it. Here is an example:

> That, if you do not mind my saying so, is a pretty ugly hat.

Notice that with this remark I *do* say that the hat is pretty ugly. Telling someone that he is wearing an ugly hat is not exactly polite. The parenthetical remark acknowledges this and, to some extent, neutralizes it. (Of course, tone of voice will also make a difference here.)

The word "parenthetically" can also be used parenthetically. In writing a graduate school recommendation, a professor says:

> Gilbert is a first-rate mathematician and, parenthetically, a world class swimmer.

It is not hard to see what is going on here: the parenthetical expression is connected to a rule of relevance. Being a world class swimmer is not relevant in any obvious way to future success in a graduate school, but it is to some extent an indication of a generally good character. Words like "incidentally" and "by the way" can also be used in this way. They get the fact in, but in a way that does not give it too much weight.

There seems to be no limit to the jobs that parentheticals can do. They can be used to give assurances:

> Jones, as you will soon discover, cannot keep off the bottle.

> Jones, unless I am sadly mistaken, has run out of ideas.

They can be used for guarding:

> Daniels, rumor has it, is about to get married.

> Daniels, as far as I know, is not coming East.

They can be used in discounting:

> I don't care what you have heard; Chrysler will not fold.

[2] J. O. Urmson, "Parenthetical Verbs," *Mind,* LXI (1952), pp. 480–96.

And so on.

It is a good idea to pay close attention to parentheticals, for they are often surprisingly helpful in revealing the underlying structure of an argument.

Argumentative Performatives

In the previous chapter, we saw that our language contains a rich system of argumentative performatives that actually give our conversations an argumentative structure. We saw that expository performatives not only introduce an argumentative structure, but do so in a *clear* and *explicit* way. If someone says, "I conclude such and such . . ." there is no doubt that he or she is concluding. When people say, "I admit such and such" there is no doubt that they are admitting something. We also saw that argumentative performatives allow us to make very subtle and complicated argumentative moves, like "I shall reserve comment until my opponent says something worth answering."

Along with parentheticals, argumentative performatives deserve close attention. Used correctly, they are powerful and subtle devices for constructing a clear, forceful argument. They can also be used incorrectly and dishonestly.

Exercise 5:
  (a) Construct three interesting examples of statements containing assuring terms.
  (b) Do the same for hedging terms.
  (c) Finally, do the same for discounting terms.

Exercise 6: In Part Two of this book there is a collection of arguments of some complexity. Take one of these arguments and label all the warranting connectives, assuring terms, discounting terms, and hedging terms.

Exercise 7: Perform Exercise 6 with an argument taken from the editorial pages of a newspaper.

Substitutes for Arguments

So far we have seen that the basic categories of the language of argument are *warranting connectives, assuring terms, hedging terms*, and *discounting terms*. We have also noticed that other devices show the

structure of an argument, in particular, *performatives* and *parentheticals*. The first task in assessing an argument is to look for these terms,
for they reveal the basic structure of the argument. Once the bare bones
of the argument have been exposed, still other questions remain, for it
is not always easy to assess the exact force of an argument. In particular,
we are sometimes misled by devices that are mere substitutes for genuine arguments. Here we shall examine a common device of this kind. It
is called *slanting*.

Slanting Although some words in our language are relatively neutral,
others carry a strong positive or negative connotation. That is, in using
many words in our language we are not only describing something, but
also evaluating it, expressing our feelings toward it, or in various other
ways indicating our attitudes concerning it. Ethnic and racial slurs are
obvious examples of this. To say that a person is a Jew is to comment
upon his or her ethnic origin: to call someone a kike conveys the same
information, but combines it with an expression of contempt. Actually,
in this area, connotations are so prevalent that we have to look to scientific language to find more or less neutral language. For example,
"white" is a positive term, whereas "whitey" (and "honkey") are negative. "Caucasian" is more or less scientific and neutral. Here we must
use the guarding expression "more or less" because all the language in
this area is highly charged. For many, "Black" is a positive term, and
"nigger" is a term of contempt, but "Negro" is not really neutral in the
way, for example, that "Mongolian" is. These tensions in the language
reflect deeper tensions in our society.

When we stop to think about it, it is surprising how many words appear in our language that are intended to express contempt. Beyond racial and ethnic slurs, our language contains a vast system of words
charged with negative connotations. Our language contains a rich system of obscenities. When we describe something using obscene language, we are usually (though not always) condemning it. There seems
to be no end to the ways in which we can describe things in demeaning,
degrading, and insulting ways. New forms of insult are constantly invented as the old ones lose their sting.

We should also notice that the connotations of a word vary with context; they depend upon who is saying what to whom. An irresponsible
conservative will accuse his liberal opponents of being communists,
thereby associating them with an organization generally held in contempt in this country. On the other hand, it wouldn't have made sense
to *accuse* Joseph Stalin of having been a communist. That's not something that Stalin would want to deny—he was proud of it. In the reverse
fashion, radicals sometimes call their more conservative opponents "fascists." Again, it would not have made sense to *accuse* Hitler or Musso-
lini of being fascists. From their point of view, being a fascist was something good, not bad. Thus, even where the descriptive meaning of a

word remains more or less fixed, the positive and negative connotations can vary with context. Calling someone a liberal can count as praise, as an attack from the right, or as an attack from the left, depending upon the speaker and the audience.

Finally, positive and negative connotations can be subtle. Consider a word like "clever." Descriptively, it indicates quick mental ability and carries a positive connotation. In contrast, "cunning," which has much the same descriptive content, often carries a negative connotation. It thus makes a difference which one of these words we choose. It also makes a difference where we apply them. You can praise a light opera by calling it clever, but it would surely be taken as a criticism if you called a grand opera clever. This, needless to say, turns upon the rule of Quantity. Grand operas are supposed to be more than clever. When something is supposed to be profound and serious, it is insulting just to call it clever. Prayers, for example, should not be clever.

Sometimes innocuous words can shift connotations. The word "too" is the perfect example of this. This word introduces a negative connotation, sometimes turning a positive quality into a negative one. Compare the following sentences:

John is smart.	John is too smart.
John is honest.	John is too honest.
John is ambitious.	John is too ambitious.
John is nice.	John is too nice.
John is friendly.	John is too friendly.

The word "too" indicates an excess, and thereby contains a criticism. If you look at the items in the second column, you will see that the criticism is sometimes rather brutal—for example, calling someone "too friendly."

Slanting and Persuasive Definitions A particularly subtle form of slanting involves the use of a definition to gain an argumentative advantage. Charles L. Stevenson calls such definitions *persuasive definitions*.[3] Here is an example:

Russian Communism is really state capitalism.

Who would say this? Certainly not a capitalist, who thinks capitalism is a *good* thing and communism is *bad*. Nor would Russian Communists say this, because they think that capitalism is *bad* and have no desire to associate their system with it. On the other hand, this is just the kind of statement that a Chinese Communist might use against the

[3] Charles L. Stevenson, "Persuasive Definitions," *Mind*, XLVII (July, 1938).

Russians. To a Chinese Communist, capitalism is a bad thing; thus calling Russian Communism "state capitalism" applies all the standard attacks against capitalism to the Russians. The pattern looks like this:

Something to be criticized.	Definitional link	Something considered bad.

Here is another example that uses the same pattern:

> Admissions quotas in favor of minorities are nothing more than reverse discrimination.

Since discrimination is usually thought to be something bad, a person will have a hard time making a case for minority quotas if he is trapped into accepting "reverse discrimination" as a defining characteristic of a system of minority quotas. Sometimes these definitions are crude and heavy handed, for example:

> Abortion is fetal murder.

Since murder is, by definition, a wrongful act of killing, this definition assumes the very point at issue. At other times the argumentative move can be quite subtle, for example:

> Abortion is the killing of an unborn person.

At first sight, this definition may seem neutral. It does not contain any obviously charged word like "murder." All the same, it is one of the central issues in the debate over abortion whether a human fetus is already a person. This is a matter to be established by argument, not by definition. In general we have a right to be suspicious of anyone who tries to gain an argumentative advantage through an appeal to definitions. Confronted with a definition in the midst of an argument, we should always ask whether the definition clarifies the issues or merely slants them.

What, then, is *slanting*? We shall say that language is slanted when the speaker uses terms with positive and negative connotations *without laying a foundation for doing so.* Here the last clause is important, for we are not proposing a rule that would reject language rich in positive and negative connotations. In the first place, no one would obey such a rule; secondly, if such a rule were followed, our language would be less interesting. The point is this: We have a right to use a term containing, say, an implicit criticism only if we have shown good reasons for this criticism. The word "scoundrel" has a negative connotation. If I simply call someone a scoundrel without giving reasons for doing so, then I am involved in slanting. On the other hand, if I give a detailed account of this person's life showing that he has taken bribes, lied under oath, neglected his duties, harmed innocent people, and been cruel to animals, then calling him a scoundrel is not slanting. It is just the word I want to express a *well-founded* negative attitude. Slanting occurs when we use words carrying a positive or negative connotation without justification. In slanting, we simply help ourselves to such words.

Exercise 8: For each of the following sentences, construct two others—one that reverses the emotive force and one that is more or less neutral. The symbol 0 stands for neutral, + for positive emotive force, and − for negative emotive force.

Example: − Professor Conrad is rude.
+ Professor Conrad is uncompromisingly honest in his criticisms.
0 Professor Conrad often upsets people with his criticisms.

1. − Martin is a lazy lout.
2. + Brenda is vivacious.
3. + John is a natural leader.
4. + Selby is a methodical worker.
5. − Marsha is a snob.
6. + Clara is imaginative.
7. − Bartlett is a buffoon.
8. − Wayne is a goody-goody.
9. − Sidney talks incessantly.
10. − Dudley is a weenie.
11. ? Floyd is a hotdog. (Decide whether this is + or −.)
12. + Martha is liberated.
13. + Ralph is sensitive.
14. + Betty is a fierce competitor.
15. − Psychology is a trendy department.
16. − This is a Mickey Mouse exercise.

Exercise 9: After reading Robin Lakoff's essay "Talking about Women" (pp. 248 ff.), test her hypothesis that the language used in talking about women often reveals a sexist bias in our society. To do this, collect a series of articles concerning women and see if they reveal the kind of bias Lakoff describes. Since many writers are now self-consciously trying to avoid the appearance of sexism, blatant examples may be less easily found in recent writing than in articles written a few years ago. One way to bring this matter into sharper focus is to compare the language used about a woman with the language used about a man in a similar context, for example, in a description of the individual's appointment to some high position.

Honors Exercise: Rewrite the following letter to the editor in the style of a neutral analysis of the sources of opposition to former President Nixon's reelection. As far as possible, do not change the factual content.

To the Editor:

Every long-haired hippie, every left-wing lunatic, every phony college professor, every socialist school teacher, every bus-crazy judge, every lazy welfare loafer, every yellow-bellied draft-dodger, every blood-stained abortionist, every dope-peddling fiend, every Communist pig, etc. (not to mention innumerable kooks, weirdos, derelicts, and degenerates) is fighting the reelection of President Nixon. Think it over. Which side are you on?

THE ART OF CLOSE ANALYSIS

4

This chapter will be largely dedicated to a single purpose: the close and careful analysis of a speech drawn from the Congressional Record, using the argumentative devices introduced in Chapter 3. The point of this study is to show in detail how these methods of analysis can be applied to an actual argument of some richness and complexity. Though this chapter will stress the importance of analyzing an argument in close detail, it will conclude with a discussion of the significance of the standpoint of the argument taken as a whole.

An Extended Example

It is now time to apply all of these notions to a genuine argument. Our example will be a debate that occurred in the House of Representatives on the question whether there should be an increase in the allowance given to members of the House for clerical help—the so-called "clerk hire allowance." The argument against the increase presented by Representative Kyl (Republican, Iowa) will be examined in detail. We will put it under an analytic microscope. The reply made by Representative Mc-Cormack (Democrat, Massachusetts) will be left for analysis as a student exercise.

The choice of this example may seem odd, for the question of clerk hire allowance is not one of the burning issues of our time. This, in fact, is one reason for choosing it. It will be useful to begin with an example where feelings do not run high in order to learn the habit of objective analysis. Later on we shall examine arguments where almost everyone has strong feelings and try to maintain an objective standpoint even there. The example is a good one for two other reasons: (1) it contains most of the argumentative devices we have listed and, (2) relatively speaking, it is quite a strong argument. This last remark may seem ironic after we seemingly tear the argument quite to shreds, but in comparison to other arguments we shall examine, it stands up quite well.

We can begin by reading through the section of the *Congressional Record*[1] without comment:

Clerk Hire Allowance, House of Representatives

Mr. FRIEDEL. Mr. Speaker, by direction of the Committee on House Administration, I call up the resolution (H. Res. 219) to increase the basic clerk hire allowance of each Member of the House, and for other purposes, and ask for its immediate consideration.

The Clerk read the resolution as follows:

Resolved, That effective April 1, 1961, there shall be paid out of the contingent fund of the House, until otherwise provided by law, such sums as may be necessary to increase the basic clerk hire allowance of each Member and the Resident Commissioner from Puerto Rico by an additional $3,000 per annum, and each such Member and Resident Commissioner shall be entitled to one clerk in addition to those to which he is otherwise entitled by law.

Mr. FRIEDEL. Mr. Speaker, this resolution allows an additional $3,000 per annum for clerk hire and an additional clerk for each Member of the House and the Resident Commissioner from Puerto Rico.

[1] *Congressional Record,* Vol. 107, Part 3 (March 15, 1961), pp. 4059–60.

Our subcommittee heard the testimony, and we were convinced of the need for this provision to be made. A few Members are paying out of their own pocket for additional clerk hire. This $3,000 is the minimum amount we felt was necessary to help Members pay the expenses of running their offices. Of course, we know that the mail is not as heavy in some of the districts as it is in others, and, of course, if the Member does not use the money, it remains in the contingent fund.

Mr. KYL. Mr. Speaker, will the gentleman yield?

Mr. FRIEDEL. I yield to the gentleman from Iowa [Mr. KYL] for a statement.

Mr. KYL. Mr. Speaker, I oppose this measure. I oppose it first because it is expensive. I further oppose it because it is untimely.

I do not intend to belabor this first contention. We have been presented a budget of about $82 billion. We have had recommended to us a whole series of additional programs or extensions of programs for priming the pump, for depressed areas, for the needy, for unemployed, for river pollution projects, and recreation projects, aid to education, and many more. All are listed as "must" activities. These extensions are not within the budget. Furthermore, if business conditions are as deplorable as the newspapers indicate, the Government's income will not be as high as anticipated. It is not enough to say we are spending so much now, a little more will not hurt. What we spend, we will either have to recover in taxes, or add to the staggering national debt.

The amount of increase does not appear large. I trust, however, there is no one among us who would suggest that the addition of a clerk would not entail allowances for another desk, another typewriter, more materials, and it is not beyond the realm of possibility that the next step would then be request for additional office space, and ultimately new buildings. Some will say, "All the Members will not use their maximum, so the cost will not be great." And this is true. If the exceptions are sufficient in number to constitute a valid argument, then there is no broad general need for this measure. Furthermore, some Members will use these additional funds to raise salaries. Competition will force all salaries upward in all offices and then on committee staffs, and so on. We may even find ourselves in a position of paying more money for fewer clerks and in a tighter bind on per person workload.

This measure proposes to increase the allowance from $17,500 base clerical allowance to $20,500 base salary allowance. No member of this House can tell us what this means in gross salary. That computation is almost impossible. Such a completely absurd system has developed through the years on salary computations for clerical hire that we have under discussion a mathematical monstrosity. We are usually told that the gross allowed is approximately $35,000. This is inaccurate. In one office the total might be less than $35,000 and in another, in complete compliance with the law and without any conscious padding, the amount may be in excess of $42,000. This is possible because of a weird set of formulae which determines that three clerks at $5,000 cost less than five clerks at $3,000. Five times three might total the same as three times five everywhere else in the world—but not in figuring clerk hire in the House.

This is application of an absurdity. It is a violation of bookkeeping principles, accounting principles, business principles and a violation of commonsense. Listen to the formula:

First, 20 percent increase of first $1,200; 10 percent additional from $1,200 to $4,600; 5 percent further additional from $4,600 to $7,000.

Second, after applying the increases provided in paragraph 1, add an additional 14 percent or a flat $250 whichever is the greater, but this increase must not exceed 25 percent.

Third, after applying the increases provided in both paragraphs 1 and 2, add an additional increase of 10 percent in lieu of overtime.

Fourth, after applying the increases provided in paragraphs 1, 2, and 3, add an additional increase of $330.

Fifth, after applying the increases provided in paragraphs 1, 2, 3, and 4, add an additional increase of 5 percent.

Sixth, after applying the increases provided in paragraphs 1, 2, 3, 4, and 5, add an additional increase of 10 percent but not more than $800 nor less than $300 a year.

Seventh, after applying the increases provided in paragraphs 1, 2, 3, 4, 5, and 6, add an additional increase of 7½ percent.

Eighth, after applying the increases provided in paragraphs 1, 2, 3, 4, 5, 6, and 7, add an additional increase of 10 percent.

Ninth, after applying the increases provided in paragraphs 1, 2, 3, 4, 5, 6, 7, and 8, add an additional increase of 7½ percent.

The Disbursing Office has a set of tables to figure house salaries for office staffs and for about 900 other employees. It contains 45 sheets with 40 entries per sheet. In the Senate, at least, they have simplified the process some by figuring their base in multiples of 60, thus eliminating 11 categories. Committee staffers, incidentally, have an $8,880 base in comparison to the House $7,000 base limitation.

Now, Mr. Speaker, I have planned to introduce an amendment or a substitute which would grant additional clerk hire where there is a demonstrable need based on heavier than average population or "election at large" and possible other factors. But after becoming involved in this mathematical maze, I realize the folly of proceeding one step until we have corrected this situation. We can offer all kinds of excuses for avoiding a solution. We cannot offer reasonable arguments that it should not be done or that it cannot be done.

Someone has suggested that the Members of this great body prefer to keep the present program because someone back in the home district might object to the gross figures. I know this is not so. When a Representative is busy on minimum wage, or aid to education, or civil rights, such matters of housekeeping seem too picayune to merit attention. The Member simply checks the table and hires what he can hire under the provisions and then forgets the whole business. But I know the

Members also want the people back home to realize that what we do here is open and frank and accurate, and that we set an example in businesslike procedures. The more we can demonstrate responsibility the greater will be the faith in Congress.

May I summarize. It is obvious that some Members need more clerical help because of large population and large land area. I have been working for some time with the best help we can get, on a measure which would take these items into consideration. Those Members who are really in need of assistance should realize that this temporary, hastily conceived proposition we debate today will probably obviate their getting a satisfactory total solution.

First, we should await redistricting of the Nation.

Second, we should consider appropriate allowance for oversize districts considering both population and total geographic area.

Finally, I hope we can develop a sound and sensible formula for computing salaries of office clerks and other statutory employees in the same category.

Mr. FRIEDEL. Mr. Speaker, I yield 2 minutes to the gentleman from California [Mr. YOUNGER].

Mr. YOUNGER. Mr. Speaker, I take this time simply to state my opposition to this bill, opposition straight across the board. I would favor an increase if it were based on the additional work or the additional population in a district; I think that is justified. It could be worked out at a certain allowance for every additional 250,000 population in the district.

I am opposed to this whole scheme as it is set up. I have had a bill before the committee for 4 or 5 years. This House would not permit any department of the Government to operate the way we operate. It is just as sensible and as profitable for a Congressman to build up a big staff as it is for the head of a bureau to build up a big staff; and in many instances big staffs are being built up right here in our own House. I think this House ought to set a determined example for the departments of Government.

I am opposed to this type of legislation.

Mr. FRIEDEL. Mr. Speaker, I yield 3 minutes to the gentleman from Massachusetts [Mr. McCORMACK].

Mr. McCORMACK. Mr. Speaker I think the RECORD should show that there is definite need for this resolution. I, as a Member of the House as well as majority leader, take my responsibility. I have never apologized to anybody for Members of this House receiving increases in salary throughout the years; as a matter of fact, I think we should further increase our salaries to $25,000. I never apologize for the Members of the House or the Members of the other body having a staff that will enable them to serve the people of their district, of their State, and as Members of Congress the people of the Nation.

Those who object on the grounds some Members raise of the lack of need, do not have to appoint additional help in their offices unless they want to; but certainly those Members should not take the position that because they do not need additional clerk hire that other Members of the House do not either.

This resolution is not for the benefit of any Member of this House; this resolution is for the benefit of the people of America to enable the Members of this House to more effectively and efficiently perform their duties as Members of Congress. So I have no hesitancy in supporting the resolution. I probably will not take advantage of it; I may and I may not. I have not up to date used all of my clerk hire. I may or I may not take advantage of this resolution should it be passed, but I would not want to deny other Members who need additional staff from having it so that they may effectively represent the people of their district here in the Halls of Congress.

Mr. YOUNGER. Mr. Speaker, will the gentleman yield?

Mr. McCORMACK. I am always glad to yield to the gentleman from California.

Mr. YOUNGER. In respect to the gentleman's last statement I may say that never in the 8 years I have been in Congress have I used all my clerk hire allowance, and I have no intention of using this additional allowance.

I think that additional allowance for clerk hire should be on the basis of need. I think in this bill we are hoodwinking the public.

Mr. McCORMACK. I think the weakness of the gentleman's argument is that it does not take into account the volume of work regardless of the number of people in a district. Some Members with a district of 300,000 might have more interested constituents requiring more attention than another Member having a district with 460,000.

In these matters we must treat all alike. As I say, the question of population is not the determining factor as to the prime responsibility of a Member of Congress. A Member from a smaller district may have tremendous mail from all over his State, in fact, from all over the country.

So I do not think a formula based on steps of population increase is a fair one or a good one.

As to the argument of the gentleman from Wisconsin that this resolution is not based on reason, I shall not enter into that at all.

I will say it is commonsense for us to pass this resolution today.

Before going any farther, it will be useful to record your general reaction to this exchange. Perhaps you think that on the whole Kyl gives a more reasoned argument than McCormack. Alternatively, you might think that Kyl is making a big fuss over nothing, trying to confuse people with numbers, and just generally being obnoxious. When you are finished examining this argument in detail, you can look back and ask yourself why you formed this original impression and how, if at all, you have changed your mind.

The first step in the close analysis of an argument is to go through the text, labelling the various argumentative components we have examined. Here some abbreviations will be useful:

warranting connective	War. Con.
assuring term	As.
hedging term	Hedge
discounting term	Dis.
argumentative performative	Arg. Perf.
parenthetical	Par.
slanting	Slant (+ or −)
persuasive definition	Per. Def. (+ or −)

Even this simple process of labelling brings out features of an argument that could pass by unnoticed. It also directs us to ask sharp critical questions. To see this, we can look at each part of the argument in detail.

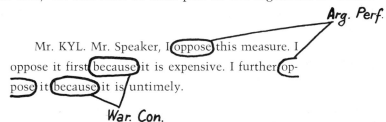

Arg. Perf.

Mr. KYL. Mr. Speaker, I oppose this measure. I oppose it first because it is expensive. I further oppose it because it is untimely.

War. Con.

This is a model of clarity. By the use of a performative utterance in the opening sentence, Kyl makes it clear that he opposes the measure. Then by twice using the warranting connective "because," he gives his two main reasons for opposing it: *it is expensive* and *it is untimely*. We must now see if he makes good each of these claims. This paragraph begins the argument for the claim that the measure is expensive:

As.

I do not intend to belabor this first contention. We have been presented a budget of about $82 billion. We have had recommended to us a whole series of additional programs or extensions of programs for priming the pump, for depressed areas, for the needy, for unemployed, for river pollution projects, and recreation projects, aid to education, and many more. All are listed as "must" activities. These extensions are not within the budget. Fur-

Dis.

thermore, if business conditions are as deplorable —— **Hedge**
as the newspapers indicate, the Government's income will not be as high as anticipated. It is not —— **Dis.**
enough to say we are spending so much now, a little more will not hurt. What we spend, we will
either have to recover in taxes, or add to the stag-
gering national debt.

(a) "I do not intend to belabor this first contention. . . ." This is a
pure example of *assuring.* The obvious conversational implication is
that the point is so obvious that little has to be said in its support. Yet
there is something strange going on here. Having said that he will *not*
belabor the claim that the bill is expensive, Kyl actually goes on to say
quite a bit on the subject. It is a good idea to look closely when someone
says that he or she is not going to do something, for often just the opposite is happening. For example, saying "I am not suggesting that Smith
is dishonest" is one way of suggesting that Smith *is* dishonest. If no
such suggestion is being made, why raise the issue at all?

(b) Kyl now proceeds in a rather flat way, stating that the proposed
budget comes to $82 billion and that it contains many new programs
and extensions of former programs. Since these are matters of public
record and nobody is liable to deny them, there is no need for guarding
or assuring. Kyl also claims, without qualification, that these extensions
are not within the budget. This recital of facts does, however, carry an
important conversational implication: Since the budget is already out of
balance, any further extensions should be viewed with suspicion.

(c) Putting the word "must" in quotation marks, or saying it in a
certain tone of voice, is a common device for discounting. The plain
suggestion is that some of these measures are *not* must activities at all.
We see the same device in a more dramatic fashion when Mark Anthony ironically repeats that "Brutus is an honorable man." Anyway,
Kyl here suggests that some of the items already in the budget are not
necessary. He does this, of course, without defending this suggestion.

(d) "If business conditions are as deplorable as the newspapers indicate . . . ." This is a clear example of hedging. Kyl is not saying that
business conditions are deplorable. For this reason the suggestion that
the government's income will be less than anticipated is not given very
strong support.

(e) "It is not enough to say we are spending so much now, a little
more will not hurt." The opening phrase is, of course, used to discount
what follows it. Kyl is plainly rejecting the argument that we are spending so much now, a little more will not hurt. Yet his argument has a peculiar twist, for who would come right out and make such an argument?
If you stop to think for a minute, it should be clear that nobody would
want to put it that way. A liberal, for example, would use quite different

phrasing. He might say something like this: "Considering the large benefits that will flow from this measure, it is more than worth the small costs." What Kyl has done is to attribute a bad argument to his opponents and then discount it in an indignant tone. This is a common device.[2] When we run into the use of a discounting phrase, it is often useful to ask whether anyone would actually argue or speak in the way suggested. When the answer to this question is no, as it often is, it is also useful to ask what the speaker's opponent would have said instead. This leads to a further question: Has the arguer even addressed himself to the *real* arguments of his opponents?

So far, Kyl has not addressed himself to the first main point of his argument, that the measure is *expensive*. This is not a criticism, because he is really making the preliminary point that the matter of expense is significant. Here he has stated some incontestable facts—for example, that the budget is already out of balance. Beyond this he has indicated, with varying degrees of strength, that the financial situation is grave. It is against this background that the detailed argument concerning the cost of the measure is actually presented in the next paragraph.

> The amount of increase does not appear large. — **Dis.**
>
> I trust, however, there is no one among us who would suggest that the addition of a clerk would not entail allowances for another desk, another typewriter, more materials, — **As.** and it is not beyond the — **Hedge** realm of possibility that the next step would then be a request for additional office space, and ultimately new buildings. Some will say, "All the Members will not use their maximum, so the cost will not be great." — **Dis.** And this is true. If the exceptions are sufficient in number to constitute a valid argument, then there is no broad general need for this measure. — **War. Con.** Furthermore, some Members will use these additional funds to raise salaries. Competition will force all salaries upward in all offices and then on committee staffs, and so on. We may even — **Hedge** find ourselves in a position of paying more money for fewer clerks and in a tighter bind on per person workload.

[2] Another example is that of a professor who spoke to student radicals in the following way: "I can understand that the younger generation wants a free ride—they want to get things without really working for them, but. . . ."

(a) "The amount of increase does not appear large." Words like "appear" and "seem" are sometimes used for hedging, but we must be careful not to apply labels in an unthinking way. The above sentence is the beginning of a *discounting* argument. As soon as you hear this sentence, you can feel that a word like "but" or "however" is about to appear. Sure enough, it does.

(b) "I trust, however, there is no one among us who would suggest that the addition of a clerk would not entail allowances for another desk, another typewriter, more materials . . . ." This is the beginning of Kyl's argument that is intended to rebut the argument that the increase in expenses will not be large. Appearances to the contrary, he is saying, the increase will be large. He then ticks off some additional expenses that are entailed by hiring new clerks. Notice that the whole sentence is covered by the assuring phrase, "I trust . . . that there is no one among us who would suggest . . . ." This implies that anyone who would make such a suggestion is merely stupid. But the trouble with Kyl's argument so far is this: He has pointed out genuine additional expenses, but they are not, after all, very large. It is important for him to get some genuinely large sums of money into his argument. This is the point of his next remark:

(c) "And it is not beyond the realm of possibility, that the next step would then be a request for additional office space, and ultimately new buildings." Here, at last, we have some genuinely large sums of money in the picture, but the difficulty is that the entire claim is totally hedged by the phrase, "it is not beyond the realm of possibility." There are very few things that *are* beyond the realm of possibility. Kyl's problem, then, is this: There are certain additional expenses that he can point to without qualification, but these tend to be small. On the other hand, when he points out genuinely large expenses, he can only do so in a hedged way. So we are still waiting for a proof that the expense will be large. (Parenthetically, it should be pointed out that Kyl's prediction of new buildings actually came true.)

(d) "Some will say, 'All the Members will not use their maximum, so the cost will not be great.' And this is true. If the exceptions are sufficient in number to constitute a valid argument, then there is no broad general need for this measure." This looks like a "tricky" argument, and for this reason alone it demands close attention. The phrase "some will say" is a standard way of beginning a discounting argument. This *is*, in fact, a discounting argument, but its form is rather subtle. Kyl cites what some will say, and then adds, somewhat surprisingly: "And this is true." To understand what is going on here, we must have a good feel for conversational implication. Kyl imagines someone reasoning in the following way:

All the Members will not use their maximum.

So the cost will not be great.

Therefore, since the measure will not be expensive, let's adopt it.

Given the same starting point, Kyl tries to derive just the *opposite* conclusion along the following lines:

All the Members will not use their maximum.

If very few use their maximums, then the cost will not be great.

But if very few use their maximum, then there is no broad general need for this measure.

Therefore, whether it is expensive or not, we should reject this measure.

In order to get clear about this argument, we can put it into schematic form:

Kyl's argument
If (1) expensive, then   → Reject

If (2) inexpensive, then, because that demonstrates no general
need,   → Reject

The opposite argument
If (1) inexpensive, then   → Accept

If (2) expensive, then, because that demonstrates a general need,
                                                              → Accept

When the arguments are spread out in this fashion, it should be clear that they have equal strength. Both are no good. The question that must be settled is this: Does a genuine need exist that can be met in an economically sound manner? If there is no need for the measure, then it should be rejected however inexpensive. Again, if there is a need, then some expense is worth paying. The real problem is to balance the need against expense and then to decide on this basis whether the measure as a whole is worth adopting. Kyl's argument is a *sophistry* because it has no tendency to answer the real question at hand. By a sophistry we shall mean a clever but fallacious argument intended to establish a point through trickery. Incidentally, it is one of the marks of a sophistical argument that, though it may baffle, it almost never convinces. I think that very few readers will have found this argument persuasive even if they could not say exactly what is wrong with it. The appearance of a sophistical argument (or even a complex and tangled argument) is a sign that the argument is weak. Remember, where a case is strong, people usually argue in a straightforward way. This is illustrated by the second half of Kyl's argument, where he argues directly and strongly that the measure is untimely.

(e) "Furthermore, some Members will use these additional funds to raise salaries. Competition will force all salaries upward in all offices and then on committee staffs, and so on." The word "furthermore" signals that further *reasons* are forthcoming. Here Kyl returns to the argument that the measure is more expensive than it might at first sight appear. Notice that he speaks here in an unqualified way; no hedging appears. Yet the critic is bound to ask whether Kyl has any right to make these projections. Beyond this, Kyl here projects a *parade of horrors*. He pictures this measure leading, by gradual steps, to quite disastrous consequences. Here the little phrase "and so on" carries a great burden in the argument. Once more, we must simply ask ourselves whether these projections seem reasonable.

(f) "We may even find ourselves in a position of paying more money for fewer clerks and in a tighter bind on per person workload." Once more, the use of a strong hedging expression takes back most of the force of the argument. Notice that if Kyl could have said straight out that the measure *will* put us in a position of paying more money for fewer clerks and in a tighter bind on per person workload, that would have counted as a very strong objection. You can hardly do better in criticizing a position than showing that it will have just the opposite result from what is intended. In fact, however, Kyl has not established this, he has only said that this is something that we "may even find."

Before we turn to the second half of Kyl's argument, which we shall see in a moment is much stronger, we should point out that our analysis has not been entirely fair. Speaking before the House of Representatives, Kyl is in an *adversary* situation. He is not trying to prove things for all time; rather, he is responding to a position held by others. Part of what he is doing is *raising objections*, and a sensitive evaluation of the argument demands a detailed understanding of the nuances of the debate. But even granting this, it should be remembered that objections themselves must be made for good reasons. The problem so far in Kyl's argument is that the major reasons behind his objections have constantly been hedged in a very strong way.

Turning now to the second part of Kyl's argument—that the measure is untimely—we see that he moves along in a clear and direct way with really no hedging.

> This measure proposes to increase the allowance from $17,500 base clerical allowance to $20,500 base salary allowance. No member of this House can tell us what this means in gross salary. — *Hedge*
> That computation is (almost) impossible. Such (a
> *Slant* — completely absurd system) has developed through

the years on salary computations for clerical hire that we have under discussion a mathematical monstrosity. — *Slant* — We are usually told that the gross allowed is approximately $35,000. This is inaccurate. In one office the total might be less than $35,000 and in another, in complete compliance with the law and without any conscious padding, the amount may be in excess of $42,000. This is possi- *Slant* — ble because of a weird set of formulae which determines that three clerks at $5,000 cost less than five clerks at $3,000. Five times three might total the same as three times five everywhere else in the world—but not in figuring clerk hire in the House.

This is application of an absurdity. It is a viola- *Slant* — tion of bookkeeping principles, accounting principles, business principles and a violation of common-sense. Listen to the formula:[3]

The main point of the argument is clear enough: Kyl is saying that the present system of clerk salary allowance is utterly confusing, and this matter should be straightened out before *any* other measures in this area are adopted. There is, of course, a great deal of negative slanting in this passage. Notice the words and phrases that Kyle uses.

completely absurd system

weird set of formulae

a violation of common sense

mathematical monstrosity

an absurdity

There is also a dash of irony in the remark that five times three might total the same as three times five everywhere else in the world, but not in figuring clerk hire in the House. Remember, there is nothing wrong with using slanted language (and irony) if it is deserved. We have a *smear job* only when negative slanting is excessive and undeserved. Looking at the nine-step formula on page 60, you can decide for yourself whether Kyl is on strong grounds in using these negative characterizations.

[3] See page 60 for the formula.

Now, Mr. Speaker, I have planned to introduce an
amendment or a substitute which would grant additional clerk hire where there is a demonstrable
need based on heavier than average population or
"election at large" and possible other factors.

(a) This passage discounts any suggestion that Kyl is unaware that
a genuine problem does exist in some districts. It also indicates that he
is willing to do something about it.

(b) The phrase "and possible other factors" is not very important,
but it seems to be included to anticipate other reasons for clerk hire that
should at least be considered.

As.

But after becoming involved in this mathematical
maze, I realized the folly of proceeding one step un-   Slant—
til we have corrected this situation.

(a) Here Kyl clearly states his reason for saying that the measure is
untimely. Notice that the reason offered has been well documented and
is not hedged in by qualifications.

(b) The phrases "mathematical maze" and "folly" are again negatively slanting, but probably justified.

Slant—

Dis.—

We can offer all kinds of excuses for avoiding a solution. We cannot offer reasonable arguments that
it should not be done or that it cannot be done.

(a) Notice that the first sentence discounts these "excuses" and that
calling them *excuses* is negatively slanting. The second sentence gives
assurances that such a solution can be found.

Someone has suggested that the Members of
this great body prefer to keep the present program
because someone back in the home district might
object to the gross figures. I know this is not so.
When a Representative is busy on minimum wage,
or aid to education, or civil rights, such matters of
housekeeping seem too picayune to merit attention. The Member simply checks the table and
hires what he can hire under the provisions and
then forgets the whole business. But I know the
Members also want the people back home to realize
that what we do here is open and frank and accurate, and that we set an example in businesslike

Dis. ———

As.

Slant +

procedures. The more we can demonstrate responsibility the greater will be the faith in Congress.

(a) Once more the seas of rhetoric run high. Someone (though not
Kyl himself) has suggested that the Members of the House wish to conceal information. He disavows the very thought that he would make
such a suggestion by the sentence "I know this is not so." All the same,
he has gotten this suggestion into the argument.

(b) Kyl then suggests another reason why the Members of the House
will not be concerned with this measure: it is too *picayune*. The last
two sentences discount the suggestion that it is too small to merit close
attention. Even on small matters, the more the House is "open and
frank and accurate," the more it will "set an example in businesslike
procedures" and thus "demonstrate responsibility" that will increase
"the faith in Congress." This is actually an important part of Kyl's argument, for presumably his main problem is to get the other Members of
the House to take the matter seriously.

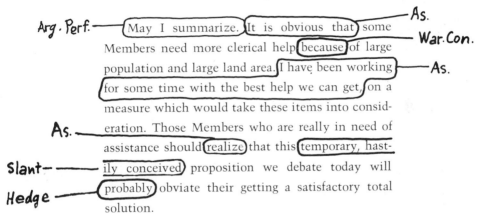

Arg. Perf. — May I summarize. It is obvious that some — As.
Members need more clerical help because of large — War. Con.
population and large land area. I have been working — As.
for some time with the best help we can get, on a
measure which would take these items into consid-
As. — eration. Those Members who are really in need of
assistance should realize that this temporary, hast-
Slant — ily conceived proposition we debate today will
Hedge — probably obviate their getting a satisfactory total
solution.

(a) This is a concise summary. Kyl once more assures the House that
he is aware that a genuine problem exists. He also indicates that he is
working on it.

(b) The phrase "temporary, hastily conceived proposition we debate
today" refers back to his arguments concerning untimeliness.

(c) The claim that "it will probably obviate their getting a satisfactory total solution" refers back to the economic argument. Notice, however, that, as before, the economic claim is hedged by the word "probably."

First, we should await redistricting of the Nation.

Second, we should consider appropriate allowance for oversize districts considering both population and total geographic area.

Finally, I hope we can develop a (sound and sen- ——— *Slant+*
sible) formula for computing salaries of office clerks
and other statutory employees in the same category.

This is straightforward except that a new factor is introduced: we
should await redistricting of the Nation. This was not mentioned earlier
in the argument, and so seems a bit out of place in a summary. Perhaps
the point is so obvious that it did not need any argument to support it.
On the other hand, it is often useful to keep track of things that are
smuggled into the argument at the very end. If redistricting was about
to occur in the *near* future, this would give a strong reason for delaying
action on the measure. Since the point is potentially so strong, we
might wonder why Kyl has made so little of it. Here, perhaps, we are
getting too subtle.

Exercise 1: Below is reprinted Representative McCormack's reply to
Representative Kyl. Some remarks by Representative Younger are also
included for continuity. Subject this speech to the same close analysis
that we have used in examining Representative Kyl's speech. Who do
you think gets the better of the exchange?

Mr. McCORMACK. Mr. Speaker I think the RECORD should show that there
is definite need for this resolution. I, as a Member of the House as well
as majority leader, take my responsibility. I have never apologized to
anybody for Members of this House receiving increases in salary
throughout the years; as a matter of fact, I think we should further increase our salaries to $25,000. I never apologize for the Members of the
House or the Members of the other body having a staff that will enable
them to serve the people of their district, of their State, and as Members
of Congress the people of the Nation.

Those who object on the grounds some Members raise of the lack
of need, do not have to appoint additional help in their offices unless
they want to; but certainly those Members should not take the position
that because they do not need additional clerk hire that other Members
of the House do not either.

This resolution is not for the benefit of any Member of this House; this
resolution is for the benefit of the people of America to enable the
Members of this House to more effectively and efficiently perform their
duties as Members of Congress. So I have no hesitancy in supporting the
resolution. I probably will not take advantage of it; I may and I may not.
I have not up to date used all of my clerk hire. I may or I may not take

advantage of this resolution should it be passed, but I would not want to deny other Members who need additional staff from having it so that they may effectively represent the people of their district here in the Halls of Congress.

Mr. YOUNGER. Mr. Speaker, will the gentleman yield?

Mr. McCORMACK. I am always glad to yield to the gentleman from California.

Mr. YOUNGER. In respect to the gentleman's last statement I may say that never in the 8 years I have been in Congress have I used all my clerk hire allowance, and I have no intention of using this additional allowance.

I think that additional allowance for clerk hire should be on the basis of need. I think in this bill we are hoodwinking the public.

Mr. McCORMACK. I think the weakness of the gentleman's argument is that it does not take into account the volume of work regardless of the number of people in a district. Some Members with a district of 300,000 might have more interested constituents requiring more attention than another Member having a district with 460,000.

In these matters we must treat all alike. As I say, the question of population is not the determining factor as to the prime responsibility of a Member of Congress. A Member from a smaller district may have tremendous mail from all over his State, in fact, from all over the country.

So I do not think a formula based on steps of population increase is a fair one or a good one.

As to the argument of the gentleman from Wisconsin that this resolution is not based on reason, I shall not enter into that at all.

I will say it is commonsense for us to pass this resolution today.

Exercise 2: Using the Congressional Record, an editorial, a letter to the editor, etc., find an interesting example of an argument and subject it to close analysis. Be sure to label the various argumentative moves and then comment on them. It is also important to get a general sense of context. In particular, you should be alert for the ironic use of an expression which, of course, reverses its normal force.

Exercise 3: Chapter 11, "An Issue of Public Concern," offers the full transcript of a television program entitled "Incident at Brown's Ferry." It contains a series of exchanges between those who favor atomic energy and those who oppose it on the grounds of safety. After reading through the script, go back and subject it to close analysis. When you have finished, review your analysis and decide whether it is fair or slanted in favor of your own position. Finally, after all this is done, decide to what extent, if at all, your own opinions on these matters have changed as a result of this activity.

Standpoints

Now that we have looked at Representative Kyl's argument in close detail, we can notice an important feature of the argument as a whole: it is presented from a particular *standpoint*. Kyl puts himself across as a tough-minded, thoroughly honest person who is willing to stand up against majority opinion. This, in fact, may be an accurate representation of his character, but by adopting this standpoint he gains an important argumentative advantage: He suggests that those who disagree with him are a bit soft-minded, not altogether candid, and, anyway, mere tools of the Democratic majority that runs the Congress. By adopting this stance, Kyl casts his opponents in a light that is hardly flattering.

This tactic of adopting a standpoint that puts one's opponent at a disadvantage is a common argumentative device that deserves close attention. A standard ploy is to claim a *middle ground* between two extreme positions. This strategy is used by Paul A. Samuelson in the opening paragraphs of an article published in *Newsweek* under the title "New York Dilemma."

> This is a hard column to write. How easy it would be if one were simpleminded and could baldly assert: "Let New York go down the drain. It couldn't happen to a nicer bunch of fellows anyway. Bankruptcy not only will teach a lesson, punish the guilty and deter those tempted in the future, but it will also be the first step on the road back to fiscal probity."
>
> Likewise, it would be an easy position to hold if one could believe with conviction: "The Federal government should take responsibility for the city's present plight. After all, *the crisis has national not local causes.* Any Puerto Rican or Southerner can freely move into the city. Any well-heeled person can freely move out to the suburbs, thereby avoiding his share of the irreducible fiscal burden of the less fortunate who are left in the city. Only the Federal government has the powers of the purse to take care of the intolerable load now being put on the city and the state . . ."
>
> Neither of these positions is tenable for an intelligent person of goodwill. But where in the wide middle ground between them is the feasible optimum for policy to be found? Here are some tentative economic considerations that may help set bounds on possible policy alternatives.[4]

We thus find Samuelson defining himself as an "intelligent person of goodwill," which is accurate enough, but not very gracious to those who might want to disagree with him in a strong way.

Another device is to seize an extreme position and accuse those who

---

[4] *Newsweek*, November 10, 1975, p. 102.

occupy a middle position of being cowardly, indecisive, or lukewarm. William Lloyd Garrison made brilliant use of this strategy in the first issue of his abolitionist newspaper *The Liberator*. Part of the opening editorial read as follows:

> Assenting to the "self evident truth" maintained in the American Declaration of Independence, "that all men are created equal, and endowed by their Creator with certain inalienable rights—among which are life, liberty and the pursuit of happiness," I shall strenuously contend for the immediate enfranchisement of our slave population. In Park Street Church, on the Fourth of July, 1829, in an address on slavery, I unreflectingly assented to the popular but pernicious doctrine of *gradual* abolition. I seize this opportunity to make a full and unequivocal recantation, and thus publicly to ask pardon of my God, of my country, and of my brethren the poor slaves, for having uttered a sentiment so full of timidity, injustice and absurdity. A similar recantation, from my pen, was published in the *Genius of Universal Emancipation* at Baltimore, in September, 1829. My conscience is now satisfied.
>
> I am aware, that many object to the severity of my language; but is there not cause for severity? I *will be* as harsh as truth, and as uncompromising as justice. On this subject, I do not wish to think, or speak, or write, with moderation. No! no! Tell a man whose house is on fire, to give a moderate alarm; tell him to moderately rescue his wife from the hands of the ravisher; tell the mother to gradually extricate her babe from the fire into which it has fallen;—but urge me not to use moderation in a cause like the present. I am in earnest—I will not equivocate—I will not excuse—I will not retreat a single inch—*AND I WILL BE HEARD*. The apathy of the people is enough to make every statue leap from its pedestal, and to hasten the resurrection of the dead.
>
> It is pretended, that I am retarding the cause of emancipation by the coarseness of my invective and the precipitancy of my measures. *The charge is not true.* On this question my influence,—humble as it is,—is felt at this moment to a considerable extent, and shall be felt in coming years—not perniciously, but beneficially—not as a curse, but as a blessing; and posterity will bear testimony that I was right. I desire to thank God, that he enables me to disregard "the fear of man which bringeth a snare," and to speak his truth in its simplicity and power.[5]

There are a great many devices for establishing an argumentative standpoint that puts the opponent at a disadvantage. Here are just a few:

The disinterested party: Although I have no personal stake in this matter . . .

[5] Richard Heffner, ed., *A Documentary History of the United States* (New York: Mentor Books, 1952), pp. 106–07.

The reasonable man: By now it should be obvious to everyone . . .

The voice in the wilderness: I don't suppose that it will help much to point out that . . .

The world-weary cynic: Are we really going to go through all this again?

Official indignation: It is high time that . . .

The mature person: When I was a child I spoke as a child . . .

The radical: You're either on the bus or off the bus . . .

The plain man: I may not have gone to Harvard but . . .

The expert: Things are not as simple as they might seem.

The agonizer: I've worried about this problem for a long time, and . . .

Sometimes these argumentative moves hit their mark and sometimes they do not. Fair or foul, however, they almost always infuriate those against whom they are directed. If the Expert tells you that things are not as simple as they might seem, this plainly suggests that you are a dope. You have to dig your way out of this hole before you can even get into the argument.

Two additional ploys are worth mentioning: these are used by the *Uplifter* and the *Debaser*. The Uplifter appeals to your better instincts, claiming that in your conscience or in your heart you really *agree*. The Uplifter strikes the pose of bringing you up to his or her level, a particularly obnoxious move when you hold that you *do* disagree, and for perfectly sound and moral reasons. The Debaser is even slimier. The strategy here is to acknowledge all sorts of base motives and low qualities, and then go on to say that everyone else is in the same boat. Where Uplifters lift you up to their preferred heights, Debasers drag you down to their acknowledged depths. Debasers often use the phrase "Let's face it."

"Let's face it, everyone is out to get what he can get for himself."

"Let's face it, you would do the same thing if you thought you could get away with it."

If you disagree, you are accused not only of being naive, but of being dishonest. Debasers pride themselves on admitting to the bad qualities they find in others. It often turns out that Debasers are not so bad as they pretend to be, and Uplifters are almost never as righteous as they assume they are. However this may be, both of these moves often produce strong—even violent—responses.

Exercise 4: Almost any political speech, editorial, or piece of social commentary will be written from a particular standpoint. It is often useful, in analyzing such writing, to identify this standpoint. Using the categories given above—or even better, using some of your own—identify the author's standpoint in a number of arguments of current interest.

Exercise 5: Sometimes a writer shifts standpoint, speaking first in one role, then in another. In the statement below, circle each occurrence of I, we, and us and identify the standpoint from which the word is written.

STATEMENT ON TUITION INCREASE

Fully mindful of the central educational and intellectual role that the residential colleges play in the life of Yale College and of the University, and of how overcrowding in the colleges undermines the achievement of the educational mission, I have recommended and the Corporation has voted to reduce the total number of students in Yale College next year. . . . Clearly, there are costs associated with reduction of college and class size, and clearly the term bill level—including room, board, and tuition—must be seen as part of the whole issue of the size of Yale College. Last year, the Consumer Price Index indicated that inflation rose at 9%. Yale, like everyone else, must live in that world. On the other hand, we must also be aware of the difficulties imposed on us—parents, friends, students—by the inflationary spiral. In order, therefore, to assist us in meeting the real costs of an education at Yale, while never forgetting the burdens on all of us, I have recommended and the Corporation has voted an increase in the term bill in Yale College of 8.5%. This means an increase of $640. . . .

FALLACIES OF CLARITY AND RELEVANCE

5

In this chapter we shall examine some of the ways in which arguments can be defective. Defects in arguments will be considered here under two main headings: <u>fallacies</u> of <u>clarity</u> and <u>fallacies of relevance.</u> Fallacies of clarity arise when language is not used precisely enough for the argumentative context. Vagueness and abiguity, two of the most common results, will be defined and discussed in detail. Fallacies of relevance arise when a claim is made which, true or not, has no tendency to establish the point at issue. Such irrelevance comes in endless forms, but only two will be given special attention here: arguments <u>ad hominem</u> and appeals to authority. A central theme of the chapter will be that, in order to speak accurately of fallacies, we must be sensitive to the context of the argument and the conversational implications within it.

Clarity

In a good argument, a person states a conclusion clearly and then, with equal clarity, gives reasons for this conclusion. The arguments of everyday life often fall short of this standard. Usually, unclear language is a sign of unclear thought. There are times, however, when people are intentionally unclear—their goal is to confuse others. This is called *obfuscation*.

Before we look at the various ways in which language can be unclear, a word of caution is needed. There is no such thing as absolute clarity. Whether something is clear or not depends upon the context in which it occurs. A botanist does not use the commonsense vocabulary in describing and classifying plants. At the same time, it would be foolish for a person to use botanical terms in describing the appearance of his backyard. Thus, Aristotle said, it is the mark of an educated person not to expect more rigor than the subject matter will allow. Since clarity and rigor are context-dependent, it takes judgment and good sense to pitch an argument at the right level.

Vagueness Perhaps the most common form of unclarity is *vagueness*. It arises in the following way. Many of our concepts admit of *borderline cases*. The standard example is baldness. A person with a full flowing head of hair is not bald. A person without a hair on his head is bald. In between, however, there is a range of cases where we are not prepared to say definitely whether the person is bald or not. Here we say something less definite, such as this person is "going" bald. Notice that our inability to apply the concept of baldness in this borderline case is not due to ignorance. It will not help, for example, to count the number of hairs on the person's head. Even if we knew the exact number, we would still not be able to say whether the person was bald or not. The same is true of most adjectives that concern properties admitting of degrees—for example, *rich, healthy, tall, wise,* and *ruthless.* We can also encounter borderline cases with common nouns. Consider the common noun *game.* Baseball is a game and so is chess, but how about tossing a frisbee? Is that a game? Is Russian roulette a game? Are prize fighting and bull fighting games? As we try to answer these questions, we feel an inclination to say Yes and an inclination to say No. This uncertainty shows that these concepts admit of borderline cases.

For the most part this feature of our language—that we use terms without sharply defined limits—causes little difficulty. In fact, this is a useful feature of our language, for suppose we *did* have to count the number of hairs on a person's head before we could say whether he was bald or not. Yet difficulties can arise when borderline cases themselves are at issue. Suppose that a state passes a law forbidding all actions that tend to corrupt the public morals. The law is backed up by stiff fines and imprisonment. There will be many cases that clearly fall under this law and many cases that clearly do not fall under it. But in a very wide range of cases, it will just not be clear whether they fall under this law or not. Here we shall say that the law is *vague;* laws are sometimes called unconstitutional for this very reason. In calling the law vague, we are *criticizing* it. We are not simply noticing the existence of borderline cases, for there will usually be borderline cases no matter how careful we are. *We shall say, then, that a concept is vague if, in a given context, it leaves open too wide a range of borderline cases for the successful use of that concept in that context.*

To further illustrate this notion of context dependence, consider the expression "light football player." There are, of course, borderline cases between those football players who are light and those who are not light. But on these grounds alone we would not say that the expression is vague. It is a perfectly serviceable expression, and we can indicate borderline cases by saying that "Jones is a bit light for a football player." Suppose, however, that Ohio State and Cal Tech wish to have a game between their light football players. It is obvious that the previous understanding of what counts as being light is too vague for this new context. At Ohio State, anyone under 210 pounds is considered light. At Cal Tech, anyone over 150 pounds is considered heavy. What is needed then is a ruling—for example, anyone under 175 pounds will be considered a lightweight. This is a common situation. A concept that is perfectly okay in one area becomes vague when applied to some other (usually more specialized) area. This vagueness is removed by adopting more precise rules. Vagueness is resolved by definition.

Exercise 1: Each of the following sentences contains words or expressions that are potentially vague. Resolve this vagueness by replacing the underlined expression with one that is more precise. To do this, you must imagine some context in which the vagueness would make a difference.

For example: Harold has a bad reputation.
    Harold is a known thief.

1. John has a nice personality.
2. Cortisone is a dangerous drug.
3. Marian is a clever girl.
4. Nancy is a terrific tennis player.
5. Mark is a fiend at chess.
6. Sam's loyalty is in question.
7. There's not enough money to go around.
8. We have runaway inflation.
9. Jones won by a landslide.
10. Johnson is no better than he has to be.

Practical problems produced by vagueness may even lead to a lawsuit. The following case turns upon the meaning of the word "chicken":

FRIGALIMENT IMPORTING CO. v. B.N.S. INT'L SALES CORP., S.D. N.Y., 1960, 190 F.Supp. 116. Plaintiff and defendant, a Swiss buyer and a New York seller, respectively, entered into a contract for the sale of "chicken." When the initial shipment arrived in Switzerland, plaintiff found it had received stewing chicken or "fowl," rather than young chicken suitable for broiling or frying, as it had expected. Plaintiff then sued for breach of contract. Judge Friendly of the Second Circuit Court of Appeals, sitting as District Judge, held for defendant.

"The issue is, what is chicken? Plaintiff says 'chicken' means a young chicken, suitable for broiling and frying. Defendant says 'chicken' means any bird of that genus that meets contract specifications on weight and quality, including what it calls 'stewing chicken' and plaintiff pejoratively terms 'fowl'. Dictionaries give both meanings, as well as some others not relevant here. To support its [construction], plaintiff sends a number of volleys over the net; defendant essays to return them and adds a few serves of its own. . . .

"When all the evidence is reviewed, it is clear that defendant believed it could comply with the contracts by delivering stewing chicken in the 2½–3 lbs. size. Defendant's subjective intent would not be significant if this did not coincide with an objective meaning of 'chicken.' Here it did coincide with one of the dictionary meanings, with the definition in the Department of Agriculture Regulations to which the contract made at least oblique reference, with at least some usage in the trade, with the realities of the market, and with what plaintiff's spokesman had said. Plaintiff asserts it to be equally plain that plaintiff's own subjective intent was to obtain broilers and fryers; the only evidence against this is the material as to market prices and this may not have been sufficiently brought home. In any event it is unnecessary to determine that issue. For plaintiff has the burden of showing that 'chicken' was used in the narrower rather than in the broader sense, and this it has not sustained."

The issue here is whether, in the contract, the word "chicken" was used in a broad or narrow sense. This shows that the word was used in a vague way in the context of this contract. In order to deal with these practical problems of vagueness, every modern society has developed complicated systems for classifying and grading products. Meats are classified as *good, choice, prime,* etc.; eggs as *extra-large, large, medium,* etc.; and in France, where these things matter, wines are classified into categories with various subcategories thrown in. Of course, even these careful and elaborate classifications cannot completely exclude borderline cases, but they limit them and for the most part avoid troublesome vagueness.

Heaps and Slippery Slopes The existence of borderline cases makes possible various styles of fallacious reasoning that have been identified (and used) since ancient times. One such argument was called the argument "from the *heap*," for it was intended to show that there are no heaps. As a variation on this, we will show that there are no rich men. The argument goes as follows:

heap argument

(1) If someone has one cent, he is not rich.

(2) If someone is not rich, then giving him one cent will not make him rich.

∴ No matter how many times you give a person a cent, he will not pass from being not rich to being rich.

Everyone will agree that there is something wrong with this argument, for if we hand over a billion pennies to someone, that person will be worth ten million dollars. If he or she started out with nothing, that would certainly count as passing from being not rich to being rich.

Although there is some disagreement among philosophers about the correct way to analyze this argument, we can see that it turns upon borderline cases in the following way: If we laid down a ruling (maybe for tax purposes) that anyone with a million dollars or more is rich and anyone with less than this is not rich, then the argument would fail. A person with $999,999.99 would pass from not being rich to being rich when given a single penny. But, of course, we do not use the word "rich" with this precision. We know of some clear cases of people who are rich and some other clear cases of people who are not rich. In between there is a fuzzy area where we are not prepared to say that people either are or are not rich. In this fuzzy area, a penny one way or the other will make no difference. Once we see the form of the argument from the heap, we see how we might "prove" that nobody is tall, fat, or bald and, finally, that there are no heaps. Wherever we find one thing passing over into its opposite through a gradual series of borderline cases, we can pull the following trick: find some increase that will not be large enough to carry us outside the borderline area, and then use the pattern of argument given above.

But what exactly is wrong with the argument from the heap? As a matter of fact, this is not an easy question to answer and remains a subject of debate. Here is one way of viewing this problem. Consider a case where we would all agree that a person would pass from being fat to being thin by losing at least 100 pounds. Now if this person lost an ounce a day for five years, he or she would have lost at least this much. Of course, there would be no particular day on which this person would pass from being fat to being thin. Yet losing an ounce a day for five years is *equivalent to* losing more than 100 pounds. So the argument from the heap seems to depend upon the idea that a series of insignificant changes cannot be equivalent to a significant change. Surely this is a strange assumption. Here we might be met with the reply that, for a change to occur, it must occur at some particular time and place. The answer is that this merely shows a misunderstanding of concepts that admit of borderline cases. We can examine this issue more closely by looking at a near cousin to arguments from the heap—so-called "slippery slope" arguments.

Slippery slope arguments exploit borderline cases in a different way than arguments from the heap. Here, instead of getting trapped in the borderline area, we inch our way through it in order to show that there is no real difference between things at opposite ends of a scale. Whereas the argument from the heap could be used to show that nobody is really bald, a slippery slope argument could be trotted out to show that there is no *real difference* between being bald and not being bald.

Slippery slope arguments are no better than arguments from the heap, but, strangely, they are sometimes taken quite seriously. Consider the difference between living and nonliving things:

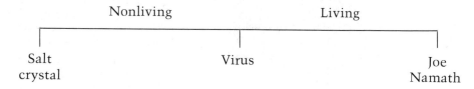

We notice first that a salt crystal is *not* alive. Yet a salt crystal is very similar to other more complex crystals, and these crystals are similar to certain viruses. We might even say that a virus just *is* a highly complex crystalline structure. But a virus is on the borderline between living and nonliving things. A virus does not take nourishment and does not reproduce itself. Instead, a virus invades the reproductive mechanisms of cells and these cells then produce the virus. As viruses become more complex, the differences between them and "higher" life forms become less obvious. Through a whole series of such small transitions, we finally reach a creature who is obviously alive: Joe Namath. So far, we have merely described a series of gradual transitions along a *continuum.* We get a slippery slope argument when we draw the following conclusion from these facts: Therefore there is no genuine difference between living and nonliving things since living processes are nothing more than complex nonliving processes. (By the way, the slippery slope argument can also be run in the opposite way by shifting emphasis: We conclude that everything is really alive, but some things, for example salt crystals, possess a very low level of life.)

Slippery slope arguments have been used to deny the difference between sanity and insanity, health and sickness, and amateur and professional athletics. (We can imagine someone saying that a professional athlete is just an athlete who gets paid more than other athletes who are called "amateurs.") All such arguments depend upon the following principles:

(1) We should not draw a sharp distinction between things that are not significantly different.

(2) If A is not significantly different from B and B is not significantly different from C, then A is not significantly different from C.

This first principle is interesting, complicated, and at least *generally* true. We shall examine it more closely in a moment. The second principle is obviously false. A series of insignificant differences can add up to a significant difference. As Senator Everett Dirksen once said, "A billion dollars here and a billion dollars there can add up to some real money."

Those who use slippery slope arguments often use the phrase "it's just a matter of degree." What is usually wrong with this phrase is the emphasis on the word "just," which suggests that differences of degree don't count. The difference between gluttony and starvation is a matter of degree—how much food you consume—but it is not *only* a matter of degree.

Where do you draw the line? We can now turn to some arguments concerning borderline cases that can be much more important. In the middle of an argument a person can offer a challenge by asking the question, "Where do you draw the line?" This challenge makes sense only when there is a range of intermediate or borderline cases where a line is difficult to draw. But sometimes, even if the line is difficult to draw, this challenge is out of place. If I say that Hank Aaron was a superstar, I am not going to be refuted if I cannot draw a sharp dividing line between athletes who are superstars and those who are not. There are some difficult borderline cases, but Hank Aaron isn't one of them. Nor will we be impressed if someone tells us that the difference between Hank Aaron and the thousands of players who never made it to the major leagues is "*just a matter of degree.*" Of course it is a matter of degree, but the difference in degree is so great that it should be marked by a special word. Arguing that we cannot distinguish things on opposite ends of a scale because we cannot justify any particular dividing point in the middle of the scale is just another variation of the slippery slope argument.

There are, however, occasions when the challenge to draw a line is relevant. For example, most schools and universities have grading systems that draw a fundamental distinction between passing grades and a failing grade. Of course, a person who barely passes a course does not perform very differently from one who barely fails a course, yet they are treated very differently. Students who barely pass a course get credit for it; those who barely fail it do not. This, in turn, can lead to serious consequences in an academic career and even beyond it. It is not unreasonable to ask for a justification of a procedure that treats cases that are so similar in such strikingly different ways. In other words, we are not just being tender-hearted; we are raising an issue of fairness or justice. It seems unfair to treat very similar cases in strikingly different ways, but this occurs any time we draw a sharp line between closely similar cases.

So the question "Where do you draw the line?" sometimes raises a genuine problem. Since drawing a line will make a great deal of difference to those who fall on one side of it or the other, how can it be drawn in a rational and fair way? This is a constant dilemma in making public policy. In considering a poverty program, it will be obvious that certain people are in need of aid and others are not. Yet the program itself must have some specific cut-off point. Those just above this point and those just below it will be treated differently even though the differences between them are negligible.

Sometimes we can find practical ways of dealing with problems of this kind. With a poverty program we can use a graduated scale based on need. Those with a greater need will receive more aid, and the aid will decrease as the cut-off point is approached. In this way, there will be only a small difference between those just below the cut-off point who receive minimal aid and those just above it who receive no aid at all. But sometimes this strategy is not available. Consider the death penalty. Most societies have reserved the death penalty for the most serious crimes. But where should we draw the line between crimes punishable by death and crimes not punishable by death? There is no possibility of introducing a sliding scale, since death does not admit of degrees. It seems to be an unavoidable consequence of the death penalty that similar cases will be treated in radically different ways. A defender of the death penalty can argue that it is fair since once the line is drawn the public will have fair warning about which crimes are subject to the death penalty. It will then be each person's decision whether to cross this line or not. It remains a matter of debate, however, whether the law can be administered in a way that makes this argument plausible. If the laws themselves are administered in an arbitrary way, arguments of this kind lose their force.

The finality and completeness of death raises a profoundly difficult problem in another area too: the legalization of abortion. There are some people who think that abortion is never justified. There are others who think that it doesn't need any justification at all. Between these extremes, there are many people who believe that abortion is justified in certain circumstances but not in others. There are also those who think that abortion should be allowed for a certain number of months of pregnancy, but not thereafter. People in the middle positions face the problem of deciding where to draw a line, and for this reason they are subject to criticism from both extreme positions. This problem admits of no easy solution. Since every line we draw will seem arbitrary to some extent, and since the issues here are profoundly important, the only way a person who holds a middle position can face this problem honestly is to argue that it is better to draw some line—even an arbitrary one—than to draw no line at all.

In an earlier discussion, we saw that, *in general,* we should not draw a sharp distinction between things that are not significantly different. This principle becomes more than a matter of logic when the distinction involves questions of life and death. Yet sometimes we abandon this principle with hardly a thought. There is surely no obvious reason why the voting age should be 18 rather than 17 or 19.[1] The previous voting age of 21 was arbitrary in the same way. But in this area, most people agree that the need to draw a clear line someplace more than outweighs the arbitrariness of drawing it in some particular place. To cite another example, most people agree that it is important to have uniform speed laws for motor vehicles even though it is arbitrary whether the limit is 50, 55, or 60 miles per hour. In other situations, arbitrariness is not so easily accepted. To summarize, the question, "Where do you draw the line?" is sometimes a variation on the slippery slope argument and so is just a quibble, whereas at other times it raises fundamental questions of fairness and justice. We must learn to distinguish the two kinds of cases—dismissing the first and doing the best we can with the second.

Exercise 2: For your own amusement, construct examples of an argument from the heap and a slippery slope argument.

Exercise 3: More seriously, discuss a case where drawing a sharp line can produce important moral, social, or political problems. The arguments on abortion given in Part Two (pp. 291–316) may serve this purpose.

Ambiguity The idea of vagueness is based upon a common feature of words in our language. Many of them leave open a range of borderline cases. When these borderline cases cause difficulty, we say that the use of such terms is vague. The notion of ambiguity is also based upon a common feature of our language. Words often have a number of different meanings. For example, *The New Merriam-Webster Pocket Dictionary* has the following entry under the word "cardinal":

> Cardinal *adj. 1:* of basic importance: Chief, Main, Primary, *2:* of cardinal red color.

[1] An answer to this is that people should be allowed to vote at 18 since they can, in times of war, be drafted at 18. This is not much of an answer, for it is also arbitrary to draft people at the age of 18.

n. 1: an ecclesiastical official of the Roman Catholic Church ranking
next below the Pope, 2: a bright red, 3: any of several American finches
of which the male is bright red.

In the plural, "The Cardinals" is the name of various athletic teams that
inhabit St. Louis; "cardinal" is also the name of the numbers used in
simple counting.

It is not likely that people could get confused about these very different meanings of the word "cardinal," but we might imagine a priest,
a bird watcher, and a baseball fan all hearing the remark: "The cardinals
are in town." The priest would prepare for a solemn occasion, the bird
watcher would get out his binoculars, and the baseball fan would head
for the stadium. If a term is used so that such confusions arise, we say
that it is used *ambiguously.*

Examples of ambiguity are perhaps more common in logic texts
than in everyday life, for context usually settles which of a variety of
meanings is appropriate. Yet sometimes genuine misunderstandings do
arise in everyday life. An American and a European discussing "football" may have two different games in mind. The European is talking
about what *we* call "soccer"; the American is talking about what *they*
call "American football." It is characteristic of the ambiguous use of a
term that when it comes to light we are likely to say something like,
"Oh, you mean *that* kind of cardinal!" or "Oh, you are talking about
American football!" In a context where the use of a word is ambiguous,
we do not know which of *two* clear meanings to attach to a word. In
a context where the use of a word is vague, we cannot attach *any* clear
meaning to the use of a word.

So far we have talked about the ambiguity of terms or individual
words. But sometimes we do not know what interpretation to give to a
phrase or a sentence because its grammar or syntax admits of more than
one interpretation. Thus if we talk about *the conquest of the Persians,*
we might be referring either to the Persians' conquering someone or to
someone's conquering the Persians. Sometimes a sentence admits of a
great many possible interpretations. For example, consider the sentence:

Only sons marry only daughters.

One thing that this might mean is that a person who is a male only
child will marry a person who is a female only child. Again, it might
mean that sons are the only persons who only marry daughters.[2]

The process of rewriting a sentence so that its meaning becomes
clear is called *disambiguating.* One way of disambiguating a sentence is
to continue it in a way that forces one interpretation. This is a way of
filling out a context. Consider the sentence, "Mary had a little lamb."

[2] This example comes from Paul Benacerraf.

Notice how the meaning changes completely under the following continuations:

(1) Mary had a little lamb; he followed her to school.

(2) Mary had a little lamb and then a little broccoli.

Just in passing, it is not altogether obvious how we should describe the ambiguity in the sentence "Mary had a little lamb." The most obvious suggestion is that the word "had" is ambiguous, meaning "owned" on the first reading and "ate" on a second reading. Notice, however, that this also forces alternative readings for the expression "a little lamb." Presumably, it was a small whole live lamb that followed Mary to school, whereas it would have been a small piece of cooked lamb that she ate. So if we try to locate the ambiguity in particular words, we must say that not only the word "had" but also the word "lamb" is being used ambiguously. This is a reasonable approach, but another is available. In everyday speech we often leave things out. Thus, instead of saying "Mary had a little *piece of meat derived from a* lamb *to eat*," we just say "Mary had a little lamb," dropping out the italicized words on the assumption that they will be understood. In most contexts, such deletions cause no misunderstanding. But sometimes deletions are misunderstood, and this can produce ambiguity.

Exercise 4: Show that each of the following sentences admits of at least two interpretations by either rewriting the sentence as a whole in two different ways or expanding the sentence two different ways in order to clarify the context.

Example: Kenneth let us down.
Rewriting: Kenneth lowered us.
              Kenneth disappointed us.
Expanding: Kenneth let us down with a rope.
              Kenneth let us down just when we needed him.

1. The Abbots have to raise all their food.
2. Reggie Jackson was safe at home.
3. Nixon followed Johnson.
4. Marion missed her friends.
5. I don't know what state Meredith is in.
6. Wendy ran the Marathon.
7. Where did you get bitten?
8. There is some explanation for everything.
9. The President sent her congratulations.
10. I cannot recommend him too highly.
11. Visiting professors can be boring.
12. The meaning of the term "altering" is changing.

Equivocation Broadly speaking, to *equivocate* means to use language in a misleading way. More specifically, people equivocate when they shift their position in the course of a discussion or argument. Equivocation is connected with vagueness and ambiguity because they provide the means for making, and masking, such a shift in position. The following series of statements illustrates equivocation:

> All those who claim to be conscientious objectors will be pardoned.
>
> By a conscientious objector we will mean those persons who actually applied for this status.
>
> In coming to a decision, a review board will consider the sincerity of this application.
>
> Evidence of sincerity includes such things as membership in a religious organization that is opposed to all wars, and willingness to accept alternative service.
>
> Only long-term members of religious organizations opposed to all wars who have volunteered for alternative hazardous duty will be considered genuine conscientious objectors.

Here we move by slow stages from a view that will pardon all conscientious objectors to one that will pardon almost none of them. We can imagine a person sincerely maintaining any one of these positions. But a person who shifts back and forth from one position to another by changing his definition of what counts as a conscientious objection is involved in equivocation.

Equivocation does not always happen in slow stages. Sometimes it takes place with blinding speed. When asked what he thought about a committee report concerning his actions, Billy Carter replied in the following way:

> "I don't think I did anything illegal, I don't think I did anything immoral. My morals may be different from anybody else's, but I don't think I did anything wrong."

Here what is said in the first sentence is promptly taken back in the second.

Exercise 5 (a light diversion): What is wrong with each of the following remarks?

1. The census can never be 100 or 101 percent accurate.
2. He averages five yards each and every time he carries the ball.
3. Success is fifty percent ability and three quarters hard work. (Paraphrasing Yogi Berra)

4. The sooner you fall behind in your work, the longer you have to catch up.
5. Smoking may knock a few years off your life, but it is not going to kill you.

Definitions It is sometimes suggested that a great many disputes could be avoided if people simply took the precaution of defining their terms. To some extent this is true; but definitions will not solve all problems, and a mindless insistence upon definitions can turn a serious discussion into a semantic quibble. Furthermore, definitions themselves can be confusing or obfuscating as, for example, when an economist tells us:

I define inflation as too much money chasing too few goods.

Not only is this definition metaphorical and obscure, it also has built into it a theory on the causes of inflation.

Definitions are, of course, important, but to use them correctly, we must realize that they come in various forms and serve various purposes. There are at least five kinds of definition that should be distinguished.

(1) *Lexical, or dictionary, definitions:* We consult a dictionary when we are ignorant about the meaning of a word in a particular language. Except for an occasional diagram, a dictionary explains the meaning of a word by using other words that, presumably, the reader already understands. If you do not happen to know what the words "jejune," "ketone," or "Kreis" mean, then you can look these words up in an English, a scientific, or a German dictionary respectively. Lexical definitions supply us with information about the standard meaning of words in a particular language.

(2) *Stipulative definitions* are used to assign a meaning to a new (usually technical) term or to assign a new or special meaning to a familiar term. Thus mathematicians introduced the term "googol" to stand for the number expressed by 1 followed by one hundred zeroes. Economists have given the term "money," which in common parlance means currency, i.e., something you can put in your pocket, a much wider meaning. For economists money includes both currency and those assets which are readily convertible into currency.

(3) *Precising definitions* are used to resolve vagueness. They are used to draw a sharp (or sharper) boundary around the extension of a term which, in ordinary usage, has a fuzzy or indeterminate boundary. For example, for most purposes it is not important to decide how big a population center must be in order to count as a city rather than as a town. We can deal with the borderline cases by using such phrases as "very small city" or "quite a large town." On most occasions it will not make much difference which phrase we use. Yet it is not hard to imagine a situation in which it might make a difference whether a center of population is a city or not: as a city, it might be eligible for redevelopment funds that are not available to towns. Here a precising definition—a def-

inition that draws a sharp boundary where none formerly existed—is essential. Precising definitions are like stipulative definitions; they involve a decision. They are not completely arbitrary, however, since they usually conform to the accepted understanding of the meaning of a term. (It would be reasonable to define a city as any population center with more than 50,000 people. It would be unreasonable to define a city as any population center with more than 17 people.)

(4) *Disambiguating definitions* tell us in which sense a word is being used. (When I said that banks were collapsing, I meant the river banks, not the financial institutions.)

(5) Finally, *theoretical definitions* are introduced to give a systematic order to a subject matter. For example, in mathematics, every term must be either a primitive (undefined) term or a term defined by means of these primitive terms. In a similar way, we might try to represent family relationships using only the primitive notions of parent, male, and female. We might construct definitions of the following kind:

"A is the brother of B."   = "A and B have the same parents and A is male."

"A is B's grandmother."   = "A is a parent of a parent of B and A is female."[3]

Things become more complicated when we try to define such notions as "second cousin once removed," yet by extending these definitions from simple to more complicated cases, our system of family relationships can be given a systematic development. This process may even prove useful in comparing our system of family relationships with that of some other society. Formulating definitions of this kind for family relationships is relatively easy, but similar activities in science and mathematics can demand the insight of a genius.

The Role of Definitions In the middle of discussions people often ask for definitions or even state, usually with an air of triumph, that everything depends upon the way you define your terms. We saw in the opening chapter that definitions are not always needed, and, in most cases, issues do not turn upon the way in which words are defined. Heavy-handed calls for definitions are unfortunate because they often derail honest discussion and can also obscure those cases in which a demand for a definition is in order. When asked for a definition, it is appropriate to reply: "What sort of definition do you want, and why do you want it?" Of course, if you are using a word in a way that departs from customary

---

[3] Notice that in these definitions an individual word is not defined in isolation; instead, a whole sentence containing the word is replaced by another whole sentence in which the defined word does not appear. Definitions of this kind are called "contextual definitions" because a context containing the word is the unit of definition.

usage, or using it in some special way of your own, or using a word that is too vague for the given context, or using a word in an ambiguous way, then the request for a definition is perfectly in order. In such cases the demand for a definition represents an important move within the argument rather than a distraction from it.

Exercise 6: Find the lexical definitions for the words "jejune" and "clarion."

Give a stipulative definition for the word "klurg." Stipulate a word to stand for the chunks of ice that form under car fenders in winter.

Give precising definitions for the words "book" and "alcoholic beverage." (Supply the context that gives your precising definitions a point.)

Give disambiguating definitions for the words "chair" and "pen."

Using the notions of parent(s), male, and female as basic, give definitions of the following family relationships:
- (1) A and B are sisters.
- (2) A is B's half brother.
- (3) A is B's niece.
- (4) A is B's cousin.

Irrelevance

In a good argument we present statements that are true in order to offer support for some conclusion. One way to mimic arguing without really arguing is to state things that are certainly true, but have no bearing upon the truth of the conclusion. Speaking and arguing in this way violates what Grice calls a rule of Relevance. Now we might wonder why irrelevant remarks can have any influence at all. The answer is that we generally assume that a person's remarks are relevant, for this is one of the conditions for smooth and successful conversation. That it is possible to exploit this natural assumption is shown in the following passage from *The Catcher in the Rye.*

> ... the new elevator boy was sort of on the stupid side. I told him, in this very casual voice, to take me up the Dicksteins' ...
>
> He had the elevator doors all shut and all, and was all set to take me up, and then he turned around and said, "They ain't in. They're at a party on the fourteenth floor."
>
> "That's all right," I said. "I'm supposed to wait for them. I'm their nephew."

He gave me this sort of stupid, suspicious look. "You better wait in the lobby, fella," he said.

"I'd like to—I really would," I said. "But I have a bad leg. I have to hold it in a certain position. I think I'd better sit down in the chair outside their door."

He didn't know what the hell I was talking about, so all he said was "oh" and took me up. Not bad, boy. It's funny. All you have to do is say something nobody understands and they'll do practically anything you want them to.[4]

It's clear what is going on here. When someone offers something as a reason, it is conversationally implied that there is some connection between it and the thing you are arguing for. In most cases the connection is obvious, and there is no need to spell it out. In other cases the connection is not obvious, but in the spirit of cooperation others are willing to assume that it exists. In the present case, there seems to be no connection between having a bad leg and sitting in one *particular* chair. Why, then, doesn't the elevator operator challenge this statement? Part of the reason is that it is not easy to challenge what people say; among other things, it is not polite. But politeness doesn't seem to hold the elevator operator back; instead, he does not want to appear stupid. The person who offers a reason conversationally implies a connection and we do not like to admit that we fail to see this connection. This combination of generosity and pride leads us to accept all sorts of irrelevant statements as reasons.

The Presidential campaign debates of 1976 also provided some splendid examples of fallacies of irrelevance. Here is one example involving an exchange with Jimmy Carter:

Question: . . . What should the role of the United States in the world be and in that connection, concerning your limited experience in foreign affairs and the fact that you take some pride in being a Washington outsider, don't you think it would be appropriate to tell the American voters, before the election, the people you would like to have in key positions . . .

After indicating that it would be inappropriate to announce his appointments at that time, he went on to say:

I've travelled the last twenty-one months among the people of this country. I've talked with them and I've listened. And I've seen it first hand in a very vivid way the deep hurt that's come to this country in

[4] J. D. Salinger, *The Catcher in the Rye* (New York: Bantam Book Co., 1964), pp. 157–58.

the aftermath of Vietnam and Cambodia and Chile and Pakistan and Angola and Watergate, CIA revelations.

Notice that the question itself is not a model of clarity. It falls into three parts. (1) A broad, unfocused question about foreign policy, (2) a reference to Carter's limited experience in foreign affairs, and (3) a direct question about appointments. Carter responds directly to the third item, but he is obviously reacting most strongly to the second aspect of the question because it challenges his qualifications to be President. He speaks of his firsthand knowledge of *the people's concern with* foreign affairs—which is not exactly to the point—and then drifts off into plain irrelevance by referring to Watergate. Hearing this, a visitor from another planet would think that Watergate was a country.

Fallacies of irrelevance are surprisingly common in everyday life. The best strategy for dealing with them is simply to cross out all irrelevant claims and then see what is left. Sometimes nothing is left. On the other hand, we should not be heavy-handed in making charges of irrelevance. Sometimes the occurrence of irrelevance is innocent; good arguments often contain irrelevant asides. More importantly, relevance is often secured by way of a conversational implication, so we really have to know what is going on in a given context in order to decide whether a remark is irrelevant or not.

We can illustrate this last point by examining two classical fallacies of irrelevance: the argument *ad hominem* and appeals to authority.

Arguments ad Hominem Literally, an *argument ad hominem* is an argument directed against the arguer rather than against his argument or against the conclusion of his argument. On the face of it, this seems to involve irrelevance, for the character of the person should have nothing to do with the truth of what he says or the soundness of what he argues. But consider a case in point:

A: It is time for the United States to develop more normal relations with Cuba.

B: Yeah, so you can make a bundle importing cigars from those Commies.

B's reply is certainly an ad hominem attack; it is an attack upon the motives of the speaker and not upon what the speaker has said. Yet the remark is not without some relevance—it is not off the wall. In a conversational exchange, we rely on the integrity of the person who is speaking, and when we have reasons to believe that the person's integrity is questionable, we sometimes say so. This is the significance of B's remark. He points to a fact that gives us some reason not to trust A's integrity in a discussion of U.S. relations with Cuba. We will therefore have to draw a distinction between an ad hominem attack and an ad hominem fallacy. In the context of an argument, we sometimes challenge a person's *right* to perform certain speech acts. Sometimes these attacks are justified, sometimes they are not. They must be judged on their own terms. On the other hand, an attack of this kind is sometimes illicitly turned into an attack upon the *truth* of what a person says or upon the soundness of that person's argument. We then have an instance of an *ad hominem fallacy*. In general, the truth of a statement or the soundness of an argument does not depend upon who produces them.

This difference is illustrated by the Biblical story of Job. Job is described as a person who "was blameless and upright, one who feared God and turned away from evil." Satan challenges God to allow him to subject Job to the worst calamities to see if Job's faith will remain unchanged. After the most extreme misfortune, Job finally cries out and asks why he should be made to suffer so.

Then the Lord answered Job out of the whirlwind:

Who is this that darkens counsel by words without knowledge?

Gird up your loins like a man.

I will question you, and you shall declare to me.

Where were you when I laid the foundations of the earth?

Tell me, if you have understanding.

God then continues with a long list of matters about which Job is completely ignorant. If we read all this as an answer to Job's complaints, then it must seem an ad hominem fallacy, for how can talk about Job's ignorance justify his apparently unmerited suffering? On the other hand, if we interpret God's statements as an attack upon Job's right to ask such a question, then they will not be read as answers to it, and no fallacy has been committed.

Although there is an important difference between ad hominem attacks and ad hominem fallacies, there is no shortage of the latter. One mark of an ad hominem fallacy is that the personal attack may have nothing to do with the matter at hand. A person's physical appearance, ethnic background, sex, bathing habits, or dress may *sometimes* give us reason to challenge his or her speech acts, but usually they do not. Ad hominem fallacies deal almost exclusively in such matters.

Exercise 7: (1) Ad hominem fallacies are so common that you should have little difficulty finding examples in political speeches, editorials, etc. Collect as many as you can.

(2) Chapter 12 reprints two articles concerning protesters, one by Jeffrey Hart entitled "Protesters are 'Ugly, Stupid,' " the other by Ian Menzies entitled "A Record of Being Right." As the titles themselves indicate, one article is sharply critical of protesters, whereas the other strongly approves of them. Analyze each of these arguments in the light of the discussion of slanting in earlier chapters and this chapter's treatment of ad hominem attacks vs. ad hominem fallacies. Decide in each case whether the description of protesters is fair and accurate. Then decide whether either article commits a fallacy of relevance by converting unfavorable or favorable remarks about the protesters themselves into either a criticism or a defense of their views.

Appeals to Authority Often in the midst of an argument we cite an authority to back up what we say. As we saw in Chapter 3, this is a standard way of offering assurances. In citing an authority, instead of giving reasons for what we say, we indicate that someone (the authority cited) could give them. Although logicians sometimes speak of the *fallacy* of appealing to authorities, we should notice in the first place that there is often nothing wrong with citing authorities or experts to support what we say. An authority is a person or institution with a privileged position concerning certain information. Through training, a doctor is an expert on certain diseases. A person who works in the Department of Agriculture can be an expert on America's soybean production. Someone who grew up in the swamps might be an expert on trapping muskrats. Since some people stand in a better position to know things than others, there is nothing wrong with citing them as authorities. In fact, an appeal to experts and authorities is essential if we are to make up our minds on subjects outside our own range of competence.

At the same time, appeals to authority can be abused, and there are some obvious questions we should ask whenever such an appeal is made. Most obviously, we should always ask *whether the authority cited is, in fact, an authority in the area under discussion.* If the answer to this question is *No,* then we are dealing with a fallacy of *relevance.* For example, being a movie star does not qualify a person to speak on the merits of a particular brand of elbow macaroni. Endorsements by athletes of hair cremes, deodorants, beer, and automobiles are in the same boat. Of course, we have to be careful in making this charge. It is possible that certain athletes make systematic studies of deodorants before giving one deodorant their endorsement. But it is not likely.

Of course, most people realize that athletes, movie stars, and the like are featured in advertisements primarily to attract attention and not because they are experts concerning the products they are promoting. It is more surprising how often non-authorities or the wrong authorities are brought in to judge serious matters. To cite one example, Uri Geller had little difficulty in convincing a group of distinguished British scientists that he possessed psychic powers. In particular, he was able to convince them that he could bend spoons by mental powers alone. In contrast, James Randi, a professional magician, had little difficulty in detecting and unmasking the tricks that bamboozled the scientific observers.[5] The remarkable feature of this case was not that a group of scientists could be fooled by a magician, but rather that these scientists assumed that they had the expertise necessary to decide whether a paranormal phenomenon had taken place or not. After all, the most obvious explanation of Geller's feats was that he had somehow cheated. To test this possibility, what was needed, as it turned out, was not a scientist with impeccable scholarly credentials, but a magician who could do the same tricks himself and therefore knew what to look for.

It is, of course, difficult to decide whether someone is an expert in a field when you yourself are not. There are, however, certain clues that will help you make this decision. If the "expert" spends a great deal of time showing off knowledge that is not relevant to the matter at hand, then you have reason to be suspicious. Furthermore, if the authority claims to have detailed knowledge of things that he or she could not possibly know—for example, about what was said in private conversations that he or she did not hear or, even more strikingly, about the thoughts that were taking place in other people's minds, then you have very little reason to trust whatever else that person has to say. You know,

[5] For an entertaining and instructive account of this case, see James Randi's *The Magic of Uri Geller* (New York: Ballantine Books, 1975).

for example, that he or she has no qualms about making things up, that is, about lying. Finally it is often possible to spot-check certain claims in order to make sure that they are correct. It may take one expert to tell another, but it often takes very little more than good common sense and an unwillingness to be fooled to detect a fraud.[6]

Apart from cases where the opinions of the "authority" cited are obviously irrelevant to the matter at hand, we can still ask *whether the question is of the kind that can be settled by expert opinion.* It is important to raise this issue because experts often disagree. In a criminal trial, one set of expert witnesses may testify that the defendant had been brainwashed and was in no way responsible for his or her actions. A second set of expert witnesses will testify that the defendant was as sane and sober as a judge at the time of the crime. A bewildered jury must decide which (if any) of the experts to trust.

To get a sense of this problem, imagine yourself sitting in the jury trying to decide the following case. In 1920 Mrs. Andree Hahn of Kansas City, Missouri, purchased a painting (entitled *La Belle Ferronnière*) that was supposedly painted by Leonardo da Vinci. On hearing of this sale, Sir Joseph Duveen, an international art dealer, declared that the painting was a fake. He did this publicly, without actually having seen Mrs. Hahn's painting. Such a remark, made by a leading art dealer, naturally lowered the value of the painting and Mrs. Hahn sued. Duveen summoned a gallery of art experts to testify in his behalf that the painting was indeed a fraud. Duveen's leading witness was Bernard Berenson, an art critic of international renown. Part of Berenson's deposition and subsequent cross-examination by Hyacinthe Ringrose, Mrs. Hahn's attorney, has been summarized by Laurie Adams:

> Berenson was Duveen's first Paris witness; his deposition lasted two days and was taken at the offices of the Guaranty Trust Co., 1 rue des Italiens. In view of Berenson's international renown as an art critic, Duveen's attorney opened the deposition with questions on the nature of expertise.
>
> "You have to know the pictures," Berenson explained, "no matter how few or how many, and all the other works of art that practically nobody questions as being by that master. You then get a sense . . . this sort of sixth sense that comes from accumulated experience . . . a sense of the quality of the master, a sense of what that master is up to, what he is likely to do, able to do, and what he is not likely to be able to do. Then you control this by trying to find out what characteristics are recurrent in him and that do not occur in that one picture exclusively. For instance, a certain kind of ear, a certain type of hand, a certain lay

---

[6] As an illustration of the remarkable results that can be obtained by asking just these questions, see the essay by Richard Kusche on the Bermuda Triangle reprinted in Part Two, pp. 354 ff.

of hair, a certain kind of eye, of chin, and so on; certain folds of draperies. When all these things go together in picture after picture, we conclude and are allowed to conclude by all people who allow for evidence, that that is the right kind of evidence; and if that occurs in the picture, then you say that it is a picture by the said master."

Later, under cross-examination, Ringrose launched into an attack on Berenson's description of his own expertise by bringing up the idea of the painter's unconscious. "Do you think it is possible for anybody to identify the unconscious characteristics of a painter?"

"Yes, it is the easiest thing in the world, because he was not trying to disguise them."

"The mystical characteristics?" Ringrose persisted, trying to discredit Berenson's technique by implying that it was vague, unscientific, even ridiculously magical.

"Not at all," asserted Berenson confidently, "It was what he was doing unconsciously; or what he was doing by rote—we all do most of our work by rote. What we do habitually, we always do in the same fashion."

"Didn't you use the word 'mystical' and say that you had ascertained the unconscious characteristics of Leonardo da Vinci by a sort of sixth sense?"

"I did not use it in that sense. I used it in expressing that the moment I see a picture my sixth sense tells me what it is; but not when I describe it. . . . You must distinguish in art criticism between the instantaneous impression, then the attempt to control it by all sorts of other detailed evidence and then the further effort to get the kind of evidence which would appeal to the other man, after you have convinced yourself. . . ."

"Is there any value at all in this so-called 'sixth sense'?"

"To me it is of the highest value, but I keep it to myself. I wouldn't give any value to it unless it was entirely vouched for by detailed counter-examination, counterproof. . . . It is a phrase which is accepted universally and may be called 'accumulated experience.' A man who has been working on a job for forty years gets an accumulated experience which gives him an instantaneous reaction within his field of competence. That is all I mean."[7]

After listening to this testimony—and to other testimony like it—the majority of the jury (9 - 2) decided that Duveen's experts had not produced credible evidence that Mrs. Hahn's painting was a fraud. The art world was, of course, thunderstruck to see its experts repudiated in this way.

To return to the main point, before we accept expert opinion, we must decide whether expert opinion really exists in a given area. In

[7] Laurie Adams, *Art on Trial* (New York: Walker and Company, 1976), pp. 80–81.

Hahn v. Duveen, the majority of a jury came to the conclusion that for the authenticity of Italian Renaissance painting, the answer is No.

Although this may seem obvious, we often forget to ask *whether the authority has been cited correctly.* When a person cites an authority, he or she is making a factual claim that so and so holds some particular view. Sometimes the claim is false. Here is an example:

> According to medical authorities, poison ivy is contagious when it is oozing.

This is false, for according to medical authorities, poison ivy is never contagious. Yet many people hold that it is contagious, and they think that they have medical opinion on their side. It is hard to deal with people who cite authorities incorrectly, for we do not carry an almanac or encyclopedia around with us. Yet it is a good idea to spot-check appeals to authority, for, short of lying, people often twist authorities to their own opinions.

It is also worth asking *whether the authority cited can be trusted to tell the truth.* To put this more bluntly, we should ask ourselves whether a particular authority has any good reason to lie or misrepresent facts. Presumably, the officials who know most about Russian food production will be the heads of the various agricultural bureaus. But it would be utterly naive to take their reports at face value. Failures in agricultural production have been a standing embarrassment of the Russian economy, and, as a consequence, there is pressure at every level to put a good face on things. Even if the state officials were inclined to tell the truth, which is a charitable assumption, the information they receive is probably not very accurate. But we do not have to consider totalitarian regimes to find instances of deliberate falsification. Oskar Morgenstern remarks that "central banks in many countries, the venerable Bank of England not excepted, have for decades published deliberately misleading statistics, as, for example, when part of the gold in their possession is put under 'other assets' and only part is shown as 'gold.' "[8] Of course, the officials of central banks do not misrepresent their gold holdings out of simple malice; they think that they can gain some advantage through such misrepresentations. So in assessing the trustworthiness of an authority we must really ask two questions: First, is the authority really in a position to know, and secondly, do we have good reason to believe that the authority is telling the truth.

One last question we can ask is *why the appeal to authority is being made at all.* To cite an authority is to give assurances and, as we noticed earlier, we usually give assurances to strengthen the weak points in our arguments. It is surprising how often we can see what is wrong

---

[8] Oskar Morgenstern, *On the Accuracy of Economic Observations* (Princeton, N. J.: Princeton University Press, 1963), p. 20.

with an argument just by noticing where it is backed by appeals to authority. Beyond this, we should be suspicious of arguments that rely on too many authorities. (We might call this the fallacy of excessive footnotes.) Good arguments tend to stand on their own.

To go back to the beginning, in our complicated and specialized world, reliance on experts and authorities is unavoidable. Yet we can still be critical of appeals to authority by asking these questions:

(1) Is the authority cited in fact an authority in the areas under discussion?

(2) Is this the kind of question that can be settled by expert opinion?

(3) Has the authority been cited correctly?

(4) Can the authority cited be trusted to tell the truth?

(5) Why is an appeal to authority being made at all?

Exercise 8: A striking example of disagreements between authorities occurred in a television program mentioned earlier. This script is reproduced in its entirety in Part Two of this book (pp. 229–46). Give your own evaluation of the various authorities. Include the narrator in your assessment.

OTHER USES OF ARGUMENTS

6

In earlier chapters we have spoken about arguments as if their only function were to prove something or to justify some claim. This chapter will attempt to correct this one-sided view by exploring uses of argument other than justification. Sometimes the primary intention of an argument is not to establish some truth, but to criticize or refute an argument. The patterns of successful refutations mirror the criteria for a sound and significant argument, for the point of a refutory argument is to show that one of these criteria has not been met. Another very important use of arguments is to formulate explanations. In seeking an explanation, we are not trying to prove that something is true; we are trying to understand why it is true. One way of making sense out of a perplexing fact is to show how it can be derived from understood principles. Scientific explanations often have this form.

Refutations

To refute an argument is to show that it is no good. Given the nature of an argument, this can be done in two main ways: (1) we can argue that some of the reasons offered are themselves dubious (or even false) or (2) we can argue that the conclusion does not follow from the reasons presented. It is important to note that a refutory argument does *not* have to prove the opposite of what someone else is arguing. A refutation is sufficient if it raises objections that cannot be answered.

Consider the following example. For centuries many people have believed in astrology. That is, they have believed that their lives are determined by, and therefore can be predicted from, the configuration of the stars at their birth. As evidence for this, astrologers point to successful predictions that they have made. There are two ways in which we might attack the astrologer's claim. First, we might examine the evidence to see just how accurate the predictions were. A second, and often more elegant, form of refutation is to grant the evidence and then argue that it does not establish the conclusion. A beautiful argument of this kind is found in St. Augustine's *Confessions*. St. Augustine was captivated by astrology until his conversion to Christianity. He then abandoned it, he says, for the following simple reason:

> I turned my attention to the case of twins, who are generally born within a short time of each other. Whatever significance in the natural order the astrologers may attribute to this interval of time, it is too short to be appreciated by human observation and no allowance can be made for it in the charts which an astrologer has to consult in order to cast a true horoscope. His predictions, then, will not be true, because he would have consulted the same charts for both Esau and Jacob and would have made the same predictions for each of them, whereas it is a fact that the same things did not happen to them both. Therefore, either he would have been wrong in his predictions or, if his forecast was correct, he would not have predicted the same future for each. And yet he would have consulted the same chart in each case. This proves that if he had foretold the truth, it would have been by luck, not by skill.[1]

It may take a few moments to see the full force of this simple argument, but consider what replies an astrologer might make. He could argue that the small difference in time between the births does make a difference, but since past horoscopes have not been cast on this basis, they must all be incorrect and their success simply luck. On the other

[1] St. Augustine, *Confessions*, R. S. Pine-Coffin, trans. (Harmondsworth, England: Penguin Books, 1961), p. 142.

side, if these past horoscopes were correct in ignoring the small time differences, then astrology fails to explain why twins often lead such different lives.

One way for the astrologers to avoid St. Augustine's argument would be to make their claim more modest. Instead of saying that our entire lives are *determined* by the configuration of the heavens at our birth, they could hedge their position by saying that this configuration has an important *influence* on our lives. This move takes some of the excitement out of astrology, for in admitting to *other* influences on our lives, the astrologer can no longer make detailed predictions without having knowledge of the natural and social sciences. But the advantage of this hedging move is that it will allow the astrologer to explain away a great many mistaken predictions. Whenever a particular prediction fails, the astrologer can always say that some other influence interfered with the influence of the stars. If the astrologer is willing to make this move no matter how many predictions come out wrong, then the position is *self-sealing* and so empty of content. (We will examine this notion of a self-sealing position later in this chapter.) So astrologers who wish to maintain that the stars have any influence at all on our lives must produce positive statistical evidence to support their claim. The status of such statistical evidence is examined in a recent textbook on astronomy:

> From time to time astrologers have presented statistical "proofs" of astrology, but without exception when they are checked over by competent mathematicians they are found to be baseless.[2]

That's just like arguing . . . We know that an argument is no good if it starts from true premises and leads to a false conclusion. Often, however, we cannot point this out to refute an argument because the truth or falsity of the conclusion is the very thing at issue. Here a typical device is to point out that by arguing in the same way, we *can* get a result that is unsatisfactory. A wonderfully simple example of this style of argument occurred in the English Parliamentary debate on capital punishment. One member of Parliament was defending the death penalty on the grounds that the alternative, life in prison, was much more cruel. He was met with the following reply: On this principle, those found guilty of first-degree murder ought to be given life in prison and the death penalty should be given to those who commit some lesser offense. Notice that the reply is not decisive as it stands. The first speaker could go on to call for the abolition of life imprisonment and then keep the death penalty as the most severe punishment. Alternatively, he could simply

[2] George O. Abell, *Exploration of the Universe*, 3rd ed. (New York: Holt, Rinehart and Winston, 1975), p. 33.

accept the idea that life imprisonment—not the death penalty—is the most severe penalty and apply it to first-degree murder. In point of fact, however, the first speaker was certainly unwilling to accept either of these alternatives. He simply tried a rhetorical trick and got caught.

Refuting an argument by showing that it is *just like another* argument that is obviously no good is a common device in everyday discussions. Here is another example:

A: If I had a higher salary, I could buy more things, so if everyone had higher salaries, everyone could buy more things.

B: That's just like arguing that if one person stands up at a ball game he will get a better view, so if everyone stands up, everyone will get a better view.

At first sight, it may not be obvious whether A's style of reasoning is valid or not. B's response shows that it is invalid by providing an instance where the same style of reasoning takes us from something true to something false. This, then, is the general method for showing that an argument is invalid: give an example of an argument with the same basic form, where the inference clearly takes us from something true to something false. Admittedly, this procedure is not precise, for we have given no explanation of the notion that two arguments have the *same basic form*. (This topic will be discussed more carefully in Chapters 9 and 10.) Yet it remains a fact that people can often see that two arguments have the same basic form and, through seeing this, decide that an argument presented to them is invalid. This ability is the basis of sound logical judgment. It is also the basis of wit. It's at best mildly funny to say that if God had wanted us to fly, he would have given us wings. You have to be fairly clever to reply at once: "If God had wanted us to stay on the ground, he would have given us roots."

Exercise 1: For each of the following arguments, find another with the same basic form where the premise or premises are true and the conclusion is false.

1. If tea is dangerous, so is coffee.
   Tea isn't dangerous, so coffee isn't either.

2. If a country becomes wealthy, then its people become wealthy as well.

3. You cannot pass a law against dangerous drugs because there is no way of drawing a sharp line between dangerous and nondangerous drugs.

4. If you have never written a novel, then you are in no position to make judgments about novels.

5. If a person has nothing to hide, he or she should not object to being investigated.

6. Women are the natural persons to raise children because they are the ones who give them birth.

7. Radicals should not be granted freedom of speech because they deny this freedom to others.

8. Since everyone acts from his or her own motives, everyone's actions are selfish.

9. Why not smoke? The longer you smoke the longer you live.

Counter-examples So far we have looked at refutations of *arguments*. We have seen that they take two basic forms—they show that the pattern of reasoning is invalid, or they show that the premises themselves are not well-founded. When an argument is refuted, its conclusion has not been shown to be false. As we have seen, we can refute all of the arguments in behalf of astrology but, for all that, the claims of astrologers could still be true. Of course, if we refuted all of these arguments, there would be no *reason* to think that these claims are true.

In contrast, we also speak about refuting a *statement*. This *does* mean showing it to be false. Refutations take various forms, depending upon the form of the statement under attack. For example, if a person claims that all snakes lay eggs, then we need only find one species of snake that does not lay eggs in order to refute the claim. (Here we can cite the black snake, for it bears its young alive.) If the person retreats to the somewhat weaker claim that *most* snakes lay eggs, it becomes much harder to refute his claim. A single example of a snake that bears its young alive is not enough; to refute this claim we would have to show that a majority of snakes do not lay eggs. Here, instead of trying to refute his statement, we may ask him to produce his *argument* in behalf of it. We can then attack this argument. Finally, if the person retreats to the very weak claim that at least some snakes lay eggs, then his statement becomes very difficult to refute. Even if it were false (which it is not), to show this we would have to check every fool snake and establish that it does not lay eggs. So, as a rough-and-ready rule, we can say that the stronger a statement is, the more subject it is to refutation; the weaker it is, the less subject it is to refutation.

Citing the fact that black snakes bear their young alive in order to refute the claim that all snakes lay eggs is called presenting a *counterexample*. The pattern of reasoning is perfectly simple: If someone claims that *everything* of a certain kind has a certain feature, we need find only *one* thing of that kind lacking that feature in order to refute the claim. Although the pattern of argument is simple in form, it is not always easy to think of counter-examples. Some people are much better at it than others. Socrates was a genius in this respect. He wandered through the streets of ancient Athens questioning various people—often important political figures—challenging them to explain what they meant by various terms such as *justice, knowledge, courage, friendship*, and *piety*. As narrated by Plato, these exchanges all fall into a standard pattern: Socrates asks for a definition of some important notion; after some skirmishing, a definition is offered; Socrates immediately finds a counter-example to this definition; the definition is then changed or replaced by another; once more Socrates produces a counter-example; etc. With effortless ease, Socrates seemed able to produce counter-examples to any definition or any principle that others offered. There is no better introduction to the art of giving counter-examples than some specimens of the Socratic method.

In *The Republic*, Socrates is inquiring into the nature of justice. He begins by interrogating Cephalus, an old and distinguished citizen of Athens. Cephalus, in discussing the value of wealth, suggests that justice consists in telling the truth and restoring things we have been entrusted with. The dialogue goes as follows:

> *Cephalus:* Now in this, as I believe, lies the chief value of wealth, not for everyone, perhaps, but for the right-thinking man. It can do much to save us from going to that other world in fear of having cheated or deceived anyone even unintentionally or of being in debt to some god for sacrifice or to some man for money. Wealth has many other uses, of course; but, taking one with another, I should regard this as the best use that can be made of it by a man of sense.
>
> *Socrates:* You put your case admirably, Cephalus.... But take this matter of doing right: can we say that it really consists in nothing more nor less than telling the truth and paying back anything we may have received? Are not these very actions sometimes right and sometimes wrong? Suppose, for example, a friend who had lent us a weapon were to go mad and then ask for it back, surely anyone would say we ought not to return it. It would not be "right" to do so; nor yet to tell the truth without reserve to a madman.
>
> *Cephalus:* No, it would not.
>
> *Socrates:* Right conduct, then, cannot be defined as telling the truth and restoring anything we have been trusted with.[3]

Whereas many of Plato's *Dialogues* show Socrates making fools—and also enemies—of people who claim to know things that they do not

---

[3] *The Republic of Plato*, Francis M. Comford, trans. (New York: Oxford University Press, 1941), p. 7.

know, other dialogues have a different quality. They show Socrates and his interlocutors involved in a cooperative activity searching after philosophical understanding. The *Theaetetus* is a dialogue of this kind. Theaetetus was a brilliant young man, gifted in mathematics. In the dialogue he and Socrates try (unsuccessfully) to arrive at a correct definition of *knowledge*. They notice an important difference between knowledge and mere belief: It is possible for someone to *believe* something that is false, but it is not possible for someone to *know* something that is false. This leads Theaetetus to suggest a simple definition of knowledge: Knowledge equals true belief. After all, someone cannot have a true belief concerning something that is false. This proposed definition is refuted in the following exchange.

> *Socrates:* [There is] a whole profession to prove that true belief is not knowledge.
>
> *Theaetetus:* How so? What profession?
>
> *Socrates:* The profession of those paragons of intellect known as orators and lawyers. There you have men who use their skill to produce conviction, not by instruction, but by making people believe whatever they want them to believe. You can hardly imagine teachers so clever as to be able, in the short time allowed by the clock, to instruct their hearers thoroughly in the true facts of a case of robbery or other violence which those hearers had not witnessed.
>
> *Theaetetus:* No, I cannot imagine that; but they can convince them.
>
> *Socrates:* And by convincing you mean making them believe something.
>
> *Theaetetus:* Of course.
>
> *Socrates:* And when a jury is rightly convinced of facts which can be known only by an eye-witness, then, judging by hearsay and accept a true belief, they are judging without knowledge, although, if they find the right verdict, their conviction is correct?
>
> *Theaetetus:* Certainly.
>
> *Socrates:* But if true belief and knowledge were the same thing, the best of jurymen could never have a correct belief without knowledge. It now appears that they must be different things.[4]

One thing to notice about both of these counter-examples is that they are *completely decisive*. Cephalus does not stand by his position and argue that it would be right to return the sword to his demented

[4] Plato, *Theaetetus*, Francis M. Cornford, trans., in his *Plato's Theory of Knowledge* (New York: Liberal Arts Press, 1957), p. 141.

friend, nor does Theaetetus dig in his heels and insist that the ignorant members of the jury do know that the person is innocent provided only that they believe it and it is true. Faced with the counter-examples, they both retreat at once. Why is this? Why not stay with the definition and reject the counter-examples as false? The answer is that for many concepts there is general agreement about their application to particular cases, even if there is no general agreement about a correct definition. To take an extreme example, everyone agrees that Hitler was a dictator (even Hitler), and no one supposes that Thomas Jefferson was a dictator (even his enemies). So any definition of *a dictator* that would lead us to say that Hitler was not a dictator and Thomas Jefferson was a dictator must be wrong. A less extreme example is the notion of negligence—an idea important in the law. We have some perfectly clear cases of negligence: a person amusing himself by setting off skyrockets in the Sistine Chapel, for example. On the other hand, a person who deliberately drives off a road to avoid striking a child is clearly *not* acting negligently. In between these clear cases there are any number of difficult ones that help give lawyers a living. Because of these borderline cases, no perfectly exact definition of negligence is possible. But any definition of negligence that does not square with the clear cases is just plain wrong, and this can be shown by citing one of these clear cases as a counter-example.

Ethics is an area where arguments often turn upon counter-examples. Although various forms of relativity remain fashionable, in our day-to-day life there is a surprisingly wide range of agreement concerning what actions are right and what actions are wrong. That is, whatever theory we might hold, we usually agree about particular cases. We tend not to notice this agreement because disagreement is interesting and exciting, whereas agreement is not. The task of an ethical theory is to discover those principles which tell us what actions are right and what actions are wrong. One important test of an ethical theory is whether it squares with these clear cases where agreement exists.

Consider the Utilitarian Principle. According to that principle, an action is right if it is the action that will produce the greatest possible total happiness. Admittedly, the idea of happiness is vague and stands in need of explanation. For this discussion, however, we can ignore this complication. At first sight, this principle has much to recommend it. How, we might ask, could it ever be better to act in a way that produces less happiness than would be produced by acting in another way? Furthermore, the world would be a much better place if people uniformly followed this principle. All the same, the Utilitarian Principle is subject to a counter-example that has led most—though not all—philosophers to reject it as the *single* basic principle of ethics. One version of this counter-example goes as follows: It is certainly possible for a society to exist where a small slave population leading a wretched life allows the rest of the population to lead a blissfully happy life. In such a society, any other arrangement would, in fact, lower the total happiness. For example, any attempt to improve the lives of the slaves would be overbalanced by a loss of happiness in the slave-holding class. This may seem like a far-fetched situation, but if it were to occur, the utilitarian would have to approve of this society and argue against any changes in it. To most people this is unacceptable, for it offends our sense of fairness. "Why," we want to ask, "should one segment of society be assigned wretched lives so that others can be happy? How can the society be morally sound when human rights are infringed upon in this way?" Considerations of this kind have led most philosophers to abandon strict utilitarianism as the single principle of morality. Some philosophers have modified the principle to meet objections; some have supplemented it with other principles; some have simply rejected it in favor of some other theory.

Sometimes counter-examples force clarification. Consider the traditional moral precept, "Do unto others as you would have them do unto you." Like utilitarianism, this principle captures an important moral insight, but, if taken quite literally, it is even more subject to counter-examples. Jones, a sado-masochist, enjoys beating other people. When asked whether he would like to be treated in that way, he replies, "Yes." It is obvious that the Golden Rule was not intended to approve of Jones's behavior. The task, then, is to reformulate its principle to avoid this counter-example.

No discussion of counter-examples is complete without a mention of the Morgenbesser Retort. Though the exact story is now shrouded in the mists of time, it has come down to us from the 1950s in the following form. In a lecture, a British philosopher remarked that he knew of many languages where a double negative means an affirmative, but not one language where a double affirmative means a negative. From the back of the room came Morgenbesser's famous retort: "Yeah, Yeah."

Exercise 2: Find a counter-example to each of the following claims.

Examples: Claim: All prime numbers are odd.
Counter-example: 2 is a prime number, but it is not odd.

Claim: "Sugar" is the only word where an s is pronounced sh.
Counter-example: Oh sure.

1. Lightning never strikes twice in the same place.
2. Three points determine a plane.
3. What you don't know can't hurt you.
4. Only the plate umpire can call balls and strikes.
5. You cannot be religious without believing in God.
6. Without poverty there would be no crime.
7. It is always wrong to lie.

Here are two more difficult cases:
1. If it is wrong for one person to do something, then it must be wrong for everyone to do it.
2. There are no rights without corresponding duties.

Self-Sealers and Vacuity It is characteristic of certain positions that no evidence can *possibly* refute them. This may seem like a wonderful feature for a position to have. In fact, however, it usually makes the position useless. We can start with a silly example. A Perfect Sage claims to be able to predict the future in detail. The Perfect Sage's predictions take the following form:

Two weeks from today at 4:37 you are going to be doing . . . *exactly* what you will be doing.

This prediction cannot possibly be wrong, but, of course, it doesn't tell us anything in particular about the future. Whatever happens, the prediction is going to be true, and this is just what is wrong with it. The prediction is *empty* or *vacuous.*

People do not, of course, go around making predictions of the kind just noticed, but, strange to say, they sometimes hold positions that are empty or vacuous in just the same way. A clairvoyant claims to be able to predict the future, but every time a prediction fails, he says that this just proves that someone set up bad vibrations that interfered with his visions. If the prediction comes true, that shows his clairvoyance; if it does not come true, that proves interference. No matter what happens, then, the clairvoyant cannot be wrong. So his predictions are as empty and vacuous as those of the Perfect Sage.

Positions that are set up in this way so that nothing can possibly refute them we will call *self-sealers.*[5] A self-sealing position is one that is so constructed that no criticism can possibly be brought against it. This shows its vacuity, and it is precisely for this reason that we reject it.

People do not usually hold self-sealing positions in a blatant way— they tend to back into them. A person who holds that the American economy is controlled by an international Jewish conspiracy will point out people of Jewish extraction (or with Jewish names) who occupy important positions in financial institutions. This at least counts as evidence, though not very strong evidence. There are a great many people in these institutions who are not Jews. To counter this claim, the person now argues that many of these other people are secretly Jews or are tools of the Jewish conspiracy. The Jews have allowed some non-Jews to hold

[5] I owe this phrase to Ted Honderich. I now know that he owes it, directly or indirectly, to Leon Lipson.

important positions in order to conceal their conspiracy. What evidence is there for this? Well, really none, but that only helps to prove how clever the conspiracy is. The position has now become self-sealing, for all evidence cited *against* the existence of the conspiracy will be converted into evidence *for* its cleverness. Unlike our previous examples, which were artificial, reasoning of this kind actually does take place.

Self-sealing arguments are hard to deal with, for people who use them will often shift their ground. A person will begin by holding a significant position that implies that facts are one way rather than another, but under the pressure of criticism he will self-seal it so that no evidence can possibly count against it. That is, he will slide back and forth between two positions—one that is not self-sealed, and so is significant, but subject to criticism, and another that is self-sealed, and so is not subject to criticism, but insignificant. The charge that is leveled against a theory that vacillates in this way is that it is either *trivial* or *false:* trivial if self-sealing, false if not.

One way of challenging a self-sealing position is to ask what possible fact could prove it wrong. This is a good question to ask, but it can be misunderstood and met with the triumphant reply: "Nothing can prove my position wrong, because it is true." A better way to show the insignificance of a self-sealing theory is to put the question in a different form: If your position has any significance, it should tell us that certain things will occur whereas certain other things will not occur. If it cannot do this, it really tells us nothing at all; so please make some specific predictions and we will see how they come out.

Ideologies and world views tend to be self-sealing. The Marxist ideology has this quality. If a revolution occurs, then this was predicted by one part of the theory; if it does not occur, then that too was predicted by another part of the theory. The position also has another quite special twist. If you fail to see the truth of the Marxist ideology, that just shows that your social consciousness has not been raised. The very fact that you reject the Marxist ideology shows that you are not yet capable of understanding it and that you are in need of re-education. This is perfect self-sealing. Sometimes psychoanalytic theory gets involved in this same kind of self-sealing. People who disagree with certain psychoanalytic claims can be accused of repressing these facts. If a boy *denies* that he wants to murder his father and sleep with his mother, this itself is taken as evidence of the strength of these desires and of his unwillingness to acknowledge them. If this kind of reasoning gets out of hand, then psychoanalytic theory also becomes self-sealing and empty. Freud was aware of this danger; this was the basis of his remark that sometimes a cigar is just a cigar.

So far, we have seen two ways in which an argument can be self-sealing: (1) it can invent an *ad hoc* or arbitrary way of dismissing every possible criticism. The clairvoyant and the astrologer can always point to interfering conditions without going to the trouble of saying what they are. The anti-Semite can always cite Jewish cleverness to explain away counter-evidence. (2) A theory can counter criticism by attacking its critics. The critic of Marxism is charged with having a decadent bourgeois consciousness which blinds him to the facts of class conflict. The critic's response to psychoanalytic theory is analyzed (and then dismissed) as repression, a reaction formation, or something or other.

Yet another form of self-sealing is this: Words are used in such a way that a position becomes true *by definition.* For example, a person makes the strong claim that all human actions are selfish. This is an interesting remark, but it seems to be false, for it is easy to think of cases where people have acted in self-sacrificing ways. To counter these obvious objections, the argument takes the following turn: When a person acts in a self-sacrificing way, what he *wants* to do is help another, even at his own expense. This is his desire or his motive, and that is what he acts to fulfill. So the action is selfish after all. It should be obvious that this is a self-sealing move, for it will not help to cite any behavior— even self-destructive behavior—as counter-evidence. If a person desires to harm himself, then he acts to fulfill his desire and the act is again selfish.

It is not hard to see what has happened in this case. The arguer has chosen to use the word "selfish" in a new and peculiar way. A person is said to act selfishly if he acts to do what he desires to do. This is not what we usually mean by this word. We say that a person acts selfishly if he is too much concerned with his own interests at the expense of the interests of others. On this standard use of the word "selfish" there are any number of counter-examples to the claim that all human actions are selfish. But these counter-examples do not apply when the word "selfish" is used in a new way, where "acting selfishly" comes close to meaning just "acting." The point is that under this new meaning of "selfish" it becomes empty (or almost empty) to say that all human actions are selfish. We are thus back to a familiar situation: Under one interpretation (the ordinary interpretation), the claim that all human actions are selfish is interesting, and false. Under another interpretation (an extraordinary interpretation), the claim is true but uninteresting. The position gets all its *apparent* interest and plausibility from a rapid two-step back and forth between these positions.

Self-sealing arguments are not easy to handle, for they change their form under pressure. The best strategy is to begin by charging a person who uses such an argument with saying something trivial, vacuous, or boring. If, to meet this charge, he or she says something quite specific and important, then argument can proceed along normal lines. But it is not always easy to get down to brass tacks in this way. This becomes clear if you examine an argument between a Marxist and a non-Marxist, or between individuals with different religious views. Their positions are sealed against objections from each other, and the arguments are almost always at cross purposes.

Explanations

Explanations answer questions about *how* or *why* something happened. We explain how a mongoose got out of his cage by pointing to a hole he dug under the fence. We explain why Smith was acquitted by saying that he got off on a technicality. The purpose of explanations is to make sense out of things. The character of explanations will depend upon the subject matter and the audience. Explanations in science are more technical than those of everyday life, because scientists are addressing their colleagues who are familiar with the subject matter. We explain things in different ways to children and adults. Sometimes simply filling in the details of a story makes an explanation. For example, we can explain how a two-year-old girl foiled a bank robbery by saying that the robber tripped over her while fleeing from the bank. Here we have made sense out of an unusual event by putting it in the context of a plausible *narrative*. It is unusual for a two-year-old girl to foil a bank robbery, but there is nothing unusual about a person tripping over a child when running recklessly at full speed.

Very many of our explanations in everyday life have this narrative form. One standard puzzle specifically calls for this kind of explanation. We are told, for example, of a person who, when alone, always rides an elevator to the eighteenth floor, gets off, and then walks up the remaining five floors to her apartment. We want to know why she behaves in this way. Various lame suggestions are made: she likes to visit people on her way home; she's taking exercise; etc. None of these explanations makes sense because none accounts for the *invariability* of her behavior. Surely she isn't visiting friends when she comes home at five in the morning, nor is this a reasonable time for taking exercise. Her behavior is completely explained, however, when we are told a single fact: that she is quite short and can reach only up to the button for the eighteenth floor. When she is alone, that is as far as she can take the elevator.

Although the narrative is probably the most common form of explanation in everyday life, we also use *arguments* for giving explanations. We can explain a certain event by deriving it from established principles and accepted facts. This derivation has the form of an argument. Although explanations of this kind do occur in daily life, the clearest examples come from science. A scientist can explain the movements of a complex mechanism by deriving them from the laws of mechanics. A psychologist can explain a person's apparently strange behavior by citing laws governing the unconscious mind. Broadly speaking, the pattern of explanation will employ an argument of the following form.

Accepted principles or laws.
A statement of initial conditions.
∴ A statement of the phenomenon to be explained.

By "initial conditions" we mean those facts in the context which, together with the accepted principles and laws, allow us to derive the result that the event to be explained will occur.

This sounds very abstract, which it is, but one extended example should clarify these ideas. Suppose we put an ice cube into a glass and then fill the glass to the very brim. It will look something like this:

What will happen when the ice cube melts? Will the water overflow? Will it remain at the same level? Will it actually go down? Here we are asking for a *prediction* and it will, of course, make sense to ask a person to *justify* whatever prediction he or she makes.

Stumped by this question, we let the ice cube melt to see what happens. In fact, the water level remains unchanged. We are no longer faced with a problem of prediction, for we can now see what happened: When ice cubes melt (or, anyway, when *this* ice cube melts), the water level stays the same (or, at least, it stayed the same in *this* case). After a few experiments we convince ourselves that this result always occurs. We now have a new question: *Why* does this occur? In short, we want an explanation of this phenomenon. The explanation turns upon the law of buoyancy:

> An object is buoyed up by a force equal to the weight of the water it displaces.

So if we put an object in water, it will continue to sink until it displaces a volume of water whose weight is equal to its own weight. (An object heavier than water will continue to sink, but it will feel lighter under water.) With all this in mind, go back to the original problem. In the following diagram, the shaded area indicates the volume of water displaced by the ice cube.

We know from the law of buoyancy that the weight of the ice cube will be equal to the weight of the volume of water it displaces. But an ice cube is itself simply water in a solid state. It is a quantity of water equal to the quantity of water it displaces. More simply, when it melts, it will exactly fill in the volume of water it displaced, so the water level will remain unchanged.

We can now see how this explanation conforms to the argumentative pattern mentioned above:

Accepted principles or laws.	(Primarily the law of buoyancy.)
Initial conditions.	(An ice cube floating in a glass of water filled to the brim.)
∴ Phenomenon to be explained.	(The level of the water remaining unchanged after the ice cube melts.)

There are some things to notice about this explanation. First of all, it is a pretty good explanation. People with only a slight understanding of science can follow it and see why the water level remains unchanged. We should also notice that it is not a *complete* explanation, for certain things are simply taken for granted—for example, that things do not change weight when they pass from a solid to a liquid state. To put the explanation into perfect argumentative form, this assumption and many others would have to be stated explicitly. This is never done in everyday life, and is only rarely done in the most exact sciences.

Here is an example of an explanation that is less technical. Houses in Indonesia sometimes have their electrical outlets in the middle of the wall rather than at floor level. Why? A beginning of an explanation is that flooding is a danger in the Netherlands. Citing this fact does not help much, however, unless one remembers that Indonesia was formerly a Dutch colony. Even remembering this leaves gaps in the explanation. We can understand why the Dutch might put their electrical outlets above floor level in the Netherlands. It is safer in a country where flooding is a danger. Is flooding, then, a similar danger in Indonesia? Apparently not. So why did the Dutch continue this practice in Indonesia? To answer this question we must cite another broad principle: Colonial settlers tend to preserve their home customs, practices, and styles. In this particular case, the Dutch continued to build Dutch-looking houses with the electrical outlets where (for them) they are normally placed— that is, in the middle of the wall rather than at floor level.

Even though this is not a scientific explanation, notice that it shares many features of the scientific explanation examined previously. First we have a curious fact: the location of electrical outlets in some houses in Indonesia. By way of explanation, certain important facts are cited:

Indonesia was a Dutch colony.

Flooding is a danger in the Netherlands.

And so on.

These facts are then woven together by certain general principles:

Where flooding is a danger, it is safer to put electrical outlets above floor level.

Colonial settlers tend to preserve their home customs, practices, and styles even when their practical significance is diminished.

And so on.

Taken together, these facts and principles make sense of an anomalous fact, i.e., they explain it.[6]

Explanations are satisfactory for *practical* purposes if they remove bewilderment or surprise. An explanation is satisfactory if it tells us *how* or *why* something happened in a way that is relevant to the concerns of a particular context. But how far can explanations go? In explaining why the water level remains the same when the ice cube melts, we cited the law of buoyancy. Now why should that law be true? What explains it? To explain the law of buoyancy, we would have to derive it from other laws that are more general and, perhaps, more intelligible. In fact, this has been done. Archimedes simultaneously proved and explained the Law of Buoyancy by deriving it from the Laws of the Lever.[7] How about the Laws of the Lever? Can they be proved and explained by deriving them from still higher and more comprehensible laws? Perhaps. Yet reasons give out, and sooner or later explanation and justification come to an end. It is the task of science and all rational inquiry to move that boundary further and further back.

[6] This example comes from my former teacher Alan Ross Anderson.
[7] This proof, which is a model of elegant scientific reasoning, is given in Part Two of this book (pp. 318–23).

Exercise 3: Experts found the facts reported in the following newspaper article puzzling. Can you think of some explanation for them?

LOCKED DOORS NO BAR TO CRIME, STUDY SAYS

WASHINGTON (UPI) — Rural Americans with locked doors, watchdogs or guns may face as much risk of burglary as neighbors who leave doors unlocked, a federally financed study says.

The study, financed in part by a three-year $170,000 grant from the Law Enforcement Assistance Administration, was based on a survey of nearly 900 families in rural Ohio.

Sixty percent of the rural residents surveyed regularly locked doors, but were burglarized more often than residents who left doors unlocked.

The figures puzzled investigators, too. "A precise explanation of this finding is not possible from these data," they said.

The report also painted a picture of the rural vandal as a youth from a broken home who viewed vandalism as amusement and was involved with a group smoking marijuana or drinking alcohol at the time of the offense.

The survey, released Sunday, was conducted with the help of federal funds by the Ohio State University extension service and the Farm Bureau.

Seventy-eight percent of the residents surveyed kept watchdogs, but the report found they faced as much chance of being victims of burglary, theft or vandalism as neighbors who had no dog.

And while 76 percent of the rural residents surveyed kept guns for protection, they, too, faced the same chance of being a victim of crime as someone without a gun.[8]

Exercise 4: Write a brief explanation of one of the following:

1. Why a lighter-than-air balloon rises.

2. Why there is an infield fly rule in baseball.

3. Why there is an international date line.

4. Why there are more psychoanalysts in New York City than in any other city or, for that matter, in most countries in the world.

5. Why the cost of food tends to be higher in city slums than in wealthy suburbs.

What facts and what general principles are employed in your explanations? (Don't forget those principles that may seem too obvious to mention.)

Excuses

Sometimes when we have acted in an improper or particularly stupid way, we are asked to explain our actions or explain ourselves. "Why in the world did you do that?" is a request for an explanation of our behav-

---

[8] *Santa Barbara, Calif., News-Press,* Wednesday, February 16, 1977, p. C-11.

ior. Although such explanations lack the rigor of a scientific explanation, they share some of its features. In explaining our behavior we point to certain facts and general principles that together make sense out of what we have done. Take a simple example:

A: Why did you shove Harold into the gulch?

B: He was about to be shot by an assassin.

Here the response makes sense out of a piece of peculiar behavior by citing a single fact: An assassin was about to shoot Harold. But this explanation also depends upon some general principles that are so obvious that we simply take them for granted. For example, we assumed that saving a person's life is, in general, a good thing; that a person in a gulch is less likely to be struck by a bullet than a person standing in plain view; that the amount of harm that might come from falling into a gulch is much less than the harm that would be caused by being struck by a bullet. Against the background of these principles and others, B's remark explains his otherwise inexplicable conduct.

Staying with this same example, we can see that B's remark also justifies his conduct. Not only can we make sense out of what he has done, we are also likely to approve of it. Next, notice what happens when we change the example in the following way:

A: Why did you shove Harold into the gulch?

B: I mistakenly thought that he was about to be shot.

B's remark still explains why he acted as he did. That is, we can still understand his behavior. It no longer justifies, or at least fully justifies, his conduct. Here we would say that B is offering an *excuse* for what he did. Broadly speaking, an excuse is an explanation of human behavior intended to put it in the best possible light. It will often happen that the best possible light will involve the admission of some wrongdoing. In the second dialogue, B admits to having made a mistake. In some contexts this might be a serious admission, but in the present context B does better admitting that he was, perhaps, stupid, rather than acknowledging that he shoved poor Harold into the gulch as a simple act of malice.

We evaluate excuses in much the same way that we evaluate other explanations. An excuse will involve statements of fact and these may be either true or false. We can also challenge the background principles employed in the excuse. We will not be impressed by someone who tells us that he ran seven stoplights so that he would not be late for a kickoff. Getting to a kickoff on time does not warrant such obviously dangerous behavior. Finally, as with other explanations, the facts together with the background principles should make sense out of a piece of behavior.

Presented with an excuse, we can ask the following questions:

(1) Broadly speaking, what are the facts?

(2) With what is the person liable to be charged?

(3) What lesser wrong will the person settle for instead?

(4) How does the explanation accomplish this task?

In our example, (1) B shoved Harold into a gulch. (2) On the face of it, this looks like an attempt to injure Harold. (3) B is willing to admit that he made a mistake of fact. (4) Given this admission, his action can be seen as a laudable, if flawed, attempt to save Harold from death or serious injury.

Exercise 5: Imagine that you have written a letter home asking for money. In the closing paragraph, you feel called upon to offer some excuse for not writing for two months. Write such an excuse (not just an apology) in a perfectly natural way, and then analyze it, using the questions given above.

Exercise 6: In William Shakespeare's Much Ado About Nothing, Benedict, after previously denouncing women and marriage in the strongest terms, is trapped into falling in love with Beatrice. In the following passage he attempts to explain his sudden turnabout. Using the questions given above, analyze this passage.

I may chance have some odd quirks and remnants of wit broken on me because I have railed so long against marriage. But doth not the appetite alter? A man loves the meat in his youth that he cannot endure in his age. Shall quips and sentences and these paper bullets of the brain awe a man from the career of his humor? No, the world must be peopled. When I said I would die a bachelor, I did not think I should live till I were married.[9]

Exercise 7: Find an example of a public official offering an excuse for something he or she has done. Analyze its structure using the four questions above.

[9] William Shakespeare, *Much Ado About Nothing*, Act III, Sc. 1.

BETWEEN PREMISE AND CONCLUSION

7

Arguments in everyday life are rarely spelled out explicitly. In fact, important premises are often omitted altogether and, at times, even the conclusion is left unstated. Such omissions are tolerable because we are able to convey a great deal of information by conversational implication. In order to give a critical assessment of an argument, it is often necessary to make explicit these unstated parts of the argument and then put the whole argument into systematic order. After this is done, we are better placed to decide upon the soundness or unsoundness of the argument in question. This chapter will present methods for restating or reconstructing arguments so that they may be evaluated in a systematic fashion.

Suppressed Premises

If we think of arguments as pathways between premises and conclusions, it becomes obvious that some of these pathways are more complicated than others. Yet even the simplest arguments reveal hidden complexities when examined closely. For example, there is no question that the following argument is valid:

Harriet is in New York with her son.

Therefore, Harriet's son is in New York.

If asked why this conclusion follows from the premises, it would be natural to reply that you cannot be someplace with somebody unless that person is there too. This is not something we spell out, but, nonetheless, it is the principle that takes us from the premise to the conclusion.

One thing to notice about this principle is that it is quite general, that is, it does not depend upon any special features of the people or places involved. If Benjamin is in St. Louis with his daughter, then Benjamin's daughter is in St. Louis. Although the references have changed, the general pattern of the argument has remained the same. Furthermore, the principle that lies behind this inference will seem obvious to anyone who *understands the words used to formulate it.* For this reason we shall say that principles of this kind are basically *linguistic* in character.

If we look at arguments as they occur in everyday life, we will discover that almost all of them turn upon unstated linguistic principles. To cite just one more example, if a wife is taller than her husband, then there is at least one woman who is taller than at least one man. We do not usually state these linguistic principles, for to do so will often violate the rule of strength. (Try to imagine a context in which you would come right out and say, "Husbands, you know, are men." Unless you were speaking to someone just learning the language, this would be a very peculiar remark.) But even if in most cases it would be peculiar to come right out and state such linguistic principles, our arguments typically presuppose them. This observation reveals yet another way in which our daily use of language moves within a rich, though largely unnoticed, framework of rules.

Not only do our arguments often depend upon *linguistic* principles (for example, that husbands are men), but, as noted briefly in Chapter 2, they often depend upon unstated facts understood by those involved in the conversation. Thus, if we are told that Chester Arthur was a President of the United States, we have a right to assume a great many things about him, for example, that at the time he was President, he was a live human being and, more particularly, a native-born citizen of the United States. Appeals to facts of this kind lie behind the following arguments:

Benjamin Franklin could not have been our second President because he died before the second election was held.

Alexander Hamilton could not have been President because he was born in the West Indies.

The first argument obviously turns on a question of fact: did Franklin die before the second presidential election was held? (He did.) But the argument also depends upon a more general principle that ties the premise and conclusion together, that is, that the dead are not eligible for the presidency. It might, however, have been otherwise. We can imagine a society in which the deceased are elected to public office as an honor (something akin to posthumous induction into the Baseball Hall of Fame). But our national government is not like that, and this is something that most Americans know. Therefore it would be odd to come right out and say that the deceased cannot hold public office. (In most settings this would involve a violation of the rule of Strength.) Even so, this fact plays a central role in the argument.

Traditionally, logicians have called premises that seem too obvious to mention *suppressed premises*. An argument depending upon suppressed premises is called an *enthymeme* or is said to be *enthymematic*. If we look at arguments that occur in daily life, we discover that they are, almost without exception, enthymematic. Therefore, in order to trace out the pathway between premises and conclusion, it is usually necessary to fill in these suppressed premises as connecting links.

The second argument given above is more complicated. Why should being from the West Indies disqualify someone from being President of the United States? It seems odd that the Founding Fathers should have something against that particular part of the world. The answer is that the argument depends upon a more general suppressed premise:

Only a native-born American citizen may become President of the United States.

Thus the argument can be unpacked in the following way:

Hamilton was born in the West Indies.

The West Indies has never been part of the United States.

Therefore, Hamilton was not a native-born United States citizen.

Only a native-born United States citizen may become President of the United States.

Therefore, Hamilton could not become President of the United States.

The argument has been broken down into two steps, and each step contains a suppressed premise. The first step is intended to show that Hamilton was not a native-born United States citizen, and it relies on the unstated premise that the West Indies has never been part of the United States. This seems straightforward enough, but notice that the argument further depends upon a *linguistic* suppressed premise concerning what we mean by a "native-born United States citizen." The second part of the argument contains the key idea, namely, that only native-born citizens of the United States are eligible for its presidency. It is this provision of the United States Constitution that lies at the heart of the argument. Knowing this provision is, of course, a more special piece of knowledge than knowing that you have to be alive to be President. (The Founding Fathers felt no need to mention this qualification in the Constitution.) For this reason, more people will see the force of the first argument than the second. The second argument assumes an audience with more specialized knowledge.

To summarize what we have seen thus far: It is only in rare cases that the conclusion of an everyday argument follows immediately from its stated premises. Even for most simple arguments, filling in is necessary if justice is to be done to the force of the argument. Logicians call these unstated facts or principles *suppressed premises.* In the first place, linguistic principles are often suppressed because they are known to virtually all speakers of the language. Nonetheless, they often play an important role in connecting the premises to the conclusion. A second kind of suppressed premise concerns facts that, presumably, are acknowledged by those involved in the conversational exchange. Most people educated in the United States know that you must be a native-born United States citizen to be eligible for the presidency; thus when addressing this audience, there is usually no need to mention the fact. When done appropriately, the suppression of linguistic and factual premises can add greatly to the efficiency of language. Indeed, without the judicious suppression of obvious premises, many arguments would become too cumbersome to be effective.

There are then good pragmatic reasons for not spelling everything out. There are also dangers involved. What is not stated explicitly may escape scrutiny. At times, in fact surprisingly often, the key move in an argument is not given explicit statement and therefore slips by unnoticed and unchallenged.

As an illustration, consider the following style of argument, which, in one form or another, is commonly used:

Since Garvey has already had four hits in a row, his chances of getting a fifth hit are very slight.

The general form of the argument could hardly be simpler: from the premise "Garvey has had four hits already" we are given the conclusion, "His chances of getting a fifth hit are very slight." Pretty obviously, further premises are needed to take us from the premise to the conclusion.

We can notice in the first place that the premise is a straightforward statement of fact, and any dispute concerning it could be settled by checking the records. The conclusion, however, is quite vague; we will have to fix its sense with more precision before we can look for additional premises that might establish it. When we speak of chances being slight, we mean slight relative to some standard or other. If a person has only one chance in ten of surviving an operation, then we would probably say that his chances of survival are slight. On the other hand, if we were told that the chances of an atomic power plant blowing up within the next year were one in ten, we would not call this a slight chance, but rather an unacceptably high probability. Now even very good batters have not much more than one chance in three of getting a hit in a given time at bat; their chances are not particularly favorable. Thus, if the conclusion is to have conversational significance, it must mean something like this:

Garvey's chances of getting a hit *are much lower than usual.*

To say that his chances are much lower than usual would mean much lower than his batting average would indicate. Suppose that up to now Garvey has been a .333 hitter; then the conclusion would mean that his chances are much less than one in three of getting a hit.

With the conclusion thus clarified, we can now ask why someone might think that the fact that Garvey has had four hits in a row makes his chances of getting a fifth consecutive hit much lower than his average would indicate? What are the suppressed premises that connect the stated premise to the conclusion? More than likely, the person is reasoning in the following way:

Garvey has had four hits already.

Another hit will make it five in a row.

The chances of getting five hits in a row are very slight.

Therefore, Garvey's chances of getting a hit are much lower than usual.

This expanded argument contains two new premises. The first premise ("Another hit will make it five in a row") is a linguistic truism and will not be a subject for dispute. The second premise poses problems. First of all, like the original conclusion, it is vague, since no determinate sense has been given to the expression "very slight." To remedy this, we can approximate the probability of Garvey, a .333 hitter, getting five hits in a row. If his chances of getting a hit at a single time at bat are 1 in 3, then his chances of getting five consecutive hits are $(1/3 \times 1/3 \times 1/3 \times 1/3 \times 1/3)$ or 1 chance in 243. Thus, if the argument is correct, Garvey's chances of getting a hit are, indeed, much lower than usual.

With the argument spread out before us, we can look more carefully at the premises. The first two premises are clear and not likely to be the subject of the dispute. What are we to make of the third premise which, after all, is the very heart of the argument? Is it true that Garvey's chances of getting five consecutive hits are very slight—something like 1 chance in 243? At the beginning of the game that probably is a pretty good approximation of his chances. Anyway, we will grant this. But that there is something wrong with this argument can be shown in the following way. After he gets his first hit, his chances of hitting five straight are improved. After two hits they are improved even more, and with three consecutive hits they are improved considerably. Finally, after four hits in a row the odds on a fifth are reduced to the probability of his getting a hit in any single time at bat. That, for a .333 hitter, is 1 chance in 3.

We can now state more carefully how the argument goes wrong. Starting from scratch, a batter like Garvey has about 1 chance in 243 of getting five consecutive hits. Taken this way, the argument will have the following form:

Garvey has had four straight hits.

Another hit will make five straight hits.

Starting from scratch, the chances of getting five straight hits are very slight.

Therefore, Garvey's chances of getting another hit are very slight.

Spelled out this way, the argument is plainly invalid, since the third premise does not apply to Garvey. He *is not starting from scratch;* he has four hits already. We can next try to change the premise so that it does apply to the present case:

After getting four straight hits, the chances of getting a fifth are very slight.

When the suppressed premise is put this way, the conclusion does follow validly, given the premises. They, however, cannot establish the conclusion; for, as we have seen, when taken this way, the third premise is false. Garvey's chances of getting a fifth hit are just his ordinary chances of getting a hit.[1]

In analyzing this argument, we have encountered a common situation: the argument depends upon a premise that, when read so as to be

---

[1] The fallacy revealed in this argument is called the Gambler's Fallacy. The confusion involves a failure to distinguish antecedent probabilities, i.e., the initial probability that a series of events will occur, from the probability that a series will occur given the fact that part of the series has already occurred. The persistence of this fallacy may be part of the reason that gambling houses make money whereas gamblers, as the saying goes, die broke.

true, does not provide valid support for the conclusion; and when read so that it does support the conclusion logically, the premise is not true. No reading gives us premises that are true and an argument that is valid. The argument gains its apparent persuasiveness by sliding back and forth between the two interpretations of the premise. Furthermore, this crucial premise is unstated or suppressed, allowing the shortcomings of the argument, which are obvious once the premise is revealed, to be hidden from sight.

There are times that we feel that an argument is "fishy" although we cannot say exactly why. The best way to deal with such an argument is to make the steps in it as explicit as possible, using the following procedure:

(1) List the explicit premises and the conclusion.

(2) Clarify the premises and conclusion where necessary.

(3) Attempt to fill in a line of reasoning that will take you from the premises to the conclusion.

(4) Under each interpretation, assess the argument for soundness, that is, for the truth of the premises and the validity of the argument.

We are already familiar with the first step in this procedure from Chapter 3, which dealt with the language of argument. No further comment is needed here. In the second step of this procedure, we attempt to make the premises sufficiently clear for logical analysis. The goal here is not perfect clarity, for there probably is no such thing. The degree of clarity needed is a function of context. For example, the argument we began with had as its conclusion a vague statement to the effect that there is not much chance of Garvey getting another hit. We gave this conclusion a more determinate content by interpreting it to mean that his chances of getting a hit were much lower than usual. This, in turn, was interpreted to mean that his chances of getting a hit were significantly lower than his batting average would indicate. This notion is also vague, but it proved good enough for our purposes. Given this reasonable interpretation of the conclusion, we then asked whether the argument supported it.

The third step of the procedure is complicated, indeed, more complicated than our discussion thus far has suggested. In fact, it must be carried out in tandem with the fourth step, assessing the argument for its soundness. If we are trying to give an argument a charitable interpretation, that is, trying to decide for ourselves whether it is acceptable or not, we set as our goal a reconstruction of the argument that shows that it can be filled out with true suppressed premises that validly imply the conclusion. Two problems typically arise when we make this effort:

(1) When we find a set of premises strong enough to support the conclusion, at least one of these premises is false.

(2) When we modify the premises to avoid falsehood, the conclusion no longer follows from them.

The reconstruction of an argument typically involves shifting back and forth between the demand for a valid argument and the demand for true premises. Eventually, we either show the argument to be sound or we abandon the effort, concluding that the argument in question has no sound reconstruction. In assessing the argument intended to show that Garvey's chances of getting another hit after four in a row are very slight, we suggested a number of suppressed premises, but we found it impossible to find a set of suppressed premises that would show the argument to be sound. Now it is entirely possible that *we* were at fault, that we did not show enough ingenuity in looking for suppressed premises that would do the trick. There is, in fact, no purely formal or mechanical way of dealing with this search; we must simply pay close attention to the context of the argument. A person putting forward an argument may reasonably leave out steps provided that they can easily be filled in by those to whom the argument is addressed. The argument we have just examined obviously had something to do with probabilities and, more particularly, with probabilities that occur after a batter has had four hits in a row. But, when we tried to find a suppressed premise that shows the argument to be sound, we found it quite impossible to do so. Of course, it is still abstractly possible that there are suppressed premises other than the ones we tried that would do the trick. Perhaps batters get very tired or bored after getting four hits in a row; perhaps they limit their consecutive hits to avoid humiliating the opposing pitcher; or perhaps they dislike dragging a game out too long. Although these suggestions are abstractly possible, none is very plausible; and the search for suppressed premises should be governed by pragmatic rules. In analyzing an argument, we should be charitable, but our charity can have limits. After a reasonable search for suppressed premises, we have a right to blame the person who formulated the argument for not making it clear.

Once more it is important to remember that presenting an argument is a complex conversational act governed by the same kinds of rules that govern other speech acts. Thus the suppression of premises is seldom just a matter of laziness or sneakiness. Rather, in most instances, it represents the influence of rules that tell us to include in conversational exchanges neither more nor less than is needed for the present purposes. An argument that suppresses no premises will almost surely violate these rules by saying too much. An argument that suppresses too many premises will violate the rule of Strength by withholding information relevant to the given context. In general, however, it is better that an argument say too much rather than too little.

An awareness of conversational setting can also help us understand the relationship between the explicit statement of an argument and its suppressed premises. In using a warranting connective, we commit ourselves to the position that certain statements (the premises) offer adequate justification for another statement (the conclusion). If, as is typically the case, the conclusion is not established by the stated premises alone, then our presentation of the argument implies that there are suppressed premises that, together with the stated premises, do establish the conclusion. Only in rare cases is everything made explicit; in general, conversational arguments imply suppressed premises. Furthermore, the content of the stated or explicit premises suggests the form that these suppressed premises must take. Thus, as we saw, the argument "Benjamin Franklin could not have been our second President because he died before the second election was held" plainly relies upon a principle connecting being President with not being dead. The principle that you have to be alive to be President is so widely known that no useful purpose would be served in stating it explicitly. We have seen also that the argument "Alexander Hamilton could not have been President of the United States because he was born in the West Indies" conversationally implies a connection between place of birth and eligibility for the presidency. It also presupposes knowledge of geography, namely, that the West Indies is not part of the United States. It is therefore obvious that the kinds of premises that can or cannot be suppressed will depend upon the audience to whom the argument is addressed. This last point is more obvious in our discussion of Garvey's chances of getting a fifth hit after getting four in a row. To follow this argument at all, we must have some understanding of baseball; for example, we must know what hits are, that they are relatively hard to get, and so on. Indeed, the argument can make sense only to the small portion of the world's population with the knowledge necessary to understand the implied suppressed premises.

Of course, our treatment of the Garvey example has differed from our treatment of the two previous examples in an important way. In discussing the two presidential arguments we were able to point out suppressed premises that show the conclusion could be established by the premises. This was not possible with the baseball example: as far as we could see, there was no set of acceptable suppressed premises that could be added to the stated premises to make the argument sound. In the first two cases, reconstruction *vindicated* the arguments; in the third case, failure to find a vindicating reconstruction led us to reject the argument. Were we fair in this assessment of the argument? The explicit argument clearly implies some sort of connection between getting four hits in a row and the diminished chances of getting a fifth. (It was argued that *because* he had four hits in a row, Garvey's chances of getting a fifth are very slight.) Our search, however, did not turn up any plausible principles that allowed us to connect the premise to the conclusion. But our analysis had more than this merely negative result. We saw that a natural suppressed premise admitted of two distinct interpretations and that the argument could well gain its apparent force by sliding back and forth between these two interpretations. We rejected the argument as unsound, but we also discovered why people who did not examine it closely might find it persuasive.

Exercise 1: Supply the obvious suppressed premises that connect premises to conclusion in the following simple arguments:

1. Olympia Snow cannot be one of New Hampshire's representatives; she is from Maine.

2. Some husbands are better cooks than their wives, so some men are better cooks than some women.

3. America cannot compete with Japanese imports because the Japanese pay their workers much lower wages.

4. You cannot put June and Brian on the committee; they have been political enemies for years.

5. We cannot make a soufflé tonight because we are out of eggs.

Exercise 2: During the presidential campaign of 1980, the Republicans made the state of the economy a central part of their attack upon the record of the Carter administration. For example, candidate Ronald Reagan made the following statement:

"When Mr. Carter became President, inflation was 4.8 percent. . . . It is now running at 12.7 percent."

This statement is obviously intended as criticism. Starting with the most obvious, list the suppressed premises (or assumptions) that give the statement this force.

You Can Draw Your Own Conclusions

Although it is easy to see why premises are often suppressed, it may seem peculiar to suppress a conclusion. After all, we assume that the point of an argument is to establish the conclusion. It is hard to see how this purpose can be accomplished in an efficient way if the conclusion is not even mentioned. Nonetheless, in conversational arguments, conclusions are quite commonly suppressed. The reasons are many. Sometimes the conclusion follows so obviously from the premises that there is no need to draw the inference explicitly. In fact, in certain contexts, it would be insulting to do so. Someone might tell you that the milk has turned sour so that you do not drink it, but it would be at least faintly insulting for that person to say "The milk has turned sour so don't drink it." This statement would suggest that you might stupidly go on to drink the milk even though you now know that it is sour. One reason, then, for suppressing the conclusion of an argument is that it follows so obviously from the stated premises that there is no need to state it.

Conclusions are sometimes suppressed for rhetorical or dramatic effect. The facts are simply laid out and the audience is asked to draw the conclusion for itself. At the end of a murder mystery the detective shows a diagram of the victim's mansion and says, "Ira Schoenfeld, who could go from his room through the basement then up the narrow laundry chute, is the only person who could have reached the victim's room unnoticed." The stunned listeners realize the implication at once: Schoenfeld is the murderer.

Another reason conclusions are sometimes suppressed is that the person wishes to keep the conclusion indeterminate or unspecified. This wish may be a matter of prudence, that is, the conclusion may be disrespectful, embarrassing, or inflammatory. More often than not, however, a conclusion is suppressed and thus left indeterminate because the person wishes to suggest (or insinuate) it without taking full responsibility for it. Thus, a mother tells her son, "It doesn't take you this long to get dressed when there is no work to be done," plainly implying that her son is a lazy lout. The route from premise to conclusion is obvious: the premise implies that the son is getting dressed less quickly than he often does. In the absence of a physical malady, this fact suggests that he is intentionally getting dressed slowly. To his mother, the obvious reason is that he wishes to delay starting work. Acting on such a wish shows that he is a lazy lout.

Often a conclusion is insinuated by means of a rhetorical question. A asks B: "Did you buy that coat at a rummage sale?" plainly implying that the coat is outdated, ugly, worn, filthy, or in some other way defective. This in turn implies that the person wearing the coat lacks style, is stingy, or, perhaps, is a slob. Only if given the specific context can we tell what precisely is being implied by such a rhetorical question, and sometimes, even if we know the specific context, it is not possible to determine the implication more precisely because no precise implication is intended. A may have nothing more in mind than to launch a free-floating unstructured insult in B's direction. B, of course, will find it very difficult to defend against such an insult.

As another example of an argument with a suppressed conclusion, consider the bumper-sticker slogan, "When Guns Are Outlawed Only Outlaws Will Have Guns." Interpreted one way, it permits a perfectly valid inference: If a law is passed making it illegal for anyone to possess a gun, then anyone possessing a gun will be in violation of that law and thus an outlaw. It is not likely, however, that those who display the bumper sticker are interested in making this fine point of logic. They are obviously arguing against gun control laws or, at least, very stringent gun control laws. Spelled out, their underlying argument looks like this:

> Gun control laws will not be effective in keeping guns out of the hands of criminals.
>
> They will, however, deprive honest citizens of the right to have guns and thus deprive them of the protection guns would give.
>
> Therefore, gun control laws would make honest citizens more, rather than less, subject to criminal assault.
>
> Therefore, gun control laws should not be enacted.

When the argument is spelled out this way, we leave the realm of bumper-sticker rhetoric and confront a series of sharply focused questions. We must examine various proposals for gun control legislation and then try to predict, to the extent possible, what effects such legislation will have. Only in the light of such information can an intelligent discussion of gun control legislation take place.

Speaking to an economist, someone remarks, "If you're so smart, why ain't you rich?" This pointed question plainly implies that the economist is not rich. (Imagine the stunned silence if the economist replied, "As a matter of fact, I am rich; I made a bundle on tin futures.") The question suggests the following line of reasoning:

> 1. Anyone who can become rich will become rich.
>
> Therefore
> 2. This person would become rich if he could.
> 3. A person who can predict the future of the economy can become rich.
> 4. A smart economist can predict the future of the economy.
>
> Therefore
> 5. A smart economist can become rich.
> 6. This person is not rich.
>
> Therefore
> 7. This person is not a smart economist.

With the argument spread out this way, it is possible to formulate specific replies to the (implied) criticism contained in the original rhetorical question. Contrary to the first premise, there are people who are not interested in becoming rich or would find the effort needed to do so either tiring or boring. Contrary to the fourth premise, a person can be a smart or able economist without being able to predict the course of the economy in sufficient detail to make substantial wealth through investments.

(Even so, the questioner's suspicion may remain. Economists who speak with great confidence and detail about the economy but show no signs of having profited from their expertise have the credibility of the bald barber who sells hair restoring lotion.)

Exercise 3: People opposed to the military draft sometimes remark "If the members of Congress were subject to be drafted, they would not vote for the draft." Although on the surface this looks like a statement of fact, it obviously contains an implied criticism of the enactment of the draft by Congress. A person who makes such a remark is probably putting forward an argument of the following kind:

If members of Congress were eligible for the draft, they would not vote for it.

Therefore, it is wrong for members of Congress to vote for the draft.

Using the procedures discussed in this chapter, try to find a set of suppressed premises that captures the force of this argument. After giving the argument a charitable reconstruction, evaluate its soundness.

Exercise 4: Perform the same kind of analysis for the following remarks, where again a conclusion and, perhaps, some premises are plainly implied but not stated:

1. "As Governor of California, Ronald Reagan could not start a war, as President of the United States he could." — Gerald Ford

2. If a six-year-old can find a drug dealer in New York, why can't the police?

3. There are no atheists in foxholes.

4. "... I've noticed that everybody that is for abortion has already been born." — Ronald Reagan

FUNDAMENTAL ISSUES

The techniques for reconstructing arguments developed in the previous chapter can serve another important function: they can clarify the lines of dispute between contesting points of view. This is particularly useful when we are dealing with fundamental moral or political conflicts, in which disagreement can be sharp, emotions can run high, and the level of tolerance for opposing views can be negligible. The first step in dealing with disagreements on fundamental issues is to reconstruct the arguments on both sides so that the bases of the disagreement are made evident. Such a clarification may not settle the dispute, but it can aid in bringing intelligence and good will to bear upon it.

Rock Bottom Disagreements

In the previous chapter, we filled out arguments by supplying suppressed premises and then assessed their soundness. At times this proved a simple task, for the suppressed premises were easy to find, and, once the argument was reconstructed in this way, it was not difficult to assess its soundness. Of course, some of these arguments proved more difficult to assess than others; for example, it was not immediately obvious what principles lay at the heart of the argument that Garvey has a very slight chance of getting a fifth hit after four hits in a row. But even in this case we were able to find the underlying form of the argument and decide that it was unsound.

In this chapter we shall examine arguments that do not admit of such straightforward reconstruction and that may not, in the end, admit of a final resolution concerning soundness or unsoundness. We shall examine arguments concerning fundamental issues, issues that often lead to rock bottom disagreements. By fundamental issues, we mean those that turn upon basic principles of morality, religion, politics, and world view. For the most part, discussions in daily life do not reach these principles, but they lie in the background where they are taken for granted. In a domestic political discussion Americans do not usually go back to question whether a representative democracy is superior to a monarchy. We live in a representative democracy, and the principles of that form of government shape our discussion even when they are not explicitly mentioned. There are times, however, when we are unavoidably led into discussions of fundamental principles. We cannot discuss such matters as capital punishment, abortion, mercy killing, and the military draft without raising basic moral questions. Discussions concerning the Equal Rights Amendment, affirmative action programs, gay liberation, and so on have the same tendency to take us, almost at once, to basic questions concerning society and its morality.

How, then, do we deal with arguments concerning fundamental issues? To begin with, we treat them in the same way that we treat any argument. We first analyze their surface structure and then, to borrow a notion from geology, we look at their bedrock formation. It is often the case that discussions of fundamental issues are highly charged emotionally, and principles of charity and tolerance that hold in other areas are largely set aside. Thus those who disagree concerning abortion are likely to consider their opponents not only wrong but wicked, and much of the argument on both sides will consist of stating just how wicked the opponent is. The first step, then, in analyzing an argument on a fundamental issue is to clear away the fog of rhetorical excess so that the substantive questions can be brought into focus. The second step—the bedrock analysis—is the search for those principles that connect the conclusion with the reason or reasons offered in its behalf. This is precisely what we have been doing already, only the seriousness of the issues has increased.

Capital Punishment

It has been argued before the Supreme Court that the death penalty should be declared unconstitutional because it violates the constitutional provision against "cruel and unusual punishments." The explicitly stated argument has the following form:

> The death penalty violates the constitutional provision against cruel and unusual punishments.
>
> Therefore, the death penalty should be ruled unconstitutional.

The argument plainly depends upon two suppressed premises:

> *SP1:* The death penalty involves cruel and unusual punishment.
>
> *SP2:* Anything that violates a constitutional provision should be declared unconstitutional.

So the argument more fully spelled out looks like this:

(1) *SP:* The death penalty involves cruel and unusual punishment.

(2) The Constitution prohibits cruel and unusual punishments.

(3) *SP:* Anything that violates a constitutional provision should be declared unconstitutional.

(4) Therefore, the death penalty should be declared unconstitutional.

This reconstruction seems to be a fair representation of the original argument.

Let us turn now to an assessment of the expanded argument. First, we can agree that it is valid in form: given the premises, the conclusion follows from it. Therefore we can next ask whether the premises are acceptable. The second premise causes no special problems. If we look to the Constitution, we do find a provision prohibiting cruel and unusual punishment (see the Eighth Amendment). The third premise seems uncontroversial as well. Indeed, it may sound like a truism to say that anything that violates a constitutional provision should be declared unconstitutional. As a matter of fact, this notion was once a controversial matter, for nothing in the Constitution gives the courts the right to declare acts of legislators unconstitutional and hence void. The courts acquired and consolidated this right in the years since 1789, and it is still sometimes challenged by those who think that it gives the courts too much power. But even if the judiciary's power to declare laws unconstitutional is not itself a constitutionally stated power, it is so much an accepted part of our system that no one would challenge it in a *courtroom* procedure.

Although the third premise has a more complicated backing than most people realize, it is obviously the first premise—"The death penalty involves cruel and unusual punishment"—that forms the heart of the argument. What we would expect, then, is a good argument to be put forward in its behalf. When we look at the second premise closely we discover at once a problem of interpretation. Does the constitutional provision exclude *both* cruel punishment and unusual punishment or does it exclude only those punishments that are *both* cruel and unusual? For example, someone might argue that, while the death penalty is cruel, it is not unusual and that it is therefore not unconstitutional. For the moment, at least, we shall adopt this second reading and assume that, in order to be covered by the provision, a punishment must be *both* cruel and unusual.

Consider the following argument intended to establish this double claim:

> That taking a person's life is cruel should go without saying. The important issue is whether such a penalty is unusual. That execution is an unusual penalty is seen from examining court records. Whether a person committing a particular crime will be given the death penalty depends upon the kind of legal aid he is given, his willingness to enter into plea bargaining, the personality of the judge, the beliefs and attitudes of the jury, and a great many other considerations. In fact, only in a small percentage of the cases in which it might apply is the death penalty actually handed down.

Let us concentrate on the part of this argument intended to show that the death penalty is an unusual punishment. Of course, in civilized nations the death penalty is reserved for a small range of crimes; but the fact that it is not widespread is hardly the point at issue. The point of the argument is that the death penalty is unusual even for those crimes that are punishable by death. Calling such crimes *capital offenses,* we can restate the argument more carefully as follows:

> Only a small percentage of those found guilty of committing a capital offense are given the death sentence.

> Therefore, the death penalty is, in the relevant sense, an unusual punishment.

We can spread the entire argument out before us:

(1) Taking a human life is a cruel act.

(2) The death penalty is therefore cruel.

(3) Only a small percentage of those found guilty of committing capital offenses are given the death penalty.

(4) Therefore, the death penalty is an unusual punishment.

(5) Therefore, the death penalty is both cruel and unusual.

(6) The Constitution prohibits cruel and unusual punishments.

(7) Anything that violates the Constitution should be declared unconstitutional.

(8) Therefore, the death penalty should be declared unconstitutional.

These propositions provide at least the skeleton of an argument with some force; for the conclusion does seem to follow from the premises, and the premises themselves seem plausible. It seems, then, that we have devised a charitable reconstruction of the argument, and we can now see how an opponent might respond to it.

One response is particularly probing. It goes like this:

It is certainly true that only a small percentage of those who commit capital offenses are actually sentenced to death, but this fact does not reflect badly on the law but on its administration. If judges and juries met their obligations, more people who deserve the death penalty would receive it, and the use of it would no longer be unusual. What is needed, then, is judicial reform and not the removal of the death penalty on constitutional grounds.

This response is a probing one because it insists upon a distinction between a law and the effects of its application or, more pointedly, its misapplication. To meet this rejoinder, the original argument could be strengthened in the following way:

A law should not be judged in isolation from the likely effects of implementing it. Given the nature of our system of criminal justice, for the foreseeable future, the death penalty will continue to be applied to only a small percentage of capital offenders. It will therefore remain an unusual punishment and so be unconstitutional.

We can spell this argument out in the following way:

(1) A law should be declared unconstitutional if its likely consequences are contrary to the Constitution.

(2) A law that uses the death penalty as a punishment will have as its likely consequence a penalty that is cruel and unusual.

(3) Cruel and unusual punishments are explicitly forbidden by the Constitution.

(4) Therefore, any law that employs the death penalty should be declared unconstitutional.

Both the first premise and second premise will lead to further debate. Should a law be declared unconstitutional because there is a good chance that it will be abused in ways that infringe on constitutional rights? Of course, a great many laws have this potential, for example, all laws involving police power. However, only an extremist would suggest that we should abolish all police powers because of this risk of unconstitutional abuse. Yet certain police powers have been limited by court ruling because they have this potential for unconstitutional abuse. Strict rules governing the use of evidence gained from wiretaps are one result. So those who argue in favor of the death penalty must show either that there is a good chance that the application of the death penalty can be made more uniform or show that this failure of uniform application is not sufficiently important to be considered constitutionally intolerable.

The supporter of the death penalty can offer a sharper criticism of the second premise of our last argument. It goes like this:

> Those who argue against the constitutionality of the death penalty on the grounds that it is a cruel and unusual punishment use the expression "cruel and unusual" in a way wholly different from that intended by the framers of the Eighth Amendment. By "cruel" they had in mind punishments that involved torture. By "unusual" they did not mean rare, for in a good society all punishment would be rare. What they were opposed to were bizarre or ghoulish punishments of the kind that often formed part of public spectacles, especially in barbaric times. Modern methods of execution are neither cruel nor unusual in the constitutionally relevant sense of these words. Therefore laws demanding the death penalty cannot be declared unconstitutional on the grounds that they either directly or indirectly involve a punishment that is cruel and unusual.

The core of this counter-argument can be expressed as follows:

(1) In appeals to the Constitution, its words must be taken as they were originally intended.

(2) Modern methods of carrying out a death penalty are neither "cruel" nor "unusual" if these words are interpreted as they were originally intended.

(3) Therefore the death penalty cannot be declared unconstitutional on the grounds that it violates the amendment against cruel and unusual punishments.

The second premise of this argument states a matter of historical fact that might not be altogether easy to verify. The chances are, however, that it comes close to the truth. Given this, the opponent of the death penalty must either attack the first premise or find some other grounds for holding that the death penalty should be declared unconstitutional.

The first premise may seem like a truism, for how can we be guided by a document if everyone is free to give it the meaning he or she chooses? The literal meaning of the document is simply its meaning; everything else is interpretation. Of course, there are times when it is not easy to discover what the literal meaning is. (In the present case, for example, it is not clear whether the Eighth Amendment prohibits punishments that are *either* cruel *or* unusual or only those that are *both* cruel and unusual.) It seems unlikely, however, that those who drafted the Eighth Amendment used either the word "cruel" or the word "unusual" in the ways they are employed in the anti-capital punishment argument.

Does this last concession end the debate in favor of those who reject the anti–capital punishment argument we have been examining? The argument certainly seems to be weakened, but there are those who would take a bold course by simply denying the first premise of the argument used to refute them. *They would deny, that is, that we are bound to read the Constitution in the way intended by its framers.* An argument in favor of this position might look something like this:

> The great bulk of the Constitution was written in an age almost wholly different from our own. To cite just two examples of this: women were denied fundamental rights of full citizenship, and slavery was a constitutionally accepted feature of national life. The Constitution has remained a live and relevant document just because it has undergone constant reinterpretation. So even if it is true that the expression "cruel and unusual" meant something quite special to those who framed the Eighth Amendment, plainly a humane desire to make punishment more civilized lay behind it. The present reading of this amendment is in the spirit of its original intention and simply makes it applicable to our own times.

The argument has now moved to an entirely new level: one concerning whether the Constitution should be read strictly in accord with the original intentions of those who wrote it or more freely to accommodate modern realities. But we shall not pursue the discussion further into these complex areas; instead, we should consider how we were led into them. Our original argument did not concern the *general* question of whether capital punishment is right or wrong, nor did it simply concern the question of whether capital punishment is unconstitutional. The argument turned upon a much more specific point: Does the death penalty violate the Eighth Amendment's prohibition against cruel and unusual punishments? The argument with which we began seemed to be a straightforward proof that it does. Yet, as we explored principles that lay in back of this deceptively simple argument, the issue became broader and more complex. We finally reached a point at which the force of the original argument was seen to depend upon what we consider the proper way to interpret the Constitution—strictly or more freely.

Exercise 1: The final argument presented in our examination of whether the death penalty violates the Constitutional provision against cruel and unusual punishments attempts to show that the Constitution must be read in a free or liberal way that makes it relevant to present society. Filling in suppressed premises where necessary, restate this argument as a sequence of explicit steps. After you have given the argument the strongest restatement you can, evaluate it for its soundness.

Abortion

Another issue that has been the source of profound disagreement between members of our society is whether (or in what circumstances) abortion should be made illegal. A similar question has arisen concerning so-called mercy killing, or euthanasia. Those who oppose both abortion and euthanasia could defend their position by invoking a general principle of the following kind:

It is always wrong to take a human life.

But this principle by itself does not rule out either abortion or euthanasia. To reach these conclusions, we need further premises of the following kind:

A fetus is a human being.

An utterly comatose person is still a human being.

Given these premises, the anti-abortion and the anti-euthanasia argument will have the following form:

(1) Abortion involves taking the life of a fetus.

(2) A fetus is a human being.

(3) It is always wrong to take the life of a human being.

(4) Therefore, abortion is wrong.

(1) Euthanasia involves taking the life of a person who is ill.

(2) A living person, however ill, is still a human being.

(3) It is always wrong to take the life of a human being.

(4) Therefore, euthanasia is wrong.

Stated this way, we can see why so much of the debate concerning abortion and euthanasia turns on the question of whether a fetus is already a human being and whether a patient suffering from so-called "brain death" continues to be a human being. But the argument so stated is not characteristically used by most people who adopt a strong anti-abortion or anti-euthanasia position. In particular, very few of those who espouse these positions will accept the third premise of each of these arguments. This comes out in the following way. Many of those who oppose abortion or euthanasia are in favor of the death penalty for certain crimes. Therefore, they do not accept the general principle that it is always wrong to take a human life. Similarly, those who support abortion or euthanasia are not simply indifferent to human life, for these very same people often oppose capital punishment. The question, then, that must be put to those on both sides of the debate is this: What principle allows the taking of a human life in some instances but not in others?

Those who are opposed to abortion or euthanasia could reformulate the third premise in these words:

It is always wrong to take the life of an innocent human being.

Here the word "innocent" allows an exception for the death penalty being imposed on those who are guilty of certain crimes. Even stated this way, however, the principle seems to admit of exceptions. If someone's life is threatened by a madman, it is generally thought that the person has the right to use whatever means are necessary against the madman to prevent this. This may include killing him, yet the insane are usually thought to be innocent of their deeds. So the principle must be modified again:

It is always wrong to take the life of an innocent human being except in certain cases of self-defense.[1]

---

[1] It is possible to find difficulties with this principle that will force further modifications or clarifications. Children, for example, are often the innocent victims of bombing raids, yet the raids are often thought to be justified even though they will have this predictable consequence. At this point it is common to modify the principle again by including a reference to intentions: although the death of a certain number of innocent children is a foreseeable consequence of the bombing raid, it is not what is intended. We cannot, however, pursue this complex line of reasoning here.

We have arrived, then, at a principle that seems to make sense out of a position that is against abortion but in favor of the death penalty. With these modifications included, the argument now looks like this:

(1) Abortion is taking the life of a human fetus.

(2) A human fetus is a living human being.

(3) A human fetus is an innocent human being.

(4) It is always wrong to take the life of an innocent human being except in cases of self-defense.

(5) Therefore, abortion is always wrong.

But, having made the premises more plausible, we confront a new problem: the argument is invalid as it stands, since the qualification "except in cases of self-defense" has been dropped from the conclusion. The proper conclusion of the argument should be:

(5) Abortion is always wrong except in cases of self-defense.

Rewriting the conclusion in this way has an important consequence: the argument no longer leads to a conclusion that abortion is *always* wrong. The qualified conclusion could permit abortion in those cases in which it is needed to defend the life of the bearer of the fetus. It could then be argued that there is no important difference between our right to defend ourselves against an irrational assailant and a non-rational fetus. In both cases we grant the innocence of the party whose life must be taken, but think that the right to life of the victim in one case or the bearer of the fetus in the other overrides this. In fact, this is the position that many people opposed to abortion take: abortion is wrong except in those cases in which it is plainly needed to save the life of the mother. This is a strong anti-abortion position, since it would condone abortion in only a few exceptional cases. It is the view, in fact, of many who consider themselves strongly opposed to abortion.[2]

The contours of the debate between those who are opposed to abortion and those who are in favor of it are now becoming more clear. Those who oppose abortion need not hold an absolute position banning all abortion. They usually admit that in certain exceptional cases abortion is permitted. They then try to give some reasoned ground for admitting these exceptions. Similarly, those who favor abortion rarely suggest that there should be no constraints on its use. They hold instead that abortion should be permitted in a much wider range of cases than their opponents

[2] A stronger, but still not absolute, anti-abortion position is that abortion is permitted when it is needed to save the life of the mother and there is no chance of the fetus surviving in any case.

admit. It makes more sense, then, to speak about a liberal and a conservative view of abortion rather than simply about a pro-abortion and an anti-abortion position. (There is a tendency for those engaged in this debate to saddle their opponents with as extreme a position as possible. This merely shows that zeal for a cause can corrupt intellectual honesty.)

We can now examine the way that those who adopt the liberal position will attack the conservative argument as it has just been spelled out. The first premise, which simply defines abortion, should not be a subject for controversy. Nor does it seem likely that the third premise will be attacked on the ground that the fetus is not innocent. To the best of my knowledge, no one has argued that abortion can be justified as a punishment of the fetus. (Justification in terms of saving the bearer's life is altogether different from this.)

The second premise will be a center of controversy, for if it is admitted that a fetus is a human being, then moral and legal considerations will apply directly to it, and the burden of proof will shift and force those who maintain the liberal position to show why these legal and moral considerations should be set aside, or at least modified. An argument intended to show that a fetus is not a human being—or perhaps not a human being up to a certain time after conception—must proceed from some idea of what it is to be a human being. Such arguments often proceed along the following lines:

> No moral significance attaches to being a member of one biological species rather than another, for example, *Homo sapiens* (man) rather than *Quercus rubra* (a red oak). We accord human beings special rights because of their capacity to suffer pain and enjoy pleasure, because they can plan their lives and make choices, because they are subject to praise and blame, and so on. A human fetus lacks these qualities.

A person who uses this line of argument may admit that the fetus differs from an acorn since it is *potentially* a creature that will be endowed with special rights, and this potential itself may have moral significance. The point, however, is that the fetus is not yet a person and therefore the problem is no longer viewed as a choice between the rights of two persons, the bearer and the fetus.

At first it may seem that the question whether a fetus is a human being is merely a quibble. In fact, it raises questions that take us to bedrock issues. The liberal position just sketched gives human beings a special moral status in virtue of their capacities (to suffer, choose, assume responsibility, and the like). On this approach, a fetus will have no—or, at best, greatly diminished—human rights. On the other side, a person with a religious orientation might reject this "image of man" completely. Human beings have special moral significance because they have been created by God in His image; they possess an immortal soul; and so on.

If these features are attributed to the fetus, then, once more, the fetus has human rights that cannot be set aside except, possibly, in extreme cases.

How does one deal with such bedrock disagreements? The first thing to see is that logic alone will not settle them. Starting from a certain conception of man, it is possible to argue coherently for a liberal view on abortion; starting from another point of view, it is possible to argue coherently for a conservative view on abortion. The important thing to see is that it is possible to *understand* an opposing view, that is, get a genuine feeling for its inner workings, even if you disagree with it completely. Logical analysis may show that particular arguments are unsound or have unnoticed and unwanted implications. This may force clarification and modification. But the most important service that logical analysis can perform is to lay bare the fundamental principles that lie beneath surface disagreements. Analysis will sometimes show that these disagreements are fundamental and perhaps irreconcilable. Dealing with such irreconcilable differences in a humane way is one of the fundamental tasks of a society dedicated to freedom and a wide range of civil liberties.

In examining the conservative position on abortion, it proved useful to ask how commitments on this issue squared with commitments in other areas. It proved particularly interesting to ask how a person could simultaneously be a conservative on abortion and a proponent of the death penalty for certain criminal offenses. We saw that this apparent inconsistency could be overcome by insisting upon the innocence of the fetus and the guilt of the capital offender as significant factors. People who take a liberal stand on abortion also adopt positions that may seem inconsistent. For example, it is quite common to find a person with a very liberal approach to abortion who also rejects capital punishment altogether. It will be useful to ask how these apparently anti-life, pro-life positions can be combined.

Once more, the question whether a fetus is already a human being (in the sense of a person) may form an important part of the discussion. The criminal is, after all, a human being. If the fetus is not, then the cases are separated and there is no conflict between always being opposed to taking the life of a criminal and not always being opposed to taking the life of a fetus. This, however, is probably not the whole story or even the most important part of it. Those who adopt a liberal position on abortion often do so on the basis of an argument from *human welfare.* They argue that abortion can sometimes be justified in terms of the welfare of the woman who bears the fetus, or in terms of the welfare of the family it will be born into, or even in terms of the welfare of the child itself if it were to be born into an impoverished situation. On the other side, it is argued that the death penalty does not benefit human welfare. In itself it is a harsh and dehumanizing practice and in its effects does not serve as a useful deterrent. So the cases are distinguished once more: abortion at least sometimes contributes to human welfare, whereas the death penalty does not. This argument, when spelled out, looks like this:

(1) An action that best contributes to human welfare is correct.

(2) Abortion sometimes is the best way of maximizing human welfare.

(3) Therefore, abortion is sometimes correct.

It is then claimed that a similar argument cannot be produced justifying the death penalty because it does not maximize human welfare. It is argued, in particular, that it does not serve as a deterrent to capital offenses.

What are we to say about this argument from human welfare? It seems valid in form, so we can turn to the premises themselves and ask if they are acceptable. The first (and leading) premise of the argument is subject to two immediate criticisms. First of all, it is vague. Probably what a person who uses this kind of argument has in mind by speaking of human welfare is a certain level of material and psychological well-being. More simply, an action is said to be right if it best makes people happy. Of course, this is still vague, but it is clear enough to make the premise a target of the second, more important, criticism. While maximizing human welfare may, in general, be a good thing, it is not the only relevant consideration in deciding how to act. To cite the standard example used against positions of this kind, it might be true that our society would be much more prosperous on the whole if 10 percent of the population were designated slaves who would do all menial work. In this way the general level of prosperity and happiness might be much higher than the level that could be achieved without a slave caste. Yet, even if a society could be made generally happy in this way, most people would reject such a system on grounds that it is unfair to the slave class. For reasons of this kind, most people would modify the first premise of the argument we are now examining in the following way:

(1) An action that best increases human welfare is right, provided that it is fairly applied.

But if the first premise is modified in this way, then the entire argument must be restated to reflect this revision. It will now look like this:

(1) An action that best increases human welfare is right, provided that it is fairly applied.

(2) Abortion is sometimes an action that best increases human welfare.

(3) Therefore, abortion is sometimes right provided that it is fairly applied.

It should be obvious how conservatives on abortion will reply to this argument: they will maintain that abortion always (or almost always) involves unfair application, namely, to the fetus. Once more we have encountered a standard situation: given a strong premise (Premise 1), it is possible to derive a particular conclusion, but this strong premise is subject to criticism and therefore must be modified. When the conclusion is modified, it no longer supports the original conclusion that the person presenting the argument wishes to establish. (A like situation arose in examining the conservative position on abortion on page 305.)

The argument does not stop here. A person who holds a liberal position on abortion might reply in a number of ways. Again, the burden of the argument may shift to the question of whether or not a human fetus is a human being and therefore possessed of the right to fair treatment. It might also be argued that sometimes, at least, questions of human welfare are more important than the issue of fair or equal treatment. During war, for example, members of a certain segment of the population are called upon to risk their lives for the good of the whole. Indeed, in many emergencies, fair and equal treatment must be set aside or modified for the sake of preserving the society as a whole.

When the argument is put on this new basis, the question then becomes this: Are there circumstances in which matters of welfare become so urgent that the rights of the fetus (here assuming that the fetus has rights) are overriden? The obvious case in which this might happen is when the life of the bearer of the fetus is plainly threatened. For many conservatives on abortion, this does count as a case in which abortion is permitted. Those who hold to the liberal position will maintain that severe psychological, financial, or personal losses may also take precedence over the life of the fetus. How severe must these losses be? From our previous discussion of slippery slope arguments, we know that we should not expect a sharp line to exist here, and, indeed, people will tend to be spread out in their opinions in a continuum ranging from a belief in complete prohibition to no prohibition. Very few people occupy the end points on this continuum, yet it still leaves room for profound disagreements on fundamental issues.

Weighing Factors Our discussion has brought us to the following point: disagreements concerning abortion cannot be reduced to a yes-no dispute. Most conservatives on abortion acknowledge that it is permissible in some (though very few) cases. Most liberals on abortion admit that there are some (though not restrictively many) limitations on its use. The way people place themselves on this continuum does not depend on any simple acceptance of one argument over another, but instead on the *weight* they give certain factors. To what extent does a fetus have human rights? The conservative position we examined earlier grants the fetus full (or close to full) human rights. The liberal position usually grants diminished rights to the fetus. (Only rarely does the liberal deny the fetus any rights at all.) In what areas do questions of welfare override certain individual rights? The conservative in this matter usually restricts this to those cases in which the very life of the mother is plainly threatened. As the position on abortion becomes more liberal, the range of cases in which the rights of the fetus are set aside in favor of the rights of the bearer of the fetus becomes more extensive.

Where a particular person strikes this balance is not only a function of basic moral beliefs, but also a function of different weights assigned to them. Except for those who occupy extreme positions, there is surprising agreement in moral principles between the conservatives concerning abortion and those who are liberal concerning it. In an ideal world, the rights of the fetus and the rights of the bearer of the fetus would never conflict, and the profound and often tragic issue of weighing one moral demand against another would not arise. Logical analysis is not capable of solving such fundamental problems as this, but it can help us understand their underlying structure and in this way help bring honest intelligence to bear upon them.

Exercise 2 (suitable for a term project): An anti-abortion measure known as the Hyde Amendment has been attached to various appropriation bills over the last few years. It has been stated in a variety of ways, but a version that was held constitutional by the Supreme Court has the following form:

None of the funds provided for in this paragraph shall be used to perform abortions except where the life of the mother would be endangered if the fetus were carried to term, or except in such medical procedures necessary for the victims of rape or incest, where such rape or incest has been reported promptly to a law enforcement agency or public health service.

Using the techniques developed in this chapter, construct the strongest possible argument that will give a reasoned basis for both the overall anti-abortion standpoint of the Hyde Amendment and the three exceptions it allows. This will involve presenting arguments in support of the three exceptions that do not, at the same time, undercut the general (anti-abortion) intention of the amendment. You must spell out all of these arguments in detail. After giving the position a fair statement, assess its plausibility.

Exercise 3 (suitable for a term project): Chapter 14 contains two essays concerning the morality of abortion. Using the techniques developed in this chapter, show the fundamental structure of one of these two positions and assess its strength.

THE FORMAL ANALYSIS OF ARGUMENT: PART ONE

This chapter will examine some more technical procedures for analyzing arguments. In particular, it will consider the notion of <u>validity</u>, for this is the central concept of logic. The first part of the chapter will show how the notion of validity first introduced in Chapter 3 can be developed rigorously in one area, the so-called <u>Propositional Logic</u>. This branch of logic deals with those connectives like "and" and "or" that allow us to build up complex propositions from simpler ones. Throughout most of the chapter, the focus will be theoretical rather than immediately practical. It is intended to provide insight into the concept of validity by examining it in an ideal setting. The chapter will close with a discussion of the relationship between the ideal language of symbolic logic and the language we ordinarily speak.

Validity and Formal Analysis of Argument

When we carry out an informal analysis of argument, we pay close attention to the key terms used to present the argument and then ask ourselves whether these key terms have been used properly. The procedure is informal because, so far, we have no exact techniques for answering the question: Is such and such a term used correctly? We rely, instead, on logical instincts which, on the whole, are pretty good.

Except in complicated or tricky cases, most people can tell whether one claim follows from another. But if we ask the average intelligent person *why* the one claim follows from the other, he or she will probably have little to say except, perhaps, that it is obvious. That is, it is often easy to see that one claim follows from another, but to explain why turns out to be difficult. This quality of "following from" is called validity, as we saw in Chapter 3. The purpose of this chapter is to get some better idea of this notion—to begin, at least, to understand what we are saying when we assert that one claim follows from another.

The focus of our attention will be the *concept* of validity. We are not, for the time being at least, interested in whether this or that argument is valid—we want to understand validity itself. To this end, the arguments we will examine are so simple that you will not be able to imagine anyone not understanding them at a glance. Who needs logic to deal with arguments of this kind? There is, however, good reason for dealing with simple—*trivially simple*—arguments at the start. The analytic approach to a complex issue is first to break it down into subissues, repeating the process until we reach problems simple enough to be solved. After these simpler problems are solved, we can reverse the process and construct solutions to larger and more complex problems. When done correctly, the *result* of such an analytic process may seem dull and obvious—and it often is. The *discovery* of such a process, in contrast, often demands the insight of genius.

The Propositional Calculus

Conjunction The first system of arguments that we shall examine concerns sentential (or propositional) connectives. Sentential connectives are terms that allow us to combine two or more sentences into a single sentence. For example, given the propositions "John is tall" and "Harry is short," we can use the term "and" to *conjoin* them forming a single compound proposition "John is tall and Harry is short." Now let us look carefully at this simple word "and" and ask how it functions. "And," in fact, is a curious word, for it doesn't seem to stand for anything, at least in the way in which a proper name ("Churchill") and a common noun ("dog") seem to stand for things. Instead of asking what this word stands for, we can ask a different question: What *truth conditions* govern this connective? That is, under what conditions are propositions containing this connective true? To answer this question, we imagine every possible way in which the component propositions can be true or false. Then for each combination we decide what truth value to assign to the entire proposition. This may sound complicated, but an example will make it clear:

John is tall.	Harry is short.	John is tall and Harry is short.
T	T	T
T	F	F
F	T	F
F	F	F

Here the first two columns cover every possibility for the component propositions to be either true or false. The third column states the truth value of the whole proposition for each combination. Pretty obviously, the conjunction of two propositions is true if both of the component propositions are true; otherwise it is false.

It should also be obvious that our reflections have not depended upon the particular sentences we have selected. We could have been talking about dinosaurs instead of people, and we still would have come to the conclusion that the conjunction of two propositions is true if both propositions are true, but false otherwise. In order to reflect the generality of our conclusion, we can drop reference to particular sentences altogether and use *variables* instead. Just as the letters x, y, and z can stand for arbitrary numbers in mathematics, we can let the letters p, q, r, s, . . . stand for arbitrary propositions in logic. We will also use the symbol "&" for "and."

Consider the expression "p & q." Is it true or false? There is obviously no answer to this question. This is not because we do not know what "p" and "q" stand for, for in fact "p" and "q" do not stand for anything at all. Thus "p & q" is not a statement, but a pattern for a whole series of statements. To reflect this, we shall say that "p & q" is a *statement form*. It is a pattern, or form, for a whole series of statements, including "John is tall and Harry is short." To repeat the central idea, we can pass from a statement to a statement form by uniformly replacing statements with statement variables.

Statement	*Statement form*
John is tall and Harry is short.	$(p$ & $q)$

When we proceed in the opposite direction by uniformly substituting statements for statement variables, we get what we shall call a *substitution instance* of that statement form.

Statement form	*Substitution instance*
$(p$ & $q)$	Roses are red and violets are blue.

Thus, "John is tall and Harry is short" and "Roses are red and violets are blue" are both substitution instances of the statement form "*p* & *q*." These ideas are perfectly simple, but to get clear about them, it is important to notice that "*p*" can also be a statement form, with "Roses are red and violets are blue" as one of its substitution instances. There is no rule against substituting complex statements for statement variables. Perhaps a bit more surprisingly, our definitions allow "Roses are red and roses are red" to be a substitution instance of "*p* & *q*." We get a substitution instance of a statement form by uniformly replacing the same variable by the same statement throughout. We have not said that different variables must be replaced by different statements throughout. Different variables may be replaced by the same statement, but different statements may not be replaced by the same variable. To summarize this discussion:

"Roses are red and violets are blue" is a substitution instance of "*p* & *q*."

"Roses are red and violets are blue" is a substitution instance of "*p*."

"Roses are red and roses are red" is a substitution instance of "*p* & *q*."

"Roses are red and roses are red" is a substitution instance of "*p* & *p*."

"Roses are red and violets are blue" is not a substitution instance of "*p* & *p*."

"Roses are red" is not a substitution instance of "*p* & *p*."

Exercise 1: The statement "The night is young and you're so beautiful" is a substitution instance of which of the following statement forms?
   1. p
   2. p & q
   3. p & r
   4. p & p
   5. p or q

Exercise 2: Find three statement forms for which the following statement is a substitution instance:

"The night is young and you're so beautiful and my flight leaves in thirty minutes."

The expression "*p* & *q*" is neither true nor false because it is a *statement form*, not a statement. We get a statement (something that is either true or false) only when we replace these variables by statements. When such a substitution is made, we get a true statement if both substituted statements are true; otherwise, we get a false statement. These reflections are summarized in the following truth-table definition for conjunction, now using variables where previously we used specific statements.

p	q	p & q
T	T	T
T	F	F
F	T	F
F	F	F

Next we can look at an argument involving conjunction. Here is one that is ridiculously simple:

Harry is short and John is tall.
_____
∴ Harry is short.

This argument is obviously valid. But why is the argument valid? Why does the conclusion follow from the premise? The answer in this case seems obvious, but we will spell it out in detail as a guide for more difficult cases. Suppose we replace these particular statements by statement forms, using a different variable for each distinct statement throughout the argument. This yields what we shall call the following *argument form:*

p & q
_____
∴ p

This is a pattern for endlessly many arguments, each of which is called a substitution instance of this argument form. Every argument that has this general form will also be valid. It really doesn't matter which propositions we put back into this schema; the resulting argument will be valid—so long as we are careful to substitute the same statement for the same variable throughout.

Let us pursue this matter further. If an argument has true premises and a false conclusion, then we know at once that it is invalid. But in saying that an argument is *valid,* we are not only saying that it does not have true premises and a false conclusion; we are saying that the argument *cannot* have a false conclusion when the premises are true. By that we mean that the argument has a structure that rules out the very possibility of true premises and a false conclusion. We can appeal to the notion of an argument form to make sense out of this idea. A somewhat more complicated truth table will make this clear:

		Premise	Conclusion
p	q	p & q	p
T	T	T	T
T	F	F	T
F	T	F	F
F	F	F	F

The first two columns give all the combinations for the truth values of the statements that we might substitute for p and q. The third column gives the truth value of the premise for each of these combinations and, finally, the fourth column gives the truth value for the conclusion for each combination. (Here, of course, this merely involves repeating the first column. Later on, things will become more complicated and interesting.) If we look at this truth table, we see that no matter how we make substitutions for the variables, we never get a case where the premise is true and the conclusion is false. Here it is important to remember that a valid argument can have false premises, for one proposition can follow from another that is false. Of course, an argument that is sound cannot have a false premise, since a sound argument is defined as a valid argument with true premises.[1]

Let us summarize this discussion. In the case we have examined, validity depends upon the form of an argument and not upon its particular content. A first principle, then, is this:

An argument is valid if it is an instance of a valid argument form.

So the argument "Harry is short and John is tall, therefore Harry is short" is valid because it is an instance of the valid argument form "p & q ∴ p." Next we must ask what makes an argument form valid. The answer to this is given in this principle:

An argument form is valid if it has no substitution instances where the premises are true and the conclusion is false.

We have just seen that the argument form "p & q ∴ p" meets this test. The truth-table analysis showed that. Incidentally, we can use the same truth table to show that the following argument is valid:

John is tall.	p
Harry is short.	q
∴ John is tall and Harry is short.	∴ $(p \& q)$

---

[1] The difference between validity and soundness is explained in Chapter 3.

The argument on the left is a substitution instance of the argument form on the right, and a glance at the truth table will show that there is never a case where all the premises (i.e., p and q) are true and the conclusion (i.e., p & q) is false. This pretty well tells the story of the logical properties of the connective we call conjunction.

Notice that we have not said that *every* argument that is valid is so by virtue of its form. There may be arguments where the conclusion plainly does follow from the premises but where we cannot show that the argument's validity is a matter of its logical form. Explaining validity by means of logical form has been an ideal of logical theory, but there are arguments, many of them quite commonplace, where this ideal has not been fulfilled. At present, however, we shall only consider cases where the strategy we used for analyzing conjunction continues to work.

Disjunction Just as we can form a conjunction of two propositions by using the connective "and," we can form a *disjunction* of two propositions by using "or," as in the following compound sentence:

John will win or Harry will win.

Again, it is easy to see that the truth of this whole statement depends upon the truth of the component statements. If they are both false, then the statement as a whole is false. If just one of them is true, then the statement as a whole is true. But suppose they are both true, what shall we say then? Sometimes when we say "either–or" we seem to rule out the possibility of both. "You may have chicken or steak" probably means that you cannot have both. Sometimes, however, both is not ruled out—for example, when we say to someone, "If you want to see tall mountains, go to California or Colorado." So one way (in fact, the standard way) to deal with this problem is to say that "or" has two meanings: one *exclusive*, which rules out both, and one *inclusive*, which does not rule out both. We could thus give two truth-table definitions, one for each of these senses of the word "or":

	Exclusive			Inclusive	
p	q	p or q	p	q	p or q
T	T	F	T	T	T
T	F	T	T	F	T
F	T	T	F	T	T
F	F	F	F	F	F

For reasons that will become clear in a moment, we will adopt the inclusive sense of the word "or." Where necessary, we will define the exclusive sense using the inclusive sense as a starting point. Logicians symbolize *disjunctions* using the connective "v." The truth table for this connective has the following form:

p	q	p v q
T	T	T
T	F	T
F	T	T
F	F	F

We shall look at some arguments involving this connective in a moment.

Negation With conjunction and disjunction, we begin with two propositions and construct a new proposition from them. There is another way in which we can construct a new proposition from another—through *denying* it. Given the proposition "John is clever," we can get a new proposition "John is not clever" simply by inserting the word "not" in the correct place in the sentence. What, exactly, does the word "not" mean? This can be a difficult question to answer, especially if we begin with the assumption that all words stand for things. Does it stand for nothing or, maybe, nothingness? Although some respectable philosophers have sometimes spoken in this way, it is important to see that the word "not" does not stand for anything at all. It has an altogether different function in the language. To see this, think how conjunction and disjunction work. Given two propositions, the word "and" allows us to construct another proposition that is true only when both original propositions are true, and is false otherwise. Turning to disjunction, given two propositions, the word "or" allows us to construct another proposition that is false only when both the original propositions are false, and true otherwise. (Our truth-table definitions reflect these facts.) Using these definitions as a model, how should we define *negation*? A parallel answer is that the negation of a proposition is true just in case the original proposition is false and it is false just in case the original proposition is true. Using the symbol ~ to stand for negation, this gives us the following truth-table definition:

p	~p
T	F
F	T

How Truth Functional Connectives Work We have now defined *conjunction, disjunction,* and *negation.* That, all by itself, is sufficient to complete the branch of modern logic called Propositional Logic. The definitions themselves may seem peculiar. They do not look like the definitions we find in a dictionary. But the form of these definitions is important, for it tells us something interesting about the character of

such words as "and," "or," and "not." Two things are worth noting:
(1) These expressions are used to construct new propositions from old.
(2) The newly constructed proposition is always a *truth function* of
the original propositions—that is, the truth value of the new proposition
is always determined by the truth value of the original propositions.
For this reason they are called *truth functional connectives*. (Of course,
with negation, we start with a *single* proposition.) For example, suppose
that A and B are two true propositions and G and H are two false propositions. We can then determine the truth values of more complex
propositions built from them using conjunction, disjunction, and negation. Sometimes the correct assignment is obvious at a glance:

A & B	True
A & G	False
~G	True
A v H	True
~A & G	False

As in mathematics, parentheses can be used to distinguish groupings.
Parentheses bring out an important difference between the following
two expressions:

$$\sim A \ \& \ G \qquad \sim(A \ \& \ G)$$

Notice that in one expression the negation symbol applies only to the
proposition A, whereas in the other expression it applies to the entire
proposition (A & G). The first expression above is false, then, and the
second expression is true.

As expressions become more complex, we reach a point where it is
no longer obvious how the truth values of the component propositions
determine the truth value of the entire proposition. Here a regular
procedure is helpful. The easiest method is to fill in the truth values of
the basic propositions and then, step by step, make assignments progres-
sively wider, going from the inside out. For example:

```
~((A v G)  &  ~(~H & B))
   (T v F)  &  ~(~F & T)
   (T v F)  &  ~(T & T)
       T  &  ~(T)
      ~(T  &  F)
      ~  (F)
         T
```

With very little practice, you can master this technique in dealing with
even highly complex examples.

Exercise 3: Given that A, B, and C are true propositions and X, Y, and Z are false propositions, determine the truth values of the following complex propositions.

1. (A v Z) & B
2. ~(Z v Z)
3. ~~(A v B)
4. (A v X) & (B v Z)
5. (A & X) v (B & Z)
6. ~(A v (Z v X))
7. ~(A v ~(Z v X))
8. ~Z v (Z & A)
9. A v ((~B & C) v ~(~B v ~(Z v B)))
10. A & ((~B & C) v ~(~B v ~(Z v B)))

But what is the point of all this? In everyday life we rarely run into an expression as complicated as the one given in our example. Our purpose here is to sharpen our sensitivity concerning the way in which truth functional connectives work, and then to express our insights in clear ways. This is important because the validity of many arguments depends upon the logical features of these truth functional connectives. We can now turn directly to this subject.

Earlier we saw that every argument of the form "*p* & *q* ∴ *p*" will be valid. This is obvious in itself, but we saw that this claim could be justified by an appeal to truth tables. A truth-table analysis shows us that an argument of this form can never have an instance where the premise is true and the conclusion is false. We can now apply this same technique to arguments that are more complex. In the beginning we will take arguments that are still easy to follow without the use of technical help. At the end, we will consider some arguments that most people cannot follow without guidance.

Consider the following argument:

Harry is spending his summer in Florida or California. Harry is not spending his summer in California or New York. Therefore, Harry is spending his summer in Florida.

We can use the following abbreviations:

A = Harry is spending his summer in Florida.
B = Harry is spending his summer in California.
C = Harry is spending his summer in New York.

Using these abbreviations, and then substituting the variables *p, q,* and *r,* the argument looks like this:

A v B   p v q
~(B v C)   ~(q v r)
—————   ————————
∴ A   ∴ p

The expression on the right gives the argument *form* of the argument
presented on the left. To see whether the argument is valid, we ask if
the argument form is valid. The procedure is cumbersome, but perfectly
mechanical:

			Pr.	Pr.	Pr.	Cn.
p	q	r	(p v q)	(q v r)	~(q v r)	p.
T	T	T	T	T	F	T
T	T	F	T	T	F	T
T	F	T	T	T	F	T
T	F	F	T	F	T	T
F	T	T	T	T	F	F
F	T	F	T	T	F	F
F	F	T	F	T	F	F
F	F	F	F	F	T	F

Notice that there is only one combination of truth values where both
premises are true, and in that case the conclusion is true as well. So the
original argument is valid since it is an instance of a valid argument form,
i.e., an argument form with no instances of true premises combined with
a false conclusion.

This last truth table may need some explaining. First, why do we get
eight rows in this truth table where before we got only four? The answer
to this is that we need to test the argument form for *every possible
combination of truth values* for the component propositions. With two
variables, there are four combinations: (TT), (TF), (FT), and (FF). With
three variables, there are eight combinations: (TTT), (TTF), (TFT), (TFF),
(FTT), (FTF), (FFT), and (FFF). The general rule is this: If an argument
form has n variables, the truth table used in its analysis must have 2^n
rows. For four variables there will be sixteen rows; for five variables,
thirty-two rows; for six variables, sixty-four rows; etc. You can be sure
that you capture all possible combinations of truth values by using the
following pattern in constructing the columns of your truth table:

First column	*Second column*	*Third column*	*Etc.*
First half T's, second half F's	First quarter T's, second quarter F's	First eighth T's, second eighth F's	

A glance at the earlier examples in this chapter will show that we have been using this pattern. Of course, as soon as an argument becomes very complex, these truth tables become very large indeed. But there is no need to worry about this, since we will not consider complex arguments. (Those who do turn to a computer for help.)

The style of the truth table above is also significant. The premises (Pr.) are plainly labeled and so is the conclusion (Cn.). A line is drawn under every row where the premises are all true. (In this case, there is only one such row.) If the conclusion on this line is also true, it is marked "O.K." If every line where the premises are all true is okay, the argument form is valid. Marking all this out may seem rather childish, but it is worth doing. First, it helps guard against mistakes; more importantly, it draws one's attention to the purpose of the procedure being used. Cranking out truth tables without understanding what they are about does not enlighten the mind or elevate the spirit.

For the sake of contrast, we can next consider an invalid argument:

Harry is spending his summer in Florida or California.
Harry is not spending his summer both in California and New York.

∴ Harry is spending his summer in Florida.

Using the same abbreviations as earlier for Harry's vacation plans, this becomes:

Argument	Argument form
A v B	p v q
~(B & C)	~(q & r)
∴ A	∴ p

Truth-table analysis:

			Pr.		Pr.	Cn.	
p	q	r	(p v q)	(q & r)	~(q & r)	p	
T	T	T	T	T	F	T	
T	T	F	T	F	T	T	O.K.
T	F	T	T	F	T	T	O.K.
T	F	F	T	F	T	T	O.K.
F	T	T	T	T	F	F	
F	T	F	T	F	T	F	NO *Invalid*
F	F	T	F	F	T	F	
F	F	F	F	F	T	F	

This time, we find four rows where all the premises are true. In three cases the conclusion is true as well, but in one case the conclusion is false. The argument form is thus invalid, since it is possible for it to have a substitution instance where all the premises are true and the conclusion is false. In the present case, this possibility arises in the sixth row of the truth table, where *A* would be false, *B* true, and *C* false.

Exercise 4: Using the truth-table technique outlined above, test the following argument forms for validity:

1. p ∨ q
   p
   _____
   ∴ ~q

2. ~(p ∨ q)
   _____
   ∴ ~q

3. ~(p & q)
   ~q
   _____
   ∴ ~p

4. p
   ~(p ∨ q)
   _____
   ∴ ~q

5. p
   ~(p ∨ q)
   _____
   ∴ r

6. (p & q) ∨ (p & r)
   _____
   ∴ p & (q ∨ r)

7. (p ∨ q) & (p ∨ r)
   _____
   ∴ p & (q ∨ r)

8. p & q
   _____
   ∴ (p ∨ r) & q

Some Further Connectives

We have developed the logic of propositions using only three basic notions corresponding (perhaps roughly) to the English words "and," "or," and "not." Now let us go back to the question of the two possible senses —exclusive and inclusive—of the word "or." Sometimes "or" seems to rule out the possibility that both options are open; at other times "or" seems to allow this possibility. This is the difference between exclusive and inclusive disjunction, respectively.

Suppose we use the symbol ⩔ to stand for exclusive disjunction. (After this discussion, we will not use it again.) We could then define this new connective in the following way:

$$(p ⩔ q) = (\text{by definition}) ((p \lor q) \& \sim(p \& q))$$

It is not hard to see that the expression on the right side of this definition captures the force of exclusive disjunction. Since we can always define exclusive disjunction when we want it, there is no need to introduce it into our system of basic notions.

> **Exercise 5**: Construct a truth-table analysis of the expression on the right side of the above definition and compare it with the truth-table definition of exclusive disjunction given on page 159.

Actually, in analyzing arguments we have been defining new logical connectives without much thinking about it. For example, *not both p and q* was symbolized as "~(p & q)." *Neither p nor q* was symbolized as "~(p v q)." Let us look more closely at the example "~p & q." Perhaps we should have symbolized it as "~p & ~q." As a matter of fact, we could have used this symbolization, for the two expressions amount to the same thing. Again, this may be obvious, but we can prove it by using a truth table in yet another way. Compare the truth-table analysis of these two expressions:

p	q	~p	~q	(~p & ~q)	(p v q)	~(p v q)
				*		*
T	T	F	F	F	T	F
T	F	F	T	F	T	F
F	T	T	F	F	T	F
F	F	T	T	T	F	T

Under "~p & ~q" we find the column (FFFT), and we find the same sequence under "~(p v q)." This shows that for every possible substitution we make, these two expressions will yield statements of the same truth value. We shall say that these statement forms are *truth-functionally equivalent.*

Given the notion of truth-functional equivalence, the possibility of more than one translation can often be solved. If two translations are truth-functionally equivalent, then it does not matter which one we use in testing for validity. Of course, some translations will seem more natural than others. For example, "p v q" is truth-functionally equivalent to:

$\sim((\sim p \ \& \ \sim p) \ \& \ (\sim q \ v \ \sim q))$

The first expression is obviously more natural than the second, even though they are truth-functionally equivalent.

So far in this chapter we have seen that by using conjunction, disjunction, and negation, it is possible to construct complex statements out of simple statements. A distinctive feature of compound statements constructed in these three ways is that the truth of the compound statement is always a function of the truth of its component propositions. Thus, these three notions allow us to construct truth-functionally compound statements. Some arguments depend for their validity simply upon these truth-functional connectives. When this is so, it is possible to test for validity in a purely mechanical way. This can be done through the use of truth tables. Thus, in this area at least, we are able to give a clear account of validity and to specify exact procedures for testing for validity. Now we shall go on to examine an area where the application of this approach is more problematic. It concerns *conditionals.*

Conditionals

Conditionals often occur in arguments. They have the form, "If _____, then _____." Sometimes conditionals appear in the indicative mood:

If it rains, the crop will be saved.

Sometimes they occur in the subjunctive mood:

If it had rained, the crop would have been saved.

There are also conditional imperatives:

If a fire breaks out, call the fire department first!

There are conditional promises:

If you get into trouble, give me a call and I promise to help you.

Indeed, conditionals get a great deal of use in our language, and they very often appear in arguments. It is important, therefore, to understand them.

Unfortunately, there is no general agreement among experts about the correct way to analyze conditionals. We shall simplify matters by considering only *indicative* conditionals, but even here there is no settled opinion about the correct position to adopt. It may seem surprising that disagreement should exist concerning such a simple and fundamental notion as the if-then construction. Nonetheless, be prepared that this discussion will have none of the settled character of the previous one. First we shall describe the most standard treatment of conditionals; second, we shall consider a number of alternatives to it.

For conjunction, disjunction, and negation, the truth-table methods provided an approach that was at once plausible and effective. An indicative conditional is also compounded out of two simpler propositions, and this suggests that we might be able to offer a truth-table definition for conditionals as well. What should the truth table look like? When we try to answer this question, we get stuck almost at once, for it is unclear how we should fill in the table in three out of four cases.

p	q	If p, then q.
T	T	?
T	F	F
F	T	?
F	F	?

Let us call "*p*" the *antecedent* of this conditional and "*q*" its *consequent*. It seems obvious that a conditional cannot be true if the antecedent is true and the consequent false. We record this by putting an F in the second row. But suppose *p* and *q* are replaced by two arbitrary true propositions, say, "two plus two equals four" and "Chile is in South America." What shall we say about the conditional:

If two plus two equals four, then Chile is in South America.

The first thing to say is that this is a very strange statement, because the arithmetic remark in the antecedent doesn't seem to have anything to do with the geographical remark in the consequent. So this conditional is odd—indeed, extremely odd—but is it true or false? At this point a reasonable response is bafflement.

Now consider the following argument, which is intended to solve all these problems by giving good reasons for assigning truth values in each row of the truth table. One thing that seems obvious is that if "If p, then q" is true, then it is not the case that "p" is true and "q" is false. That in turn means that "$\sim(p \; \& \sim q)$" must be true. Now let's reason in the opposite direction. Suppose that we know that "$\sim(p \; \& \sim q)$" is true. For this to be true, "$p \; \& \sim q$" must be false. We know that from the truth-table definition of negation. Next let us suppose that "p" is true. Then "$\sim q$" must be false. We know that from the truth-table definition of conjunction. Finally, if "$\sim q$" is false, then "q" itself must be true. This line of reasoning is supposed to show that we can derive "If p, then q" from "Not both p and not q." The first step in the argument was intended to show that we can derive "Not both p and not q" from "If p, then q." But if each of these expressions is derivable from the other, this suggests that they are equivalent. We use this background argument as a justification of the following definition:

If p, then q = (by definition) Not both p and not q.

We can put this into symbols using a horseshoe to symbolize conditionals:

p ⊃ q = (by definition) ~(p & ~q)

Given this definition, we can now construct the truth table for indicative conditionals. It is simply the truth table for "$\sim(p \; \& \sim q)$":

p	q	~(p & ~q)	(p ⊃ q)	(~p v q)
T	T	T	T	T
T	F	F	F	F
F	T	T	T	T
F	F	T	T	T

Notice that "$(\sim p \; v \; q)$" is also truth-functionally equivalent to the other expressions. We have included "$(\sim p \; v \; q)$" because traditionally it has been used to define "$p \supset q$." For reasons that are now obscure, when a conditional is defined in this truth-functional way, it is called a *material conditional*.

Now let us suppose, for the moment, that the notion of a material conditional corresponds exactly with our idea of an indicative conditional. What would follow from this? The answer is that we could treat conditionals in the same way in which we have treated conjunction, disjunction, and negation. A conditional would be just one more kind of truth-functionally compound statement capable of definition by truth tables. Furthermore, arguments that depend upon this notion (together with conjunction, disjunction, and negation) could be settled by appeal to truth-table techniques. Let us pause for a moment to examine this.

One of the most common patterns of reasoning is called *modus ponens*. It looks like this:

If p, then q.   p ⊃ q
p   p
∴ q   ∴ q

The truth-table definition of material implication shows at once that this pattern of argument is valid.

Pr.		Pr.	Cn.	
p	q	p ⊃ q	q	
T	T	T	T	O.K. *Valid*
T	F	F	F	
F	T	T	T	
F	F	T	F	

Exercise 6: Show that the argument form called modus tollens is valid. It looks like this:

p ⊃ q
~q
∴ ~p

These same techniques allow us to show that one of the traditional fallacies is, indeed, a fallacy. It is called the fallacy of denying the antecedent, and it looks like this:

p ⊃ q
~p
∴ ~q

The truth-table analysis showing the invalidity of this argument has the following form:

		Pr.	Pr.	Cn.	
p	q	p ⊃ q	~p	~q	
T	T	T	F	F	
T	F	F	F	T	
F	T	T	T	F	NO *Invalid*
F	F	T	T	T	*OK.*

Exercise 7: A second standard fallacy is called affirming the consequent. It looks like this:

p ⊃ q

q
_____

∴ p

Using truth-table techniques, show that this argument form is invalid.

We can examine one last argument that has been historically significant. It is called the *hypothetical syllogism* and has the following form:

p ⊃ q
q ⊃ r
_____
∴ p ⊃ r

Since we are dealing with an argument form containing three variables, we must perform the boring task of constructing a truth table with eight rows:

			Pr.	Pr.	Cn.	
p	q	r	p ⊃ q	q ⊃ r	p ⊃ r	
T	T	T	T	T	T	O.K.
T	T	F	T	F	F	
T	F	T	F	T	T	Valid
T	F	F	F	T	F	
F	T	T	T	T	T	O.K.
F	T	F	T	F	T	O.K.
F	F	T	T	T	T	
F	F	F	T	T	T	O.K.

This is fit work for a computer, not for a human being, but it is important to see that it actually works.

Why is it important to see that these techniques work? Most people, after all, could see that hypothetical syllogisms are correct without going through all this tedious business. We seem only to be piling boredom on top of triviality. This protest deserves an answer. Suppose we ask someone *why* he or she thinks that the conclusion follows from the premises in a hypothetical syllogism. The person might answer that anyone can see that—something, by the way, that is false. Beyond this he or she might say that it all depends upon the meanings of the words, or that it is all a matter of definition. But if we go on to ask *which words* and *what definitions*, most people will fall silent. What we have done is to discover that the validity of some arguments depends upon the meanings of such words as "and," "or," "not," and "if–then." We have then gone on to give explicit definitions of these terms—definitions, by the way, that help us to see how these terms function in an argument. Finally, by getting all these *simple* things right, we have produced what is called a *decision procedure* for determining the validity of every argument involving conjunction, disjunction, negation, and conditionals. Our truth-table techniques give us an automatic procedure for settling questions of validity in this area. In fact, truth-table techniques have practical applications, for example, in computer programming. But the important point here is that through understanding how these techniques work, we can gain a deeper insight into the notion of validity.

Exercise 8: Using the truth-table techniques employed above, test the following argument forms for validity. (For your own entertainment, guess about the validity of the argument form before working it out.)

1. $p \supset q$

   $\therefore q \supset p$

2. $p \supset q$

   $\therefore \sim q \supset \sim p$

3. $(p \lor q) \supset r$

   $\therefore p \supset r$

4. $(p \& q) \supset r$

   $\therefore p \supset r$

5. $p \supset q$
   $q \supset r$

   $\therefore p \supset (q \& r)$

6. $(p \lor q) \& (p \lor r)$
   $\sim r$

   $\therefore \sim q \supset p$

7. $(p \supset q) \& (p \supset \sim r)$
   $r \& \sim q$

   $\therefore \sim p$

8. $p \supset q$
   $q \supset r$

   $\therefore \sim r \supset \sim p$

9. $p \supset (q \supset r)$
    _____
    $\therefore (p \ \& \ q) \supset r$

10. $p \supset (q \supset r)$
    $p \supset q$
    _____
    $\therefore r$

Logical Language and Everyday Language

Early in this chapter we started out by talking about such common words as "and" and "or," and then slipped over to talking about *conjunction* and *disjunction*. The transition was a bit sneaky, but intentional. To understand what is going on here, we can ask how closely these logical notions we have defined match their everyday counterparts. We will start with conjunction, and then come back to the more difficult question of conditionals. At first sight, the match seems to be very bad indeed.

In everyday discourse, we do not go about conjoining random bits of information. We do not say, for example, that two plus two equals four and Chile is in South America. We already know why we do not say such things, for unless the context is quite extraordinary, this is bound to violate the rule of Relevance. But if we are interested in validity, the rule of Relevance—together with all other pragmatic rules—is simply beside the point.

The formal notion of conjunction is also insensitive to another important feature of our everyday discourse: context. It reduces all conjunctions to their bare truth-functional content. We have already seen that the following remarks have a very different force in the context of an argument:

The ring is beautiful, but expensive.
The ring is expensive, but beautiful.

These two remarks will mean opposite things in the context of an actual argument, but from a purely formal point of view they are equivalent. We can translate the first sentence as "*B & E*" and the second as "*E & B.*" Their truth-functional equivalence is too obvious to need proof.

It might seem that if formal analysis cannot distinguish an "and" from a "but," then it can hardly be of any use at all. This is not true. A formal analysis of an argument will tell us just one thing: whether the argument is valid or not. If we expect the analysis to tell us more than this, we will be disappointed. It is important to remember two things:

(1) we expect arguments to be valid; (2) usually we expect much more than this from an argument. To elaborate upon the second point, we usually expect an argument to be sound as well as valid—we expect the premises to be true. Beyond this, we expect the argument to be informative, intelligible, convincing, and so forth. Validity, then, is an important aspect of an argument and formal analysis helps us to evaluate it. But validity is not the only aspect of an argument that concerns us; in many contexts it is not even our chief concern.

We can now look at our analysis of conditionals, for here we find some striking departures between the logician's analysis and everyday use. The following arguments are all valid:

(1) p
_____
∴ q ⊃ p

(2) ~p
_____
∴ p ⊃ q

(3) p & ~p
_____
∴ q

(4) q
_____
∴ p v ~p

We can see that these arguments are all valid by checking them with the following truth table:

p	q	~p	~q	q ⊃ p	~p ⊃ q	p & ~p	p v ~p
T	T	F	F	T	T	F	T
T	F	F	T	T	T	F	T
F	T	T	F	F	T	F	T
F	F	T	T	T	F	F	T

Yet, though valid, all these argument forms seem odd—so odd that they have actually been called *paradoxical.* The first argument form seems to say this: if a proposition is true, then it is implied by any proposition whatsoever. Here is an example of an argument that satisfies this argument form and is therefore valid:

Lincoln was President.

If water is hard, Lincoln was President.

This is a *very* peculiar argument to call valid. First we want to know what water has to do with Lincoln's having been President. Beyond this, how can his having been President depend upon the falsehood that water is hard? We can give these questions even more force by noticing that even the following argument is valid:

Lincoln was President.

If Lincoln was not President, then Lincoln was President.

This is an instance of the valid argument form: "$p \therefore \sim p \supset p$."

The other three argument forms are also paradoxical. They seem to say the following things: (2) A false proposition implies anything whatsoever. (3) Anything whatsoever follows from a contradiction. ("$p \& \sim p$" is the statement form for a *contradiction*, or what people sometimes call a self-contradiction. Look at the truth table and you will see that it is false for all possible truth value combinations.) (4) A tautology may be validly inferred from any proposition whatsoever. (Logicians call "$p \lor \sim p$" the statement form for *tautologies*. Just the reverse of a contradiction, a tautology is true no matter what truth values are assigned to its constituent parts.)

At this point, nonphilosophers become impatient, whereas philosophers become worried. We started out with principles that seemed to be both obvious and simple. Now, quite suddenly, we are being overwhelmed with a whole series of peculiar results. What in the world has happened, and what should be done about it? Philosophers remain divided in the answers they give to these questions. The responses fall into two main categories: (1) Simply give up the idea that conditionals can be defined truth-functionally and search for a different and better analysis of conditionals that avoids the difficulties involved in truth-functional analysis. (2) Take the difficult line and argue that there is nothing wrong with calling the above argument forms valid.

The first approach is highly technical and cannot be pursued in detail in this book. The general idea is this: Instead of identifying "If p, then q" with "Not both p and not q," identify it with "Not *possibly* both p and not q." This provides a stronger notion of a conditional and avoids some—though not all—of the suspicious arguments noticed above. This theory is given a systematic development by offering a logical analysis of the notion of *possibility*. This branch of logic is called *modal logic*, and has shown remarkable development in recent years.

Paul Grice, whose theories played a prominent part in Chapter 2, has taken the second line. He acknowledges—as anyone must—that the four argument forms above are decidedly odd. He denies, however, that this oddness has anything to do with *validity*. Validity concerns one thing and one thing only: An argument is valid if it is an instance of an argument form that never takes us from true premises to a false conclusion. The above arguments are valid by this definition of validity. Of course, arguments can be defective in all sorts of other ways. Look at the third and fourth arguments. Since "q" can be replaced by any proposition (true or false), the rule of Relevance will often be violated. It is worth pointing out violations of the rule of Relevance, but, according to Grice, this has nothing to do with validity. Now if we look at the first two arguments we see that they can also lead to arguments that contain a violation of the rule of Relevance. They also invite violations of the rule of Quantity. A conditional will be true just in case the consequent is true. Given this, it doesn't matter whether the antecedent is true or false. Again, a conditional is true just in case the antecedent is false—and it doesn't matter, given this, whether the consequent is true or false. Yet it can be very misleading to *use* a conditional on the basis of these logical features. For example, it would be very misleading for a museum guard to say, "If you give me five dollars, then I will let you into the exhibition," when, in fact, he will let you in in any case. For Grice, this is misleading since it violates the rule of Quantity. Yet, strictly speaking, it is not false. Strictly speaking, it is true.

The Grice line is attractive, for, among other things, it allows us to accept the truth-functional account of conditionals with all its simplicity. Yet sometimes it is difficult to swallow. Consider the following remark:

If God exists, then there is evil in the world.

If Grice's analysis is correct, even the most pious will have to admit that this conditional is true provided only that he is willing to admit that there is evil in the world. Yet this conditional plainly suggests that God's existence has something to do with the evil in the world, and the pious will wish to deny this suggestion. Grice would agree: The conditional plainly suggests that there is some connection between God's existence and the evil in the world—presumably, that is the point of connecting them in a conditional. All the same, this is something that is suggested, not asserted, and once more we come to the conclusion that this conditional is misleading—and therefore in need of criticism and correction—but still, strictly speaking, true.

Philosophers and logicians have had various responses to Grice's position. No consensus has emerged on this issue. The author of this book finds it on the whole convincing and we shall adopt it in this book. This will have two advantages: (1) This appeal to pragmatics fits in well with our previous discussions and (2) it provides a way of keeping the logic simple and within the range of a beginning student. Other philosophers and logicians continue to work toward a definition superior to the truth-table definition for indicative conditionals.

Other Conditionals in Ordinary Language So far we have considered only one form in which conditionals appear in everyday language: the indicative conditional "If p, then q." But, as we have noted, conditionals come in a variety of forms and some of them demand subtle treatment.

We can first consider the contrast between constructions using "if" and those using "only if":

(1) I'll clean the barn *if* Hazel will help me.
(2) I'll clean the barn *only if* Hazel will help me.

Adopting the following abbreviations:

B = I'll clean the barn
H = Hazel will help me

the first sentence is translated as follows:

(1) H ⊃ B

Notice that in the prose version of (1), the antecedent and consequent appear in reverse order. "*q* if *p*" means the same thing as "If *p*, then *q*."

How shall we translate the second sentence? Here we should move slowly and first notice what seems incontestable: If Hazel does not help me, then I will not clean the barn. This is translated in the following way:

(2) ~H ⊃ ~B

And that is equivalent to:

(2) B ⊃ H²

A more difficult question arises when we ask whether an implication runs the other way. When I say that I will clean the barn only if Hazel will help me, am I committing myself to cleaning the barn if she does help me? There is a strong temptation to answer this question "yes" and then give a fuller translation of (2) in the following way:

(2) (B ⊃ H) & (H ⊃ B)

Logicians call such two-way implications *biconditionals*, and we shall discuss them in a moment. But adding this second conjunct is almost surely a mistake, for we can think of parallel cases where we would not be tempted to include it. A government regulation might read as follows:

A person is eligible for retirement only if he or she is past 65.

From this it does not follow that anyone past 65 is eligible for retirement, for there may be other requirements as well.

Why were we tempted to use a biconditional in translating sentences containing the connective "only if"? Why, that is, are we tempted to think that the statement "I'll clean the barn only if Hazel will help me" implies "If Hazel helps me, then I will clean the barn"?

---

² If this equivalence is not obvious, it can be quickly established by using a truth table.

The answer turns upon the notion of conversational implication first met in Chapter 1. If I am *not* going to clean the barn, whether Hazel helps me or not, then it will be misleading—a violation of the rule of Quantity—to say that I will clean the barn only if Hazel helps me. For this reason, in many contexts, the use of a sentence of the form "*p* only if *q*" will conversationally imply a commitment "*p* if and only if *q*."

We can next look at sentences of the form "*p* if and only if *q*"—so-called biconditionals. If I say that I will clean the barn if and only if Hazel will help me, then I am saying that I will clean it if she helps and I will not clean it if she does not help. Translated, this becomes:

$$(H \supset B) \ \& \ (\sim H \supset \sim B)$$

This is equivalent to:

$$(H \supset B) \ \& \ (B \supset H)$$

We thus have an implication going both ways—the characteristic form of a biconditional. In fact, constructions containing the expression "if and only if" do not often appear in everyday speech. They appear almost exclusively in technical or legal writing. In ordinary conversation, we capture the force of a biconditional by saying something like this:

I will clean the barn, but only if Hazel helps me.

The decision whether to translate a remark of everyday conversation into a conditional or a biconditional is often subtle and difficult. We have already noticed that the use of sentences of the form "*p* only if *q*" will often conversationally imply a commitment to the biconditional "*p* if and only if *q*." In the same way, the *use* of the conditional "*p* if *q*" will also often carry this same implication. If I plan to clean the barn whether Hazel helps me or not, it will certainly be misleading—again, a violation of the rule of Quantity—to say that I will clean the barn *if* Hazel helps me.

So far, then, we have the following results:

(1) "*q* if *p*" translates "$(p \supset q)$." However, the use of "*q* if *p*" often has the conversational force of a biconditional.

(2) "*q* only if *p*" translates "$(q \supset p)$." However, the use of "*q* only if *p*" often has the conversational force of a biconditional.

(3) "*q* if and only if *p*" translates "$(p \supset q) \ \& \ (q \supset p)$." The biconditional, "*q* if and only if *p*," is more often conversationally implied than explicitly stated in everyday discourse.

We can close this discussion by considering one further, rather difficult, case. What is the force of saying *"p unless q"*? Is this a biconditional, or just a conditional? If it is just a conditional, which way does the implication go? There is a strong temptation to treat this as a biconditional, but the following example shows this to be wrong:

Carter will not win re-election unless he carries the Northeast.

This sentence clearly indicates that Carter will not win re-election if he does not carry the Northeast. Using abbreviations:

N = Carter will carry the Northeast.
W = Carter will win reelection.
~N ⊃ ~W

The original statement does not imply—even conversationally—that he will win re-election if he does carry the Northeast. The expression *"~p unless q"* means the same thing as the expression *"p only if q,"* and they both translate:

(p ⊃ q)

Summary In this chapter we have tried to get a clear conception of the notion of validity in one particular area. We have studied the logic of truth-functionally compound statements. These are arguments that depend for their validity on the logical properties of *conjunction, disjunction, negation,* and *material implication.* We have offered truth-table definitions of these notions and laid down a truth-table method for testing the validity of arguments that turn upon these connectives. Although we have not shown this, we have, in fact, developed a method for testing the validity of *all* arguments whose validity depends upon the character of these truth-functional connectives.

Exercise 9: Translate each of the following sentences into symbolic notation, using the suggested symbols as abbreviations.

(1) The Reds will win only if the Dodgers collapse. (R,D)
(2) The Steelers will win if their defense holds up. (S,D)
(3) If it rains or snows, the game will be called off. (R,S,O)
(4) Unless there is a panic, stock prices will continue to rise. (P,R)
(5) If the house comes up for sale and if I have money in hand, I will bid on it. (S,M,B)
(6) You can be a success if only you try. (S,T)

(7) You will get a good bargain provided you get there early. (B,E)

(8) You cannot lead a happy life without friends. (Let H = "You can lead a happy life," and let F = "You have friends.")

Exercise 10: Translate each of the following arguments into symbolic notation. Then (1) test the argument for validity using truth-table techniques and (2) comment upon any violations of conversational rules.

Example: Harold is clever, so if Harold isn't clever, then Anna isn't clever either. (H, A)

H	p
~H ⊃ ~A	~p ⊃ ~q

(1)

	Pr.			Cn.
p	q	~p	~q	~p ⊃ ~q
T	T	F	F	T	O.K.
T	F	F	T	T	O.K.
F	T	T	F	F
F	F	T	T	T

(2) The argument violates the rule of Relevance.

(1) Jones is brave, so Jones is brave or Jones is brave. (J)

(2) The Democrats will run either Jones or Smith. If Smith runs they will lose the South and if Jones runs they will lose the North. So the Democrats will lose either the North or South. (J, S, D, N)

(3) Although Brown will pitch, the Rams will lose. If the Rams lose, their manager will get fired, so their manager will get fired. (B, L, F).

(4) America will win the Olympics unless Russia does and Russia will win the Olympics unless East Germany does, so America will win the Olympics unless East Germany does. (A, R, E).

(5) If you dial 0, you will get the operator, so if you dial 0 and do not get the operator, then there is something wrong with the telephone. (D, O, W)

(6) The Republicans will carry either New Mexico or Arizona, but since they will carry Arizona they will not carry New Mexico. (A, N).

(7) John will play only if the situation is hopeless, but the situation will be hopeless, so John will play. (P, H)

(8) a. Carter will win the election whether he wins Idaho or not, therefore Carter will win the election. (C, I).

b. Carter will win the election, therefore Carter will win the election whether he wins Idaho or not. (C, I).

c. Carter will win the election, therefore Carter will win the election whether he wins a majority or not. (C, M).

(9) If you flip the switch then the light will go on, but if the light goes on, then the generator is working; so if you flip the switch, then the generator is working. (F, L, G)
(This example is due to Charles L. Stevenson.)

THE FORMAL ANALYSIS OF ARGUMENT: PART TWO

10

In Chapter 9 we saw how validity can depend upon the external connections between propositions. By examining in detail the theory of immediate inference and the theory of the categorical syllogism, this chapter will demonstrate how validity can depend on the internal structure of propositions. Our interest in these two aspects of logic is mostly theoretical. Understanding the theory of the syllogism deepens our understanding of validity even if this theory is, in most cases, difficult to apply directly to complex arguments in daily life.

Armed with the techniques developed in Chapter 9, we can look at the following argument:

> All squares are rectangles.
> All rectangles have parallel sides.
> _____
> ∴ All squares have parallel sides.

At a glance it is obvious that the conclusion follows from the premises —it is a valid argument. Furthermore, if it is valid, it must be valid in virtue of its *form*. In order to show the form of this argument, we might try something of the following kind:

$$p \supset q$$
$$q \supset r$$
$$\overline{}$$
$$p \supset r$$

BUT THIS IS A MISTAKE, and a bad mistake. We have used the letters "*p*," "*q*," and "*r*" as *propositional variables*—they stand for arbitrary propositions. But the proposition "All squares are rectangles" is not it-self composed of two propositions.

In fact, if we attempt to translate the above argument into the language of the propositional calculus, we get the following result:

$$p$$
$$q$$
$$\overline{}$$
$$\therefore r$$

This, of course, is not a valid argument form. But if we look back at the original argument we see that it is obviously valid. This shows that the Propositional Logic—however adequate it is in its own areas—is not ca-pable of explaining the validity of *all* valid arguments. To broaden our understanding of the notion of validity, we will examine a branch of logic developed in ancient times, *the theory of the syllogism*.

Categorical Propositions

In the argument above, the first premise asserts some kind of relation-ship between squares and rectangles; the second premise asserts some kind of relationship between rectangles and things with parallel sides; finally, *in virtue of this*, the conclusion asserts a relationship between squares and things having parallel sides. Our task, now, is to understand these relationships as clearly as possible so that we can discover the *ba-sis* for the validity of this argument. Again we shall adopt the strategy of starting from very simple cases and using the insights gained there for dealing with more complicated cases.

A natural way to represent the relationships expressed by the propositions in an argument is through diagrams. Suppose we draw one circle standing for all things that are squares and another circle standing for all things that are rectangles. The claim that all squares are rectangles may be represented by placing the circle representing squares completely inside the circle representing rectangles.

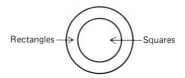

Another way of representing this relationship is to begin with overlapping circles.

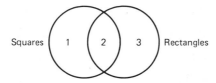

We then shade out the portions of the circles that represent nothing. Since all squares are rectangles, there is nothing that is a square that is not a rectangle—that is, there is nothing in region 1. So our diagram looks like this:

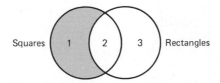

Either method of representation seems plausible. We shall, however, use the system of overlapping circles because in the long run they actually work better. They are called Venn diagrams.

Having examined *one* relationship that can exist between two classes, it is natural to wonder what other relationships might exist. Going to the opposite extreme from our first example, two classes may have *nothing* in common. The proposition "No triangles are squares" expresses such a relationship. We diagram this by indicating that there is nothing in common between squares and triangles.

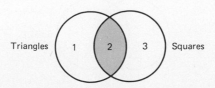

In these first two extreme cases we have indicated that one class is either completely included in another ("All squares are rectangles") or completely excluded from another ("No triangles are squares"). Sometimes, however, we make the weaker remark that two classes have at least *some* things in common. We say, for example, that "some aliens are spies." How shall we indicate this on the following diagram?

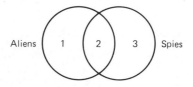

In this case, we do not want to cross out any whole region. We do not want to cross out region 1 because we are not saying that *all* aliens are spies. Plainly, we do not want to cross out region 2, for we are actually saying that some persons are both aliens and spies. Finally, we do not want to cross out region 3, for we are not saying that all spies are aliens. Saying that some aliens are spies does not rule out the possibility that some spies are homegrown.

It is plain, then, that we need some new device to represent claims that two classes have at least *some* members in common. We shall do this in the following way:

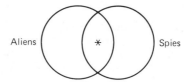

Here the asterisk indicates that there is at least one person who is both an alien and a spy. Notice, by the way, that we are departing a bit from an everyday way of speaking. "Some" is usually taken to mean *more than one;* here we let it mean *at least one.* In fact, this makes things simpler and will really cause no trouble.

Given this new method of diagramming class relationships, we can immediately think of other possibilities. The following diagram indicates that there is someone who is an alien but not a spy. In more natural language, it represents the claim that *some aliens are not spies.*

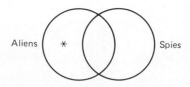

Next we can indicate that there is someone who is a spy but not an alien. More simply, we are representing the claim that *some spies are not aliens.*

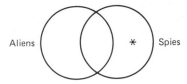

Finally, we can indicate that there is someone who is neither a spy nor an alien:

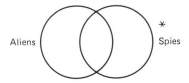

Domain of Discourse

The last example raises a special problem. When we try to think of something that is neither a spy nor an alien, we naturally think of a *person*—say, Dorothy Hamill. But how about Mt. Whitney and the number seven? Neither of these things is either a spy or an alien. Yet it seems odd to say that Mt. Whitney is neither a spy nor an alien. How could it be either of these things? Talk about spies and aliens typically concerns people. We can put it this way: Talking about spies and aliens normally *presupposes* that we are considering only persons. To reflect the notion of limiting our discussion to a certain kind of thing, we will make our diagrams a bit more elaborate. We will enclose the intersecting circles with a box that indicates the *domain of discourse* (DD). Some examples will make this clear:

    1. All squares are rectangles (domain of discourse: plane figures):

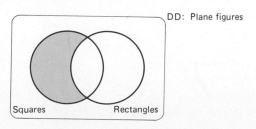

2. Some aliens are not spies (domain of discourse: people):

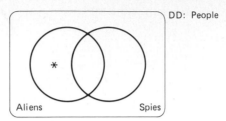

Deciding upon a domain of discourse is somewhat arbitrary. It de-pends upon good sense and present interests. In the first example, we might have taken *four-sided figures* as the domain of discourse, and per-haps in the second example *people in the United States* might have done perfectly well. Actually, we will be quite casual about specifying a domain of discourse, and will only do so when it serves some useful purpose.

The Four Basic Propositions

It is easy to see that two classes can be related in a great many different ways. Nonetheless, it is possible to examine all these relationships in terms of four basic propositions:

A: All A is B. I: Some A is B.
E: No A is B. O: Some A is not B.

The diagram for each of these propositions is given below.

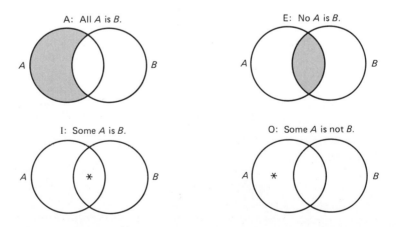

These basic propositions, together with their labels and diagrams, should be memorized because they will be used constantly.

Exercise 1: Using just the four basic propositions, indicate what information is given in each of the following diagrams:

Example:

No A is B.
Some A is not B.
Some B is not A.
No B is A.

1.

2.

3.

4.

5.

6.

Existential Import

We must now turn to a difficult problem that logicians have not fully settled. Usually when we make a statement it is obvious that we are *talking about* certain things. If someone claims that all whales are mammals, he is then talking about whales and saying that they are mammals. That is, in making this statement about whales, he *seems to be taking for granted the existence of whales.* He is not exactly saying that there are whales, yet his remark commits him to the existence of whales. To mark this commitment, we can put an asterisk (*) into our diagram for the *A* proposition:

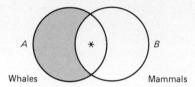

Whales   Mammals

We now see at once that if *all whales are mammals,* then *at least some whales are mammals.* This is not a very exciting inference, but one that strikes us as valid. We can now see why this inference is valid by noticing that the diagram for the A proposition given above already contains the information contained in the I proposition given below:

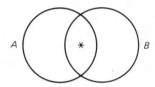

In the same way, we can see why the proposition "No aliens are spies" implies the proposition "Some aliens are not spies." In saying that no aliens are spies, we seem to be committing ourselves to the existence of aliens and saying of them that none of them are spies. If we reflect this commitment in the diagram for the E proposition, as follows,

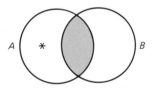

we see at once that it implies the O proposition which, as we know, is represented in the following way:

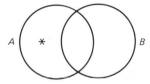

So far, then, everything seems simple enough. We can understand the relationships between the A and I as well as the E and O propositions simply by marking the commitment to existence in the A and E propositions. The difficulty is that we sometimes seem to use both the A and E propositions without any such existential commitment. If I say that all dwarfs are small, I am not committing myself to the existence of dwarfs; I am speaking about fictitious or mythical creatures. There are problems concerned with fictitious things, but they will not concern us here. A more difficult problem arises with a remark of the following kind: "All trespassers will be fined." In saying this, I am not committing myself to the existence of trespassers; I am only saying, *"If there are trespassers, then they will be fined."* Given this one example of an A proposition that carries no commitment concerning things referred to in the subject term, it is easy to think of many others.

Once more, then, we must make a decision. (Remember that we had to make decisions concerning the truth-table definitions of both disjunction and implication.) Classical logic was developed on the assumption that both the A and E propositions carry existential import. Modern logic makes the opposite decision, treating the claim that all men are mortal as equivalent to the claim that if someone is a man, then he is mortal. This way of speaking carries no commitment to the existence of men. If we want to indicate the existence of men, then we must say so explicitly. The difference is shown in the following diagrams:

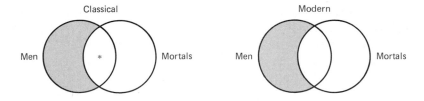

An important consequence of this difference is that in the classical approach the A proposition implies the I proposition, whereas in the modern approach it does not.

Which approach shall we adopt? In the long run, the modern approach has proved a more powerful method. All the same, there is something beautiful about the classical approach and it is worth exploring in its own right. Our decision, then, is this: We will adopt the modern approach and not assign existential import to the A and E propositions. At the same time, we can develop the classical approach simply by adding an indication of existential commitment where it is needed. In this way we can examine both the modern and the classical approach to this area of logic.

The Classification of the Basic Propositions

Traditionally, these basic propositions have been classified under the following distinctions:

Quality: Affirmative/Negative
Quantity: Universal/Particular

Quality The A and I propositions are affirmative propositions, and the E and O propositions are negative propositions. The intuitive difference between an affirmative proposition and a negative proposition seems obvious: In an affirmative proposition we *affirm* something; in a negative proposition we *deny* or *negate* something. Yet it is not always easy to apply this distinction to particular cases. Is the following proposition affirmative or negative?

John is absent.

If you decide that it is negative because absent just means "not here," then how do you classify this proposition?

John is not absent.

It seems odd to call a proposition affirmative when it has the transparent form of a denial.

Fortunately, in the present context, we do not have to worry about such questions. We shall classify propositions in terms of their form and not in terms of the meaning of the subject and predicate words. Thus the same thought can be expressed in propositions of different forms. For example:

All clergy are noncombatants.
No clergy are combatants.

Although these propositions express the same thought, the first is an A proposition, the second is an E proposition. For evident reasons, then, we call the E and the O propositions negative, and the A and the I propositions affirmative.

Quantity The A and E propositions are *universal* propositions, and the I and O propositions are *particular* propositions. The distinction between universal and particular propositions turns upon the character of the subject term in the proposition. In a universal proposition we speak about *all* of the members of the subject class; in a *particular* proposition we speak about *some* of them. So the A proposition is said to be universal and the I and O propositions are said to be particular. It does not take much thought to see that the E proposition is universal. If I say that no A is B, I am plainly speaking of *all* the things that are A and saying that none of them is B. We can summarize this nomenclature in the following table:

		Quality	
		Affirmative	Negative
Quantity	Universal	A	E
	Particular	I	O

The Square of Opposition

We can now examine some logical relationships that obtain between these four basic propositions. The first system of relationships form what has been called the *square of opposition*. The approach here is classical, with existential commitment indicated for the A and E propositions.

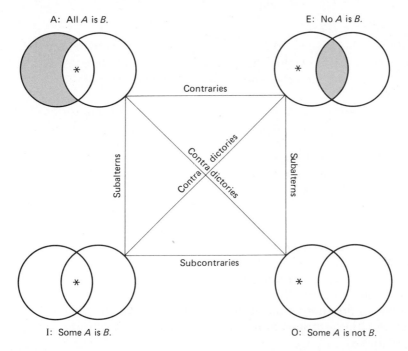

A: All *A* is *B*.

E: No *A* is *B*.

Contraries

Subalterns

Contradictories

Contradictories

Subalterns

Subcontraries

I: Some *A* is *B*.

O: Some *A* is not *B*.

This diagram shows the relationship that each proposition has to the other three. All of these relationships have specific names which are explained below.

Contraries The A and E propositions are *contraries* of one another. That is, they are so related that:

(1) They cannot both be true.

(2) They can, however, both be false.

In common life, the idea of contraries is captured by the notion that one thing is the *complete opposite* of another. The complete opposite of "Everyone is here" is "No one is here." Clearly, such complete opposites cannot both be true at once. If we look at the diagrams for the A and E propositions, we see this at once. The middle region of the A proposition diagram shows the existence of something that is both *A* and *B*, whereas the middle region of the E proposition diagram is shaded out, showing that nothing is both *A* and *B*. It should also be clear that both the A and E propositions may be false. Suppose that there is some *A* that is *B* and also some *A* that is not *B:*

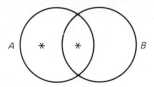

Going from left to right, the first asterisk shows that "All *A* is *B*" is false; the second asterisk shows that "No *A* is *B*" is false.

Contradictories The A and O propositions are contradictories of one another, and so are the E and I propositions. The most obvious example of a contradictory pair of propositions is a proposition and its explicit denial, i.e., pairs of the form: "*p*" and "~*p*." If we look at the square of opposition, we see that the O proposition is the denial of the A proposition. These contradictory pairs are so related that:

(1) They cannot both be true.

(2) They cannot both be false.

More simply, contradictory pairs of propositions always have *opposite* truth values.

Once more these relationships are reflected in the diagrams we have drawn for these propositions. Here we will only examine the A and O propositions.

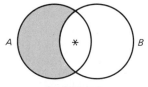

A: All *A* is *B*.

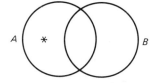

O: Some *A* is not *B*.

It is easy to see that these two propositions cannot both be true, for the second diagram has an asterisk in a region that is shaded out in the first diagram. But why must at least one of these propositions be true? Actually, it is rather easy to explain this in the *modern* approach, where there is no existential commitment for the A and E propositions. The explanation in the classical approach is more complicated.

In the modern approach we can represent the denial of a proposition by a simple procedure. The only information given in our diagram is represented either by *shading out* some region, thereby indicating that nothing exists in it, or by *putting an asterisk* in a region, thereby indicating that something does exist in it. We are given no indication about unmarked regions. To represent the denial of a proposition, we simply reverse the information in the diagram. That is, where there is an asterisk, we put in shading; where there is shading, we put in an asterisk. Everything else is left unchanged. Thus in the modern approach, we can see at once that the A and O propositions are denials of one another so that they must always take opposite truth values.

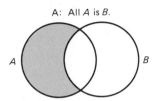

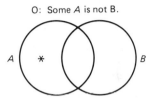

The situation in the classical interpretation is much less tidy. The basic idea in the classical approach is that in asserting that all *A* is *B*, we are committing ourselves to the existence of things that are *A*. We reflect this commitment by putting an asterisk in the middle region of the diagram for the A proposition. But now the interpretation of the denial of this proposition is no longer a straightforward business of reversing information. The following is *not* what we want:

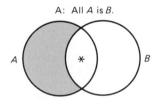

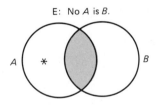

Here we have wound up with the wrong result, for we want the O proposition to be the contradiction of the A proposition and not the E proposition. The result we do want is this:

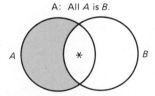

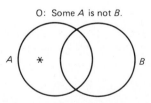

To get the right result, we shall make the following ruling: Even in the classical approach we shall ignore existential import, except in those cases where a particular inference depends upon it. In those cases, *we*

shall plug in the existential import only after all other logical maneu-
vers have been made. So we are back to our simple modern diagram:

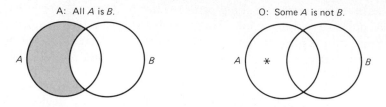

There is no need here to further decorate this diagram with indications
of existential import, since nothing turns upon it.

Subcontraries The I and O propositions are *subcontraries* of one another. Here the pattern is just the reverse of the pattern of contraries:

(1) Both can be true.

(2) Both cannot be false.

As with contraries, this relationship holds on the classical approach because of the commitment to the existence of items in the classes we
speak about. (The relationship of subcontraries does not hold on the
modern approach.) To see how this works out, compare the diagrams for
the I and O propositions:

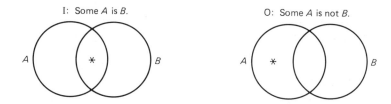

Consider just the left-hand side of this diagram:

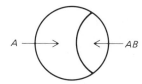

We know that in the classical approach, a presuppositional asterisk
must go into this diagram somewhere. But if the asterisk goes into the
overlapping region *AB*, then the I proposition is true; if the asterisk goes

into the nonoverlapping region of *A*, then the O proposition is true. So at least one of them is true. Finally, nothing rules out the possibility that there might be an asterisk in each region. In that case both the I and the O propositions would be true, and the situation would look like this:

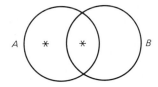

Subalternation *Subalternation* is the relationship that holds down the sides of the square of opposition. Quite simply, the A proposition implies the I proposition and the E proposition implies the O proposition. Again, this relationship depends upon the existential commitment found in the classical approach, and does not hold in the modern approach. We can use our diagrams for testing these implications in the following way: First diagram the premise, and then diagram the conclusion. If the inference from premise to conclusion is valid, then the information contained in the diagram for the conclusion must already be contained in the information given in the diagram for the premise. The validity for subalternation is illustrated by the following diagrams:

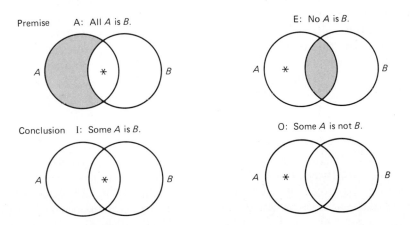

Another way of describing this test is as follows: Draw both the diagram for the premise and the conclusion, and then try to add the information contained in the diagram for the conclusion to the diagram for the premise. If the argument is valid, that information is already present in the diagram for the premise and no addition to it is needed.

We can summarize the information given by the classical square of opposition using two charts. We shall ask two questions. First, for each proposition, what consequences follow from the assumption that it is true?

		A	E	I	O
	A	T	F	T	F
Assumed true	E	F	T	F	T
	I	?	F	T	?
	O	F	?	?	T

Secondly, for each proposition, what consequences follow from the assumption that it is false?

		A	E	I	O
	A	F	?	?	T
Assumed false	E	?	F	T	?
	I	F	T	F	T
	O	T	F	T	F

Pragmatics and the Square of Opposition

As we have examined the classical treatment of the square of opposition, we have seen that at almost every turn the argument depended upon the notion of existential commitment. The one exception was the relationship of contradictories, but in all other cases we have to make this commitment explicit in order to show that the relationships hold. We might say that the classical approach depends upon making *explicit* what is *implicit* in the use of these basic propositions.

We can now look at a different approach that is familiar to us from earlier discussions. Instead of saying that the A proposition *implies* the existence of things that are *A*, we can say that the *use* of an A proposition *normally conversationally implies that the person believes that there are things that are A*. We have to speak in this qualified way because there are times when the use of an A proposition has no such conversational implication. Remember the example of someone saying, "All trespassers will be fined." This does not conversationally imply that the person who says it believes that there will be trespassers. (Having announced this, he may now believe just the opposite.) Reflections of this kind lead to a different way of treating the square of opposition. We can take the logically simple approach of dropping the assumption that the A and E propositions carry existential import. We then get the result that *only* the relationships of contradictories continue to hold. All the other relationships now fail.

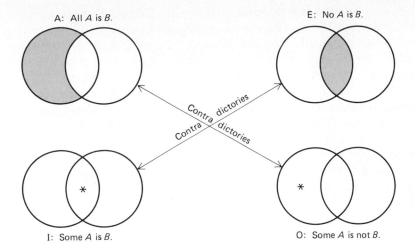

This is all that is left of the traditional square of opposition in the modern approach.

We can, however, reflect more of the traditional relationships by adding to this square the conversational implications that arise in standard contexts:

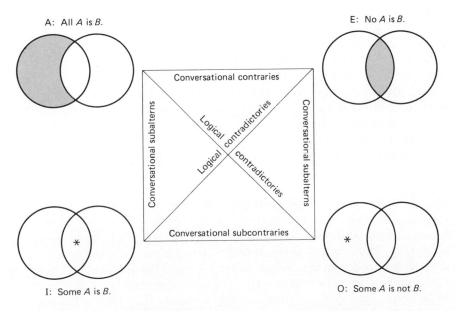

Here only the relationship of contradictories is a logical one; all the other relationships depend upon conversational implication and thus are labeled as conversational relationships.

Will it make much difference whether we adopt the classical or the modern approach to the propositions that form the square of opposition?

For some purposes it will hardly make any difference at all. In the practical affairs of life it usually does not make any difference whether something is logically implied *by what is said* or conversationally implied *by the saying of it.* In fact, it is only relatively recently that philosophers have become aware of this difference in something like a clearheaded way. Yet from the point of view of logical theory, the distinction is crucial. When we mix up logical implications and conversational implications, our logic first of all becomes very complicated. This comes out, for example, in trying to explain contradictories on the classical square of opposition.

Beyond leading to complications, mixing up logical and conversational implication can actually lead to inconsistency. This can be illustrated by noticing another way that conversational rules apply to the use of the propositions on the square of opposition. The use of these propositions is governed by Grice's rule of Quantity—that is, where justified, we are expected to use the stronger A or E propositions rather than the weaker I or O propositions. Thus when we use either the I or O propositions, we conversationally imply that we are not in a position to use the stronger A or E propositions. A simple example will show how this works: Filled with greed, a person takes every last piece of candy from a box. When asked if he has taken the candy, he replies, "I took some of the candy." Now, strictly speaking, this is true. The person did take some of the candy. Yet his remark plainly suggests that he took *only* some of it. Here the violation of the conversational rule is so extreme that it is tempting to call the person's reply an outright lie. In general, then, the use of an I proposition by a speaker contextually implies that the speaker does not believe the A proposition to be true; sometimes it implies, even more strongly, that he knows the A proposition to be false. We get this stronger implication when the speaker is in a position to know whether the A proposition is true or not. For example, the person who takes all the candy is obviously in a position to know what he has done. It is for this reason that his remark conversationally implies the *denial* of the assertion that he took all of the candy.

Now the very same relationship holds between the weak O proposition and the strong E proposition. The use of an O proposition by a speaker conversationally implies that the speaker does not believe the E proposition, and sometimes, even more strongly, that he knows it not to be true. This leads to a result that squares with our commonsense understanding of language: When someone says, "Some are . . ." this conversationally implies "Some are not . . ."; conversely, when someone says, "Some are not . . ." this conversationally implies "Some are. . . ." In general, then, the use of one subaltern conversationally implies that the use of the other subaltern is also okay.[1]

[1] Remember that conversational rules, unlike logical rules, hold only in general, for one conversational rule can be affected and overridden by another.

We are now in a position to see how mixing up conversational rules with logical rules can lead to lunacy. Consider the following line of reasoning.

(1) All aliens are spies.
∴ (2) Some aliens are spies.
∴ (3) Some aliens are not spies.
_____
∴ (4) If all aliens are spies, some aliens are not spies.

In this strange argument, we wind up with a proposition implying its own denial, a result we expect to get *only* when we start out from a self-contradictory proposition. It is not hard to see what has gone wrong here. The step from (1) to (2) is a logical implication in the classical approach, and a conversational implication in the modern approach. On the other hand, the step from (2) to (3) must be a conversational implication in either approach. In the conclusion both steps are treated as logical implications, and disaster results.

Exercise 2: Give a similar explanation of the fallacies in the following lines of reasoning:

(1) If you have an obligation to do something, then you are permitted to do it.
If you are permitted to do something, then you are permitted not to do it.
_____
∴ If you have an obligation to do something, then you are permitted not to do it.

Less seriously:

(2) If something is good, then it is not bad.
If something is not bad, then it is not so good.
_____
∴ If something is good, then it is not so good.

This last example shows that mixing up logical implications with conversational implications can lead to unwanted results. This, however, does not settle the issue between the classical and the modern approach to the existential import of these basic propositions. A logician is free to argue that existential import is logically implied—not merely conversationally implied—by the A and E propositions. He can then develop his theory accordingly. There is nothing incoherent about such an approach. This text adopts the modern approach for three reasons:

(1) It yields a simpler logical system.

(2) It is part of a much wider system that has proved extraordinarily successful.

(3) It fits in well with the general approach of distinguishing logical implications from conversational implications.

The Theory of Immediate Inference

The theory of immediate inference concerns arguments with the following features:

(1) They have a single premise. (That is why the inference is called immediate.)

(2) They involve only the four basic propositions.

Of course, there are all sorts of other arguments involving just one premise, but those involving the four basic propositions have been singled out for special attention. These inferences deserve special attention because they occur quite often in everyday reasoning.

We already know about one immediate inference: subalternation. In the classical theory, but not in the modern theory, we can always derive an I proposition from an A proposition, and we can always derive an O proposition from an E proposition. Here we shall consider three standard patterns of immediate inference: conversion, obversion, and contraposition. We will adopt the modern approach, but we will notice where the classical approach differs from it.

Conversion *Conversion* is the simplest immediate inference we shall consider. We convert a proposition simply by reversing the subject term and the predicate term. By the subject term, we simply mean the term that occurs in the grammatical subject; by the predicate term, we mean the term that occurs in the grammatical predicate. In the proposition "All spies are aliens," "spies" is the subject term and "aliens" is the predicate term. In this case identifying the predicate term is straightforward, since the grammatical predicate is a noun—a predicate nominative. Often, however, we have to change the grammatical predicate from an adjective to a noun phrase in order to get a noun that refers to a class of things. Though it is a bit artificial, we can always use this device. "All spies are dangerous" becomes "All spies are dangerous things." Here "spies" is the subject term and "dangerous things" is the predicate term. The reason we must make this change is that when we convert a proposition, we need a noun phrase to go into the place of the gram-

matical subject. In English we cannot say "All dangerous are spies," but
we can say "All dangerous things are spies."

We want to know when this operation of conversion is legitimate.
That is, we want to know when conversion yields a *valid* immediate inference. To answer this question we can examine the four basic propositions to see what happens when conversion is attempted. Two cases are
obvious at first sight. Both the I and the E propositions validly convert.
From the I proposition, "Some *S* is *P*," we may validly infer "Some *P*
is *S*."

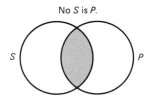

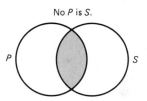

From the E proposition, "No *S* is *P*," we may validly infer "No *P* is *S*."

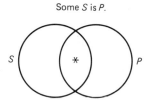

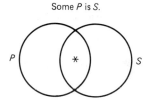

Notice that in these cases the converse of the proposition has exactly
the same diagram as the original proposition. This shows that the I
proposition not only *implies* its converse, but is *logically equivalent* to
it; the implication runs both ways. It should also be obvious that the O
proposition cannot, in general, be converted validly. From "Some *S* is
not *P*," we may not, in general, infer "Some *P* is not *S*."[2]

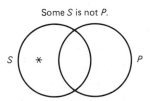

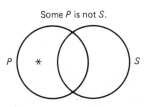

[2] There are some strange cases—logicians call them degenerate cases—where inferences of
this pattern are valid. For example, from *Some men are not men,* we may validly infer
that *Some men are not men.* Here, by making the subject term and the predicate term the
same, we trivialize conversion. Keeping cases of this kind in mind, we must say that in
general, but not always, the conversion of an O proposition does not yield a valid inference. In contrast, the set of valid inferences holds in all cases, including degenerate cases.

Finally, we can see that the A proposition does not validly convert, either. From "All *S* is *P*," we may not, in general, infer "All *P* is *S*."

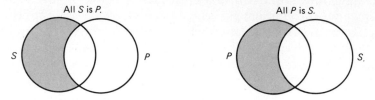

Everything that we have said so far is true in both the modern and the classical approach. To see this, we need only add the symbols indicating existential commitment to the above diagrams and then notice that the reasoning remains unchanged. But there is one important difference between the classical and the modern approach. Given the existential commitment in the classical approach, we may infer from *All S is P* that *Some P is S*. That inference does not hold in the modern approach:

Classical: All *S* is *P*.   *Some P is S.*

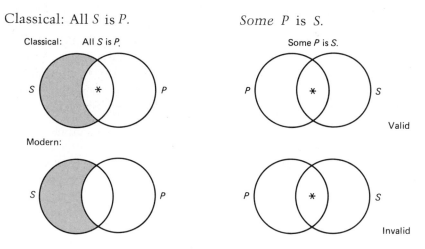

The classical conversion of an A proposition into an I proposition is called *conversion by limitation* since the original universal claim is limited to a particular claim. The following table summarizes these relationships:

Proposition	Conversion	Status
A: All *S* is *P*.	Some *P* is *S*.	Implication by limitation— classical theory only
E: No *S* is *P*.	No *P* is *S*.	Logically equivalent
I: Some *S* is *P*.	Some *P* is *S*.	Logically equivalent
O: Some *S* is not *P*.	Some *P* is not *S*.	Does not hold

Obversion Before we can deal with *obversion,* we must define the notion of a *complementary class.* The idea is simple enough: given any class C, its complementary class is just all of those things that are not in C. One standard way of referring to a complementary class is to use the prefix "non." Here are some examples:

Class	Complementary class
Republicans	Non-Republicans
Voters	Nonvoters
Combatants	Noncombatants

If we look at the class of non-Republicans, we see that it is a mixed bag, for as we have defined the notion it includes everything that is not a Republican. This includes coyotes, subatomic particles, prime numbers, the top ten record hits, and the British royal family. Of course, in everyday life we certainly do not wish to include all these things in our notion of a non-Republican. When we speak about non-Republicans, the context will usually make it clear that we are referring to politicians, voters, or party members. We can capture this idea by using a notion introduced earlier: that of a *domain of discourse.* We might say that the domain of discourse here includes all those who are members of American political parties. A non-Republican is someone in this domain of discourse who is not a Republican. We can represent this using the following diagram:

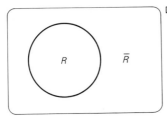

DD: Members of American political parties

A bar over a letter indicates a complementary class. In this case $\bar{R}$ means the class of non-Republicans. As indicated earlier, sometimes it is useful to specify the domain of discourse, sometimes it is not. In this book we will worry about the domain of discourse only when it serves some useful purpose.

We can now define the immediate inference called *obversion.* To pass from a basic proposition to its obverse:

(1) We reverse the *quality* of the proposition, from affirmative to negative or negative to affirmative as the case may be.

(2) We replace the predicate term by its complementary term.

Starting with "All men are mortal," this two-step process works as follows:

All men are mortal.

(1) Reversing the quality yields: No men are mortal.

(2) Replacing the predicate term by its converse yields: No men are nonmortal.

This final proposition is the obverse of "All men are mortal."

. We now want to know when this operation of obversion is legitimate—that is, we want to know when obversion yields a valid immediate inference. The answer to this is that a proposition is always *logically equivalent* to its obverse in both the classical and the modern interpretation. To show this, we can run through the four propositions. Since all these equivalences hold between a proposition and its *obverse*, there is no need to draw a diagram twice. The reader should, however, check to see whether the diagram is accurate for both propositions.

A: "All *S* is *P*" is logically equivalent to "No *S* is non-*P*."

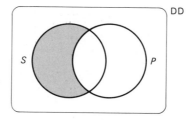

In this diagram, the class of things that are non-*P* includes all those things in the domain of discourse that are not in *P*. We can see that there is nothing in the class of things that are *S* that is also in the complimentary class of *P*, because all the things in *S* are in the class *P*. This may sound a bit complicated, but with a very little thought the validity of inferences through obversion becomes quite obvious.

E: "No *S* is *P*" is logically equivalent to "All *S* is non-*P*."

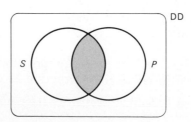

I: "Some *S* is *P*" is logically equivalent to "Some *S* is not non-*P*."

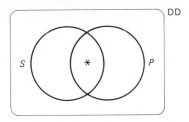

O: From "Some *S* is not *P*," we may validly infer that "Some *S* is non-*P*."

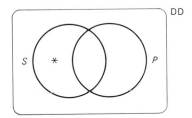

It is important to see that the final inference is a genuine inference and not a mere repetition. "Some *S* is not *P*" is an O proposition, whereas "Some *S* is non-*P*" is an I proposition. That is, the first proposition formulates a negative proposition—it indicates that there is at least one thing that is not in a certain class. The second proposition is an affirmative proposition, for it indicates that something is in a given class—in this case, a complementary class.

Contraposition *Contraposition* is the final relationship we shall examine. We get the contrapositive of a proposition by the following two-step process:

(1) We convert the proposition.

(2) We replace *both* terms by their complementary terms.

For example, starting with "All men are mortal," this two-step process works as follows:

All men are mortal.

(1) Converted, this proposition becomes:
All mortal (things) are men.

(2) Replacing each term by its complementary term we get:
All nonmortal (things) are non-men.

This final proposition is the contrapositive of "All men are mortal."
Following our previous pattern, we must now ask when the contrapositive can be validly inferred from a given proposition. Here the situation is pretty much the reverse of what we discovered for conversion:

A: "All S is P" is logically equivalent to "All non-P is non-S."

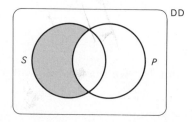

E: From "No S is P" we may not, in general, infer "No non-P is non-S."

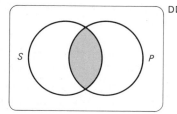
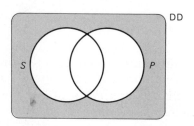

But in the classical approach, though not in the modern approach, *contraposition by limitation* does hold, i.e., from "No S is P" we may infer "Some non-P is not non-S."[3]

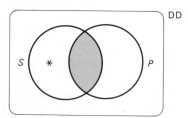
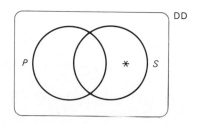

I: From "Some S is P," we may not, in general, infer "Some non-P is non-S."

[3] At first sight this proposition may seem hard to understand, but with a little thought it actually makes sense.

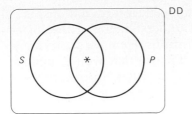 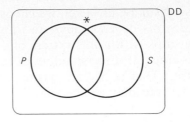

O: "Some S is not P" is logically equivalent to "Some non-P is not non-S."

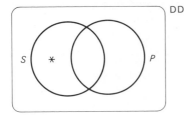 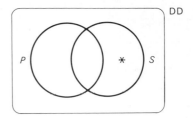

The following table summarizes all these equivalence relationships. The two items in parentheses are not equivalent but are only implied, and they hold only in the classical interpretation.

Proposition	Obversion	Conversion	Contraposition
All S is P.	No S is non-P.	(Some S is P.)	All non-P is non-S.
No S is P.	All S is non-P.	No P is S.	(Some non-P is not non-S.)
Some S is P.	Some S is not non-P.	Some P is S.	XXXXXXXXXX
Some S is not P.	Some S is non-P	XXXXXXXXXX	Some non-P is not non-S.

If we compare some of the propositions we have been studying with remarks that we make in everyday life, some of them, at least, will seem very artificial. It is hard to imagine a case where we would actually say "Some nonspies are not nonaliens." It would certainly be easier to say "Some nonspies are aliens," which is its equivalent through *obversion*. We can then *convert* this: "Some aliens are nonspies." This is still somewhat unnatural, so by using obversion again we get the natural remark, "Some aliens are not spies." Actually, we could have gotten this result immediately through applying *contraposition* to the original remark. (This shows that the contrapositive of a proposition is the obverse of the converse of the obverse of that proposition—something you need not commit to memory!)

In fact, we do *sometimes* find ourselves in contexts where we use some of these complicated sentences. Discussing the voting patterns of nonresidents, we might find ourselves saying that some nonresidents are not nonvoters. Given the context, this remark loses much of its oddness. Usually, however, we choose simple clear formulations; the ability to do this depends upon an implicit understanding of the logical relationships within this system of propositions. Here we are trying to bring this implicit understanding to the surface so that we can understand it better. That is, we are trying to give clear rules for inferences that we make routinely in everyday life.

Exercise 3: For each of the following propositions, decide by using appropriate diagrams which of the above immediate inferences hold. For example:

All ministers are noncombatants.

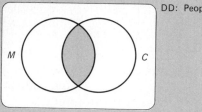

Obverse: No ministers are combatants.

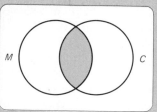

Converse: All noncombatants are ministers.

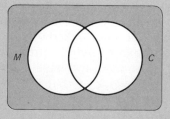

Contrapositive: All non-noncombatants are nonministers. Or more simply: All combatants are nonministers.

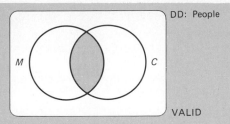

DD: People

VALID

(1) Some dudes are not cowards.
(2) All nonresidents are taxpayers.
(3) Some nonaligned nations are wealthy (nations).
(4) No daughters are sons.
(5) No nonnegotiable stocks are safe (stocks).
(6) All that glitters is not gold.
(7) Some people cannot be bought.
(8) There is no such thing as a bad boy.

Exercise 4: Put the following sentences into plain, respectable English. Indicate the immediate inference or immediate inferences you have used to do so. (Be careful!)
(1) No noncombatant is a minister.
(2) Some nonresident is not a non-nonvoter.
(3) Not all snakes are not dangerous (things).
(4) No all-the-time losers are non-nonpersons.

The Theory of the Syllogism

In an immediate inference, we draw a conclusion directly from a single proposition. The traditional theory of immediate inference explores such inferences as they arise for the basic A E I O propositions. The square of opposition answers the following question: Given the truth or falsity of one of these basic propositions, what, if anything, may we infer concerning the truth or falsity of the remaining basic propositions? We have now extended the theory of immediate inference to include the *conversion* of terms and the construction of *complementary* classes.

The next step in developing the traditional theory concerning these basic propositions is to consider arguments containing two premises rather than just one. An important group of such arguments is called *categorical syllogisms*. The basic idea behind these arguments is commonsensical. Suppose I wish to prove that "All S is P"—whatever S or P might be. A proof should present some *link* or *connection* between S and P. This link can be some other term we shall label M. In a syllogism we establish a relationship between the terms S and P through some middle term M.

We can now define a categorical syllogism more carefully.

(1) A categorical syllogism is constructed from the basic A, E, I, and O propositions.

(2) Given that the conclusion will contain two terms S and P, we can place the following restrictions on the premises.
  (i) There are only two premises.
  (ii) One premise contains the term S. (This is called the minor premise.)
  (iii) One premise contains the term P. (This is called the major premise.)
  (iv) Each premise contains the middle term M.

Traditionally, the major premise is stated first, the minor premise second. Here are some examples of syllogisms.

> All rectangles have four sides.   (Major premise)
> All squares are rectangles.   (Minor premise)
> ───────────────────────
> ∴ All squares have four sides.   (Conclusion)

> Subject term   = Squares
> Predicate term = Being four-sided
> Middle term   = Rectangles

Schematically, the argument looks like this:

> All M is P
> All S is M
> ─────────
> ∴ All S is P.

Here is a syllogism containing a negative premise.

> No ellipses have sides.
> All circles are ellipses.
> ─────────────────
> ∴ No circles have sides.

Schematically:

> No M is P.
> All S is M.
> ─────────
> ∴ No S is P.

Finally, here is an example of a syllogism containing a particular proposition.

> All squares have equal sides.
> Some squares are rectangles.
> ∴ Some rectangles have equal sides.

Schematically:

> All *M* is *P*.
> Some *M* is *S*.
> ∴ Some *S* is *P*.

Valid and Invalid Syllogisms

The examples given so far have all been of valid syllogisms—it should be obvious in each case that the conclusion does follow from the premise. It is possible to construct an argument that meets the definition of a categorical syllogism but is still invalid. A glaringly invalid argument will make this clear.

> Some figures are circles.
> Some figures are squares.
> ∴ All squares are circles.

This is a dreadful argument, but still it is a categorical syllogism. It is an *invalid* categorical syllogism.

Since some categorical syllogisms are valid whereas others are invalid, it will be important to have some systematic method for evaluating them. This subject has been explored for more than two thousand years, and a variety of analytical techniques has been developed. We shall use Venn diagrams.

Venn Diagrams for Syllogisms

In the previous section we used Venn diagrams to test the validity of immediate inferences. In a categorical syllogism, three terms appear; thus we are dealing with three classes. To reflect this, we will use diagrams of the following kind:

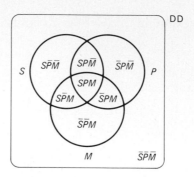

The diagram has eight different compartments:

$$
\begin{array}{ccc}
S & P & M \\
S & P & \overline{M} \\
S & \overline{P} & M \\
S & \overline{P} & \overline{M} \\
\overline{S} & P & M \\
\overline{S} & P & \overline{M} \\
\overline{S} & \overline{P} & M \\
\overline{S} & \overline{P} & \overline{M}
\end{array}
$$

Notice that if something is not an S nor a P nor an M, it falls completely outside the system of overlapping circles. In every other case, a thing is assigned to some compartment within the system of overlapping circles.

To test the validity of a syllogism using Venn diagrams, we first fill in the diagram to reflect the content of the premises. If the argument is valid, then the conclusion will already be contained in the diagram. To see this, consider the diagrams for examples already considered:

All rectangles are four-sided.
All squares are rectangles.
_____
∴ All squares are four-sided.

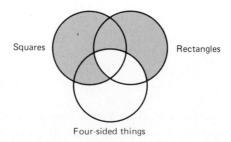

Notice that all the things that are squares are corralled into the region of things that are four-sided. So the argument is valid.

No ellipses have sides.
All circles are ellipses.
_____

∴ No circles have sides.

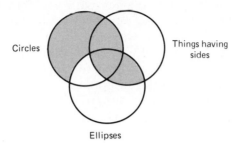

We diagram the conclusion "No circles have sides" as follows:

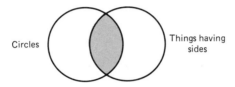

That information is already contained in the Venn diagram for the premises.

All squares have equal sides.
Some squares are rectangles.
_____

∴ Some rectangles have equal sides.

It is a good strategy to diagram a universal proposition before we diagram a particular proposition. The diagram for the above argument looks like this:

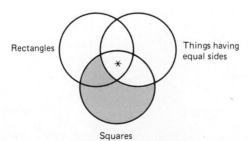

The conclusion—that there is something that is a rectangle that is equal-sided—appears in the diagram for the premises.

Existential Import

In the discussion of immediate inferences, we raised the question whether the universal propositions—the A and the E propositions—carried existential import. That is, when we assert that "All S is P" or that "No S is P," are we committing ourselves to the existence of Ss and Ps? The ruling for traditional logic was that these propositions *do* carry existential import. The same ruling holds for the traditional theory of the syllogism. So far we have continued to employ the modern approach that does not assign existential import to the A and E propositions.

We can begin our study of this matter with an example that has had a curious history:

> All rectangles are four-sided.
> All squares are rectangles.
> ─────────────────────────
> ∴ *Some* squares are four-sided.

The argument is peculiar because the conclusion is weaker than it needs to be. We could, after all, conclude that *all* squares are four-sided. The argument thus violates the conversational rule of Quantity; perhaps for this reason, this syllogism was often not included in traditional lists of valid syllogisms. Yet the argument is valid on the traditional interpretation of existential import and our diagram should show this.

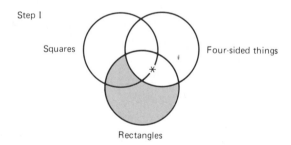

Notice that the asterisk is placed on the line dividing regions SPM and $\overline{S}PM$ since we are not in a position to put it into one region rather than the other. We now draw in the second premise:

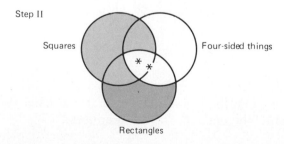

As expected, the conclusion that some squares are four-sided is already diagrammed, so the argument is valid—provided that we commit ourselves to the existential import of A propositions.

Since classical logicians tended to ignore the previous argument, their writings did not bring out the importance of existential import in evaluating it. There is, however, an argument that did appear on the classical lists that makes clear the demand for existential commitment. These are syllogisms of the following kind:

All *M* is *P*.
All *M* is *S*.
_____
∴ Some *S* is *P*.

This is diagrammed as follows:

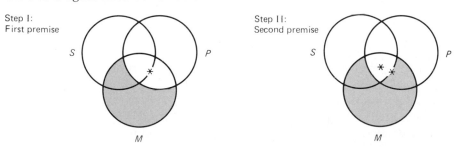

Again we see that the conclusion follows, but only if we diagram the universal propositions to indicate existential import. This, then, is an argument that was declared valid in the traditional approach, but invalid in the modern approach.

So far we have looked only at valid arguments. Here are some patterns for invalid arguments. The conclusion is diagrammed at the right. It is evident that this diagram is not already contained in the diagram for the premises. The arrows show differences in informational content.

All *M* is *P*.
All *M* is *S*.
_____
∴ All *S* is *P*.   All *S* is *P*.

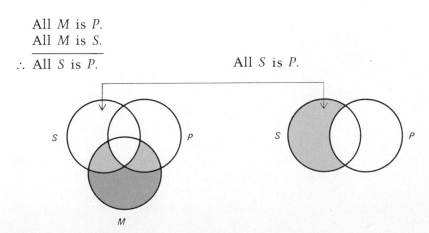

Some *M* is *P*.
Some *S* is *M*.
———————
∴ Some *S* is *P*.   Some *S* is *P*.

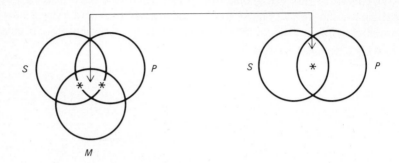

Examine this diagram closely. Notice that in saying "Some *M* is *P*," we had to put the asterisk *on* the line dividing *S* and *P*, since we were not given information saying whether anything falls into *S* or not. For the same reason we had to put the asterisk *on* the line dividing *S* and *P* when diagramming "Some *M* is *S*." The upshot was that we did not indicate that anything exists in the region of overlap between *S* and *P*. But this is what the conclusion demands, so the argument is invalid.

No *M* is *P*.
No *S* is *M*.
———————
∴ No *S* is *P*.   No *S* is *P*.

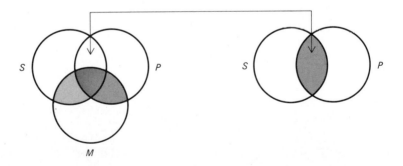

Again we see that this argument is invalid.

The method of Venn diagrams is adequate for deciding the validity or invalidity of all possible syllogisms. Furthermore, it is easy to distinguish between syllogisms that are classically valid and those that are valid in the modern interpretation of existential import. To get the classical theory, we simply include the presuppositions of existential import in our diagrams; in the modern approach we do not do this.

Exercise 5: Adopting the modern approach, test the following syllo-gisms for validity by using Venn diagrams.

1. All M is P.
    All M is S.
    _____
    ∴ All S is P.

2. No M is P.
    Some S is M.
    _____
    ∴ Some S is not P.

3. No P is M.
    Some S is not M.
    _____
    ∴ Some S is not P.

4. All M is P.
    Some S is not M.
    _____
    ∴ Some S is not P.

5. Some P is M.
    Some S is not M.
    _____
    ∴ Some S is not P.

6. All M is P.
    No S is M.
    _____
    ∴ No S is P.

7. All P is M.
    No S is M.
    _____
    ∴ No S is P.

8. All P is M.
    All S is M.
    _____
    ∴ All S is P.

9. No S is M.
    Some M is P.
    _____
    ∴ Some S is P.

10. No P is M.
    Some S is M.
    _____
    ∴ Some S is not P.

Problems in Applying the Theory of the Syllogism

After students have mastered the techniques for evaluating syllogisms, they naturally turn to arguments that arise in daily life and attempt to use these newly acquired skills. They are usually disappointed with the results. The formal theory of the syllogism seems to bear little relationship to everyday arguments, and there doesn't seem to be any easy way to bridge the gap.

This gap between formal theory and its application occurs for a number of reasons. First, as we saw in Chapter 2, our everyday discourse leaves much unstated. Many things are conversationally implied rather than explicitly asserted. Moreover, we do not feel called upon to say many things that are matters of common agreement. Before we can apply the theory of the syllogism to everyday arguments, these things that are simply understood must be *made explicit*. This is often illuminating and sometimes boring, but it usually involves a great deal of work. Second, the theory of the syllogism applies to statements only in a highly stylized form. Before we apply the theory of the syllogism to an argument, we must cast its premises and conclusion into the basic A, E, I, and O forms. This is not always easy either. Finally, there are arguments that the theory of the syllogism is not adequate to evaluate. We saw earlier in this chapter that propositional logic is not adequate to evaluate arguments whose validity depends upon the *internal* structure of propositions. For this reason, we went beyond propositional logic to study the theory of immediate inference and the theory of the syllogism, which do explore this internal structure of propositions. Although this is still a matter of some dispute, most logicians agree that developments beyond the theory of immediate inference and the theory of the syllogism are needed for the analysis of many, quite ordinary, arguments. Here is one example:

> George is taller than Harry by a head.
> _____
> ∴ George is taller than Harry.

It is hard to imagine an argument that is more obviously valid, yet its validity cannot be shown by the classical theory of immediate inference or syllogism. (In fact, the correct analysis of this argument is still a matter of debate.)

Why study the theory of the syllogism at all, if it is hard to apply in some circumstances and perhaps impossible to apply in others? The answer to this question was given at the beginning of Chapter 9: The study of formal logic is important because it deepens our insight into the central notion of logic, *validity*. Furthermore, the argument forms we have studied do underlie much of our everyday reasoning, but so much else is going on in a normal conversational setting that this dimension is hardly evident. By examining arguments in idealized forms, we can study their validity in isolation from all the other factors at work in a rich conversational setting.

There is a difference, then, between the techniques developed in Chapters 1 to 8 and the techniques developed in these last two chapters. The first eight chapters presented methods of *informal* analysis that may be applied directly to the rich and complex arguments that arise in everyday life. These methods of analysis are not wholly rigorous, but they do provide practical guides for the analysis and evaluation of actual arguments. These two chapters concerning *formal* logic have the opposite tendency. In comparison with the first eight chapters, the level of rigor is very high, but the range of application is correspondingly smaller. In general, it is accurate to say that the more rigor and precision you want, the less you can talk about.

A System of Rules for Evaluating Syllogisms

The method of Venn diagrams that we have used in this chapter is probably the most natural technique for analyzing syllogisms, since the relationship between overlapping figures is a clear analogy for the relationship between classes. Another method for evaluating syllogisms employs a system of rules. While this system has less intuitive appeal than Venn diagrams, it is easier to apply. The procedure is to lay down a set of rules such that any syllogism that satisfies all of the rules is valid and any syllogism that fails to satisfy any one of them is invalid. A concise summary of one such system is presented here.

Distribution The central idea for one system of rules is that of the *distribution* or *extension* of a term. The basic idea is that a term is used distributively in a proposition if it is used to refer to the whole of a class or to all of the members in it. We shall first simply state the distributional properties for each of the basic A, E, I, and O propositions and then try to make sense out of this notion.

Proposition	Subject	Predicate
A	Distributed	Undistributed
E	Distributed	Distributed
I	Undistributed	Undistributed
O	Undistributed	Distributed

The two universal propositions A and E have distributed subject terms. In the I and the O propositions we speak about *some S*, therefore the subject term is undistributed for these propositions.

The reasoning runs smoothly for the subject term, but the predicate term is not so easy to deal with. Notice that there is no word like "some" or "all" governing the predicate term.

The reasoning concerning the predicate term usually proceeds along the following lines: Suppose we assert that no squares are circles.

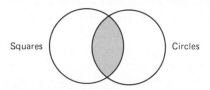

For this to be true, there can be no square that is identical with *any* circle. The appearance of the word "any" shows that the predicate term is distributed in the E proposition. Consider next the O proposition. Some *S* is not *P*. For this to be true, there must be some *S* that is not identical with *any* S. Again, the appearance of the word "any" shows that the predicate term is distributed. Our test for the distribution of terms is then to compare the basic A E I O proposition with a counterpart identity statement as follows:

A: All *S* is *P*. For *any* S there is *some P* that is identical with it.

E: No *S* is *P*. For *any* S there is not *any P* that is identical with it.

I: Some *S* is *P*. For *some S* there is *some P* that is identical with it.

O: Some *S* is not *P*. For *some S* there is not *any P* that is identical with it.

This comparison gives the pattern for the distribution of terms noticed earlier.

Quality Along with the notion of distribution, the system of rules we are discussing here also uses the idea of the *quality* of a proposition—whether it is affirmative or negative. The following rules are adequate for testing the validity of categorical syllogisms.

Quality:

(1) Nothing follows from two negative premises.

(2) If one premise is negative, then the conclusion must be negative as well.

(2') If the conclusion is negative, then one premise must be negative.[1]

Distribution:

(3) The middle term must be distributed at least once.

(4) The subject term may not be distributed in the conclusion if it is not distributed in the premises.

(5) The predicate term may not be distributed in the conclusion if it is not distributed in the premises.

The fallacies that result from violating these rules are called by the following names:

Quality:

(1) The Fallacy of Two Negative Premises

(2) The Fallacy of Drawing an Affirmative Conclusion from an Argument with a Negative Premise.

(2') The Fallacy of Drawing a Negative Conclusion from an Argument with two Affirmative Premises

Distribution:

(3) The Fallacy of the Undistributed Middle

(4) The Fallacy of the Illicitly Distributed Subject

(5) The Fallacy of the Illicitly Distributed Predicate

Quantity The rules on distribution and quality are adequate for the analysis of syllogisms in the classical interpretation. The modern interpretation requires a further rule of *quantity*.

Quantity:

(6) A particular conclusion cannot be derived from two universal premises.

Corresponding to this there is, in the modern approach, a fallacy:

(6) The Fallacy of Deriving a Particular Conclusion from Universal Premises

The following devices facilitate the application of these rules. Mark the propositions in the syllogism "+" or "−" to indicate quality. Circle

[1] Rule 2' is not needed in the modern interpretation of existential import, since any syllogism that violates it will also violate rule 6 below. It is, however, needed in the classical interpretation, which lacks rule 6.

all terms that are distributed, leaving all undistributed terms uncircled. This makes it easy to see if the first five rules of the syllogism have been satisfied, and so whether the syllogism is valid or invalid in the classical approach. No special devices are needed to check the additional sixth rule needed in the modern approach.

The following examples illustrate these methods:

(1) + All Ⓜ is P
    + All Ⓢ is M   Valid
∴ + All Ⓢ is P

(2) − No Ⓜ is Ⓟ
    + Some S is M   Valid
∴ − Some S is not Ⓟ

(3) + All Ⓜ is P   Valid classically
    + All Ⓜ is S   Invalid in modern approach (Rule 6)
∴ + Some S is P

(4) + All Ⓜ is P   Invalid—
    + All Ⓜ is S   Illicitly Distributed Subject
∴ + All Ⓢ is P

(5) + All Ⓟ is M   Invalid—
    + All Ⓢ is M   Undistributed Middle
∴ + All Ⓢ is P

(6) − No Ⓟ is Ⓜ   Invalid—
    − No Ⓢ is Ⓜ   Two Negative Premises
∴ − No Ⓢ is Ⓟ

Exercise 6: Using the system of rules we have developed, test the syllogisms given on page 219 for validity. Where a fallacy occurs, give the name of that fallacy.

Honors Exercise: To a person familiar with computer programming, this system of rules immediately suggests that a program can be written for the evaluation of syllogisms. In fact, such a program can be written and is only moderately difficult. The first problem is to find some method for encoding all possible syllogisms. After this, the notions of distribution and quality must be given mathematical analogues. In writing such a program, there is a good chance that the programmer will discover on his own large portions of Medieval logic.

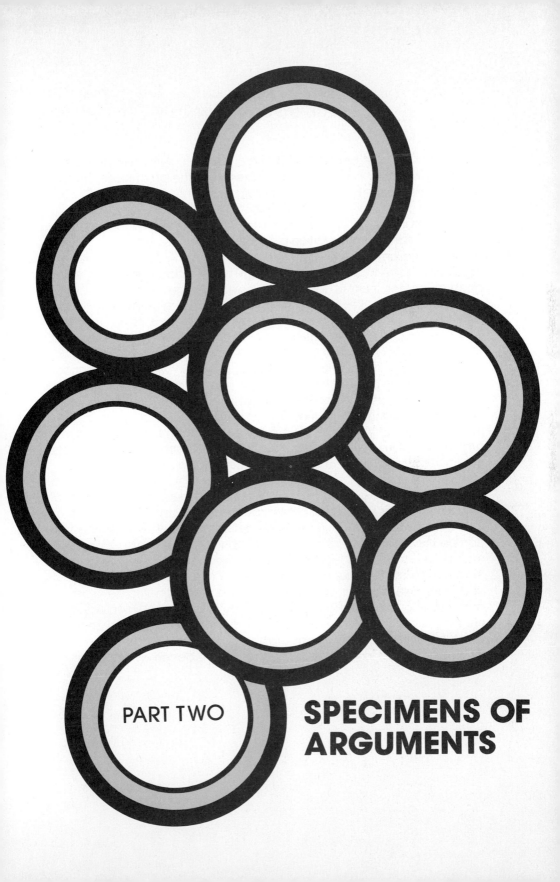

PART TWO

SPECIMENS OF ARGUMENTS

PART TWO
SPECIMENS OF ARGUMENTS

The arguments collected in Part Two are meant to serve two purposes. The first is to supply case material for exercising the art of close analysis. This is the primary intention of the material presented in Chapter 11, "An Issue of Public Concern," and in Chapter 12, "Language and Contemporary Issues." In Part I, Chapter 4 carefully examined a speech made by Representative Kyl on clerk hire allowances—not a matter to arouse strong emotions or rabid interest. The blandness of the issue, together with the high quality of the argument, made this speech a good model for analysis, for a disinterested attitude toward the content of an argument makes it easier to concentrate upon its structure. It would be misleading, however, to consider only bland topics, for in daily life we often have strong feelings concerning the arguments we encounter. Therefore, Chapters 11 and 12 will consider arguments on topics that are both of current interest and controversial, topics on which the American citizen is likely to be asked to express an opinion at the ballot box.

The second purpose of Part Two is to examine the distinctive character of arguments as they arise in different fields or areas. The procedures developed in Part I are general enough to be applied to arguments in any field, but Chapters 13–17 will illustrate that arguments arising in law, morals, science, and philosophy each have distinctive features. This fact may be obvious in regard to legal argument, for specific rules have been laid down that control them within a system of laws, precedents, and constitutional guarantees. Legal arguments thus take on a personality that reflects the distinctive role they play. The same can be said about scientific and philosophical arguments. Of course, as matters become more technical, it becomes harder for the general reader to follow the nuances of a particular argument. But with patience and close attention, it is possible for the nonprofessional to develop appreciation for the brilliance and subtlety of a legal opinion or the elegance of a scientific explanation. And eventually, the degree to which arguments in these areas are similar, in both their strengths and their weaknesses, to arguments in everyday life becomes apparent.

AN ISSUE OF PUBLIC CONCERN

As citizens of a democracy, we are often called upon to make decisions on complex public issues. Sometimes we express our decisions indirectly by voting for leaders who represent or support certain policies. Sometimes, though less frequently, we express our opinions directly by participating in a public referendum. Often a reasonable and intelligent person will find these public issues profoundly perplexing. The available facts may be scattered and fragmentary. Our informants may be biased and interested parties. We may find ourselves drawn in opposite directions by competing moral and social principles. We may have prejudices of our own to overcome. The problem in a situation of this kind is to find ways of bringing intelligence to bear upon the question. Methods of close analysis will not do this automatically or infallibly, but they do help to guide our reflections and make them more self-consciously critical.

Safety in Nuclear Power Plants

Our specimen of a public debate shows how bewildering a public issue can be. The debate concerns the safety of atomic power plants. First of all, the problem is urgent. During a time of energy shortage, we must either build atomic power plants or immediately develop alternative sources of energy. Furthermore, the stakes are high. If atomic power plants are unsafe, then the potential danger could be catastrophic. On top of this, there are sharp disagreements among experts on a whole range of topics beyond the safety of atomic power plants. This includes their effects on the environment, their immunity to terrorist attack, and so on. As responsible citizens we cannot simply consult experts on such questions; we must choose between them. Finally, and not insignificantly, the fear of an atomic holocaust is deeply engrained in our psyches. Whether fears concerning atomic power plants are reasonable fears is itself a question of importance.

We derive our information concerning public issues from a number of sources, including news reports, editorials, paid advertisements, and, likely as not, television specials. The material given below is the "unofficial public service transcript" of a television program entitled "Incident at Brown's Ferry," produced by WGBH in Boston for *Nova*. The incident in question was a fire that occurred at the nuclear power plant in Brown's Ferry, Alabama, causing 150 million dollars in damages and losses. *Nova* used this event as the starting point for a program examining the growing issue of the safety of nuclear power plants. The program was produced a number of years before the famous nuclear incident at Three Mile Island in Pennsylvania. The days of suspense in that incident cast sharper light on the issues raised in the debate.

A close analysis of this transcript will involve virtually all of the techniques discussed in Part I of this book. One of the main problems is deciding upon the credibility of various experts in an area where few citizens have technical knowledge of their own. It is also important to pay close attention to the role of the narrator in this transcript. He does not pretend to be a neutral observer, but quite plainly advocates one side of the issue. There is nothing improper about this. It is simply important to remember that the narrator is one of the parties to the dispute, not the judge.

The transcript raises a whole series of questions for close analysis. Is the program reasonably fair in presenting all sides of the issue? Are the critics of atomic energy clear-headed and precise in their objections? Are the defenders of atomic energy responsive to these criticisms? Beyond such broad questions, the transcript contains many subtle details that are worth examining. Notice the two closing graphics. One states that "the Nuclear Regulatory Commission declined repeated invitations to appear in this film"; the other cites Albert Einstein's statement that it is important for the people of America to participate in the formulation of national policies concerning atomic energy. Why does the program end in just this way?

Incident at Brown's Ferry
NOVA

NARRATOR: On March 22, 1975 a workman in the world's largest nuclear power plant was checking for air leaks by using a candle flame. A fire started. . . . It went out of control . . . burned for 7 hours . . . resulted in 150 million dollars in damage and loss to this plant. The chief government investigator of this incident at Brown's Ferry, Alabama concluded it raised embarrassing questions about the safety of reactors throughout the United States. If the Brown's Ferry incident had been the worst possible nuclear accident, a recent government study called the Rasmussen Report predicts it could have immediately killed over 3,000 people, 45,000 more would have been severely injured from radiation, 300,000 more would suffer long-term health problems, including cancer and genetic defects. An area the size of the state of Pennsylvania would have been contaminated, and there would have been 15 billion dollars in property damage. But on the other hand, the Rasmussen Report predicts that the odds of any single individual getting killed in a nuclear plant accident in any given year are only 1 in 5 billion. Despite this predicted low risk, nuclear power as a safe energy source has become an emotional public issue that won't go away. Protests like this one [shown] at Seabrook, New Hampshire in 1976, ballot measures, lawsuits, grassroots action in America and European cities . . . the cutting edge of the environmental movement.

In this film NOVA examines the growing nuclear safety issue. How the issue is resolved could have consequences affecting everyone on this planet. The 57 nuclear plants now operating in the United States supply 9 percent of the nation's electricity. About 150 plants operate in other countries around the world. Another 260 are under construction, and as many as one thousand are planned for completion by the year two thousand. If the nuclear industry has its way, they will be supplying half of the world's energy as the 21st century begins. The nuclear safety debate emerged in the early 1970's as a public issue after decades of private scientific dispute. In early 1975 pioneer nuclear physicist Ralph Lapp organized a petition in which eminent scientists declared themselves in favor of nuclear power as a safe energy source.

LAPP: In my opinion nuclear power is the very real answer to generating adequate amounts of electricity in the future for a dynamic American economy.

NARRATOR: A few months after Lapp's petition, another group of eminent scientists released a counter statement urging caution and stressing development of alternate energy sources. A leader in this drive was Henry Kendall, MIT physics professor and founder of the Union of Concerned Scientists.

KENDALL: Almost any source of energy in our society has less inherent risk than nuclear power, in my opinion. Nuclear power, with its enormous accumulations of radioactivity, can cause prompt death, can cause death by cancer, birth defects, and many other kinds of damage. It is potentially the most hazardous thing that we can incorporate in our society.

NARRATOR: Willard Libby, Nobel chemist, former member of the Atomic Energy Commission, a signer of the Lapp petition.

LIBBY: I think atomic power is an absolute necessity, and we have every reason to believe in its safety. We have a marvelous record. No major industry has ever been started that has a better record than the atomic power industry.

NARRATOR: Linus Pauling, another Nobel chemist and Nobel Peace Prize winner for alerting the world to radiation dangers from nuclear bomb testing. He supported Henry Kendall's declaration.

PAULING: I believe that nuclear power plants are unsafe, that they damage human beings, and are a real hazard.

NARRATOR: With scientists lining up on opposing sides, it was almost inevitable that the issue developed into a ballot measure question. In 1976, voters in seven different states struggled with the issue as they tried to decide how to vote.

MAN: Are we going to have enough electricity to continue living the style of life that we have been . . . that I at least, I've been living?

WOMAN: The only thing I hear is money and comfort. Does it mean anything safe for our kids, or is it all the time material? I hear material, that's all I hear. This is a housewife talking baby talk.

SECOND WOMAN: I'm really very worried about the genetic problem that can be caused by radioactivity. I don't like the thought of my children having children that are mutants. That really upsets me a great deal.

SECOND MAN: You're making damn sure that they're not gonna have these plants unless they're so safe that you could put all the babies in Oregon in them and they'd be in terrific shape.

THIRD MAN: But the fact is, when you're dealing with nuclear power and radioactive materials, there's a higher standard of care. And there has to be, and you know there is a dispute, you know, on it, how safe should it be? And we're saying that it should be safer than it is.

NARRATOR: Anthony Roisman, a Washington attorney representing nuclear power opponents.

ROISMAN: I don't think that anybody is able to say at this time that nuclear power is safe, but I'm not sure that anybody can say conclusively that it's not safe. I think it's a question which has not yet been resolved. The issue is what do you do if you don't know the answer.

NARRATOR: If the answer can be figured out, it begins with knowing how a nuclear plant works. In the simplest terms, you start with uranium pellets . . . the pellets are fitted into 30 to 40 thousand fuel rods . . . long thin tubes made of a special metal alloy . . . the core—or heat source—of a large modern nuclear reactor. Control rods are interspersed with the fuel rods. All the rods are enclosed in a reactor vessel, in turn enclosed by larger and larger protective structures, often ending with the familiar dome. The fission process—the splitting of uranium atoms—begins when the control rods are separated from the fuel rods. Water surrounding the rods is heated under pressure to 600 degrees by the fission process and turns into steam. The steam circulates under pressure of one thousand pounds per square inch. Three hundred and fifty thousand gallons of water travel through the reactor core every minute. Then, in the form of pressurized steam, it travels through pipes—at high speed—and turns huge turbine generators that produce electricity. The process is similar to a coal or oil plant, except for the fuel and its special problems. If a large cooling pipe breaks this would stop the normal flow of water that keeps the fuel rods safely covered. Radioactive 600 degree water would spurt out of the pipe under great pressure as radioactive steam. As the water level dropped, the core would get hotter, a dangerous uncontrollable melting of the fuel rods would begin, leading to massive release of radiation—resulting in death, disease, contamination and long-term genetic defects. Plant designers recognize that pipe ruptures could occur. So all modern reactors have emergency systems to maintain the supply of coolant to the reactor core. But this emergency water must reach the core within a few minutes to prevent a melting and the release of radiation. All emergency systems are monitored and can be operated, if necessary, in the control room. Here, personnel are alerted to the need to use emergency systems by a vast array of lights and gauges. These devices are connected to a large number of cables, which are collected in long trays in a cable-spreading room, beneath the control room. The thousands of cables—a kind of central nervous system for the plant— are sorted out and routed to the valves, pumps and instruments that make the emergency systems work. It is extremely complex and crucial to the safety of the plant and to the ultimate safety of the public. Nuclear plants contain enormous amounts of radioactive materials. So extraordinary measures are normally taken inside the plants to protect workers from excessive irradiation. Workers routinely wear protective clothing and masks. They check themselves daily with radiation monitors to make sure they are not contaminated. In some plants workers are checked periodically from head to toe, in a Whole Body Counter. This is to make sure that radiation accumulated in their bodies has not exceeded government established permitted limits. These are fixed at two levels: one for workers, a lower one for the public. But some scientists contend both levels increase the chances of illness, especially cancer. The only really safe radiation level, they believe, is no radiation, inside or outside the plants. Ralph Lapp sees it another way.

LAPP: People who travel in airplanes get more radiation dose than the whole nuclear industry put together. That's on the basis of high altitude air travel where because of the fact that you're closer to space—more radiation comes through from outer space—you get a radiation dose. What I would urge is that the American people understand that radiation is all around you. You live in a sea of it.

PAULING: This natural background causes about 10 percent, an estimated 10 percent of the defective children who are born; the gene mutations producing these defective children. And about 10 percent of cases of cancer. This doesn't mean that it's all right to add another one percent as might be done by the high energy radiation from nuclear power plants, if there were a lot of them. This additional one percent means thousands of additional defective children born into the world, and thousands of additional cases of cancer. So this argument is a false and misleading one.

NARRATOR: Beyond this permitted radiation hazard to workers and the public, there is the larger fear of an accidental and catastrophic radiation release.

How close was the Brown's Ferry incident to such a catastrophe? March 22, 1975. 12:20 P.M. Unit One of the plant. Polyurethane—a spongy foam—was being used to fill a 2" by 4" hole in the wall, where cables lead from the cable room to the reactor building. This was done to prevent any potential escape of radiation from the reactor building into the main part of the plant, and perhaps out into the surrounding area. To make sure the foam had in fact sealed the hole, a candle was lit and workers watched the flame to see if it was moved by escaping air. The foam caught on fire. Then the cable insulation. The air draft sucked the fire into the hole, then began to burn cable insulation inside the cable room. After fifteen minutes spent trying to snuff the fire out with rags, a decision was made to sound the fire alarm inside the plant. And so the incident at Brown's Ferry was underway. Superintendent Jim Green.

GREEN: I think there's a lot of misunderstanding on just what the fire was. Now, it was confined to one room, and the room was a concrete room and it was confined entirely to wiring. It was not a nuclear accident and we demonstrated that even under these most adverse conditions the plant could be shut down safely.

KENDALL: The Brown's Ferry accident was a very close call. I've studied it, my colleagues have studied it. We've talked to nuclear engineers at the Brown's Ferry plant who wish to remain anonymous and they've told us, and we agree, that that accident was in fact a close call.

NARRATOR: What exactly happened at Brown's Ferry? The record shows that it was the third fire caused by candle flames and foam. The first two were minor, but no change in airleak-testing procedure was made. After this fire began, like in so many accidents, a series of incredible unpredicted human and mechanical failures had started. Wrong numbers were posted and called to sound the fire alarms. There was insufficient breathing apparatus for fire-fighters and the system to refill the air supply was broken. After the fire was over, insurance inspectors said that it was "inexcusable" that the trays holding the cables were so crowded together that ordinary fire extinguishers would not reach in. As the fire spread, the chemical fire extinguisher in the cable room which was supposed to trigger automatically didn't. A metal plate covered the hand switch so it couldn't even be turned on manually. The spray nozzle of a hose would not let the water reach the flames. Twenty minutes after the fire started, operators in the control room noticed smoke leaking in, lights randomly blinking on and off, a drop in the power output of the reactor. They noticed that all the emergency cooling systems pumps had unexpectedly started. At 12:51, a half-hour after the fire began, the problem had become so severe it was decided to "scram" the reactor, which means reinserting the control rods between the fuel rods to shut the operation down. The heat in the core cannot turn off instantly; it continues to be produced for months after a "scram." So cooling water must constantly cover the fuel, even after the control rods are in, to prevent a meltdown and release of radiation. Despite earlier specific warnings by government inspectors, some of the cables for the main emergency system as well as its backup systems were all in the same or nearby cable trays. This was in direct violation of federal safety regulations. As the insulation around the cables continued to burn, the emergency cooling systems were shorted out. At 12:55 the entire electrical supply to control and power these systems was lost. By then crucial monitoring instruments had failed. Engineers could no longer measure temperature or radiation in the core. Athens, Alabama is the nearest town with a fire department, ten miles away. Chief Artie Bumpus takes up the story:

BUMPUS: Well, they called us a little after one o'clock and when we arrived there was some wires afire, a lot of wires, several hundred. And they was using their chemicals on it, dry chemicals and CO_2. We surveyed the situation and we also tried the chemicals they was using and some of ours, but it failed to put the fire out. And we saw right off that we was going to have to use something else and of course water, being the best extinguishing agent, we recommended that.

NARRATOR: With the fire still burning, and the emergency systems out of action, the water level dropped from its normal 200″ down to an alarming 48″. After several hours it was discovered that depressurizing the water would allow a low pressure pump—not part of the emergency systems—to supply enough water to keep the core covered. This makeshift arrangement is what saved the core from a catastrophic meltdown. Around 7 o'clock Chief Bumpus' suggestion to use water was finally listened to and the cable fire was put out in 15 minutes. Why didn't they use water 5 hours earlier?

BUMPUS: We didn't, could not get permission to use it. We was under their supervision down there and they wouldn't let us use water.

NARRATOR: Problems were not confined to the interior of the plant. The cable fire inside made it impossible to use automatic monitors to check for possible radiation release around the outside of the plant. Air samples were taken in two towns close to Brown's Ferry. But in Decatur, directly downwind, the man who was sent to check the radiation monitor had a surprise.

SAYWELL: This monitor was not operable at all on the day of the fire.

NARRATOR: If radioactive material from Brown's Ferry had been carried downwind to Decatur, instant knowledge was essential to protect the public. Because the first monitor was not working, it was necessary to drive to another. But that air sampler was not designed to give instant information. The filter had to be sent to a laboratory hundreds of miles away for analysis, which took two days. And local civil defense officials—in charge of evacuation plans—did not hear about the fire until two days after it was over.

GREEN: The core was never in danger of melting down throughout the fire event.

KENDALL: The circumstances of that accident would only had to have been casually different and there could well have been—almost certainly could have been—a catastrophic release of radioactivity. That's no cause for complacency. That's a severe and sharp warning.

NARRATOR: Both superintendent Green and Kendall's views appear to be justified: radiation did not leak out of the plant, but it seems to have been a close call. How could a major safety problem develop at a facility like Brown's Ferry? There had been two major safety reviews of the plant by the federal government, 207 on-site safety inspections between 1966—when they began construction— and the 1975 fire. Brown's Ferry was presumably licensed to operate under the strictest of federal regulations.

KENDALL: The worst accident we've had in the nuclear program, the fire at Brown's Ferry, was almost entirely the result of regulatory failure to correct problems that had been identified, to reduce the sensitivity of emergency systems to total failure.

LAPP: I find that the regulation of nuclear power plants is extremely tough, tougher than it was in the past; and I think that the regulation is perhaps going overboard. I think we're getting too much regulation.

ROISMAN: They've always regulated them to the possible, not to what is required. And I think that that is probably the single biggest flaw in the theory that the agency is vigorously regulating nuclear power. If it were regulating nuclear power, at least one utility sometime would have found the regulations so onerous that they would have sued them or sought relief. That's never happened. And I think that suggests that the agency has always been careful to be just as tough as the industry could take, but never any tougher. And I don't think that that is sufficiently tough.

NARRATOR: The Atomic Energy Act, signed by President Eisenhower in 1954, set up an agency that both promoted and regulated commercial use of the new peaceful atom. Under the Atomic Energy Commission—the A.E.C.—small experimental plants were begun. But private firms resisted getting into the atomic business without insurance protection, and insurance firms were unwilling to provide adequate coverage for this new hazard. Congress urged the A.E.C. to study power plant safety, hoping the findings would encourage insurance firms to provide coverage. The report came out in 1957, but was not generally publicized. It concluded that the outside limits of damage from a nuclear plant accident would result in 3,400 people killed within 15 miles of the plant; 43,000 would suffer severe radiation sickness in an area 44 miles from the plant; 182,000 people in a 200-mile circle would double their chances of getting cancer from radiation exposure. And there would be 7 billion dollars in property damage. With these gloomy figures in mind, A.E.C. Chairman Lewis Strauss led efforts to get the Price-Anderson Act passed. This meant federal tax money provided most of the 560 million dollars in insurance coverage since private insurance was reluctant. Commercial utilities then began to move into atomic energy on a larger scale. Larger, presumably safer, nuclear plants began operation. So with this experience record and the Price-Anderson Act up for possible renewal, it was expected that a new 1965 A.E.C. safety study would present a more favorable insurance picture. By this time—even with evacuation taken into account —27,000 deaths were estimated from a major accident; 73,000 would suffer severe radiation sickness; 300,000 would have greater risk of cancer. Property damage would total 17 billion dollars. The Price-Anderson Act was renewed, still at the 560 million dollar level. How enough people could get out of a major metropolitan center in enough time was not clarified. Significantly, the study concluded there was no rational way of working out the chances of such a disaster ever occurring, because there had not been a long enough history of nuclear plant operations on which to base a responsible prediction. They went on to say that it was "difficult to prove that nuclear power plants were safe enough to build." At first the A.E.C. claimed the new, ominous figures did not exist. Instead, leaving out the numbers, they reported that a major nuclear plant accident would "not be less, and under some circumstances would be substantially more, than the consequences reported" in 1957. The actual figures were kept secret for eight years, until Henry Kendall and the Union of Concerned Scientists used the Freedom of Information Act to open A.E.C. files. They found the safety regulators of the agency had been consistently overruled by the more powerful reactor-development branch. As a result in 1974 the agency was abolished. The Energy Research and Development Administration took over nuclear power promotion; N.R.C.—the Nuclear Regulatory Commission—now licenses plants and regulates safety. Ralph Lapp welcomed the change.

LAPP: The Atomic Energy Commission hadn't always behaved in the best way in the public sense. But now we have an open agency. You can get in. I can get in and do get into the Energy Research and Development Administration and the Nuclear Regulatory Commission. And to my mind, the openness of the industry is a real requirement, and I think it's satisfied today.

NARRATOR: The secret 1965 study decided it was impossible to determine the odds of an accident occurring in a nuclear plant. Nevertheless, with increased pressure by concerned scientists the A.E.C. began a new study in 1972. This was led by Norman Rasmussen, M.I.T. professor of nuclear engineering. The four million dollar study was released by the new Nuclear Regulatory Commission in October, 1975. For the first time, the government tried to estimate both chances and consequences of nuclear plant accidents.

RASMUSSEN: What we did was examine the plant and find out what kind of failures could release significant amounts of radioactivity. As engineers that's not so hard to do. And then we examined how likely it was to have failures of this type in the plant. Let's presume one of these failures is the rupture of a large pipe. How do we know how likely that is? Well, we examine how often pipes have failed in nuclear power plant accidents, in oil refineries, in fossil fuel plants, in chemical plants. We took the accumulated experience of the last few decades to get an idea of how likely that event was to occur. The same kind of investigation was made to find out how likely a valve is to fail, or a motor is to fail to operate, or any one of a number of the components in the plant that might contribute to the release of radioactivity.

NARRATOR: The Rasmussen Report rekindled the safety debate because it claimed to have examined, identified and established—with computer analysis —the risk of every possible radiation-releasing accident that could occur in a nuclear plant. Keith Miller of the University of California, computer consultant to the N.R.C., has his own outspoken private views.

MILLER: The entire basis of the Rasmussen Report is that somehow we trust them to have been able to think of every possible thing which could go wrong in a nuclear reactor, and analyze it. Here we've got a relatively new product, we've got thousand megawatt reactors and there's only a few units in operation for only a few years. Nevertheless, they seem to claim to have the analytical ability by testing this component, testing that component, guessing this probability, and that probability, to totally analyze the system, everything that might humanly go wrong with this manufacturer's operation, and end up telling us that here's a new product and it's going to be reliable for twenty thousand years. As an applied mathematician, I'm just amazed. I just can't believe it. What you can do with a large scale computer and a little of mathematical analysis.

RASMUSSEN: We as engineers can think of only the failures that we as engineers have come to recognize or imagine can happen in these kinds of systems. There may be a kind of failure that we've never thought of and never seen. However, for that to be true, it would also have to be a very unlikely failure because we've been looking and working with systems of this kind for nearly a century. That is, systems that pump water, pipe it around, turn turbine valves and so on. So for there to be a whole new mechanism that we've never thought of or contemplated it would have to be very unlikely. If it's very unlikely then it isn't going to contribute very much to the probability of failure of the plant.

KENDALL: In order to prove that a reactor is safe—and this has never been done —one has to identify all the important accidents, each one in this complex structure. Rasmussen claims he's done that. I don't believe it. And we have too many examples in our society of unexpected events and this is even more true in the complex and intricate structure of a nuclear reactor.

NARRATOR: We live in a dangerous world. The Rasmussen study compared the chances of a nuclear plant accident with a variety of natural and man-created accidents. The average chance of any individual dying in a fire in a given year is one in 25,000. The odds of any person dying from an airplane crash in any given year are one in 100,000 . . . of dying from an auto accident, one in 4,000. The odds of someone drowning, perhaps from a flood like the Teton Dam disaster in Idaho, are one in 30,000. The odds diminish when it comes to natural disasters like hurricanes or tornadoes . . . one in 2-and-a-half million. Without taking into account long-term radiation effects, Rasmussen's study contends that the odds are one in 5 billion that any individual will die in any given year from a nuclear plant accident—about as remote as you can get. George Kistiakowsky, Harvard chemistry professor, Science Advisor to President Eisenhower at the time the Atomic Energy Act was passed.

KISTIAKOWSKY: It is very difficult for me to accept assertions of the Rasmussen Report. And I should say that that's partly, this is because of my long experience with Atomic Energy Commission bureaucracy. In all my many years dealing with Washington, I would say that that bureaucracy is the most arrogant bureaucracy in the federal government. It's one whose motto seems to be the public be damned. And yet it is not the most intelligent, most competent bureaucracy. And it's the same bureaucracy which prepared, under Rasmussen's management, that report. So why should I believe it?

NARRATOR: The critics reject Rasmussen's odds. What do they think are the correct odds of a major nuclear plant disaster?

KENDALL: I believe and many colleagues agree with this, that if the program continues as it is now that within the next ten years, twenty years, perhaps twenty-five years, that there will be an accident of important size, one that would cause a crippling of the nuclear reactor program in the United States.

NARRATOR: Carl Hocevar, who resigned from the nuclear industry in 1974, has a more fundamental reservation about the Rasmussen Report.

HOCEVAR: Rasmussen does not take into the, take into account at all the possibility that the safety system itself may be improperly designed. He assumes that it is properly designed, and that occasionally a pump or something might fail. Okay? That is one of the reasons why he gets so, gets such relatively low probabilities for an accident. We don't know that that safety system will work 99 times out of a hundred. He's just assuming it will work that many times, and there's test data to prove, or to indicate that that may very well not be the case.

NARRATOR: For many years the government has been running tests trying to prove that the emergency systems in already operating nuclear plants will work, if a major cooling pipe breaks. These tests are done using computer analysis and scale models of nuclear plants. Until 1976 all tests failed. The heated pressurized water in the scale models did not allow the emergency cooling water to get to the core. And the computers couldn't accurately predict what was going to happen. So if a cooling pipe in a full-size plant actually does break, no one can yet say with certainty that the emergency systems will really work. Most of the tests are being done at the National Engineering Laboratory in Idaho. In this test, a miniature heating system is being subjected to a "blowdown"—the term describing what happens when a large cooling pipe breaks.

MAN: Three ... two ... one ... zero. We've got a blowdown.

NARRATOR: Temperature changes, water flows, pressures and other measurements from the small-scale system are combined into a computer code. Results from tests on full-scale reactor components are also included. This computer code is then used to predict how a full-scale reactor will behave during a real pipe break accident. It is not entirely theoretical, but it is not exactly the real thing either. Carl Hocevar, who worked on the project, had doubts about it.

HOCEVAR: We're taking a computer code which has been partially verified, with a system that is only one two-thousandth as large as the big machine, and we're saying that, on the basis of what we know on a small scale, we can predict what's going to happen on a big scale. And physics doesn't work that way.

NARRATOR: One partial answer to this problem may be the LOFT reactor—standing for Loss Of Fluid Test. Using nuclear fuel, LOFT will be subjected to a real pipe break accident, and the emergency core cooling system tested. But LOFT is still a scale model, one sixtieth the volume of a full-scale nuclear plant. Are scale model tests of nuclear plants adequate? Manager of the LOFT test program, Dr. Larry Ybarrando.

YBARRANDO: Scale models that we are using are indeed somewhat similar also to scale models which are used in other industries, for instance in the modeling of dams and flood situations, where people predict when the river is going to crest and how much land it is going to flood and for how long. The Army Corps of Engineers uses scale models for those types of things. For years we have tested aircraft in wind tunnels, rockets in wind tunnels.

MILLER: We have here with reactors a situation which is much, much more highly complex, much more difficult to do than aerodynamics. Yet in aerodynamics only recently have we been able to use computer programs with great success for the design of aircraft. And there, of course, we build the aircraft, and there we have constant interconnections between the computer programs, and we can check them out against wind tunnel tests. We build the aircraft, we fly it. We put a pilot in it, a test pilot. We don't go loading the public on this based completely on computer predictions.

LAPP: Large-scale, or full-scale testing of safety systems is not common to engineering. One does not test the San Francisco Golden Gate Bridge full-scale because it's too expensive. Nor does one test the Empire State Building full-scale by starting a fire in the basement and seeing if you can put it out. I mean, you just don't do it that way. What you do is you take the best engineering judgement that you can of the systems and where it is necessary to scale up a system, you do, but you do it on the basis of reasonable extrapolation or extension of your knowledge. Thus it is probably never going to be possible to test a nuclear reactor full-scale unless there is a true accident.

NARRATOR: With full-scale testing out of the question, all that seems to be left is a legacy of test failures using disputed computer codes. These same computer models are the basis for the licensing of nuclear plants by the federal government.

MILLER: Licensing computer models on which we test whether the present pressurized water reactors have adequate core coolant systems, depends upon the same codes which for 5 years have been unable to predict what happens in these small-scale experiments. Now when we go to the full size, there's room for a vast margin of error. We may be fooling the American government and public, and, what's more disturbing to me, we have indications that we're actually fooling the Nuclear Regulatory Commission and the licensing people within that commission. And there's just not enough leeway with the present system for error in our computerized analysis. If we make too many mistakes in our computerized analysis, this system will not be effective. It won't work.

NARRATOR: The Idaho facility primarily deals with pressurized water reactors. General Electric, which designs and manufactures boiling water reactors, the other major type, does its own safety testing in San Jose, California. G.E. does a variety of safety tests—this one tests the ability of separate parts of nuclear plants to withstand severe earthquakes. The fundamental behavior of steam injected into cold water is investigated. This test relates to what may happen if the emergency system is called into play. Sections of metal pipe are broken to study the behavior of cracks. Ultrasonic scanners verify that the pipes and welding used in the plants have no flaws. In early 1976 three nuclear engineers who worked at the San Jose facility quit because in spite of the testing programs, they felt nuclear power can never be made safe. One was Richard Hubbard.

HUBBARD: I resigned from my management position with General Electric because of my concerns about reactor safety. Design deficiencies that we were finding in the field and in our new, larger scaled-up products, in the regulatory deficiencies, and the quality deficiencies that I had experienced.

NARRATOR: Salomon Levy is General Electric's chief nuclear engineer in San Jose.

LEVY: I want to assure you that safety comes first in any of our work. Profits or economics clearly are secondary. You know that I could tell you personally that I would quit this corporation if at any time I felt that I had to do one thing for profit when I felt that I had to do the opposite for safety.

NARRATOR: Hubbard and his colleagues testified before Congress and the California legislature on what they thought had been going wrong.

HUBBARD: We pointed out that the G.E. containment on 19 of the operating plants in the United States—nearly a third of them—could not contain an accident. That over 20 forces had not been considered. Well, in this case the regulatory process worked because soon thereafter those plants were ordered to update their containment. We brought up that there are vibrations inside the cores of the reactors that weren't understood. Pipes were cracking and instruments were vibrating against fuel channels. Well, G.E.'s response to that was—we're building an 18 million dollar test facility. And I read in our San Jose newspaper last week that they may have it built by 1978. Maybe we'll have some tests by 1980.

LEVY: I think in reality the issues they've raised were on the way to being solved . . . I think there was some acceleration of the programs because they have focused attention on some of these problems and, clearly, as I have indicated before, we believe we have to be responsive to these criticisms.

NARRATOR: As chief nuclear engineer Levy indicates, resignations from the industry has led to acceleration in some safety testing. But that still leaves the public waiting until 1980 when vital tests are scheduled for completion. And what if these tests in San Jose or Idaho show that emergency systems in currently operating nuclear plants are faulty? Should the plants then be refitted to include better systems?

LAPP: Well, I think that you're limited there by the practicality of engineering a system that's been in operation and it would seem to me that the real issue is what is the safety margin that is built into the system, what is the probability that you would have an accident? That has been, I think, carefully examined by the Rasmussen study, and you see that whole emergency core cooling system is called into play only in the event of emergency. So you must ask yourself how likely is the emergency, and then back it up by saying, then, how probable is it that the emergency system will not work.

NARRATOR: If, as Ralph Lapp suggests, existing emergency systems cannot be changed even if tests show they are inadequate, then why bother to do the tests? James Zane of the Idaho testing program.

ZANE: The work we're doing today is trying to get an in-depth understanding or to get precision in our analytical models so we can make a case for perhaps removing some of those conservatisms in the licensing process. Perhaps give them a little more latitude in the power densities they run at.

NARRATOR: In other words, it appears that the computer and scale model Idaho tests are not designed to make plants safer, but to verify the safety of existing plants and possibly relax licensing standards for new plants. Keith Miller sees potential safety problems with this strategy.

MILLER: It's bad enough that they're telling the American leaders in public that these things are so grossly safe, but perhaps even worse is that there's indications that people within the Nuclear Regulatory Commission, the commissioners themselves—I have a letter from the chairman of the Nuclear Regulatory Commission—these people themselves are believing these grossly optimistic predictions. And that can be extremely dangerous. We can just wipe away certain problems in nuclear safety research and, such as trying to design a more adequate emergency core coolant system because we say, ah, that's totally improbable. And that can lead to a great relaxation in standards. It can lead to a great inadequacy in our safety systems for our nuclear industry.

NARRATOR: How do the critics propose that the problems of possibly inadequate safety systems can be solved? Attorney Anthony Roisman.

ROISMAN: I think a good starting point for knowing that plants are safe is to have the Advisory Committee on Reactor Safeguards, which reports to the Nuclear Regulatory Commission, issue a report that says there are no more unresolved safety problems in our judgment. Their last report had about 30 and they have had that number for quite a few years.

LAPP: Yes, the Nuclear Regulatory Commission has an Advisory Committee on Reactor Safeguards, which lists a number of unresolved technical issues. But that does not mean they are without solution. What that means is that the experts are requiring additional verification, additional research to give us an added margin of safety for those issues. I think that the whole question of technical issues of safety has been blown into the open now, the sunshine has come in because of these three G.E. engineers who resigned and who essentially cleaned the files out; they purged the system.

NARRATOR: In September, 1976 Unit One of Brown's Ferry—a plant designed by General Electric with safety systems tested in San Jose—went back into operation: the world's largest nuclear plant, supplying 1,000 megawatts of power to the Tennessee Valley in northern Alabama. Superintendent Jim Green.

GREEN: As a result of the fire we've certainly had a number of safety reviews and incorporated a number of modifications so that the plant is now safer than it was before.

BUMPUS: Since the fire they have put in sprinkler systems down there to protect these wires and they also put in more stand-pipe fire hose and things. The old saying is, "Wait 'til the mule gets out and then close the barn door."

NARRATOR: The cables where the fire had started have been realigned so that emergency systems are separated. And the cables are now covered with a fireproof material. G.E.'s chief nuclear engineer agrees that the incident at Brown's Ferry led to design changes in other plants.

LEVY: Subsequent to that plant, I think we have made some design changes in some of these plants. Learning from that experience we have assured ourselves that if a fire would take place it would be terminated quite a bit more rapidly and have arranged our electrical cables in a way that if a fire occurs in one area, we could still get the signals to all of our instruments by having the cable come from a completely separated area.

NARRATOR: Meanwhile, the new policy for checking air leak at Brown's Ferry, according to the Alabama press, is to use feathers. What are the odds of another incident like the one that happened at Brown's Ferry? Norman Rasmussen.

RASMUSSEN: Sure it could happen again. The crudest kind of statistics would say, we've now had about 250 to 300 plant years of operation. We've had one such event. So the first rough estimate statistically is that the occurrence of such an event is one in 200 per plant per year.

NARRATOR: The fact is that, worldwide, the nuclear industry has never produced the ultimate catastrophe. However, there have been many nuclear plants where unanticipated problems have occurred. At Windscale, England there was a fire and partial core meltdown in 1957. Radioactive materials escaped to nearby pastureland; traces were found hundreds of miles away. Radioactive Iodine 131, passed on to humans through contaminated cows' milk, can cause leukemia and thyroid cancer. Thousands of gallons of milk were dumped. In 1966 at Unit One of the Fermi plant near Detroit where there was another partial core meltdown. The plant has closed permanently. In 1970 the huge Commonwealth Edison plant near Chicago was shut down after 50,000 gallons of radio-active water and steam escaped from the reactor vessel. There were 17 major shutdowns in the first 19 months of operation of the Vermont Yankee plant because of safety violations, fuel rods buckling, and other equipment failures. At Millstone in Connecticut pipe cracks and leaks of sea water into the cooling system led to a six-month shutdown in 1972. Turkey Point near Miami, Florida—five failures of cooling pumps, leakage of radioactive water. Indian Point, near New York City—the government safety inspector quit in 1976, urging the plant be shut down immediately because "it's almost an accident waiting to happen." Indian Point is still operating. In another plant whose name still remains secret, radioactive water was mixed up with water for the plant's drinking fountains. In 1974 reporting on the many nuclear plant incidents, an A.E.C. report said that none threatened public health, but added "The absence of more serious effects is largely the result of good luck." Strict licensing and regulation should provide greater assurance than "good luck"—but will it ever be possible that the licensing process can guarantee that a Brown's Ferry-type accident—or worse—won't occur in another nuclear plant? Carl Hocevar.

HOCEVAR: The licensing process is basically only as good as man is. If we're in-fallible and we can think of all the things that can occur, maybe we can develop a failsafe licensing process. Since we didn't anticipate what happened at Brown's Ferry, and I suspect we can't anticipate a lot of other things that are going to happen in the future—I'm basing that on past experience—we do not have an in-fallible licensing process.

NARRATOR: Infallible or not, billions of dollars have been invested in hundreds of new plants that are planned or under construction, no matter what the critics say. Do the critics want to close this huge industry down?

MILLER: I'm not suggesting that we do away with nuclear power. We have some serious technical difficulties with nuclear power right now though, and these need to be solved.

KENDALL: If the problems can be resolved, nuclear power can make a useful contribution to the nation's energies. If these safety problems cannot be re-solved, then nuclear power is an unacceptable energy source and ultimately will simply have to be phased out.

ROISMAN: Put it on the back shelf, use the technologies in other areas—energy conservation and other kinds of energy that we know are safe—until such time as nuclear power is either proven to be safe, or proven to be not safe. And in the meantime, phase out those construction permits and operating licenses that are in existence and halt the issuance of new ones.

KENDALL: The nuclear program in this country has developed for 25 years. There are immense investments in it now. There's professional pride associated with it, and there's been the hope for many years that nuclear power would supply cheap, inexpensive safe electricity. As someone said, too cheap to meter. This promise is a bit tarnished now. In order to turn this around one needs citizen action because of the immense size of the industry. Its immense political clout. But this can be done. It's being done now in the area of nuclear reactor safety by citizens groups and it needs the support of the American people.

NARRATOR: Citizen groups have indeed organized successful drives to put nuclear plant safety on state ballots. Volunteers and voters at large focused on the growing controversy.

LINORE: I don't consider myself on any level an expert, but I just understand that I want to take care of the environment. And if I can do it this way, by just saying, "Hey, let's be reasonable. Let's just be careful," and I think that's all the proposition is. It's just a plea to be careful.

DOCTOR: Not having tested the safety systems and not having any solution for the waste storage, to me is incredible. Because the amount of radioactivity that's there now is exceedingly toxic and there are a great number of people in the medical community that are very much worried and very concerned with the consequences of a massive accident.

DARLENE: My children and myself, we're the ones who are going to pay the price if nuclear power is not safe enough. And, therefore, I think we need to be very actively involved in the decision.

NARRATOR: The nuclear industry—with federal help—fought back. They stressed their safety records, and introduced economic fears, as this campaign ad demonstrates.

KATHY HIGLEY: Hello, I'm Kathy Higley. I'm majoring in physical chemistry at Reed College, and I operate our research nuclear reactor. A lot of students like myself will soon be out of school and looking for jobs. Our energy supply is very important to us. No energy—no jobs. Please join me and vote "no" on measure 9. It would ban further development of nuclear power, a clean and safe energy source. Vote "no" on 9, and beat the ban.

NARRATOR: As nuclear power becomes a public issue, the technical complications are reduced to bumper stickers and 30-second TV spots, as in this advertisement.

ANNOUNCER FROM AD: The utilities say nuclear power is safe, but ask about radioactive waste leaks and that series of so-far small accidents, and they admit there are a few bugs. Still they say, it's worth the danger. But is it? Shouldn't we prove that nuclear emergency systems are safe before we build more plants? Measure 9 simply says, yes. But then you're taking the risk. You have to decide.

NARRATOR: All 1976 ballot measures lost, but the debate is not over. The California legislature did pass three laws that achieved the goals of the ballot proponents in that state. President Carter endorsed the Oregon ballot measure in his election campaign. Congress is taking a new look. New state ballot drives are underway, so citizens will continue to be asked to decide these issues. But should this be a voting matter, or should it simply be left to the experts?

PAULING: Everyone should decide these important questions. I do think that scientists have a special role to play. They may understand the technical aspects of these problems better than other people. I think that they have the duty of explaining them. Not only explaining, presenting the facts, but also expressing their own opinions. That's why I say that I am opposed to nuclear power plants and I say why I am.

LAPP: I happen to believe that the citizen has a very real interest in nuclear safety because, after all, he is the person who is at risk. On the other hand, there's a great gap separating the public from the expert. The expert presumably knows what the technology is, what its risks are; but the expert is also a specialist who has a limited frame of reference and sometimes a limited vocabulary. And the public is not apt to understand him very well. Therefore, it seems to me that this is a question of great delicacy for democracy, because sooner or later you have to trust somebody, and if you don't trust government, who do you trust?

DARLENE CARLSON: On the one hand, the industry says everything is fine. On the other hand, we hear people in positions of importance saying everything is not fine. And so I'm caught in the middle then. Whom am I supposed to believe?

NARRATOR: Leading international scientists disagree, so how can the ordinary citizen ever make a sound voting decision?

RASMUSSEN: Leading international scientists disagree on most everything is, ah, certainly true, especially when they're talking about things outside their field of expertise. And so one has to judge how well a man has studied and understood the issue he's talking about. Does he fully know the details of it, because scientists are no better than anybody else at making a decision in a technical area, unless it's one that they've studied.

KENDALL: Citizens are able to understand these issues. They are able to resolve the conflicting claims, and the whole history of the nuclear program with its difficulties, its poor reliability, its poor accident record speaks for itself, and is one of the reasons why the nuclear program is in so much trouble presently.

NARRATOR: Pressure by citizen groups, scientists and the growing number of people who quit the industry and the government agencies, all have helped focus attention on the whole question of whether or not nuclear power has yet been proven to be a safe energy source. For any improvements or changes, it seems likely the same kind of pressure will have to intensify. Those opposed to our growing dependence on nuclear power will have to press for major commitments to energy conservation, and intensive development of alternate energy sources. Those in favor will have to hope that the ultimate accident will never happen. Meanwhile, nuclear power plant risks continue—how high or low we probably will never really know. Should we continue to live with a technology with such potential hazards? A technology that—like the incident at Brown's Ferry—can be disrupted by a candle flame?

GRAPHIC: "The Nuclear Regulatory Commission declined repeated invitations to appear in this film."

GRAPHIC: ". . . to the village square we must carry the facts of atomic energy . . . from there must come America's voice."   Albert Einstein

LANGUAGE AND CONTEMPORARY ISSUES

12

This chapter will present three essays that either contend or show that the way we speak about a given subject—in particular, the words we choose—can be indicative of our fundamental beliefs, attitudes, and perceptions. The first essay is "Talking about Women," by Robin Lakoff, which is taken from her book *Language and Women's Place.* Applying the methods of modern linguistic analysis, Lakoff argues that the language we use in speaking about women is indicative of the role they are expected to play in society.

The second and third essays give contrasting pictures of political protesters. In both, the language is highly charged; the first speaks against protesters, the second in favor of them. Still the differences in language are so sharp that they indicate not only a disagreement in political position, but in perception of fact as well. In all likelihood, both Jeffrey Hart and Ian Menzies are giving accurate accounts of the way protesters appeared to them. Each writer attempts to support his political position, at least in part, by trying to get us to perceive them in the same way.

Talking About Women *

ROBIN T. LAKOFF

When a word acquires a bad connotation by association with something unpleasant or embarrassing, people may search for substitutes that do not have the uncomfortable effect—that is, euphemisms. Since attitudes toward the original referent are not altered by a change of name, the new name itself takes on the adverse connotations, and a new euphemism must be found. It is no doubt possible to pick out areas of particular psychological strain or discomfort—areas where problems exist in a culture—by pinpointing items around which a great many euphemisms are clustered. An obvious example concerns the various words for that household convenience into which human wastes are eliminated: toilet, bathroom, rest room, comfort station, lavatory, water closet, loo, and all the others.

In the case of women, it may be encouraging to find no richness of euphemism; but it is discouraging to note that at least one euphemism for "woman" does exist and is very much alive. The word, of course, is "lady," which seems to be replacing "woman" in a great many contexts. Where both exist, they have different connotations; where only one exists, there is usually a reason to be found in the context in which the word is uttered.

Related to the existence of euphemistic terms for "woman" is the existence of euphemistic terms for woman's principal role, that of "housewife." Most occupational terms do not have coexisting euphemisms: these seem to come into being only when the occupation is considered embarrassing or demeaning. Thus there is no euphemism for "professor," "doctor," "bank president"; but we do find "mortician" and "funeral director" for "undertaker"; "custodian" and "sanitary engineer" for "janitor"; "domestic" for "cleaning woman"; and so forth. Similarly one keeps running into hopeful suggestions, principally in the pages of women's magazines, that the lot of the housewife would be immeasurably improved if she thought of herself as "homemaker," "household executive," "household engineer," or any of several others. I am not sure what to make of the fact that none of these (unlike those of the bona fide occupational euphemisms) has taken hold: is it because the "housewife" doesn't consider her status demeaning? Then why the search for euphemisms? Or does she feel that there is no escape through a change in nomenclature, or lack pride in her job to such an extent that she doesn't feel up to making the effort? This is a question for the sociologist.

It may be objected that *lady* has a masculine counterpart, namely *gentleman*, occasionally shortened to *gent*. But I don't think this is a fair comparison. *Lady* is much more common than *gent(leman)*, and, since *gent* exists, the reason is not ease of pronunciation. *Lady* is really a euphemism for *woman*, but *gentleman* is not nearly frequent enough to classify as a euphemism for *man*. Just as we do not call whites "Caucasian-Americans," there is no felt need to refer to

* *Language and Women's Place* (New York: Harper & Row, 1975), pp. 19–42.

men commonly as "gentlemen." And just as there is a need for such terms as "Afro-Americans," there is similarly a felt need for "lady." One might even say that when a derogatory epithet exists, a parallel euphemism is deemed necessary. (The term WASP, white Anglo-Saxon Protestant, may occur to the reader as a possible derogatory term which has no parallel euphemism. But in fact, WASP is not parallel in usage to *nigger, polack,* or *yid.* One can refer to himself as a WASP, as one cannot refer to himself as a *nigger* without either a total lack of self-pride or bitter sarcasm. Thus one can say: "Sure I'm a WASP, and proud of it!" but probably not: "Sure I'm a nigger, and proud of it!" without special sarcastic inflection in the voice suggesting that it is an imitation of the addressee.) To avoid having to resort to terms like "Afro-American," we need only get rid of all expressions like "nigger"; to banish "lady" in its euphemistic sense from the vocabulary of English, we need only first get rid of "broad" and its relations. But of course, . . . we cannot achieve this commendable simplification of the lexicon unless we somehow remove from our minds the idea that blacks *are* niggers, and that women *are* broads. The presence of the words is a signal that something is wrong, rather than (as too often interpreted by well-meaning reformers) the problem itself. The point here is that, unless we start feeling more respect for women and, at the same time, less uncomfortable about them and their roles in society in relation to men, we cannot avoid *ladies* any more than we can avoid *broads.*

In the past, some ethnic groups that today are relatively respectable were apparently considered less so. And in looking at reports of the terms used to describe those groups at the earlier time, we find two interesting facts: first, there is a much greater incidence of derogatory epithets for that group (as might be expected); and second (which one might not be led to expect automatically) there exist euphemistic terms for that group that are no longer in general use. One can only conclude that euphemisms vanish as they are no longer needed. The example I have in mind is that of the words used to describe Jews. Aside from the uncomplimentary epithets which still exist today, though not encountered very often, one finds, in reading novels written and set more than half a century ago, a number of euphemisms that are not found any more, such as "Hebrew gentleman" and "Israelite." The disappearance of the euphemisms concurrently with the derogatory terms suggests that women will be *ladies* until some more dignified status can be found for them.

It might also be claimed that *lady* is no euphemism because it has exactly the same connotations as woman, is usable under the same semantic and contextual conditions. But a cursory inspection will show that this is not always the case. The decision to use one term rather than the other may considerably alter the sense of a sentence. The following are examples:

(1) *(a)* A (woman) that I know makes amazing things out of shoelaces and
     (lady)   old boxes.
   (b) A (woman) I know works at Woolworth's.
      (lady)
   (c) A (woman) I know is a dean at Berkeley.
      (lady)

(These facts are true for some speakers of English. For others, *lady* has taken over the function of *woman* to such an extent that *lady* can be used in all these sentences.)

In my speech, the use of *lady* in (1) *(c)* imparts a frivolous or nonserious tone to the sentence: the matter under discussion is one of not too great moment. In this dialect, then, *lady* seems to be the more colloquial word: it is less apt to be used in writing, or in discussing serious matters. Similarly in (1) *(a)*, using *lady* would suggest that the speaker considered the "amazing things" not to be serious art, but merely a hobby or an aberration. If *woman* is used, she might be a serious (pop art) sculptor.

Related to this is the use of *lady* in job terminology. For at least some speakers, the more demeaning the job, the more the person holding it (if female, of course) is likely to be described as a *lady.* Thus, *cleaning lady* is at least as common as *cleaning woman, saleslady* as *saleswoman.* But one says, normally, *woman doctor.* To say *lady doctor* is to be very condescending: it constitutes an insult. For men, there is no such dichotomy. *Garbageman* or *salesman* is the only possibility, never *garbage gentleman.*[1] And of course, since in the professions the male is unmarked, we never have *man (male) doctor.*

Numerous other examples can be given, all tending to prove the same point: that if, in a particular sentence, both *woman* and *lady* might be used, the use of the latter tends to trivialize the subject matter under discussion, often subtly ridiculing the woman involved. Thus, for example, a mention in the San Francisco *Chronicle* of January 31, 1972, of Madalyn Murray O'Hair as the "lady atheist" reduces her position to that of scatterbrained eccentric, or at any rate, one who need not be taken seriously. Even *woman atheist* is scarcely defensible: first, because her sex is irrelevant to her philosophical position, and second, because her name makes it clear in any event. But *lady* makes matters still worse. Similarly a reference to a *woman sculptor* is only mildly annoying (since there is no term *male sculptor,* the discrepancy suggests that such activity is normal for a man, but not for a woman), but still it could be used with reference to a serious artist. *Lady sculptor,* on the other hand, strikes me as a slur against the artist, deliberate or not, implying that the woman's art is frivolous, something she does to fend off the boredom of suburban housewifery, or at any rate, nothing of moment in the art world. Serious artists have shows, not *dilettantes.* So we hear of *one-woman shows,* but never *one-lady shows.*

Another realm of usage in which *lady* contrasts with *woman* is in titles of organizations. It seems that organizations of women who have a serious purpose (not merely that of spending time with one another) cannot use the word *lady* in their titles, but less serious ones may. Compare the *Ladies' Auxiliary* of a men's group, or the *Thursday Evening Ladies Browning and Garden Society* with *Ladies' Lib* or *Ladies Strike for Peace.*

---

[1] In conformity with current linguistic practice, throughout this work an asterisk (*) will be used to mark a sentence that is inappropriate in some sense, either because it is syntactically deviant or used in the wrong social context.

What is curious about this split is that *lady* is, as noted, in origin a euphemism for *woman*. What kind of euphemism is it that subtly denigrates the people to whom it refers, suggests that they are not to be taken seriously, are laughing stocks? A euphemism, after all, is supposed to put a better face on something people find uncomfortable. But this is not really contradictory. What a euphemism is supposed to do, actually, is to remove from thought *that part* of the connotations of a word that creates the discomfort. So each of the euphemisms for toilet, starting with *toilet*, seems to be trying to get further from the notion of excrement, by employing successively more elegant terminology that seems designed to suggest that the piece of furniture in question has really other primary uses, for performing one's toilette, for washing, for comfort, for resting, but never for those other things. Perhaps the notion of the nonseriousness of women is not the thing that makes men—the devisers of euphemism—as well as women, uncomfortable. Perhaps it is some other aspect of the man-woman relationship. How can we determine whether this is in fact the case?

One way of identifying the precise source of discomfort is, perhaps, by looking at the derogatory terms for something. Many of the terms for blacks refer to their physical characteristics. And the latest euphemism for blacks, *Afro-Americans*, seems to be a specific attempt to get away from color names. (The term *black* is not a euphemism, but rather an attempt to confront the issue squarely and make color into a source of pride.) And as has often been noted, derogatory terms for women are very often overtly sexual: the reader will have no difficulty recalling what I allude to here.

The distinction between *lady* and *woman*, in those dialects of American English in which it is found, may be traceable to other causes than the sexual connotations present in *woman*. Most people who are asked why they have chosen to use *lady* where *woman* would be as appropriate will reply that *lady* seemed more polite. The concept of politeness thus invoked is the politeness used in dignifying or ennobling a concept that normally is not thought of as having dignity or nobility. It is this notion of politeness that explains why we have *cleaning lady*, but not, normally, *lady doctor*. A doctor does not need to be exalted by conventional expressions: she has dignity enough from her professional status. But a cleaning woman is in a very different situation, in which her occupational category requires ennobling. Then perhaps we can say that the very notion of womanhood, as opposed to manhood, requires ennobling since it lacks inherent dignity of its own: hence the word *woman* requires the existence of a euphemism like *lady*. Besides or possibly because of being explicitly devoid of sexual connotation, *lady* carries with it overtones recalling the age of chivalry: the exalted stature of the person so referred to, her existence above the common sphere. This makes the term seem polite at first, but we must also remember that these implications are perilous: they suggest that a "lady" is helpless, and cannot do things for herself. In this respect the use of a word like *lady* is parallel to the act of opening doors for women—or ladies. At first blush it is flattering: the object of the flattery feels honored, cherished, and so forth; but by the same token, she is also considered helpless and not in control of her own destiny. Women who protest that they *like* receiving these little courtesies, and object to being liberated from them, should reflect a bit on their deeper meaning and see how much they like *that*.

This brings us to the consideration of another common substitute for *woman*, namely *girl*. One seldom hears a man past the age of adolescence referred to as a boy, save in expressions like "going out with the boys," which are meant to suggest an air of adolescent frivolity and irresponsibility. But women of all ages are "girls": one can have a man, not a boy, Friday, but a girl, never a woman or even a lady, Friday; women have girl friends, but men do not—in a nonsexual sense—have boyfriends. It may be that this use of *girl* is euphemistic in the sense in which *lady* is a euphemism: in stressing the idea of immaturity, it removes the sexual connotations lurking in *woman*. Instead of the ennobling present in *lady*, *girl* is (presumably) flattering to women because of its stress on youth. But here again there are pitfalls: in recalling youth, frivolity, and immaturity, *girl* brings to mind irresponsibility: you don't send a girl to do a woman's errand (or even, for that matter, a boy's errand). It seems that again, by an appeal to feminine vanity (about which we shall have more to say later) the users of English have assigned women to a very unflattering place in their minds: a woman is a person who is both too immature and too far from real life to be entrusted with responsibilities and with decisions of any serious nature. Would you elect president a person incapable of putting on her own coat? (Of course, if we were to have a married woman president, we would not have any name for her husband parallel to *First Lady*, and why do you suppose that is?)

Perhaps the way in which *lady* functions as a euphemism for *woman* is that it does not contain the sexual implications present in *woman*: it is not "embarrassing" in that way. If this is so, we may expect that, in the future, *lady* will replace *woman* as the primary word for the human female, since *woman* will have become too blatantly sexual. That this distinction is already made in some contexts at least is shown in the following examples:

(2) *(a)* She's only twelve, but she's already a woman.
*lady

(b) After ten years in jail, Harry wanted to find a woman.
*lady

(c) She's my woman, see, so don't mess around with her.
*lady

It may be, finally, that the reason the use of *lady* rather than *woman* in a sentence creates the impression of frivolity discussed above is precisely because of the euphemistic nature of *lady*. In serious discussion, one does not typically employ euphemisms. So, for instance, a sentence like (3) *(a)* is more suited to cocktail party chitchat by returning tourists than to learned discussion by anthropologists, who would be more likely to use a technical term, as in (3) *(b)*:

(3) *(a)* When the natives of Mbanga want to use the little boys' room, first they find a large pineapple leaf. . . .

(b) When the natives of Mbanga wish to defecate, first they find a large pineapple leaf. . . .

Perhaps the discomfort men suffer in contemplating, more or less unconsciously, the sexuality of women is traceable to guilt feelings on their part. The
guilt arises, I should think, not only because they think sex is inherently dirty
(that is another problem) but because if one deals with women as primarily sexual
beings, one is in effect automatically relegating them to object status; if women
are there for the use and enjoyment of men, they are not fully human beings in
their own right. But women are in most other respects evidently human. So a
man feels somewhat ambivalent—more or less consciously—and reacts all the
more strongly for that reason. Hence, perhaps, the rather hysterical ridicule
heaped on Women's Lib in the media. In any case, throughout English one finds
evidence of many sorts that women are viewed (by women as well as men) as
secondary beings: as having an existence only when defined by a man.

These facts about women's position should cause us to question one of the
commonest criticisms made of women's behavior, as opposed to men's: one often
hears that women are vain and self-centered, concerned only about their appearance and how others view them. A little thought should convince anyone that,
in fact, it is men who are self-centered and egocentric and that women's seeming
vanity is not that at all.

As noted above, a woman's reputation and position in society depend almost
wholly on the impression she makes upon others, how others view her. She must
dress decoratively, look attractive, be compliant, if she is to survive at all in the
world. Then her overattention to appearance and appearances (including, perhaps,
overcorrectness and overgentility of speech and etiquette) is merely the result of
being forced to exist only as a reflection in the eyes of others. She does not,
cannot, do anything in her own behalf or purely for her own pleasure or aggran-
dizement. (Rather ironically, the only way she can increase her own comfort,
pleasure, and security is through her husband's advancement, and thus she can
achieve material comforts only through someone else's efforts. What seem to be
self-centered efforts are really aimed at the opinions of others, and what appear
to be efforts for someone else are really the only ones permissible for a woman's
own behalf. It is no wonder women lack an identity and feel they have no place
of their own.)

In fact, men are the vain sex. Men may derive pleasure directly from their
own works. Men do things purely for their own satisfaction, not caring nearly so
much how it will look to others. This, surely, is the true egocentricity. Further,
it seems to me that the ultimate vanity or self-centeredness is to be found in
eccentricity. The eccentric alone truly cares only for himself and his own pleasure: he does not concern himself with how his actions affect others or look to
others. And eccentricity is far more common and far more tolerated in men than
in women. A strong personality in general, a mark of egocentricity, is again
valued in men much more than in women. For these reasons, women are not
very successful in business or politics, where both vanity and eccentricity of
certain sorts can be marks of distinction rather than objects of ridicule.

Sociologically it is probably fairly obvious that a woman in most subcultures
in our society achieves status only through her father's, husband's, or lover's

position. What is remarkable is that these facts show up linguistically in non-obvious ways.

Suppose we take a pair of words which, in terms of the possible relationships in an earlier society, were simple male-female equivalents, analogous to bull: cow. Suppose we find that, for independent reasons, society has changed in such a way that the primary meanings now are irrelevant. Yet the words have not been discarded, but have acquired new meanings, metaphorically related to their original senses. But suppose these new metaphorical uses are no longer parallel to each other. By seeing where the parallelism breaks down, we can intuit something about the different roles played by men and women in this culture. One good example of such a divergence through time is found in the pair *master* and *mistress*. Once used with reference to one person's power over another, these words became unusable in their original sense as the master-servant relationship became nonexistent. But the words are still common as used in sentences (4) and (5):

(4) *(a)* He is a master of the intricacies of academic politics.
     (b) *She is a mistress . . .

(5) *(a)* *Harry declined to be my master, and so returned to his wife.
     (b) Rhonda declined to be my mistress, and so returned to her husband.

Unless used with reference to animals or slaves, *master* now generally refers to a man who has acquired consummate ability in some field, normally nonsexual. But its feminine counterpart cannot be used in this way. It is practically restricted to its sexual sense of "paramour." We start out with two terms, both roughly paraphrasable as "one who has power over another." But the masculine form, once one person is no longer able to have absolute power over another, becomes usable metaphorically in the sense of "have power over *something.*" The feminine counterpart also acquired a metaphorical interpretation, but the metaphor here is sexual: one's mistress "has power over" one in a sexual sense. And this expression is probably chivalrous, rather than descriptive of the real-world relationship between lovers. In terms of choice, of economic control, and so forth, it is generally the man who holds the power in such a relationship; to call a woman one's "mistress" is the equivalent of saying "please" in prefacing a request to a subordinate. Both are done for politeness and are done purely because both participants in the relationship, in both cases, know that the supposed inferiority of the mistress's lover and of the user of "please" is only a sham. Interesting too in this regard is the fact that "master" requires as its object only the name of some activity, something inanimate and abstract. But "mistress" requires a masculine noun in the possessive to precede it. One cannot say:

(6) *Rhonda is a mistress.

One must be *someone's* mistress.

And obviously too, it is one thing to be an *old master*, like Hans Holbein, and another to be an *old mistress:* the latter, again, requires a masculine possessive form preceding it, indicating who has done the discarding. *Old* in the first instance refers to absolute age: the artist's lifetime versus the time of writing. But *old* in the second really means "discarded," "old" with respect to someone else. . . .

So here we see several important points concerning the relationship between men and women illustrated: first, that men are defined in terms of what they do in the world, women in terms of the men with whom they are associated; and second, that the notion of "power" for a man is different from that of "power" for a woman: it is acquired and manifested in different ways. One might say then that these words have retained their principal meanings through time; what has changed is the kinds of interpersonal relationships to which they refer.

As a second example, the examples in (7) should be completely parallel semantically:

(7) *(a)* He's a professional.
     (b) She's a professional.

Hearing and knowing no more about the subjects of the discourse than this, what would one assume about them in each case? Certainly in *(a)* the normal conclusion the casual eavesdropper would come to was that "he" was a doctor or a lawyer or a member of one of the other professions. But it is much less likely that one would draw a similar conclusion in *(b)*. Rather, the first assumption most speakers of English seem to make is that "she" is a prostitute, literally or figuratively speaking. Again, a man is defined in the serious world by what he does, a woman by her sexuality, that is, in terms of one particular aspect of her relationship to men.

This discrepancy is not confined to English. Victor Wen has informed me that a similar situation pertains in Chinese. One may say of a man, "He's in business," and of a woman, "She's in business," lexically and grammatically parallel. The former means about what its English equivalent means. But the latter is synonymous to sentence (7) *(b)*.

James Fox tells me that in many cultures, as in English, people may be referred to metaphorically by animal names, suggesting that they have some of the attributes of that animal, real or part of the folklore. What is interesting here is that where animal names may be applied to both men and women—whether or not there are separate terms for male and female in the animal—the former may have connotations in all sorts of areas, while the latter, whatever other connotations the term may suggest, nearly always makes sexual reference as well. Compare in this regard *dog* and *bitch, fox* and *vixen*, and the difference between *he's a pig* and *she's a pig*.

The sexual definition of women, however, is but one facet of a much larger problem. In every aspect of life, a woman is identified in terms of the men she relates to. The opposite is not usually true of men: they act in the world as autonomous individuals, but women are only "John's wife," or "Harry's girl friend." Thus, meeting a woman at a party, a quite normal opening conversational gambit might be: "What does your husband do?" One very seldom hears, in a similar situation, a question addressed to a man: "What does your wife do?" The question would, to a majority of men, seem tautological: "She's my wife—that's what she does." This is true even in cases in which a woman is being discussed in a context utterly unrelated to her relationships with men, when she has attained sufficient stature to be considered for high public office. In fact, in a recent discussion of possible Supreme Court nominees, one woman was mentioned prominently. In discussing her general qualifications for the office, and her background, the *New York Times* saw fit to remark on her "bathing-beauty figure." Note that this is not only a judgment on a physical attribute totally removed from her qualifications for the Supreme Court, but that it is couched in terms of how a man would react to her figure. Some days later, President Nixon announced the nominations to his Price Board, among them one woman. In the thumbnail sketches the *Times* gave of each nominee, it was mentioned that the woman's husband was a professor of English. In the case of none of the other nominees was the existence of a spouse even hinted at, and much less was there any clue about the spouse's occupation. So here, although the existence of a husband was as irrelevant for this woman appointee as the existence of a wife was for any of the male appointees, the husband was mentioned, since a woman cannot be placed in her position in society by the readers of the *Times* unless they know her marital status. The same is not at all true of men. Similarly in the 1971 mayoral campaign in San Francisco, the sole woman candidate was repeatedly referred to as *Mrs. Feinstein*, never *Feinstein*, when her opponents were regularly referred to by first and last names or last names alone: *Joseph Alioto*, or *Alioto*, not *Mr. Alioto*. Again, the woman had to be identified by her relationship to a man, although this should bear no relevance to her qualifications for public office.

While sharp intellect is generally considered an unqualified virtue in a man, any character trait that is not related to a woman's utility to men is considered suspect, if not downright bad. Thus the word *brainy* is seldom used of men; when used of women it suggests (1) that this intelligence is unexpected in a woman; (2) that it isn't really a good trait. If one calls a woman "smart," outside of the sense of "fashionable," either one means it as a compliment to her domestic thrift and other housekeeping abilities or, again, it suggests a bit of wariness on the part of the speaker.

Also relevant here are the connotations (as opposed to the denotative meanings) of the words *spinster* and *bachelor*. Denotatively, these are, again, parallel to "cow" versus "bull": one is masculine, the other feminine, and both mean "one who is not married." But there the resemblance ends. *Bachelor* is at least a neutral term, often used as a compliment. *Spinster* normally seems to be used pejoratively with connotations of prissiness, fussiness, and so on. Some of the differences between the two words are brought into focus in the following examples:

(8) (a) Mary hopes to meet an eligible bachelor.
     (b) *Fred hopes to meet an eligible spinster.

It is the concept of an *eligible spinster* that is anomalous. If someone is a spinster, by implication she is not eligible (to marry); she has had her chance, and been passed by. Hence, a girl of twenty cannot be properly called a spinster: she still has a chance to be married. (Of course, *spinster* may be used metaphorically in this situation, as described below.) But a man may be considered a bachelor as soon as he reaches marriageable age: to be a bachelor implies that one has the choice of marrying or not, and this is what makes the idea of a bachelor existence attractive, in the popular literature. He has been pursued and has successfully eluded his pursuers. But a spinster is one who has not been pursued, or at least not seriously. She is old unwanted goods. Hence it is not surprising to find that a euphemism has arisen for *spinster*, a word not much used today, *bachelor girl*, which attempts to capture for the woman the connotations *bachelor* has for a man. But this, too, is not much used except by writers trying to give their (slick magazine) prose a "with-it" sound. I have not heard the word used in unself-conscious speech. *Bachelor*, however, needs no euphemisms.

When *bachelor* and *spinster* are used metaphorically, the distinction in connotation between the two becomes even clearer:

(9) *(a)* John is a regular bachelor.
   (b) Mary is a regular spinster.

The metaphorical connotations of "bachelor" generally suggest sexual freedom; of "spinster," puritanism or celibacy. So we might use a sentence like (9) *(a)* if John was in fact married but engaged in extramarital affairs freely. It is hard to think of other circumstances in which it might be used. Certainly it could not be used if John were married but determined to remain celibate. (9) *(b)*, on the other hand, might be used under two conditions: first, if Mary were in fact unmarried, but still of marriageable age (that is, not yet a literal spinster), and very cold and prissy; second, if Mary were married, with the same characteristics. The use of "regular," then, seems to be an indicator that the noun it modifies is to be taken purely in its connotative rather than denotative sense.

These examples could be multiplied. It is generally considered a *faux pas*, in proper society, to congratulate a girl on her engagement, while it is correct to congratulate her fiancé. Why is this? The reason here seems to be that it is impolite to remind someone of something that may be uncomfortable to him. To remind a girl that she must catch someone, that perhaps she might not have caught anyone, is rude, and this is what is involved, effectively, in congratulating someone. To congratulate someone is to rejoice with him in his good fortune; but it is not quite nice to remind a girl that getting married is good fortune for her, indeed a veritable necessity; it is too close to suggesting the bad fortune that it would be for her had she not found someone to marry. In the context of this society's assumptions about women's role, to congratulate a girl on her engagement is virtually to say, "Thank goodness! You had a close call!" For the man, on the other hand, there was no such danger. His choosing to marry is viewed as a good thing, but not something essential, and so he may be congratulated for doing a wise thing. If man and woman were equal in respect to marriage, it would be proper to congratulate either both or neither.

Another thing to think about is the traditional conclusion of the marriage service: "I now pronounce you man and wife." The man's position in the world, and in relation to other people including the bride, has not been changed by the act of marriage. He was a "man" before the ceremony, and a "man" he still is (one hopes) at its conclusion. But the bride went into the ceremony a "woman," not defined by any other person, at least linguistically; she leaves it a "wife," defined in terms of the "man," her husband. There are many other aspects of traditional marriage ceremonies in our culture that might be used to illustrate the same point.

And having discussed bachelorhood and spinsterhood, and the marital state, we arrive at widowhood. Surely a bereaved husband and a bereaved wife are equivalent: they have both undergone the loss of a mate. But in fact, linguistically at any rate, this is not true. It is true that we have two words, *widow* and *widower*; but here again, *widow* is far commoner in use. Widows, not widowers, have their particular roles in folklore and tradition, and mourning behavior of particular sorts seems to be expected more strongly, and for a longer time, of a widow than of a widower. But there is more than this, as evidenced by the following:

(10) *(a)* Mary is John's widow.
       (b) *John is Mary's widower.

Like *mistress*, *widow* commonly occurs with a possessive preceding it, the name of the woman's late husband. Though he is dead, she is still defined by her relationship to him. But the bereaved husband is no longer defined in terms of his wife. While she is alive, he is sometimes defined as Mary's husband (though less often, probably, than she is as "John's wife"). But once she is gone, her function for him is over, linguistically speaking anyway. So once again, we see that women are always defined in terms of the men to whom they are related, and hence the worst thing that can happen to a woman is not to have a man in this relationship—that is, to be a spinster, a woman with neither husband nor lover, dead or alive.

What all these facts suggest is merely this, again: that men are assumed to be able to choose whether or not they will marry, and that therefore their not being married in no way precludes their enjoying sexual activity; but if a woman is not married, it is assumed to be because no one found her desirable. Hence if a woman is not married by the usual age, she is assumed to be sexually undesirable, prissy, and frigid.

The reason for this distinction seems to be found in the point made earlier: that women are given their identities in our society by virtue of their relationship with men, not vice versa. . . .

Now it becomes clearer why there is a lack of parallelism in men's and women's titles. To refer to a man as *Mr.* does not identify his marital status; but there is no such ambiguous term for women: one must decide on *Mrs.* or *Miss.* To remedy this imbalance, a bill was proposed in the United States Congress by Bella Abzug and others that would legislate a change in women's titles: *Miss* and *Mrs.* would both be abolished in favor of *Ms.* Rather less seriously, the converse has been proposed by Russell Baker, that two terms should be created for men, *Mrm.* and *Srs.,* depending upon marital status. We may ask several questions: *(a)* Why does the imbalance exist in the first place? *(b)* Why do we feel that Baker's suggestion (even if it did not come from Baker) is somehow not to be taken as seriously as Abzug's? And *(c)* does Abzug's proposal have a chance of being accepted in coloquial speech? (One must distinguish between acceptance in official use and documents, whcre Ms. is already used to some extent, and acceptance in colloquial conversation, where I have nevcr heard it. I think the latter will be a long time in coming, and I do not think we can consider Ms. a real choice until this occurs.)

(a) A title is devised and used for a purpose: to give a clue to participants in social interaction how the other person is to be regarded, how he is to be addressed. In an avowedly class-conscious society, social ranking is a significant determining factor: once you know that your addressee is to be addressed as "lord," or "mister," or "churl," you know where he stands with respect to you; the title establishes his identity in terms of his relationship with the larger social group. For this reason, the recent suggestion that both *Mr.* and *Mrs./Miss* be abolished in favor of *Person* is unlikely to be successful: *Person* tells you only what you already know, and does not aid in establishing ranking or relationship between two people. Even in a supposedly classless society, the use of *Mr.* (as opposed to simple last name or first name) connotes a great deal about the relationship of the two participants in the discourse with respect to each other. To introduce yourself, "I'm Mr. Jones" puts the relationship you are seeking to establish on quite a different basis than saying, "I'm Jones," or "I'm John," and each is usable under quite different contextual conditions, socially speaking. As long as social distinctions, overt or covert, continue to exist, we will be unable to rid our language of titles that make reference to them. It is interesting that the French and Russian revolutions both tried to do away with honorific titles that distinguished class by substituting "citizen(ess)" and "comrade." These, however, are not purely empty like "person": they imply that speaker and addressee share a relationship in that both are part of the state and hence, by implication, both equal. In France, the attempt was not long-lived. (Although *tovarishch* is normal today in the Soviet Union, I don't know whether it is really usable under all conditions, whether a factory worker, for instance, could use it to his foreman, or his foreman's wife.)

Although, in our society, naming conventions for men and women are essentially equal (both have first and last names, and both may have additional names, of lesser importance), the social conventions governing the choice of form of address is not parallel in both sexes. Thus, as noted, a man, Mr. John Jones, may be addressed as John, as Jones, as Mr. Jones, and as Mr. John Jones. The first normally implies familiarity, the second intimacy coupled with Jones's inferiority (except in situations of nondirect address, as in professional citation; or among intimates, as a possibly more intimate form of address even than first name alone, without inferiority being implied); the third distance and more or less equality. The last is never used in direct address, and again indicates considerable distance. To address someone by first name alone is to assume at least equality with the other person, and perhaps superiority (in which case the other person will respond with *Mr.* and last name). *Mr. Jones* is probably the least-marked form of address, a means of keeping distance with no necessary suggestions of status. To address someone as *Jones* socially or in business may be an indication of his inferior status, but to refer to someone that way professionally (as at a linguistics conference, generally in indirect reference rather than direct address) seems to be a mark of his acceptance, as a colleague and a person to be taken seriously as a fellow member of the profession. In this way, perhaps, it is related to the last-name-only of familiarity: it is "we know each other well; we are equals and pals, or equals and colleagues." . . .

Aside from making apparent a dilemma arising from a social inequity, the facts noted above are of interest for other reasons: they show that titles are very much alive in our supposedly classless society, and apparently small differences in their use reflect great chasms in social position among users. The use (or misuse) of titles supplies much information to people, and hence titles are important in our language as in our society, and not about to be lightly discarded.

If then, we can reasonably assume that a title supplies information about the person to whose name it is attached, we may further assume that this information is necessary in telling people how to interact with this person. And if this sort of information is felt to be necessary for one class of people and not another, we may expect to find a distinction made in the titles for the first class, if at all, but not the second.

So it is with *Mrs., Miss,* and *Mr.* Since a significant part of the opinion one normally forms about a woman's character and social station depends on her marital status—as is not the case with men—it is obvious that the title of address should supply this information in the case of women, but not of men.

(It may seem as though a man's marital status is, under certain conditions, of crucial interest to a woman, and therefore this point is suspect. But I think we have to distinguish between importance in the eyes of a single person in a particular situation, and importance in the eyes of society at large, in a great many possible situations. At almost every turn, because of the way social and business events are arranged, one needs to know a woman's marital status, and the position held by her husband. But one does not need the same information about a man, since his social status can be gauged, generally, purely by reference to his own accomplishments.) Once again, it would seem that trying to legislate a change in a lexical item is fruitless. The change to *Ms.* will not be generally adopted until a woman's status in society changes to assure her an identity based on her own accomplishments. (Perhaps even more debasing than the *Mrs./Miss* distinction is the fact that the woman in marrying relinquishes her own name, while the man does not. This suggests even more firmly that a woman is her husband's possession, having no other identity than that of his wife. Not only does she give up her last name [which, after all, she took from her father], but often her first name as well, to become *Mrs. John Smith.)*

Although blacks are not yet fully accorded equal status with whites in this society, nevertheless *black,* a term coined to elicit racial pride and sense of unity, seems to have been widely adopted both by blacks and whites, both in formal use and in the media, and increasingly in colloquial conversation. Does this constitute a counterexample to my claim here? I think not, but rather an element of hope. My point is that linguistic and social change go hand in hand: one cannot, purely by changing language use, change social status. The word *black,* in its current sense, was not heard until the late 1960s or even 1970, to any significant extent. I think if its use had been proposed much earlier, it would have failed in acceptance. I think the reason people other than blacks can un

derstand and sympathize with black racial pride is that they were made aware
of the depths of their prejudice during the civil rights struggles of the early 1960s.
It took nearly ten years from the beginning of this struggle for the use of *black*
to achieve wide acceptance, and it is still often used a bit self-consciously, as
though italicized. But since great headway was made first in the social sphere,
linguistic progress could be made *on that basis*; and now this linguistic progress,
it is hoped, will lead to new social progress in turn. The women's movement is
but a few years old, and has, I should think, much deeper ingrained hostility to
overcome than the civil rights movement ever did. (Among the intelligentsia,
the black civil rights struggle was never a subject for ridicule, as women's liberation all too often is, among those very liberals who were the first on their
blocks to join the NAACP.) The parallel to the black struggle should indicate
that social change must precede lexical change: women must achieve some measure of greater social independence of men before *Ms.* can gain wider acceptance.

(b) There is thus a very good reason why a distinction is made in the case
of women, but not men, in the matter of marital status. But this fact suggests an
answer to the second question posed above, regarding why *Ms.* is felt to be a
more serious proposal than Baker's suggestion. It is obviously easier to imagine
obliterating an extant distinction than creating a new one: easier to learn to
ignore the marital status of a woman than to begin to pay attention to that of a
man. Moreover, we may also assume that for a woman, the use of *Ms.* is a
liberating device, one to be desired. But (as Baker suggests) the use of two titles
for men is an encumbrance, a remover of certain kinds of liberties, and something
definitely undesirable. So the two suggestions are not equivalent, and if either
were ever to be accepted, the choice of *Ms.* is the probable candidate.

(c) The third question regarding the chances *Ms.* has for real acceptance has,
in effect, already been answered. Until society changes so that the distinction
between married and unmarried women is as unimportant in terms of their social
position as that between married and unmarried men, the attempt in all probability cannot succeed. Like the attempt to substitute any euphemism for an
uncomfortable word, the attempt to do away with *Miss* and *Mrs.* is doomed to
failure if it is not accompanied by a change in society's attitude to what the titles
describe.

Protesters are "Ugly, Stupid"*

JEFFREY HART

It's an interesting question. Why do so many political protesters tend to be, to
put it mildly, physically ugly?

South Africa has been this spring's protest issue on the college campus. At
Princeton, 800 students demanded that the university withdraw its money from
corporations doing business there. A similar number turned out at Harvard, a
much smaller number at Dartmouth, etc.

---

* King Features.

For now, I want to set aside the substance, pro or con, of the investment in South Africa issue.

But it is simply a visual fact that the students and non-students marching in these picket lines with hand-lettered placards are mostly quite unattractive human beings.

First of all, the most casual glance indicates that most of them were not very well endowed by nature to begin with. They are either too fat or too thin, they tend to be strangely proportioned. Often, various features are somehow . . . wrong. They do not stride forth as if they had a valid claim on existence. They shuffle. Some move as if one leg were a couple of inches shorter than the other.

But if nature failed to give most of these people much to work with, they themselves have certainly not improved matters much. Ill-fitting blue jeans seem to be the uniform. Sloppy shirts. Hair looks unkempt, unwashed. They wear a variety of stupid looking shoes. Yuck.

But why is this?

Surely it is not logically excluded that a handsome or beautiful individual might oppose apartheid, hate it, want to do something about it. Why, then, are most of these protesters so . . . unacceptable?

It is possible, at least I here advance the theory, that the real protest of these people shuffling around has nothing much to do with South Africa. Perhaps they are really protesting against what they see when they look in the mirror. Perhaps this is a kind of cosmic protest against the way things, the way they, actually are. Comes the revolution—and, boy, it would take some revolution—they will be attractive human beings.

Their ugliness seems an act of will. Perhaps they think it symbolizes proletarian status, the great unwashed. But, of course, the actual proletariat does not consider itself ugly. The American worker has a collection of Linda Ronstadt records, a motorboat, and a Volvo.

Of course the South Africa protest marchers, most of them, implicitly desire a "socialist" solution there.

Another alternative has not occurred to them. Suppose foreign capital poured into that resource-rich region. Might it not overwhelm the musty 19th Century apartheid system with the economic pressures of modernity, make black workers much too valuable to mistreat? That, at least, is one possibility.

But it has not occurred to these dim types, shuffling along with their tired slogans. They are not only ugly, they are stupid.

A Record of Being Right*

IAN MENZIES

Seventeen years ago Rachel Carson wrote of the dangers of powerful insecticides. Today it's accepted she was right. Environmentalists warned against the dangers of nuclear energy. Three Mile Island underscores that warning. Now the target is offshore oil drilling.

* From the *Boston Globe*, Oct. 4, 1979.

They've been laughed at, taunted and ridiculed, but they haven't faltered. They've been bodily removed, knocked down and jailed but they've come back.

Call them environmentalists, conservationists, preservationists, urbanists, kooks, subversives, whatever . . . the truth is they've been right, their warnings have been justified, their causes sound.

We've seen them march across our screens, in all shapes and sizes, little old ladies in tennis shoes, lean bearded types with orange backpacks, serious-looking young women, couples holding hands and sometimes a child.

Some we haven't seen; they work anonymously, self-protectively.

Some were weaned on Lewis Mumford, some on Jane Jacobs. Some first heard the word from Ralph Nader, some from Barry Commoner or Jacques Cousteau. Some were radicalized by *Silent Spring*, some by Jane Fonda, some by the evidence of their own eyes.

All believe that Small is Beautiful. They've been called the advocates of nogrowth, for the most part unfairly. They believe in growth, but through the employment of man, not the unemployment of machines.

They are not against computers or technology per se, but against being subordinated to them, against a mindless worship of automation which they fear will diminish, dehumanize and, ultimately, if left unchecked, destroy man.

They believe in human scale, in the balance of nature, in the conservation of natural resources, in equal access, in clean air, clean water, a clean livable environment for all.

Richard Nixon, with his "rugged individualism," can't tolerate them, nor can Edward Teller with his H-bomb. Robert Moses fought them in New York, and obviously won, while economist Herman Kahn ("Growth is Good for You") ridicules and mocks them at the drop of an honorarium.

. . . The oil industry hates them. The auto industry fought them. Developers despise them. The nuclear industry arrests them.

Bankers, who once opposed them but are now finding profits in conservation, have become less critical. So also have discriminating developers.

The industries who fear and hate them the most are those that pollute the most, such as the estimated 9000 firms that have been pouring millions of gallons of toxic chemicals into the state's land and rivers for a decade or more.

It's not that all conservationists are angels. There are elitists among them, concerned only with protecting personal privilege; people who talk conservation but who frequently live in expensive walled-in city developments that block access to public places, who would bar others from the nation's beaches and wilderness areas.

But conservationists, who come from many different backgrounds, are, for the most part, egalitarian, and fight for many different causes in many different ways.

Curiously, however, conservationists have never publicly been credited with being right, perhaps because to do so would be to admit that their critics have been wrong.

But the record tells the story. Seventeen years ago Rachel Carson wrote of the dangers of DDT and other powerful insecticides. She was attacked, even by fellow scientists. Today it's accepted she was right.

Twenty years ago environmentalists warned of ever bigger automobiles and multiplying exhaust gases. Detroit laughed. The environmentalists were right. Air pollution now makes Los Angeles unlivable for days at a time. Denver's air quality is deteriorating and so is Boston's.

They warned the country against the dangers of nuclear energy. Three Mile Island underscores that warning. They propose conserving energy by first cutting back on demand and urge that power from atomic fission be used only as a last resort.

Twenty years ago Lewis Mumford decried clustering the urban poor in a new variety of ghetto barracks. He was right. He also warned that more automobiles and bigger expressways would kill cities. He was right.

Conservationists fought against building on our fragile coastal beaches and in flood plain zones. Demolishing storms have proved them right, yet we allow rebuilding at enormous public expense.

Cousteau, Commoner and others warned that the flow of industrial toxic wastes into our rivers and bays would kill our fish. It has. Now, as it gets more deeply into the water table, it's poisoning our fresh water wells.

They've been right. All along the conservationists have been right.

And now they warn that oil drilling on Georges Bank should be a last resort, that protecting the nation's greatest fish hatchery comes first. Why shouldn't they be right again?

LEGAL REASONING

At first sight, it might seem that the pattern of legal reasoning should be simple and straightforward. A legal issue, it might seem, looks like this: A criminal law exists prohibiting a certain kind of behavior and assigning a punishment to those who violate it. A person is accused of violating this law, so a trial is held to decide whether *in fact* he has done so. If the jury decides the facts show that he has, they find him guilty. The judge then hands down the punishment stated in the statute. Or, in a civil suit, one party sues another for breach of contract. Since states have laws governing the formation of contracts, once more a trial is held to decide whether *in fact* a breach of contract (as defined by these statutes) has occurred. If a breach of contract is found, then the judge awards damages as the law prescribes.

Actually, some cases do fall into this simple pattern, but the most interesting ones do not. In order for a case to be settled in this mechanical way, both the law and the facts must be clear. Often they are not. Starting from the side of the law, statutes and regulations are often vague. For example, a law may insist that people show "reasonable care" not to harm the person or property of another. Needless to say, there is no sharp line between conduct that shows reasonable care and conduct that does not. To cite another example, antitrust laws prohibit "combinations in restraint of trade"—a notion that may be widely interpreted. The situation becomes more complicated when we take into account the *common law* tradition of English and American law. A particular decision must be made in the context of past decisions and, as far as possible, be consistent with them. The most obvious difficulty with this is that the past decisions may not be consistent with each other. There can also be conflicts between statutes and the common law, between interpretations of statutes, between different statutes, between jurisdictions. We can add to this the complication that a given case may "fall between the cracks." Human beings have a remarkable ability to produce weird cases that would tax even the wisdom of Solomon.

Turning now to facts, they must be established through testimony, and this testimony can also contain conflicts. In a criminal procedure, the prosecution must establish its case beyond a "reasonable doubt" (another inherently vague expression). In a civil case the situation is different. Although the procedural rules can be very complicated, the general idea is this. The case is won by the party who shows that the *preponderance* of evidence favors his or her side of the case. Although this is a bit too simple, it is sometimes said that if the scales tip ever so slightly in favor of A rather than B, then A wins the case. The complicated rules that govern civil procedures are intended to guarantee that each party has a fair chance to show that the preponderance of evidence falls on his or her side of the case.

Together, the vagueness and conflicts within the *law* and the indeterminacy of *facts* often make it impossible to settle legal disputes in a mechanical way. Of course, vagueness and conflict are not special to the law, and it often happens that available facts are not conclusive. But outside the law, we can often just let matters ride—we can postpone a decision until further facts are established, or even declare that the issues are too vague to admit of any decision. This is rarely an option in a legal case. If A sues B, then either A or B must win. Throwing the case out of court amounts to ruling in favor of the defendant. A decision must be made, and usually in a relatively short period of time. Many legal decisions must be made in a context of vague and perhaps conflicting laws, mixed precedents, and incomplete information—all under the pressure of time.

With all this in mind, we can see why, as Edward Levy has remarked, legal reasoning is *analogical*.[1] By this he does not mean that every argument that takes place in a court of law is analogical, for many of the arguments—perhaps most—are guided by common-sense standards. But given the indeterminacies we have noticed, a legal situation may look like this:

	Laws and precedents favorable to B.
Laws and precedents favorable to A.	

Fact
situation

---

[1] Edward Levi, *An Introduction to Legal Reasoning* (Chicago: University of Chicago Press, 1963). There is no better introduction to the study of legal reasoning than this fine little book.

The attorney for A will try to establish and then stress those facts that
bring the case under laws and precedents favorable to his client's side of
the case. B's attorney will, of course, proceed in the opposite direction.
It is important to see that this debate can take place even when there
is *no* disagreement concerning facts. By stressing certain similarities
and playing down others, each attorney will try to move the case under
those laws and precedents that favor his client's side of the case. Exchanges will often have the following form:

> A: Your honor, may I remind the court that in cases of this kind
> it has always held . . .

> B: Your honor, the case before us is of an entirely different sort
> from those just cited . . .

The pattern of argument here is analogical because the whole point is
to get the court to agree that the particular case is *more like* one line
of cases than another.

Analogy in Legal Reasoning

The analogical aspect of legal reasoning is illustrated by the following
classic case from the law of contracts: *Hawkins v. McGee.* McGee performed an operation on Hawkins that proved unsuccessful, and Hawkins sued for damages. He did not sue on the basis of malpractice, however, but on the basis of breach of contract. His attorney argued that the
doctor initiated a contractual relationship by saying "I will guarantee to
make the hand a hundred percent perfect hand." The attorney for the
surgeon replied that these words, even if uttered, would not be an offer
of a contract, but merely an *expression of strong belief.* The issue before
the court, then, was to decide which is the more plausible way of interpreting this *speech act.* More precisely, the court was asked to rule on
a *question of law* as opposed to a *question of fact.* The question of fact
took the following form:

> Did the defendant make the statement attributed to him?

This is a question appropriately settled by a jury.

> If the doctor did make the statement attributed to him, would
> it amount to an offer of a contract?

This is not a question for a jury, but for a judge, to decide, and if it is
answered No, then the case should have been thrown out of court rather
than sent to the jury. This was the basis for an appeal. The court decided
that the remarks attributed to the doctor could more reasonably be

viewed as an offer of a contract than as an expression of strong belief. It thus rejected the appeal on this question of law and ruled that the lower court was correct in submitting the case to the jury for a determination of the question of fact.[2]

Hawkins v. McGee[*]

BRANCH, J. 1. The operation in question consisted in the removal of a considerable quantity of scar tissue from the palm of the plaintiff's right hand and the grafting of skin taken from the plaintiff's chest in place thereof. The scar tissue was the result of a severe burn caused by contact with an electric wire, which the plaintiff received about nine years before the time of the transactions here involved. There was evidence to the effect that before the operation was performed the plaintiff and his father went to the defendant's office, and that the defendant in answer to the question, "How long will the boy be in the hospital?" replied, "Three or four days, . . . not over four; then the boy can go home and it will be just a few days when he will go back to work with a perfect hand." Clearly this and other testimony to the same effect would not justify a finding that the doctor contracted to complete the hospital treatment in three or four days or that the plaintiff would be able to go back to work within a few days thereafter. The above statements could only be construed as expressions of opinion or predictions as to the probable duration of the treatment and plaintiff's resulting disability, and the fact that these estimates were exceeded would impose no contractual liability upon the defendant. The only substantial basis for the plaintiff's claim is the testimony that the defendant also said before the operation was decided upon, "I will guarantee to make the hand a hundred per cent perfect hand" or "a hundred per cent good hand." The plaintiff was present when these words were alleged to have been spoken, and, if they are to be taken at their face value, it seems obvious that proof of their utterance would establish the giving of a warranty in accordance with his contention.

The defendant argues, however, that even if these words were uttered by him, no reasonable man would understand that they were used with the intention of entering into any "contractual relation whatever," and that they could reasonably be understood only "as his expression in strong language that he believed and expected that as a result of the operation he would give the plaintiff a very good hand." It may be conceded, as the defendant contends, that, before the question of the making of a contract should be submitted to a jury, there is a preliminary question of law for the trial court to pass upon, i.e. "whether the

---

[2] It does not matter that nothing was put in writing. In general, verbal contracts are binding if it can be shown that the verbal agreement did take place. More technically, a signed document is not a contract but evidence of one. A verbal agreement, though sometimes harder to prove, can also be evidence of a contract.

[*] Supreme Court of New Hampshire, 1929, 84 N.H. 114, 146 A. 641.

words could possibly have the meaning imputed to them by the party who founds his case upon a certain interpretation," but it cannot be held that the trial court decided this question erroneously in the present case. It is unnecessary to determine at this time whether the argument of the defendant, based upon "common knowledge of the uncertainty which attends all surgical operations," and the improbability that a surgeon would ever contract to make a damaged part of the human body "one hundred per cent perfect," would, in the absence of countervailing considerations, be regarded as conclusive, for there were other factors in the present case which tended to support the contention of the plaintiff. There was evidence that the defendant repeatedly solicited from the plaintiff's father the opportunity to perform this operation, and the theory was advanced by plaintiff's counsel in cross-examination of defendant that he sought an opportunity to "experiment on skin grafting," in which he had had little previous experience. If the jury accepted this part of plaintiff's contention, there would be a reasonable basis for the further conclusion that, if defendant spoke the words attributed to him, he did so with the intention that they should be accepted at their face value, as an inducement for the granting of consent to the operation by the plaintiff and his father, and there was ample evidence that they were so accepted by them. The question of the making of the alleged contract was properly submitted to the jury.

The Law of Torts

Some of the most complicated legal cases have arisen in the law of torts. A *tort* is defined as a wrongful act (with the exception of those acts involving a breach of contract) for which an injured party can recover damages in a civil action. In an ideally simple situation, A acts in a negligent way that leads directly to an injury to an innocent party, B. B sues and recovers for the injuries resulting from A's action. For example, A throws a bottle out of his car window that strikes and shatters a ceramic deer on B's lawn. B sues A and recovers the cost of replacing his ceramic deer. Here the law squares with our rough-and-ready sense of justice. But cases rarely appear in this ideal form. Consider the following possible changes in this case:

(1) Actually, B threw the bottle at A, who was peacefully and legally sitting in his car, then A threw it back, accidentally shattering B's ceramic deer.

(2) The bottle was, in fact, a Molotov cocktail thrown into the car by a third party, C. A *instinctively* threw it out, shattering B's ceramic deer.

(3) Same as (2), except that it was B who threw the Molotov cocktail into A's car.

(4) Same as (3), but A quite *deliberately* threw the Molotov cocktail at B's ceramic deer as an act of retaliation.

(5) A negligently threw the bottle out of his car window, and it was then carried a half mile by a tornado before landing on and shattering B's ceramic deer.

(6) A negligently threw the bottle out of his car window, but it ricocheted off an illegally driven motorcycle before hitting and shattering B's ceramic deer.

(7) The ceramic deer was a priceless Etruscan sculpture that no reasonable person would leave in his or her yard.

(8) There was an ordinance in the town prohibiting lawn ornaments in yards facing public thoroughfares.

In law schools, a set of examples of this kind is called a *series of hypotheticals.* These hypotheticals introduce variations on the original simple case. The first four form a progression, whereas each of the last four goes off on a tangent of its own. As these hypotheticals become more complex and remote from the original paradigm, our common-sense views of justice no longer yield simple answers and the legal issues themselves become difficult. The examination of such a series of hypotheticals is ideal for studying the law governing a particular area. It also brings out the character of legal reasoning: it is not always a mechanical procedure of applying a set of laws to a set of facts.

These hypothetical cases may seem artificial. In a way they are, and in a way they are not. They are artificial because each hypothetical is intended to isolate a single aspect of the legal situation for special investigation. Genuine cases are rarely this tidy. On the other hand, if it is thought that these hypotheticals are artificial because the facts imagined are bizarre or strange, this is simply a mistake. Cases exist corresponding to each of the hypotheticals listed above, and many genuine cases are even more exotic. Consider the famous case of *Palsgraf v. Long Island Railroad Co.*[3] Helen Palsgraf sued the Long Island Railroad for injuries she received while standing on a platform of one of its stations. The extraordinary set of facts surrounding this case is given at the opening of Chief Justice Cardozo's opinion:

---

[3] Although not the stuff of a Perry Mason television show, the case was one of high legal significance—even drama. Justices Cardozo and Andrews, who wrote the opposing opinions, were distinguished legal figures, and both—quite self-consciously—thought of themselves as making legal history. A fascinating account of the actual development of the case is given in James Noonan, *Justice and the Masks of the Law* (New York: Farrar, Straus and Giroux, 1976).

Palsgraf v. Long Island Railroad Co.*

CARDOZO, C.J. Plaintiff was standing on a platform of defendant's railroad after buying a ticket to go to Rockaway Beach. A train stopped at the station, bound for another place. Two men ran forward to catch it. One of the men reached the platform of the car without mishap, though the train was already moving. The other man, carrying a package, jumped aboard the car, but seemed unsteady as if about to fall. A guard on the car, who had held the door open, reached forward to help him in, and another guard on the platform pushed him from behind. In this act, the package was dislodged, and fell upon the rails. It was a package of small size, about fifteen inches long, and was covered by a newspaper. In fact it contained fireworks, but there was nothing in its appearance to give notice of its contents. The fireworks when they fell exploded. The shock of the explosion threw down some scales at the other end of the platform, many feet away. The scales struck the plaintiff, causing injuries for which she sues.

Helen Palsgraf won her suit in the lower courts, and the Long Island Railroad carried its appeal to the highest court in the State of New York. This court ruled in favor of the Long Island Railroad, reversing the decision of the lower courts by a margin of four to three.

The leading idea of Justice Cardozo's majority opinion is that the conductors in the employ of the Long Island Railroad were in no way negligent *relative to Mrs. Palsgraf.* Presumably their conduct was negligent relative to the person who attempted to board the train. (Among other things, the door should have been closed when the train was in motion; the conductors should have warned the passenger not to board the train; they should not have helped him to do so; etc.) Yet Mrs. Palsgraf was not in the class of the foreseeable victims of this negligence. So as a *matter of law* Cardozo held that Mrs. Palsgraf had no right to recover for her injuries and, speaking for the majority of the court, reversed the decisions of the lower courts, assigning court costs to Mrs. Palsgraf.

The remainder of Cardozo's opinion, with some technical material deleted, follows:

The conduct of the defendant's guard, if a wrong in its relation to the holder of the package, was not a wrong in its relation to the plaintiff, standing far away. Relatively to her it was not negligence at all. Nothing in the situation gave notice that the falling package had in it the potency of peril to persons thus removed. Negligence is not actionable unless it involves the invasion of a legally protected interest, the violation of a right. "Proof of negligence in the air, so to speak, will not do" (Pollock, *Torts* [11th ed.], p. 455; *Martin* v. *Herzog,* 228 N.Y.

* Court of Appeals of New York. 1928, 248 N.Y. 339; 162 N.E. 99.

164, 170; *cf.* Salmond, *Torts* [6th ed.]. p. 24). "Negligence is the absence of care, according to the circumstances" (WILLES, J., in *Vaughan* v. *Taff Vale Ry. Co.*, 5 H. & N. 679; 1 Beven, *Negligence* [4th ed.], 7). The plaintiff as she stood upon the platform of the station might claim to be protected against intentional invasion of her bodily security. Such invasion is not charged. She might claim to be protected against unintentional invasion by conduct involving in the thought of reasonable men an unreasonable hazard that such invasion would ensue. These, from the point of view of the law, were the bounds of her immunity, with perhaps some rare exceptions, survivals for the most part of ancient forms of liability, where conduct is held to be at the peril of the actor. If no hazard was apparent to the eye of ordinary vigilance, an act innocent and harmless, at least to outward seeming, with reference to her, did not take to itself the quality of a tort because it happened to be wrong, though apparently not one involving the risk of bodily insecurity, with reference to some one else. "In every instance before negligence can be predicated of a given act, back of the act must be sought and found a duty to the individual complaining, the observance of which would have averted or avoided the injury." . . . "The ideas of negligence and duty are strictly correlative" (BOWEN, L.J., in *Thomas* v. *Quartermaine*, 18 Q.B.D. 685, 694). The plaintiff sues in her own right for a wrong personal to her, and not as the vicarious beneficiary of a breach of duty to another.

A different conclusion will involve us, and swiftly too, in a maze of contradictions. A guard stumbles over a package which has been left upon a platform. It seems to be a bundle of newspapers. It turns out to be a can of dynamite. To the eye of ordinary vigilance, the bundle is abandoned waste, which may be kicked or trod on with impunity. Is a passenger at the other end of the platform protected by the law against the unsuspected hazard concealed beneath the waste? If not, is the result to be any different, so far as the distant passenger is concerned, when the guard stumbles over a valise which a truckman or a porter has left upon the walk? The passenger far away, if the victim of a wrong at all, has a cause of action, not derivative, but original and primary. His claim to be protected against invasion of his bodily security is neither greater nor less because the act resulting in the invasion is a wrong to another far removed. In this case, the rights that are said to have been invaded, are not even of the same order. The man was not injured in his person nor even put in danger. The purpose of the act, as well as its effect, was to make his person safe. If there was a wrong to him at all, which may very well be doubted, it was a wrong to a property interest only, the safety of his package. Out of this wrong to property, which threatened injury to nothing else, there has passed, we are told, to the plaintiff by derivation or succession a right of action for the invasion of an interest of another order, the right to bodily security. The diversity of interests emphasizes the futility of the effort to build the plaintiff's right upon the basis of a wrong to some one else. The gain is one of emphasis, for a like result would follow if the interests were the same. Even then, the orbit of the danger as disclosed to the eye of reasonable vigilance would be the orbit of the duty. One who jostles one's neighbour in a crowd does not invade the rights of others standing at the outer fringe when the unintended contact casts a bomb upon the ground. The

wrongdoer as to them is the man who carries the bomb, not the one who ex-
plodes it without suspicion of the danger. Life will have to be made over, and
human nature transformed, before prevision so extravagant can be accepted as
the form of conduct, the customary standard to which behaviour must conform.

The argument for the plaintiff is built upon the shifting meanings of such
words as "wrong" and "wrongful", and shares their instability. What the plaintiff must show is "a wrong" to herself, *i.e.*, a violation of her own right, and not
merely a wrong to some one else, nor conduct "wrongful" because unsocial, but
not a "wrong" to any one. We are told that one who drives at reckless speed
through a crowded city street is guilty of a negligent act and, therefore, of a
wrongful one irrespective of the consequences. Negligent the act is, and wrongful in the sense that it is unsocial, but wrongful and unsocial in relation to other
travellers, only because the eye of vigilance perceives the risk of damage. If the
same act were to be committed on a speedway or a race course, it would lose
its wrongful quality. The risk reasonably to be perceived defines the duty to be
obeyed and risk imports relation; it is risk to another or to others within the
range of apprehension. . . . This does not mean, of course, that one who launches
a destructive force is always relieved of liability if the force, though known to
be destructive, pursues an unexpected path. "It was not necessary that the defendant should have had notice of the particular method in which an accident
would occur, if the possibility of an accident was clear to the ordinary prudent
eye". . . . Some acts, such as shooting, are so imminently dangerous to any one
who may come within reach of the missile, however unexpectedly, as to impose
a duty of prevision not far from that of an insurer. Even today, and much oftener
in earlier stages of the law, one acts sometimes at one's peril. . . . Under this
head, it may be, fall certain cases of what is known as transferred intent, an act
wilfully dangerous to A resulting in misadventure in injury to B. . . . These cases
aside, wrong is defined in terms of the natural or probable, at least when unintentional. . . . The range of reasonable apprehension is at times a question for the
court, and at times, if varying inferences are possible, a question for the jury.
Here, by concession, there was nothing in the situation to suggest to the most
cautious mind that the parcel wrapped in newspaper would spread wreckage
through the station. If the guard had thrown it down knowingly and wilfully, he
would not have threatened the plaintiff's safety, so far as appearances could warn
him. His conduct would not have involved, even then, an unreasonable probability of invasion of her bodily security. Liability can be no greater when the act
is inadvertent.

Negligence, like risk, is thus a term of relation. Negligence in the abstract,
apart from things related, is surely not a tort, if indeed it is understandable at
all. . . . Negligence is not a tort unless it results in the commission of a wrong,
and the commission of a wrong imports the violation of a right, in this case, we
are told, the right to be protected against interference with one's bodily security.
But bodily security is protected, not against all forms of interference or aggres-
sion, but only against some. One who seeks redress at law does not make out
a cause of action by showing without more that there has been damage to his
person. If the harm was not wilful, he must show that the act as to him had pos-

siblities of danger so many and apparent as to entitle him to be protected against the doing of it though the harm was unintended. Affront to personality is still the keynote of the wrong. . . .

The law of causation, remote or proximate, is thus foreign to the case before us. The question of liability is always anterior to the question of the measure of the consequences that go with liability. If there is no tort to be redressed, there is no occasion to consider what damage might be recovered if there were a finding of a tort. We may assume, without deciding, that negligence, not at large or in the abstract, but in relation to the plaintiff, would entail liability for any and all consequences, however novel or extraordinary. . . .

The judgment of the Appellate Division and that of the Trial Term should be reversed, and the complaint dismissed, with costs in all courts.

Starting from the same set of facts, Justice Andrews reasons along different lines and comes to the opposite conclusion. He begins by rejecting Cardozo's innovation that recovery be limited (primarily, at least) to people in the class of foreseeable victims of a negligent act. (This portion of Andrews' opinion is not given below.) He then treats the case along the more traditional lines of *proximate cause*. For Andrews, the basic question is whether the connection between the negligent actions and Mrs. Palsgraf's injuries were sufficiently close for the actions to constitute the proximate cause of the injuries. In contrast, Cardozo says that "the law of causation, remote or proximate, is . . . foreign to the case before us." Andrews attempts to explain, through a series of analogies and metaphors, what he understands by a proximate cause.

Although it is clear that Cardozo and Andrews view this case in entirely different ways, it is still not clear why they should arrive at opposing conclusions. (Indeed, as you read Andrews' opinion, you can get the feeling that he is going to come out against Mrs. Palsgraf rather than for her.) His reasoning runs as follows: the problem at hand is one of *drawing a line* between a proximate and a remote cause. This, he argues, cannot be settled as a *matter of law*, so, without either agreeing or disagreeing with the verdict, Andrews concludes that the matter was properly submitted to a jury for determination, and there is no legal basis for overturning its decision.

What is a cause in a legal sense, still more what is a proximate cause, depends in each case upon many considerations, as does the existence of negligence itself. Any philosophical doctrine of causation does not help us. A boy throws a stone into a pond. The ripples spread. The water level rises. The history of that pond is altered to all eternity. It will be altered by other causes also. Yet it will be forever the resultant of all causes combined. Each one will have an influence. How great only omniscience can say. You may speak of a chain, or, if you please, a net. An analogy is of little aid. Each cause brings about future events. Without each the future would not be the same. Each is proximate in the sense it is essential. But that is not what we mean by the word. Nor on the other hand do we mean sole cause. There is no such thing.

Should analogy be thought helpful, however, I prefer that of a stream. The spring, starting on its journey, is joined by tributary after tributary. The river, reaching the ocean, comes from a hundred sources. No man may say whence any drop of water is derived. Yet for a time distinction may be possible. Into the clear creek, brown swamp water flows from the left. Later, from the right comes water stained by its clay bed. The three may remain for a space, sharply divided. But at last inevitably no trace of separation remains. They are so commingled that all distinction is lost.

As we have said, we cannot trace the effect of an act to the end, if end there is. Again, however, we may trace it part of the way. A murder at Serajevo may be the necessary antecedent to an assassination in London twenty years hence. An overturned lantern may burn all Chicago. We may follow the fire from the shed to the last building. We rightly say the fire started by the lantern caused its destruction.

A cause, but not the proximate cause. What we do mean by the word "proximate" is that, because of convenience, of public policy, of a rough sense of justice, the law arbitrarily declines to trace a series of events beyond a certain point. This is not logic. It is practical politics. Take our rule as to fires. Sparks from my burning haystack set on fire my house and my neighbour's. I may recover from a negligent railroad. He may not. Yet the wrongful act as directly harmed the one as the other. We may regret that the line was drawn just where it was, but drawn somewhere it had to be. We said the act of the railroad was not the proximate cause of the neighbour's fire. Cause it surely was. The words we used were simply indicative of our notions of public policy. Other courts think differently. But somewhere they reach the point where they cannot say the stream comes from any one source.

Take the illustration given in an unpublished manuscript by a distinguished and helpful writer on the law of torts. A chauffeur negligently collides with another car which is filled with dynamite, although he could not know it. An explosion follows. A, walking on the sidewalk nearby, is killed. B, sitting in a window of a building opposite is cut by flying glass. C, likewise sitting in a window a block away, is similarly injured. And a further illustration: A nursemaid ten blocks away, startled by the noise, involuntarily drops a baby from her arms to the walk. We are told that C may not recover [damages] but A may. As to B it is a question for court or jury. We will all agree that the baby might not. Because, we are again told, the chauffeur had no reason to believe his conduct involved any risk of injuring either C or the baby. As to them he was not negligent.

But the chauffeur, being negligent in risking the collision, his belief that the scope of the harm he might do would be limited is immaterial. His act unreasonably jeopardized the safety of any one who might be affected by it. C's injury and that of the baby were directly traceable to the collision. Without that, the injury would not have happened. C had the right to sit in his office, secure from such dangers. The baby was entitled to use the sidewalk with reasonable safety.

The true theory is, it seems to me, that the injury to C, if in truth he is to be denied recovery, and the injury to the baby, is that their several injuries were not the proximate result of the negligence. And here not what the chauffeur had reason to believe would be the result of his conduct, but what the prudent would foresee, may have a bearing—may have some bearing, for the problem of proximate cause is not to be solved by any one consideration. It is all a question of expediency. There are no fixed rules to govern our judgment. There are simply matters of which we may take account. We have in a somewhat different connection spoken of "the stream of events". We have asked whether that stream was deflected—whether it was forced into new and unexpected channels: . . . This is rather rhetoric than law. There is in truth little to guide us other than common sense.

There are some hints that may help us. The proximate cause, involved as it may be with many other causes, must be, at the least, something without which the event would not happen. The court must ask itself whether there was a natural and continuous sequence between cause and effect. Was the one a substantial factor in producing the other? Was there a direct connection between them, without too many intervening causes? Is the effect of cause on result not too attenuated? Is the cause likely, in the usual judgment of mankind, to produce the result? Or, by the exercise of prudent foresight, could the result be foreseen? Is the result too remote from the cause, and here we consider remoteness in time and space. . . . Clearly we must so consider, for the greater the distance either in time or space, the more surely do other causes intervene to affect the result. When a lantern is overturned, the firing of a shed is a fairly direct consequence. Many things contribute to the spread of the conflagration—the force of the wind, the direction and width of streets, the character of intervening structures, other factors. We draw an uncertain and wavering line, but draw it we must as best we can.

Once again, it is all a question of fair judgment, always keeping in mind the fact that we endeavour to make a rule in each case that will be practical and in keeping with the general understanding of mankind.

Here another question must be answered. In the case supposed, it is said, and said correctly, that the chauffeur is liable for the direct effect of the explosion although he had no reason to suppose it would follow a collision. "The fact that the injury occurred in a different manner than that which might have been expected does not prevent the chauffeur's negligence from being in law the cause of the injury." But the natural results of a negligent act—the results which a prudent man would or should foresee—do have a bearing upon the decision as to proximate cause. We have said so repeatedly. What should be foreseen? No human foresight would suggest that a collision itself might injure one a block away. On the contrary, given an explosion, such a possibility might be reasonably expected. I think the direct connection, the foresight of which the courts speak, assumes prevision of the explosion, for the immediate results of which, at least, the chauffeur is responsible.

It may be said this is unjust. Why? In fairness he should make good every injury flowing from his negligence. Not because of tenderness toward him we say he need not answer for all that follows his wrong. We look back to the catastrophe, the fire kindled by the spark, or the explosion. We trace the consequences, not indefinitely, but to a certain point. And to aid us in fixing that point we ask what might ordinarily be expected to follow the fire or the explosion.

This last suggestion is the factor which must determine the case before us. The act upon which defendant's liability rests is knocking an apparently harmless package onto the platform. The act was negligent. For its proximate consequences the defendant is liable. If its contents were broken, to the owner; if it fell upon and crushed a passenger's foot, then to him; if it exploded and injured one in the immediate vicinity, to him also as to A in the illustration. Mrs. Palsgraf was standing some distance away. How far cannot be told from the record— apparently 25 to 30 feet, perhaps less. Except for the explosion, she would not have been injured. We are told by the appellant in his brief, "It cannot be denied that the explosion was the direct cause of the plaintiff's injuries." So it was a substantial factor in producing the result—there was here a natural and continuous sequence—direct connection. The only intervening cause was that, instead of blowing her to the ground, the concussion smashed the weighing machine which in turn fell upon her. There was no remoteness in time, little in space. And surely, given such an explosion as here, it needed no great foresight to predict that the natural result would be to injure one on the platform at no greater distance from its scene than was the plaintiff. Just how no one might be able to predict. Whether by flying fragments, by broken glass, by wreckage of machines or structures no one could say. But injury in some form was most probable.

Under these circumstances I cannot say as a matter of law that the plaintiff's injuries were not the proximate result of the negligence. That is all we have before us. The court refused to so charge. No request was made to submit the matter to the jury as a question of fact, even would that have been proper upon the record before us.

The Question of Constitutionality

The most fundamental questions in our legal system concern *constitutionality*. No law may conflict with rights guaranteed by the Constitution. This is an area where disagreement is possible, and the Supreme Court of the United States is the final arbiter of such disagreements. The cases that follow concern the so-called "separate but equal" doctrine that was used to justify racial segregation laws in various states. This doctrine first made its appearance in the Supreme Court in the case of *Plessy v. Ferguson* (1896). Here the Court ruled that a Louisiana statute enforcing the segregation of races in certain forms of public transportation was not unconstitutional. In particular, the Court ruled that this statute did not violate Thirteenth or Fourteenth Amendment guarantees. Justice Brown delivered the opinion of the Court, and Justice Harlan wrote the dissenting opinion. In 1954, in *Brown v. Board of Education*, the Supreme Court considered the doctrine of "separate but equal" as it applied in a different area: *public education*. It concluded that "in the field of public education the doctrine of 'separate but equal' has no place." The Court was unanimous in its decision and Chief Justice Earl Warren wrote the opinion of the Court.

These three opinions differ strikingly in style. Justice Brown's is scholarly and is carefully argued on fairly narrow legal grounds. Justice Harlan's opinion is written from a much broader historical perspective and is infused with moral concern. At first glance, the Warren opinion may seem too casual for a decision of such fundamental historical importance.

Parts of the long opinions of Justices Brown and Harlan have been omitted. The shorter Warren opinion is given almost in its entirety; only the closing instructions concerning implementation are omitted.

Plessy v. Ferguson*

Mr. Justice Brown delivered the opinion of the Court.

This case turns upon the constitutionality of an act of the general assembly of the state of Louisiana, passed in 1890, providing for separate railway carriages for the white and colored races.

The 1st section of the statute enacts "that all railway companies carrying passengers in their coaches in this state shall provide equal but separate accommodations for the white and colored races, by providing two or more passenger coaches for each passenger train, or by dividing the passenger coaches by a partition so as to secure separate accommodations: *Provided*, That this section shall not be construed to apply to street railroads. No person or persons shall be permitted to occupy seats in coaches other than the ones assigned to them, on account of the race they belong to."

By the 2d section it was enacted "that the officers of such passenger trains shall have power and are hereby required to assign each passenger to the coach or compartment used for the race to which such passenger belongs; any passenger insisting on going into a coach or compartment to which by race he does not belong, shall be liable to a fine of $25 or in lieu thereof to imprisonment for a period of not more than twenty days in the parish prison, and any officer of any railroad insisting on assigning a passenger to a coach or compartment other than the one set aside for the race to which said passenger belongs, shall be liable to a fine of $25, or in lieu thereof to imprisonment for a period of not more than twenty days in the parish prison; and should any passenger refuse to occupy the coach or compartment to which he or she is assigned by the officer of such railway, said officer shall have power to refuse to carry such passenger on his train, and for such refusal neither he nor the railway company which he represents shall be liable for damages in any of the courts of this state." . . .

The information filed in the criminal district court charged in substance that Plessy, being a passenger between two stations within the state of Louisiana, was assigned by officers of the company to the coach used for the race to which he belonged, but he insisted upon going into a coach used by the race to

* 163 U.S. 537 1896.

which he did not belong. Neither in the information nor plea was his particular race or color averred.

The petition for the writ of prohibition averred that petitioner was seven eighths Caucasian and one eighth African blood; that the mixture of colored blood was not discernible in him, and that he was entitled to every right, privilege, and immunity secured to citizens of the United States of the white race; and that, upon such theory, he took possession of a vacant seat in a coach where passengers of the white race were accommodated, and was ordered by the conductor to vacate said coach and take a seat in another assigned to persons of the colored race, and having refused to comply with such demand he was forcibly ejected with the aid of a police officer, and imprisoned in the parish jail to answer a charge of having violated the above act.

The constitutionality of this act is attacked upon the ground that it conflicts both with the 13th Amendment of the Constitution, abolishing slavery, and the 14th Amendment, which prohibits certain restrictive legislation on the part of the states.

1. That it does not conflict with the 13th Amendment, which abolished slavery and involuntary servitude, except as a punishment for crime, is too clear for argument. . . .

. . . Indeed, we do not understand that the 13th Amendment is strenuously relied upon by the plaintiff in error in this connection.

2. By the 14th Amendment, all persons born or naturalized in the United States, and subject to the jurisdiction thereof, are made citizens of the United States and of the state wherein they reside; and the states are forbidden from making or enforcing any law which shall abridge the privileges or immunities of citizens of the United States, or shall deprive any person of life, liberty, or property without due process of law, or deny to any person within their jurisdiction the equal protection of the laws. . . .

The object of the amendment was undoubtedly to enforce the absolute equality of the two races before the law, but in the nature of things it could not have been intended to abolish distinctions based upon color, or to enforce social, as distinguished from political, equality, or a commingling of the two races upon terms unsatisfactory to either. Laws permitting, and even requiring their separation in places where they are liable to be brought into contact do not necessarily imply the inferiority of either race to the other, and have been generally, if not universally, recognized as within the competency of the state legislatures in the exercise of their police power. The most common instance of this is connected with the establishment of separate schools for white and colored children, which have been held to be a valid exercise of the legislative power even by courts of states where the political rights of the colored race have been longest and most earnestly enforced. . . .

[Justice Brown next reviews a whole series of cases where statutes similar to the one in question have been upheld as constitutional.]

It is . . . suggested by the learned counsel for the plaintiff in error that the same argument that will justify the state legislature in requiring railways to provide separate accommodations for the two races will also authorize them to require separate cars to be provided for people whose hair is of a certain color, or who are aliens, or who belong to certain nationalities, or to enact laws requiring colored people to walk upon one side of the street, and white people upon the other, or requiring white men's houses to be painted white, and colored men's black, or their vehicles or business signs to be of different colors, upon the theory that one side of the street is as good as the other, or that a house or vehicle of one color is as good as one of another color. The reply to all this is that every exercise of the police power must be reasonable, and extend only to such laws as are enacted in good faith for the promotion of the public good, and not for the annoyance or oppression of a particular class. Thus in *Yick Wo* v. *Hopkins* it was held by this court that a municipal ordinance of the city of San Francisco to regulate the carrying on of public laundries within the limits of the municipality violated the provisions of the Constitution of the United States if it conferred upon the municipal authorities arbitrary power, at their own will, and without regard to discretion, in the legal sense of the term, to give or withhold consent as to persons or places, without regard to the competency of the persons applying, or the propriety of the places selected for the carrying on of the business. It was held to be a covert attempt on the part of the municipality to make an arbitrary and unjust discrimination against the Chinese race. While this was the case of a municipal ordinance a like principle has been held to apply to acts of a state legislature passed in the exercise of the police power.

So far, then, as a conflict with the 14th Amendment is concerned, the case reduces itself to the question whether the statute of Louisiana is a reasonable regulation, and with respect to this there must necessarily be a large discretion on the part of the legislature. In determining the question of reasonableness it is at liberty to act with reference to the established usages, customs, and traditions of the people, and with a view to the promotion of their comfort, and the preservation of the public peace and good order. Gauged by this standard, we cannot say that a law which authorizes or even requires the separation of the two races in public conveyances is unreasonable or more obnoxious to the 14th Amendment than the acts of Congress requiring separate schools for colored children in the District of Columbia, the constitutionality of which does not seem to have been questioned, or the corresponding acts of state legislatures.

We consider the underlying fallacy of the plaintiff's argument to consist in the assumption that the enforced separation of the two races stamps the colored race with a badge of inferiority. If this be so, it is not by reason of anything found in the act, but solely because the colored race chooses to put that construction upon it. The argument necessarily assumes that if, as has been more than once the case, and is not unlikely to be so again, the colored race should become the dominant power in the state legislature, and should enact a law in precisely similar terms, it would thereby relegate the white race to an inferior position. We imagine that the white race, at least, would not acquiesce in this assumption. The argument also assumes that social prejudices may be overcome by legislation, and that equal rights cannot be secured to the negro except by an enforced commingling of the two races. We cannot accept this proposition. If the two races are to meet on terms of social equality, it must be the result of natural affinity, a mutual appreciation of each other's merits and a voluntary consent of individuals. As was said by the court of appeals of New York in *People* v. *Gallagher*, "this end can neither be accomplished nor promoted by laws which conflict with the general sentiment of the community upon whom they are designed to operate. When the government, therefore, has secured to each of its citizens equal rights before the law and equal opportunities for improvement and progress, it has accomplished the end for which it is organized and performed all of the functions respecting social advantages with which it is endowed." Legislation is powerless to eradicate racial instincts or to abolish distinctions based upon physical differences, and the attempt to do so can only result in accentuating the difficulties of the present situation. If the civil and political rights of both races be equal, one cannot be inferior to the other civilly or politically. If one race be inferior to the other socially, the Constitution of the United States cannot put them upon the same plane. . . .

The judgment of the Court below is therefore affirmed.

Mr. Justice Harlan dissenting. . . .

In respect of civil rights, common to all citizens, the Constitution of the United States does not, I think, permit any public authority to know the race of those entitled to be protected in the enjoyment of such rights. Every true man has pride of race, and under appropriate circumstances, when the rights of others, his equals before the law, are not to be affected, it is his privilege to express such pride and to take such action based upon it as to him seems proper. But I deny that any legislative body or judicial tribunal may have regard to the race of citizens when the civil rights of those citizens are involved. Indeed such legislation as that here in question is inconsistent, not only with that equality of rights which pertains to citizenship, national and state, but with the personal liberty enjoyed by every one within the United States.

The 13th Amendment does not permit the withholding or the deprivation of any right necessarily inhering in freedom. It not only struck down the institution of slavery as previously existing in the United States, but it prevents the imposition of any burdens or disabilities that constitute badges of slavery or servitude. It decreed universal civil freedom in this country. This court has so adjudged. But that amendment having been found inadequate to the protection of the rights of those who had been in slavery, it was followed by the 14th Amendment, which added greatly to the dignity and glory of American citizenship, and to the security of personal liberty, by declaring that "all persons born or naturalized in the United States, and subject to the jurisdiction thereof, are citizens of the United States and of the state wherein they reside," and that "no state shall make or enforce any law which shall abridge the privileges or immunities of citizens of the United States; nor shall any state deprive any person of life, liberty, or property without due process of law, nor deny to any person within its jurisdiction the equal protection of the laws." These two amendments, if enforced according to their true intent and meaning, will protect all the civil rights that pertain to freedom and citizenship. . . .

These notable additions to the fundamental law were welcomed by the friends of liberty throughout the world. They removed the race line from our governmental systems. They had, as this court has said, a common purpose, namely, to secure "to a race recently emancipated, a race that through many generations have been held in slavery, all the civil rights that the superior race enjoy." They declared, in legal effect, this court has further said, "that the law in the states shall be the same for the black as for the white; that all persons, whether colored or white, shall stand equal before the laws of the states, and, in regard to the colored race, for whose protection the amendment was primarily designed, that no discrimination shall be made against them by law because of their color." We also said: "The words of the amendment, it is true, are prohibitory, but they contain a necessary implication of a positive immunity, or right, most valuable to the colored race—the right to exemption from unfriendly legislation against them distinctively as colored—exemption from legal discriminations, implying inferiority in civil society, lessening the security of their enjoyment of the rights which others enjoy, and discriminations which are steps toward reducing them to the condition of a subject race." It was consequently adjudged that a state law that excluded citizens of the colored race from juries because of their race and however well qualified in other respects to discharge the duties of jurymen was repugnant to the 14th Amendment. At the present term, referring to the previous adjudications, this court declared that "underlying all of those decisions is the principle that the Constitution of the United States, in its present form, forbids, so far as civil and political rights are concerned, discrimination by the general government or the states against any citizen because of his race. All citizens are equal before the law."

The decisions referred to show the scope of the recent amendments of the Constitution. They also show that it is not within the power of a state to prohibit colored citizens, because of their race, from participating as jurors in the administration of justice.

It was said in argument that the statute of Louisiana does not discriminate against either race, but prescribes a rule applicable alike to white and colored citizens. But this argument does not meet the difficulty. Everyone knows that the statute in question had its origin in the purpose, not so much to exclude white persons from railroad cars occupied by blacks, as to exclude colored people from coaches occupied by or assigned to white persons. Railroad corporations of Louisiana did not make discrimination among whites in the matter of accommodation for travelers. The thing to accomplish was, under the guise of giving equal accommodation for whites and blacks to compel the latter to keep to themselves while traveling in railroad passenger coaches. No one would be so wanting in candor as to assert the contrary. The fundamental objection, therefore, to the statute, is that it interferes with the personal freedom of citizens. "Personal liberty," it has been well said, "consists in the power of locomotion, of changing situation, or removing one's person to whatsoever places one's own inclination may direct, without imprisonment or restraint, unless by due course of law." If a white man and a black man choose to occupy the same public conveyance on a public highway, it is their right to do so, and no government, proceeding alone on grounds of race, can prevent it without infringing the personal liberty of each.

It is one thing for railroad carriers to furnish, or to be required by law to furnish, equal accommodations for all whom they are under a legal duty to carry. It is quite another thing for government to forbid citizens of the white and black races from traveling in the same public conveyance, and to punish officers of railroad companies for permitting persons of the two races to occupy the same passenger coach. If a state can prescribe as a rule of civil conduct, that whites and blacks shall not travel as passengers in the same railroad coach, why may it not so regulate the use of the streets of its cities and towns as to compel white citizens to keep on one side of the street and black citizens to keep on the other? Why may it not, upon like grounds, punish whites and blacks who ride together in street cars or in open vehicles on a public road or street? Why may it not require sheriffs to assign whites to one side of a court-room and blacks to the other? And why may it not also prohibit the commingling of the two races in the galleries of legislative halls or in public assemblages convened for the political questions of the day? Further, if this statute of Louisiana is consistent with the personal liberty of citizens, why may not the state require the separation in railroad coaches of native and naturalized citizens of the United States, or of Protestants and Roman Catholics?

The answer given at the argument to these questions was that regulations of the kind they suggest would be unreasonable, and could not, therefore, stand before the law. Is it meant that the determination of questions of legislative power depends upon the inquiry whether the statute whose validity is questioned is, in the judgment of the courts, a reasonable one, taking all the circumstances into consideration? A statute may be unreasonable merely because a sound public policy forbade its enactment. But I do not understand that the courts have anything to do with the policy or expediency of legislation. A statute may be valid, and yet upon grounds of public policy may well be characterized as unreasonable. Mr. Sedgwick correctly states the rule when he says that the legislative intention being clearly ascertained, "the courts have no other duty to perform than to execute the legislative will, without any regard to their views as to the wisdom or justice of the particular enactment." There is a dangerous tendency in these latter days to enlarge the functions of the courts, by means of judicial interference with the will of the people as expressed by the legislature. Our institutions have the distinguishing characteristic that the three departments of government are co-ordinate and separate. Each must keep within the limits defined by the Constitution. And the courts best discharge their duty by executing the will of the lawmaking power, constitutionally expressed, leaving the results of legislation to be dealt with by the people through their representatives. Statutes must always have a reasonable construction. Sometimes they are to be construed strictly; sometimes literally, in order to carry out the legislative will. But however construed, the intent of the legislature is to be respected, if the particular statute in question is valid, although the courts, looking at the public interests, may conceive the statute to be both unreasonable and impolitic. If the power exists to enact a statute, that ends the matter so far as the courts are concerned. The adjudged cases in which statutes have been held to be void, because unreasonable, are those in which the means employed by the legislature were not at all germane to the end to which the legislature was competent.

The white race deems itself to be the dominant race in this country. And so it is, in prestige, in achievements, in education, in wealth, and in power. So, I doubt not that it will continue to be for all time, if it remains true to its great heritage and holds fast to the principles of constitutional liberty. But in view of the Constitution, in the eye of the law, there is in this country no superior, dominant, ruling class of citizens. There is no caste here. Our Constitution is color-blind, and neither knows nor tolerates classes among citizens. In respect of civil rights, all citizens are equal before the law. The humblest is the peer of the most powerful. The law regards man as man, and takes no account of his surroundings or of his color when his civil rights as guaranteed by the supreme law of the land are involved. It is therefore to be regretted that this high tribunal, the final expositor of the fundamental law of the land, has reached the conclusion that it is competent for a state to regulate the enjoyment by citizens of their civil rights solely upon the basis of race.

In my opinion, the judgment this day rendered will, in time, prove to be quite as pernicious as the decision made by this tribunal in the *Dred Scott Case.* It was adjudged in that case that the descendants of Africans who were imported into this country and sold as slaves were not included nor intended to be included under the word "citizens" in the Constitution, and could not claim any of the rights and privileges which that instrument provided for and secured to citizens of the United States; that at the time of the adoption of the Constitution they were "considered as a subordinate and inferior class of beings, who had been subjugated by the dominant race, and, whether emancipated or not, yet remained subject to their authority, and had no rights or privileges but such as those who held the power and the government might choose to grant them." The recent amendments of the Constitution, it was supposed, had eradicated these principles from our institutions. But it seems that we have yet, in some of the states, a dominant race, a superior class of citizens, which assumes to regulate the enjoyment of civil rights, common to all citizens, upon the basis of race. The present decision, it may well be apprehended, will not stimulate aggressions, more or less brutal and irritating, upon the admitted rights of colored citizens, but will encourage the belief that it is possible, by means of state enactments, to defeat the beneficent purposes which the people of the United States had in view when they adopted the recent amendments of the Constitution, by one of which the blacks of this country were made citizens of the United States and of the states in which they respectively reside and whose privileges and immunities, as citizens, the states are forbidden to abridge. Sixty millions of whites are in no danger from the presence here of eight millions of blacks. The destinies of the two races in this country are indissolubly linked together, and the interests of both require that the common government of all shall not permit the seeds of race hate to be planted under the sanction of law. What can more certainly arouse race hate, what more certainly create and perpetuate a feeling of distrust between these races, than state enactments which in fact proceed on the ground that colored citizens are so inferior and degraded that they cannot be allowed to sit in public coaches occupied by white citizens? That, as all will admit, is the real meaning of such legislation as was enacted in Louisiana. . . .

The arbitrary separation of citizens, on the basis of race, while they are on a public highway, is a badge of servitude wholly inconsistent with the civil freedom and the equality before the law established by the Constitution. It cannot be justified upon any legal grounds.

If evils will result from the commingling of the two races upon public highways established for the benefit of all, they will be infinitely less than those that will surely come from state legislation regulating the enjoyment of civil rights upon the basis of race. We boast of the freedom enjoyed by our people above all other peoples. But it is difficult to reconcile that boast with a state of the law which, practically, puts the brand of servitude and degradation upon a large class of our fellow citizens, our equals before the law. The thin disguise of "equal" accommodations for passengers in railroad coaches will not mislead anyone, or atone for the wrong this day done. . . .

I am of opinion that the statute of Louisiana is inconsistent with the personal liberty of citizens, white and black, in that state, and hostile to both the spirit and letter of the Constitution of the United States. If laws of like character should be enacted in the several states of the Union, the effect would be in the highest degree mischievous. Slavery as an institution tolerated by law would, it is true, have disappeared from our country, but there would remain a power in the states, by sinister legislation, to interfere with the full enjoyment of the blessings of freedom; to regulate civil rights, common to all citizens, upon the basis of race; and to place in a condition of legal inferiority a large body of American citizens, now constituting a part of the political community, called the people of the United States, for whom and by whom, through representatives, our government is administered. Such a system is inconsistent with the guarantee given by the Constitution to each state of a republican form of government, and may be stricken down by congressional action, or by the courts in the discharge of their solemn duty to maintain the supreme law of the land, anything in the Constitution or laws of any state to the contrary notwithstanding.

For the reasons stated, I am constrained to withhold my assent from the opinion and judgment of the majority.

Brown v. Board of Education*

Mr. Chief Justice Warren delivered the opinion of the Court.

These cases come to us from the States of Kansas, South Carolina, Virginia, and Delaware. They are premised on different facts and different local condi-

* 347 U.S. 483 1954.

tions, but a common legal question justifies their consideration together in this consolidated opinion.

In each of the cases, minors of the Negro race, through their legal representatives, seek the aid of the courts in obtaining admission to the public schools of their community on a nonsegregated basis. In each instance, they had been denied admission to schools attended by white children under laws requiring or permitting segregation according to race. This segregation was alleged to deprive the plaintiffs of the equal protection of the laws under the Fourteenth Amendment. In each of the cases other than the Delaware case, a three-judge federal district court denied relief to the plaintiffs on the so-called "separate but equal" doctrine announced by this Court in *Plessy* v. *Ferguson.* Under that doctrine, equality of treatment is accorded when the races are provided substantially equal facilities, even though these facilities be separate. In the Delaware case, the Supreme Court of Delaware adhered to that doctrine, but ordered that the plaintiffs be admitted to the white schools because of their superiority to the Negro schools.

The plaintiffs contend that segregated public schools are not "equal" and cannot be made "equal," and that hence they are deprived of the equal protection of the laws. Because of the obvious importance of the question presented, the Court took jurisdiction. Argument was heard in the 1952 Term, and reargument was heard this Term on certain questions propounded by the Court.

Reargument was largely devoted to the circumstances surrounding the adoption of the Fourteenth Amendment in 1868. It covered exhaustively consideration of the Amendment in Congress, ratification by the states, then existing practices in racial segregation, and the views of proponents and opponents of the Amendment. This discussion and our own investigation convince us that, although these sources cast some light, it is not enough to resolve the problem with which we are faced. At best, they are inconclusive. The most avid proponents of the post-War Amendments undoubtedly intended them to remove all legal distinctions among "all persons born or naturalized in the United States." Their opponents, just as certainly, were antagonistic to both the letter and the spirit of the Amendments and wished them to have the most limited effect. What others in Congress and the state legislatures had in mind cannot be determined with any degree of certainty.

An additional reason for the inconclusive nature of the Amendment's history, with respect to segregated schools, is the status of public education at that time. In the South, the movement toward free common schools, supported by general taxation, had not yet taken hold. Education of white children was largely in the hands of private groups. Education of Negroes was almost non-existent, and practically all of the race were illiterate. In fact, any education of Negroes was forbidden by law in some states. Today, in contrast, many Negroes have achieved outstanding success in the arts and sciences as well as in the business and professional world. It is true that public school education at the time of the Amendment had advanced further in the North, but the effect of the Amendment on Northern States was generally ignored in the congressional debates. Even in the North, the conditions of public education did not approximate those existing today. The curriculum was usually rudimentary; ungraded schools were common in rural areas; the school term was but three months a year in many states; and compulsory school attendance was virtually unknown. As a consequence, it is not surprising that there should be so little in the history of the Fourteenth Amendment relating to its intended effect on public education.

In the first cases in this Court construing the Fourteenth Amendment, decided shortly after its adoption, the Court interpreted it as proscribing all state-imposed discriminations against the Negro race. The doctrine of "separate but equal" did not make its appearance in this Court until 1896 in the case of *Plessy* v. *Ferguson* involving not education but transportation. American courts have since labored with the doctrine for over half a century. In this Court, there have been six cases involving the "separate but equal" doctrine in the field of public education. In *Cumming* v. *County Board of Education* and *Gong Lum* v. *Rice* the validity of the doctrine itself was not challenged. In more recent cases, all on the graduate school level, inequality was found in that specific benefits enjoyed by white students were denied to Negro students of the same educational qualifications. In none of these cases was it necessary to re-examine the doctrine to grant relief to the Negro plaintiff. And in *Sweatt* v. *Painter* the Court expressly reserved decision on the question whether *Plessy* v. *Ferguson* should be held inapplicable to public education.

In the instant cases, that question is directly presented. Here, unlike *Sweatt* v. *Painter*, there are findings below that the Negro and white schools involved have been equalized, or are being equalized, with respect to buildings, curricula, qualifications and salaries of teachers, and other "tangible" factors. Our decision, therefore, cannot turn on merely a comparison of these tangible factors in the Negro and white schools involved in each of the cases. We must look instead to the effect of segregation itself on public education.

In approaching this problem, we cannot turn the clock back to 1868 when the Amendment was adopted, or even to 1896 when *Plessy* v. *Ferguson* was written. We must consider public education in the light of its full development and its present place in American life throughout the Nation. Only in this way can it be determined if segregation in public schools deprives these plaintiffs of the equal protection of the laws.

Today, education is perhaps the most important function of state and local governments. Compulsory school attendance laws and the great expenditures for education both demonstrate our recognition of the importance of education to our democratic society. It is required in the performance of our most basic public responsibilities, even service in the armed forces. It is the very foundation of good citizenship. Today it is a principal instrument in awakening the child to cultural values, in preparing him for later professional training, and in helping him to adjust normally to his environment. In these days, it is doubtful that any child may reasonably be expected to succeed in life if he is denied the opportunity of an education. Such an opportunity, where the state has undertaken to provide it, is a right which must be made available to all on equal terms.

We come then to the question presented: Does segregation of children in public schools solely on the basis of race, even though the physical facilities and other "tangible" factors may be equal, deprive the children of the minority group of equal educational opportunities? We believe that it does.

In *Sweatt* v. *Painter* in finding that a segregated law school for Negroes could not provide them equal educational opportunities, this Court relied in large part on "those qualities which are incapable of objective measurement but which make for greatness in a law school." In *McLaurin* v. *Oklahoma State Regents* the Court, in requiring that a Negro admitted to a white graduate school be treated like all other students, again resorted to intangible considerations: ". . . his ability to study, to engage in discussions and exchange views with other students, and, in general, to learn his profession." Such considerations apply with added force to children in grade and high schools. To separate them from others of similar age and qualifications solely because of their race generates a feeling of inferiority as to their status in the community that may affect their hearts and minds in a way unlikely ever to be undone. The effect of this separation on their educational opportunities was well stated by a finding in the Kansas case by a court which nevertheless felt compelled to rule against the Negro plaintiffs:

> "Segregation of white and colored children in public schools has a detrimental effect upon the colored children. The impact is greater when it has the sanction of the law; for the policy of separating the races is usually interpreted as denoting the inferiority of the negro group. A sense of inferiority affects the motivation of a child to learn. Segregation with the sanction of law, therefore, has a tendency to [retard] the educational and mental development of negro children and to deprive them of some of the benefits they would receive in a racial[ly] integrated school system."

Whatever may have been the extent of psychological knowledge at the time of *Plessy* v. *Ferguson,* this finding is amply supported by modern authority. Any language in *Plessy* v. *Ferguson* contrary to this finding is rejected.

We conclude that in the field of public education the doctrine of "separate but equal" has no place. Separate educational facilities are inherently unequal. Therefore, we hold that the plaintiffs and others similarly situated for whom the actions have been brought are, by reason of the segregation complained of, deprived of the equal protection of the laws guaranteed by the Fourteenth Amendment. . . .

A MORAL DEBATE

Legal reasoning is possible because there is a shared framework of laws, precedents, procedures, etc.; it is interesting and complex because conflicts (and, hence, disagreements) can arise within this framework. A parallel situation exists for moral reasoning except that the potential for disagreement seems even greater. People in our society accept a great many moral principles as a matter of course. If a policy has no other consequence but to produce widespread misery, it is rejected out of hand. We share a conception of justice that includes, among other things, equality of opportunity and equality before the law. Most people have a conception of human dignity: a human being is not merely a thing to be used and disposed of for personal advantage. To the extent that views of this kind are widely shared and generally acknowledged, a moral community exists and moral discussion, including moral *disagreement*, is possible.

The idea that moral disagreement presupposes a system of shared moral principles may seem paradoxical, but it is not. Our moral disagreements typically arise when there is a *conflict* between moral principles, and people are inclined to resolve this conflict in different ways. If a person cannot see the moral difference between eating a carrot and eating his brother-in-law, we will not be able to get on a sufficient footing with him even to disagree. (This does not mean, of course, that cannibalism is always wrong, but even cannibals recognize that human beings are not just a different food.) The most serious and perplexing disagreements take place when people agree on principles such as welfare, justice, and human dignity, and yet, by weighing these principles differently or seeing the situation in a different light, arrive at opposing conclusions. It is a disagreement of this kind that we shall examine in this chapter.

It is important to see that we are not here concerned with *ethical theory*. An ethical theory is an attempt to establish the fundamental principle (or principles) by which actions are judged morally right or wrong. A great many such theories have been developed in the history of philosophy. Each has shed some light into the character of our moral thought, but none has received general acceptance. One such theory, ethical skepticism, holds, in effect, that there are no rational procedures for settling ethical disputes. Perhaps ethical skepticism is true, but until it is shown to be true, it would be foolish to abandon our serious concern with ethical issues. In any case, there is no reason to postpone discussion of special moral problems until agreement arises concerning the correct ethical theory. No one thinks that our courts should go into recess until the basic problems in jurisprudence have been resolved.

The Question of Abortion

The two selections given below concern the moral and, to a lesser extent, the legal issues raised by abortion. This is an area where people often gravitate toward extreme positions and express themselves in extreme language. But between the extremes of abortion on demand and the absolute prohibition of abortion there is a range of positions that generate serious and complex moral argumentation. In her essay, "A Defense of Abortion," Judith Jarvis Thomson defends an extensive (though not absolute) right to abortion. Her argument depends upon stressing the similarities between this disputed right and other human rights that are generally acknowledged. Baruch A. Brody adopts a different standpoint in his essay, "Abortion and the Sanctity of Human Life." He begins with the assumption (which Thomson acknowledges, at least for the sake of argument), that the fetus is a human being with a right to life. He then asks under what circumstances the rights of the pregnant woman should take precedence over the rights of the fetus. His answer is that a woman's right to abortion is extremely limited.

Both arguments bring out the analogical character of moral reasoning in a clear-cut way. They also show that the way in which an issue is raised will have an important influence on an argument. Starting out with the rights of a pregnant woman, Thomson asks when these should be set aside in favor of the acknowledged rights of the fetus. Reasoning from this perspective, she is able to find analogical arguments that support an extensive right to abortion. In contrast, Brody takes the rights of the fetus as his starting point and then challenges those analogical arguments that would deprive the fetus of its right to life. The outcome of this reasoning is that the fetus has an extensive right to life and, therefore, the right to abortion must be very limited.

A Defense of Abortion* [1]

JUDITH JARVIS THOMSON

Most opposition to abortion relies on the premise that the fetus is a human being, a person, from the moment of conception. The premise is argued for, but,
as I think, not well. Take, for example, the most common argument. We are
asked to notice that the development of a human being from conception through
birth into childhood is continuous; then it is said that to draw a line, to choose
a point in this development and say "before this point the thing is not a person,
after this point it is a person" is to make an arbitrary choice, a choice for which
in the nature of things no good reason can be given. It is concluded that the fetus
is, or anyway that we had better say it is, a person from the moment of conception. But this conclusion does not follow. Similar things might be said about the
development of an acorn into an oak tree, and it does not follow that acorns are
oak trees, or that we had better say they are. Arguments of this form are sometimes called "slippery slope arguments"—the phrase is perhaps self-explanatory
—and it is dismaying that opponents of abortion rely on them so heavily and
uncritically.

I am inclined to agree, however, that the prospects for "drawing a line" in
the development of the fetus look dim. I am inclined to think also that we shall
probably have to agree that the fetus has already become a human person well
before birth. Indeed, it comes as a surprise when one first learns how early in
its life it begins to acquire human characteristics. By the tenth week, for example, it already has a face, arms and legs, fingers and toes; it has internal organs,
and brain activity is detectable.[2] On the other hand, I think that the premise is
false, that the fetus is not a person from the moment of conception. A newly fer-
tilized ovum, a newly implanted clump of cells, is no more a person than an
acorn is an oak tree. But I shall not discuss any of this. For it seems to me to
be of great interest to ask what happens if, for the sake of argument, we allow
the premise. How, precisely, are we supposed to get from there to the conclusion
that abortion is morally impermissible? Opponents of abortion commonly spend
most of their time establishing that the fetus is a person, and hardly any time
explaining the step from there to the impermissibility of abortion. Perhaps they
think the step too simple and obvious to require much comment. Or perhaps instead they are simply being economical in argument. Many of those who defend
abortion rely on the premise that the fetus is not a person, but only a bit of tissue that will become a person at birth; and why pay out more arguments than
you have to? Whatever the explanation, I suggest that the step they take is

* *Philosophy and Public Affairs*, Vol. 1, No. 1 (Fall 1971), pp. 47–66.
[1] I am very much indebted to James Thomson for discussion, criticism, and many helpful
suggestions.
[2] Daniel Callahan, *Abortion: Law, Choice and Morality* (New York, 1970), p. 373. This
book gives a fascinating survey of the available information on abortion. The Jewish tradition is surveyed in David M. Feldman, *Birth Control in Jewish Law* (New York, 1968), Part
5, the Catholic tradition in John T. Noonan, Jr., "An Almost Absolute Value in History,"
in *The Morality of Abortion*, ed. John T. Noonan, Jr. (Cambridge, Mass., 1970).

neither easy nor obvious, that it calls for closer examination than it is commonly given, and that when we do give it this closer examination we shall feel inclined to reject it.

I propose, then, that we grant that the fetus is a person from the moment of conception. How does the argument go from here? Something like this, I take it. Every person has a right to life. So the fetus has a right to life. No doubt the mother has a right to decide what shall happen in and to her body; everyone would grant that. But surely a person's right to life is stronger and more stringent than the mother's right to decide what happens in and to her body, and so outweighs it. So the fetus may not be killed; an abortion may not be performed.

It sounds plausible. But now let me ask you to imagine this. You wake up in the morning and find yourself back to back in bed with an unconscious violinist. A famous unconscious violinist. He has been found to have a fatal kidney ailment, and the Society of Music Lovers has canvassed all the available medical records and found that you alone have the right blood type to help. They have therefore kidnapped you, and last night the violinist's circulatory system was plugged into yours, so that your kidneys can be used to extract poisons from his blood as well as your own. The director of the hospital now tells you, "Look, we're sorry the Society of Music Lovers did this to you—we would never have permitted it if we had known. But still, they did it, and the violinist now is plugged into you. To unplug you would be to kill him. But never mind, it's only for nine months. By then he will have recovered from his ailment, and can safely be unplugged from you." Is it morally incumbent on you to accede to this situation? No doubt it would be very nice of you if you did, a great kindness. But do you *have* to accede to it? What if it were not nine months, but nine years? Or longer still? What if the director of the hospital says, "Tough luck, I agree, but you've now got to stay in bed, with the violinist plugged into you, for the rest of your life. Because remember this. All persons have a right to life, and violinists are persons. Granted you have a right to decide what happens in and to your body, but a person's right to life outweighs your right to decide what happens in and to your body. So you cannot ever be unplugged from him." I imagine you would regard this as outrageous, which suggests that something really is wrong with that plausible-sounding argument I mentioned a moment ago.

In this case, of course, you were kidnapped; you didn't volunteer for the operation that plugged the violinist into your kidneys. Can those who oppose abortion on the ground I mentioned make an exception for a pregnancy due to rape? Certainly. They can say that persons have a right to life only if they didn't come into existence because of rape; or they can say that all persons have a right to life, but that some have less of a right to life than others, in particular, that those who came into existence because of rape have less. But these statements have a rather unpleasant sound. Surely the question of whether you have a right to life at all, or how much of it you have, shouldn't turn on the question of whether or not you are the product of a rape. And in fact the people who oppose abortion on the ground I mentioned do not make this distinction, and hence do not make an exception in the case of rape.

Nor do they make an exception for a case in which the mother had to spend the nine months of her pregnancy in bed. They would agree that would be a great pity, and hard on the mother; but all the same all persons have a right to life, the fetus is a person, and so on. I suspect, in fact, that they would not make an exception for a case in which, miraculously enough, the pregnancy went on for nine years or even the rest of the mother's life.

Some won't even make an exception for a case in which continuation of the pregnancy is likely to shorten the mother's life; they regard abortion as impermissible even to save the mother's life. Such cases are nowadays very rare, and many opponents of abortion do not accept this extreme view. All the same, it is a good place to begin: a number of points of interest come out in respect to it.

1. Let us call the view that abortion is impermissible even to save the mother's life "the extreme view." I want to suggest first that it does not issue from the argument I mentioned earlier without the addition of some fairly powerful premises. Suppose a woman has become pregnant, and now learns that she has a cardiac condition such that she will die if she carries the baby to term. What may be done for her? The fetus, being a person, has a right to life, but as the mother is a person too, so has she a right to life. Presumably they have an equal right to life. How is it supposed to come out that an abortion may not be performed? If mother and child have an equal right to life, shouldn't we perhaps flip a coin? Or should we add to the mother's right to life her right to decide what happens in and to her body which everybody seems to be ready to grant— the sum of her rights now outweighing the fetus' right to life?

The most familiar argument here is the following. We are told that performing the abortion would be directly killing[3] the child, whereas doing nothing would not be killing the mother, but only letting her die. Moreover, in killing the child, one would be killing an innocent person, for the child has committed no crime, and is not aiming at his mother's death. And then there are a variety of ways in which this might be continued. (1) But as directly killing an innocent person is always and absolutely impermissible, an abortion may not be performed. Or, (2) as directly killing an innocent person is murder, and murder is always and absolutely impermissible, an abortion may not be performed.[4] Or, (3) as one's duty to refrain from directly killing an innocent person is more stringent than one's duty to keep a person from dying, an abortion may not be performed. Or, (4) if one's only options are directly killing an innocent person or

---

[3] The term "direct" in the arguments I refer to is a technical one. Roughly what is meant by "direct killing" is either killing as an end by itself, or killing as a means to some end, for example, the end of saving someone else's life. See note 6, below, for an example of its use.

[4] Cf. *Encyclical Letter of Pope Pius XI on Christian Marriage*, St. Paul Editions (Boston, n.d.), p. 32: "however much we may pity the mother whose health and even life is gravely imperiled in the performance of the duty allotted to her by nature, nevertheless what could ever be a sufficient reason for excusing in any way the direct murder of the innocent? This is precisely what we are dealing with here." Noonan (*The Morality of Abortion*, p. 43) reads this as follows: "What cause can ever avail to excuse in any way the direct killing of the innocent? For it is a question of that."

letting a person die, one must prefer letting the person die, and thus an abortion may not be performed.[5]

Some people seem to have thought that these are not further premises which must be added if the conclusion is to be reached; but that they follow from the very fact that an innocent person has a right to life.[6] But this seems to me to be a mistake, and perhaps the simplest way to show this is to bring out that while we must certainly grant that innocent persons have a right to life, the theses in (1) through (4) are all false. Take (2), for example. If directly killing an innocent person is murder, and thus is impermissible, then the mother's directly killing the innocent person inside her is murder, and thus is impermissible. But it cannot seriously be thought to be murder if the mother performs an abortion on herself to save her life. It cannot seriously be said that she *must* refrain, that she *must* sit passively by and wait for her death. Let us look again at the case of you and the violinist. There you are, in bed with the violinist, and the director of the hospital says to you, "It's all most distressing, and I deeply sympathize, but you see this is putting an additional strain on your kidneys, and you'll be dead within the month. But you *have* to stay where you are all the same. Because unplugging you would be directly killing an innocent violinist, and that's murder, and that's impermissible." If anything in the world is true, it is that you do not commit murder, you do not do what is impermissible, if you reach around to your back and unplug yourself from that violinist to save your life.

The main focus of attention in writings on abortion has been on what a third party may or may not do in answer to a request from a woman for an abortion. This is in a way understandable. Things being as they are, there isn't much a woman can safely do to abort herself. So the question asked is what a third party may do, and what the mother may do, if it is mentioned at all, is deduced, almost as an afterthought, from what it is concluded that third parties may do. But it seems to me that to treat the matter in this way is to refuse to grant to the mother that very status of person which is so firmly insisted on for the fetus. For we cannot simply read off what a person may do from what a third party may do. Suppose you find yourself trapped in a tiny house with a growing child. I mean a very tiny house, and a rapidly growing child—you are already up against the wall of the house and in a few minutes you'll be crushed to death. The child on the other hand won't be crushed to death; if nothing is done to stop him from growing he'll be hurt, but in the end he'll simply burst open the house

[5] The thesis in (4) is in an interesting way weaker than those in (1), (2), and (3): they rule out abortion even in cases in which both mother *and* child will die if the abortion is not performed. By contrast, one who held the view expressed in (4) could consistently say that one needn't prefer letting two persons die to killing one.
[6] Cf. the following passage from Pius XII, *Address to the Italian Catholic Society of Midwives:* "The baby in the maternal breast has the right to life immediately from God.— Hence there is no man, no human authority, no science, no medical, eugenic, social, economic or moral 'indication' which can establish or grant a valid juridical ground for a direct deliberate disposition of an innocent human life, that is a disposition which looks to its destruction either as an end or as a means in another end perhaps in itself not illicit. The baby, still not born, is a man in the same degree and for the same reason as the mother" (quoted in Noonan, *The Morality of Abortion*, p. 45).

and walk out a free man. Now I could well understand it if a bystander were to say, "There's nothing we can do for you. We cannot choose between your life and his, we cannot be the ones to decide who is to live, we cannot intervene." But it cannot be concluded that you too can do nothing, that you cannot attack it to save your life. However innocent the child may be, you do not have to wait passively while it crushes you to death. Perhaps a pregnant woman is vaguely felt to have the status of house, to which we don't allow the right of self-defense. But if the woman houses the child, it should be remembered that she is a person who houses it.

I should perhaps stop to say explicitly that I am not claiming that people have a right to do anything whatever to save their lives. I think, rather, that there are drastic limits to the right of self-defense. If someone threatens you with death unless you torture someone else to death, I think you have not the right, even to save your life, to do so. But the case under consideration here is very different. In our case there are only two people involved, one whose life is threatened, and one who threatens it. Both are innocent: the one who is threatened is not threatened because of any fault, the one who threatens does not threaten because of any fault. For this reason we may feel that we bystanders cannot intervene. But the person threatened can.

In sum, a woman surely can defend her life against the threat to it posed by the unborn child, even if doing so involves its death. And this shows not merely that the theses in (1) through (4) are false; it shows also that the extreme view of abortion is false, and so we need not canvass any other possible ways of arriving at it from the argument I mentioned at the outset.

2. The extreme view could of course be weakened to say that while abortion is permissible to save the mother's life, it may not be performed by a third party, but only by the mother herself. But this cannot be right either. For what we have to keep in mind is that the mother and the unborn child are not like two tenants in a small house which has, by an unfortunate mistake, been rented to both: the mother *owns* the house. The fact that she does adds to the offensiveness of deducing that the mother can do nothing from the supposition that third parties can do nothing. But it does more than this: it casts a bright light on the supposition that third parties can do nothing. Certainly it lets us see that a third party who says "I cannot choose between you" is fooling himself if he thinks this is impartiality. If Jones has found and fastened on a certain coat, which he needs to keep him from freezing, but which Smith also needs to keep him from freezing, then it is not impartiality that says "I cannot choose between you" when Smith owns the coat. Women have said again and again "This body is *my* body!" and they have reason to feel angry, reason to feel that it has been like shouting into the wind. Smith, after all, is hardly likely to bless us if we say to him, "Of course it's your coat; anybody would grant that it is. But no one may choose between you and Jones who is to have it."

We should really ask what it is that says "no one may choose" in the face of the fact that the body that houses the child is the mother's body. It may be simply a failure to appreciate this fact. But it may be something more interesting, namely the sense that one has a right to refuse to lay hands on people, even where it would be just and fair to do so, even where justice seems to require that somebody do so. Thus justice might call for somebody to get Smith's coat back from Jones, and yet you have a right to refuse to be the one to lay hands on Jones, a right to refuse to do physical violence to him. This, I think, must be granted. But then what should be said is not "no one may choose," but only "*I cannot choose,*" and indeed not even this, but "*I* will not *act,*" leaving it open that somebody else can or should, and in particular that anyone in a position of authority, with the job of securing people's rights, both can and should. So this is no difficulty. I have not been arguing that any given third party must accede to the mother's request that he perform an abortion to save her life, but only that he may.

I suppose that in some views of human life the mother's body is only on loan to her, the loan not being one which gives her any prior claim to it. One who held this view might well think it impartiality to say "I cannot choose." But I shall simply ignore this possibility. My own view is that if a human being has any just, prior claim to anything at all, he has a just, prior claim to his own body. And perhaps this needn't be argued for here anyway, since, as I mentioned, the arguments against abortion we are looking at do grant that the woman has a right to decide what happens in and to her body.

But although they do grant it, I have tried to show that they do not take seriously what is done in granting it. I suggest the same thing will reappear even more clearly when we turn away from cases in which the mother's life is at stake, and attend, as I propose we now do, to the vastly more common cases in which a woman wants an abortion for some less weighty reason than preserving her own life.

3. Where the mother's life is not at stake, the argument I mentioned at the outset seems to have a much stronger pull. "Everyone has a right to life, so the unborn person has a right to life." And isn't the child's right to life weightier than anything other than the mother's own right to life, which she might put forward as ground for an abortion?

This argument treats the right to life as if it were unproblematic. It is not, and this seems to me to be precisely the source of the mistake.

For we should now, at long last, ask what it comes to, to have a right to life. In some views having a right to life includes having a right to be given at least the bare minimum one needs for continued life. But suppose that what in fact *is* the bare minimum a man needs for continued life is something he has no right at all to be given? If I am sick unto death, and the only thing that will save my life is the touch of Henry Fonda's cool hand on my fevered brow, then all the same, I have no right to be given the touch of Henry Fonda's cool hand on my fevered brow. It would be frightfully nice of him to fly in from the West Coast to provide it. It would be less nice, though no doubt well meant, if my friends flew out to the West Coast and carried Henry Fonda back with them. But I have no right at all against anybody that he should do this for me. Or again, to return to the story I told earlier, the fact that for continued life that violinist needs the continued use of your kidneys does not establish that he has a right to be given the continued use of your kidneys. He certainly has no right against you that *you* should give him continued use of your kidneys. For nobody has any right to use your kidneys unless you give him such a right; and nobody has the right against you that you shall give him this right—if you do allow him to go on using your kidneys, this is a kindness on your part, and not something he can claim from you as his due. Nor has he any right against anybody else that *they* should give him continued use of your kidneys. Certainly he had no right against the Society of Music Lovers that they should plug him into you in the first place. And if you now start to unplug yourself, having learned that you will otherwise have to spend nine years in bed with him, there is nobody in the world who must try to prevent you, in order to see to it that he is given something he has a right to be given.

Some people are rather stricter about the right to life. In their view, it does not include the right to be given anything, but amounts to, and only to, the right not to be killed by anybody. But here a related difficulty arises. If everybody is to refrain from killing that violinist then everybody must refrain from doing a great many different sorts of things. Everybody must refrain from slitting his throat, everybody must refrain from shooting him—and everybody must refrain from unplugging you from him. But does he have a right against everybody that they shall refrain from unplugging you from him? To refrain from doing this is to allow him to continue to use your kidneys. It could be argued that he has a right against us that *we* should allow him to continue to use your kidneys. That is, while he had no right against us that we should give him the use of your kidneys, it might be argued that he anyway has a right against us that we shall not now intervene and deprive him of the use of your kidneys. I shall come back to third-party interventions later. But certainly the violinist has no right against you that *you* shall allow him to continue to use your kidneys. As I said, if you do allow him to use them, it is a kindness on your part, and not something you owe him.

The difficulty I point to here is not peculiar to the right to life. It reappears in connection with all the other natural rights; and it is something which an adequate account of rights must deal with. For present purposes it is enough just to draw attention to it. But I would stress that I am not arguing that people do not have a right to life—quite to the contrary, it seems to me that the primary control we must place on the acceptability of an account of rights is that it should turn out in that account to be a truth that all persons have a right to life. I am arguing only that having a right to life does not guarantee having either a right to be given the use of or a right to be allowed continued use of another person's body—even if one needs it for life itself. So the right to life will not serve the opponents of abortion in the very simple and clear way in which they seem to have thought it would.

4. There is another way to bring out the difficulty. In the most ordinary sort of case, to deprive someone of what he has a right to is to treat him unjustly. Suppose a boy and his small brother are jointly given a box of chocolates for Christmas. If the older boy takes the box and refuses to give his brother any of the chocolates, he is unjust to him, for the brother has been given a right to half of them. But suppose that, having learned that otherwise it means nine years in

bed with that violinist, you unplug yourself from him. You surely are not being unjust to him, for you gave him no right to use your kidneys, and no one else can have given him any such right. But we have to notice that in unplugging yourself, you are killing him; and violinists, like everybody else, have a right to life, and thus in the view we were considering just now, the right not to be killed. So here you do what he supposedly has a right you shall not do, but you do not act unjustly to him in doing it.

The emendation which may be made at this point is this: the right to life consists not in the right not to be killed, but rather in the right not to be killed unjustly. This runs a risk of circularity, but never mind: it would enable us to square the fact that the violinist has a right to life with the fact that you do not act unjustly toward him in unplugging yourself, thereby killing him. For if you do not kill him unjustly, you do not violate his right to life, and so it is no wonder you do him no injustice.

But if this emendation is accepted, the gap in the argument against abortion stares us plainly in the face: it is by no means enough to show that the fetus is a person, and to remind us that all persons have a right to life—we need to be shown also that killing the fetus violates its right to life, i.e., that abortion is unjust killing. And is it?

I suppose we may take it as a datum that in a case of pregnancy due to rape the mother has not given the unborn person a right to the use of her body for food and shelter. Indeed, in what pregnancy could it be supposed that the mother has given the unborn person such a right? It is not as if there were un-born persons drifting about the world, to whom a woman who wants a child says "I invite you in."

But it might be argued that there are other ways one can have acquired a right to the use of another person's body than by having been invited to use it by that person. Suppose a woman voluntarily indulges in intercourse, knowing of the chance it will issue in pregnancy, and then she does become pregnant; is she not in part responsible for the presence, in fact the very existence, of the un-born person inside her? No doubt she did not invite it in. But doesn't her partial responsibility for its being there itself give it a right to the use of her body?[7] If so, then her aborting it would be more like the boy's taking away the chocolates, and less like your unplugging yourself from the violinist—doing so would be de-priving it of what it does have a right to, and thus would be doing it an injustice.

And then, too, it might be asked whether or not she can kill it even to save her own life: If she voluntarily called it into existence, how can she now kill it, even in self-defense?

The first thing to be said about this is that it is something new. Opponents of abortion have been so concerned to make out the independence of the fetus, in order to establish that it has a right to life, just as its mother does, that they have tended to overlook the possible support they might gain from making out that the fetus is *dependent* on the mother, in order to establish that she has a

---

[7] The need for a discussion of this argument was brought home to me by members of the Society for Ethical and Legal Philosophy, to whom this paper was originally presented.

special kind of responsibility for it, a responsibility that gives it rights against her which are not possessed by any independent person—such as an ailing violinist who is a stranger to her.

On the other hand, this argument would give the unborn person a right to its mother's body only if her pregnancy resulted from a voluntary act, undertaken in full knowledge of the chance a pregnancy might result from it. It would leave out entirely the unborn person whose existence is due to rape. Pending the availability of some further argument, then, we would be left with the conclusion that unborn persons whose existence is due to rape have no right to the use of their mothers' bodies, and thus that aborting them is not depriving them of anything they have a right to and hence is not unjust killing.

And we should also notice that it is not at all plain that this argument really does go even as far as it purports to. For there are cases and cases, and the details make a difference. If the room is stuffy, and I therefore open a window to air it, and a burglar climbs in, it would be absurd to say, "Ah, now he can stay, she's given him a right to the use of her house—for she is partially responsible for his presence there, having voluntarily done what enabled him to get in, in full knowledge that there are such things as burglars, and that burglars burgle." It would be still more absurd to say this if I had had bars installed outside my windows, precisely to prevent burglars from getting in, and a burglar got in only because of a defect in the bars. It remains equally absurd if we imagine it is not a burglar who climbs in, but an innocent person who blunders or falls in. Again, suppose it were like this: people-seeds drift about in the air like pollen, and if you open your windows, one may drift in and take root in your carpets or upholstery. You don't want children, so you fix up your windows with fine mesh screens, the very best you can buy. As can happen, however, and on very, very rare occasions does happen, one of the screens is defective; and a seed drifts in and takes root. Does the person-plant who now develops have a right to the use of your house? Surely not—despite the fact that you voluntarily opened your windows, you knowingly kept carpets and upholstered furniture, and you knew that screens were sometimes defective. Someone may argue that you are responsible for its rooting, that it does have a right to your house, because after all you *could* have lived out your life with bare floors and furniture, or with sealed windows and doors. But this won't do—for by the same token anyone can avoid a pregnancy due to rape by having a hysterectomy, or anyway by never leaving home without a (reliable!) army.

It seems to me that the argument we are looking at can establish at most that there are *some* cases in which the unborn person has a right to the use of its mother's body, and therefore *some* cases in which abortion is unjust killing. There is room for much discussion and argument as to precisely which, if any. But I think we should side-step this issue and leave it open, for at any rate the argument certainly does not establish that all abortion is unjust killing.

5. There is room for yet another argument here, however. We surely must all grant that there may be cases in which it would be morally indecent to detach a person from your body at the cost of his life. Suppose you learn that what the violinist needs is not nine years of your life, but only one hour: all you need

do to save his life is to spend one hour in that bed with him. Suppose also that letting him use your kidneys for that one hour would not affect your health in the slightest. Admittedly you were kidnapped. Admittedly you did not give anyone permission to plug him into you. Nevertheless it seems to me plain you *ought* to allow him to use your kidneys for that hour—it would be indecent to refuse.

Again, suppose pregnancy lasted only an hour, and constituted no threat to life or health. And suppose that a woman becomes pregnant as a result of rape. Admittedly she did not voluntarily do anything to bring about the existence of a child. Admittedly she did nothing at all which would give the unborn person a right to the use of her body. All the same it might well be said, as in the newly emended violinist story, that she *ought* to allow it to remain for that hour—that it would be indecent in her to refuse.

Now some people are inclined to use the term "right" in such a way that it follows from the fact that you ought to allow a person to use your body for the hour he needs, that he has a right to use your body for the hour he needs, even though he has not been given that right by any person or act. They may say that it follows also that if you refuse, you act unjustly toward him. This use of the term is perhaps so common that it cannot be called wrong; nevertheless it seems to me to be an unfortunate loosening of what we would do better to keep a tight rein on. Suppose that box of chocolates I mentioned earlier had not been given to both boys jointly, but was given only to the older boy. There he sits, stolidly eating his way through the box, his small brother watching enviously. Here we are likely to say "You ought not to be so mean. You ought to give your brother some of those chocolates." My own view is that it just does not follow from the truth of this that the brother has any right to any of the chocolates. If the boy refuses to give his brother any, he is greedy, stingy, callous—but not unjust. I suppose that the people I have in mind will say it does follow that the brother has a right to some of the chocolates, and thus that the boy does act unjustly if he refuses to give his brother any. But the effect of saying this is to obscure what we should keep distinct, namely the difference between the boy's refusal in this case and the boy's refusal in the earlier case, in which the box was given to both boys jointly, and in which the small brother thus had what was from any point of view clear title to half.

A further objection to so using the term "right" that from the fact that A ought to do a thing for B, it follows that B has a right against A that A do it for him, is that it is going to make the question of whether or not a man has a right to a thing turn on how easy it is to provide him with it; and this seems not merely unfortunate, but morally unacceptable. Take the case of Henry Fonda again. I said earlier that I had no right to the touch of his cool hand on my fevered brow, even though I needed it to save my life. I said it would be frightfully nice of him to fly in from the West Coast to provide me with it, but that I had no right against him that he should do so. But suppose he isn't on the West Coast. Suppose he has only to walk across the room, place a hand briefly on my brow—and lo, my life is saved. Then surely he ought to do it, it would be indecent to refuse. Is it to be said "Ah, well, it follows that in this case she has a right to the touch of his hand on her brow, and so it would be an injustice in him to refuse"? So that I have a right to it when it is easy for him to provide it, though no right when it's hard? It's rather a shocking idea that anyone's rights should fade away and disappear as it gets harder and harder to accord them to him.

So my own view is that even though you ought to let the violinist use your kidneys for the one hour he needs, we should not conclude that he has a right to do so—we should say that if you refuse, you are, like the boy who owns all the chocolates and will give none away, self-centered and callous, indecent in fact, but not unjust. And similarly, that even supposing a case in which a woman pregnant due to rape ought to allow the unborn person to use her body for the hour he needs, we should not conclude that he has a right to do so; we should conclude that she is self-centered, callous, indecent, but not unjust, if she refuses. The complaints are no less grave; they are just different. However, there is no need to insist on this point. If anyone does wish to deduce "he has a right" from "you ought," then all the same he must surely grant that there are cases in which it is not morally required of you that you allow that violinist to use your kidneys, and in which he does not have a right to use them, and in which you do not do him an injustice if you refuse. And so also for mother and unborn child. Except in such cases as the unborn person has a right to demand it—and we were leaving open the possibility that there may be such cases—nobody is morally *required* to make large sacrifices, of health, of all other interests and concerns, of all other duties and commitments, for nine years, or even for nine months, in order to keep another person alive.

6. We have in fact to distinguish between two kinds of Samaritan: the Good Samaritan and what we might call the Minimally Decent Samaritan. The story of the Good Samaritan, you will remember, goes like this:

> A certain man went down from Jerusalem to Jericho, and fell among thieves, which stripped him of his raiment, and wounded him, and departed, leaving him half dead.
>
> And by chance there came down a certain priest that way; and when he saw him, he passed by on the other side.
>
> And likewise a Levite, when he was at the place, came and looked on him, and passed by on the other side.
>
> But a certain Samaritan, as he journeyed, came where he was and when he saw him he had compassion on him.
>
> And went to him, and bound up his wounds, pouring in oil and wine, and set him on his own beast, and brought him to an inn, and took care of him.
>
> And on the morrow, when he departed, he took out two pence, and gave them to the host, and said unto him, "Take care of him: and whatsoever thou spendest more, when I come again, I will repay thee."
>
> (Luke 10:30-35)

The Good Samaritan went out of his way, at some cost to himself, to help one in need of it. We are not told what the options were, that is, whether or not the priest and the Levite could have helped by doing less than the Good Samaritan did, but assuming they could have, then the fact they did nothing at all shows they were not even Minimally Decent Samaritans, not because they were not Samaritans, but because they were not even minimally decent.

These things are a matter of degree, of course, but there is a difference, and it comes out perhaps most clearly in the story of Kitty Genovese, who, as you will remember, was murdered while thirty-eight people watched or listened, and did nothing at all to help her. A Good Samaritan would have rushed out to give direct assistance against the murderer. Or perhaps we had better allow that it would have been a Splendid Samaritan who did this, on the ground that it would have involved a risk of death for himself. But the thirty-eight not only did not do this, they did not even trouble to pick up a phone to call the police. Minimally Decent Samaritanism would call for doing at least that, and their not having done it was monstrous.

After telling the story of the Good Samaritan, Jesus said "Go, and do thou likewise." Perhaps he meant that we are morally required to act as the Good Samaritan did. Perhaps he was urging people to do more than is morally required of them. At all events it seems plain that it was not morally required of any of the thirty-eight that he rush out to give direct assistance at the risk of his own life, and that it is not morally required of anyone that he give long stretches of his life—nine years or nine months—to sustaining the life of a person who has no special right (we were leaving open the possibility of this) to demand it.

Indeed, with one rather striking class of exceptions, no one in any country in the world is *legally* required to do anywhere near as much as this for anyone else. The class of exceptions is obvious. My main concern here is not the state of the law in respect to abortion, but it is worth drawing attention to the fact that in no state in this country is any man compelled by law to be even a Minimally Decent Samaritan to any person; there is no law under which charges could be brought against the thirty-eight who stood by while Kitty Genovese died. By contrast, in most states in this country women are compelled by law to be not merely Minimally Decent Samaritans, but Good Samaritans to unborn persons inside them. This doesn't by itself settle anything one way or the other, because it may well be argued that there should be laws in this country—as there are in many European countries—compelling at least Minimally Decent Samaritanism.[8] But it does show that there is a gross injustice in the existing state of the law. And it shows also that the groups currently working against liberalization of abortion laws, in fact working toward having it declared unconstitutional for a state to permit abortion, had better start working for the adoption of Good Samaritan laws generally, or earn the charge that they are acting in bad faith.

I should think, myself, that Minimally Decent Samaritan laws would be one thing, Good Samaritan laws quite another, and in fact highly improper. But we

[8] For a discussion of the difficulties involved, and a survey of the European experience with such laws, see *The Good Samaritan and the Law*, ed. James M. Ratcliffe (New York, 1966).

are not here concerned with the law. What we should ask is not whether anybody should be compelled by law to be a Good Samaritan, but whether we must accede to a situation in which somebody is being compelled—by nature, perhaps—to be a Good Samaritan. We have, in other words, to look now at third-party interventions. I have been arguing that no person is morally required to make large sacrifices to sustain the life of another who has no right to demand them, and this even where the sacrifices do not include life itself; we are not morally required to be Good Samaritans or anyway Very Good Samaritans to one another. But what if a man cannot extricate himself from such a situation? What if he appeals to us to extricate him? It seems to me plain that there are cases in which we can, cases in which a Good Samaritan would extricate him. There you are, you were kidnapped, and nine years in bed with that violinist lie ahead of you. You have your own life to lead. You are sorry, but you simply cannot see giving up so much of your life to the sustaining of his. You cannot extricate yourself, and ask us to do so. I should have thought that—in light of his having no right to the use of your body—it was obvious that we do not have to accede to your being forced to give up so much. We can do what you ask. There is no injustice to the violinist in our doing so.

7. Following the lead of the opponents of abortion, I have throughout been speaking of the fetus merely as a person, and what I have been asking is whether or not the argument we began with, which proceeds only from the fetus' being a person, really does establish its conclusion. I have argued that it does not.

But of course there are arguments and arguments, and it may be said that I have simply fastened on the wrong one. It may be said that what is important is not merely the fact that the fetus is a person, but that it is a person for whom the woman has a special kind of responsibility issuing from the fact that she is its mother. And it might be argued that all my analogies are therefore irrelevant → for you do not have that special kind of responsibility for that violinist, Henry Fonda does not have that special kind of responsibility for me. And our attention might be drawn to the fact that men and women both *are* compelled by law to provide support for their children.

I have in effect dealt (briefly) with this argument in section 4 above; but a (still briefer) recapitulation now may be in order. Surely we do not have any such "special responsibility" for a person unless we have assumed it, explicitly or implicitly. If a set of parents do not try to prevent pregnancy, do not obtain an abortion, and then at the time of birth of the child do not put it out for adoption, but rather take it home with them, then they have assumed responsibility for it, they have given it rights, and they cannot *now* withdraw support from it at the cost of its life because they now find it difficult to go on providing for it. But if they have taken all reasonable precautions against having a child, they do not simply by virtue of their biological relationship to the child who comes into existence have a special responsibility for it. They may wish to assume responsibility for it, or they may not wish to. And I am suggesting that if assuming responsibility for it would require large sacrifices, then they may refuse. A Good Samaritan would not refuse—or anyway, a Splendid Samaritan, if the sacrifices that had to be made were enormous. But then so would a Good Samaritan assume responsibility for that violinist; so would Henry Fonda, if he is a Good Samaritan, fly in from the West Coast and assume responsibility for me.

8. My argument will be found unsatisfactory on two counts by many of those who want to regard abortion as morally permissible. First, while I do argue that abortion is not impermissible, I do not argue that it is always permissible. There may well be cases in which carrying the child to term requires only Minimally Decent Samaritanism of the mother, and this is a standard we must not fall below. I am inclined to think it a merit of my account precisely that it does *not* give a general yes or a general no. It allows for and supports our sense that, for example, a sick and desperately frightened fourteen-year-old schoolgirl, pregnant due to rape, may *of course* choose abortion, and that any law which rules this out is an insane law. And it also allows for and supports our sense that in other cases resort to abortion is even positively indecent. It would be indecent in the woman to request an abortion, and indecent in a doctor to perform it, if she is in her seventh month, and wants the abortion just to avoid the nuisance of postponing a trip abroad. The very fact that the arguments I have been drawing attention to treat all cases of abortion, or even all cases of abortion in which the mother's life is not at stake, as morally on a par ought to have made them suspect at the outset.

Secondly, while I am arguing for the permissibility of abortion in some cases, I am not arguing for the right to secure the death of the unborn child. It is easy to confuse these two things in that up to a certain point in the life of the fetus it is not able to survive outside the mother's body; hence removing it from her body guarantees its death. But they are importantly different. I have argued that you are not morally required to spend nine months in bed, sustaining the life of that violinist; but to say this is by no means to say that if, when you unplug yourself, there is a miracle and he survives, you then have a right to turn round and slit his throat. You may detach yourself even if this costs him his life; you have no right to be guaranteed his death by some other means, if unplugging yourself does not kill him. There are some people who will feel dissatisfied by this feature of my argument. A woman may be utterly devastated by the thought of a child, a bit of herself, put out for adoption and never seen or heard of again. She may therefore want not merely that the child be detached from her, but more, that it die. Some opponents of abortion are inclined to regard this as beneath contempt—thereby showing insensitivity to what is surely a powerful source of despair. All the same, I agree that the desire for the child's death is not one which anybody may gratify, should it turn out to be possible to detach the child alive.

At this place, however, it should be remembered that we have only been pretending throughout that the fetus is a human being from the moment of conception. A very early abortion is surely not the killing of a person, and so is not dealt with by anything I have said here.

Abortion and the Sanctity of Human Life*
BARUCH A. BRODY

One of our most fundamental moral intuitions is that, except in the most extreme circumstances, it is wrong to take a human life. This intuition is, however, not very precise, partially because of the vagueness of "extreme circumstances" and partially because of the unclarity about what is a human life. The
problem about abortion is a difficult one just because of this latter unclarity.
There are those who, with good reason, claim that a foetus is a human being the
taking of whose life is, except in the most extreme circumstances, wrong; destroying a foetus, according to this position, is just as wrong as the taking of any
other human life. There are, however, others who claim, with equally good reason, that a foetus is not a human being and that, therefore, its destruction is permissible in many cases in which it would be wrong to take a human life. Because it is so difficult, given the vagueness of "human life," to decide which of
these claims about the foetus is correct, it is very difficult to decide when, if
ever, an abortion is morally[1] permissible.

I should like, in this paper, to consider the following issue: if a foetus is a
human being the destruction of which is as wrong as the taking of any human
life, are there any extreme circumstances in which an abortion would still be
morally permissible? In particular, would it be permissible in order to save the
life of the mother?

There are three reasons for being concerned with this question: (a) it just
may be the case that a foetus is a human being. If so, then an answer to our
question will be the answer to the question as to whether it actually is permissible to perform an abortion in order to save the life of the mother; (b) given that
we do not know whether the foetus is a human being, it would be helpful to
have an answer to our question for if (as seems possible) it is that it would still
be permissible to perform the abortion, then we will at least know that an abortion is permissible in some of the cases in which the need for it is greatest; (c)
a consideration of this issue may shed some light upon what are the extreme circumstances in which it is permissible to take a human life.

I

The most obvious reason for supposing that it is permissible to perform an
abortion in order to save the life of the mother, even though the foetus is a human being, is that such an abortion would be a permissible act of defending oneself. After all, the foetus's continued existence poses a threat to the life of the

* *American Philosophical Quarterly*, Vol. 10, No. 2 (April 1973), pp. 133–40.
[1] This is a question about morals, not about the legal question of whether there should be
laws prohibiting abortion. On that issue, see my "Abortion and the Law," *Journal of Philosophy*, 1971.

mother which she can meet, if necessary, by the taking of the life of the foetus.[2]

This simple argument from the right to kill the pursuer will not do for there is an important difference between the case of an abortion and the normal case of killing the pursuer. In the normal case of killing the pursuer, B is attempting to take A's life and is responsible for that attempt. It is this guilt which, together with the fact that A will die unless B is stopped, seems to justify the taking of B's life. In the case of an abortion, however, the situation is quite different. Leaving aside for now—we shall return to it later on—the question as to whether the foetus is attempting to take the mother's life, we can certainly agree that the foetus is not responsible for such an attempt (if it is occurring), that the foetus is therefore totally innocent, and that the taking of his life cannot therefore be compared to the ordinary case of killing the pursuer.[3]

Let us put this point another way. Consider the following case: there is just enough medicine to keep either A or B alive; B legitimately owns it, and will not give it to A. In this case, the continued existence of B certainly poses a threat to the life of A; A can survive only if B does not survive. Still, one would not say that it is permissible for A to kill B in order to save A's life. Why not? How does this case differ from the ordinary case of killing the pursuer? The simplest answer is that in this case, while B's continued existence poses a threat to the life of A, B is not guilty of attempting to take A's life; he is not even attempting to do so. On the other hand, in the ordinary case of a pursuer, B is guilty of attempting to kill A. Now if we consider the case of a foetus whose continued existence poses a threat to the life of the mother, we see that it is like the medicine-case and not like the ordinary case of killing the pursuer. The foetus does pose a threat to the life of its mother, but it is not guilty of attempting to take its mother's life. Consequently, analogously to the medicine-case, the mother (or her agent) could not justify destroying the foetus on the ground that it is a permissible act of killing the pursuer.

This objection, while persuasive, is not entirely convincing, and something more must be said about the whole matter of pursuers before we can definitely decide whether an abortion to save the life of the mother could be viewed as a permissible act of killing the pursuer. If we look again at a normal pursuer case, we see that there are three factors involved:

(1) the continued existence of B poses a threat to the life of A, a threat that can be met only by the taking of B's life,

---

[2] To be sure, it is the abortionist, and not the mother, who will destroy the fetus, but that is irrelevant. To begin with, in such cases, it is permissible for him whose life is threatened (A) to, if necessary, either take the life of him (B) who threatens him or call upon someone else to do so. And more importantly, it seems permissible (and perhaps even obligatory in some cases) for a third person to take B's life in order to save A's life even if A has not called upon him to do so (we leave aside the question as to whether it is permissible if A objects). For this reason, it seems better to say that it is permissible to take the life of the pursuer, when necessary to save the life of the pursued, rather than to say that it is permissible to take lives, when necessary for self-defense. On this point, see *Talmud Sanhedrin* 72b–75a.

[3] This is, essentially, the argument of Pius XI (in *Casti Connubii*, Section 64).

(2) B is justly attempting to take A's life,

(3) B is responsible for his attempt to take A's life.

In the medicine-case, only condition (1) was satisfied, and our intuitions that it would be wrong for A to take B's life in that case are justified by the fact that the mere satisfaction of (1) does not guarantee that killing B will be a justifiable act of killing a pursuer. But it would be rash to conclude, as we did, that all of conditions (1)-(3) must be satisfied before one has a case in which the killing of B will be a justifiable act of killing a pursuer. What would happen, for example, if conditions (1) and (2), but not (3), were satisfied?

There are good reasons for supposing that the satisfaction of (1) and (2) is sufficient for someone's being justified in taking B's life as an act of killing the pursuer. Consider, for example, a normal case of pursuit (e.g., where B is about to shoot A and the only way in which A can stop him is by killing him first) with the modification that B is a minor who is not responsible for his attempt to take A's life.[4] In this case, conditions (1) and (2) but not (3) are satisfied. Still, despite the fact that (3) is not satisfied, it seems that A may justifiably take B's life because doing so is a permissible act of killing a pursuer. So guilt of the pursuer is not a requirement for legitimate cases of killing the pursuer.[5]

Are there any cases in which the satisfaction of (1) and something weaker than (2) is sufficient for A's justifiably killing B as an act of killing a pursuer? It seems that there are. Consider, for example, the following case: B is about to press a button that apparently turns on a light and there is no reason for him to suspect what is the case, viz., that his doing so will blow up a bomb that will destroy A. Moreover, the only way in which we can stop B and save A's life is by taking B's life (there is no opportunity to warn him, etc.). In such a case, neither conditions (2) nor (3) are satisfied. B is not attempting to take A's life and, *a fortiori*, he is not responsible for, or guilty of, any such attempt. Nevertheless, one is inclined to say that this is still a case in which one would be justified in taking B's life in order to save A's life, that this is a legitimate case of killing a pursuer.

How does this case differ from the medicine-case? Or, to put our question another way, what condition (other than (2)) in addition to (1) is satisfied in this case, but not in the medicine-case, and is such that its satisfaction (together with the satisfaction of (1)) is sufficient to justify our killing B as an act of killing a pursuer? As we think about the two cases, the following idea seems to suggest itself: there is, in this case, some action that B is doing (pressing the button) that results in A's death and which is such that if B knew about this result and still did the action voluntarily he would be to blame for the loss of A's life. In this

---

[4] This point, and its significance, was first pointed out by R. Huna when he said (*Talmud Sanhedrin,* 72b) that a pursuer who is a minor can be stopped even by killing him.

[5] It should be noted that this point wreaks havoc with a very plausible analysis of why we are justified in taking the life of the pursuer. According to this analysis, B's guilt for his attempt to take A's life together with the threat that his continued existence poses for A's life justifies the taking of B's life. Or, to put this analysis another way, B's guilt makes A's life take precedence over B's. We now see that this intuitively plausible analysis cannot be right. After all, in cases where conditions (1) and (2) but not (3) are satisfied, B has incurred no guilt for his attempt to take A's life and his guilt cannot therefore be used to explain why we are justified in taking B's life in order to save A's life.

case, if B knew that A would die if he pressed the button and still pressed it voluntarily, he would be to blame[6] for the loss of A's life. In the medicine-case, on the other hand, there is no such action. It is true that B's refusing to give A the medicine does result in A's death. But even if he knows that and still voluntarily refuses to give A the medicine, he is not to blame for the loss of A's life. A man is not obligated to give up his life to save the life of another person and he is not to blame for the loss of that other person's life when he does refuse to sacrifice himself. It would seem then that it is sufficient, for A to be justified in taking B's life as an act of killing a pursuer, that, in addition to the satisfaction of condition (1), the following condition be satisfied:

(2') B is doing some action that will lead to A's death and is such that if B is a responsible person who did it voluntarily knowing that this result would come about, B will be to blame for the loss of A's life.

To summarize, then, our general discussion of killing the pursuer, we can say that if conditions (1) and (2) or (2') are satisfied, one would be justified in taking B's life in order to save A's life.[7] The satisfaction of (3) is not required.

Let us return now to the problem of abortion and, working with the assumption that the foetus is human, apply these results to the case of the foetus whose continued existence poses a threat to the life of his mother and see whether, in that case, it would be permissible, as an act of killing a pursuer, to abort the foetus in order to save the mother. The first thing that we should note is that our initial objection to the claim that the foetus could be aborted because its abortion is a permissible act of killing a pursuer is mistaken. Our objection was that the foetus is not responsible for any attempt to take the life of the mother, that the foetus is innocent. But that only means that condition (3) is not satisfied and we have seen that the satisfaction of (3) is not necessary.

Is, then, the aborting of a foetus when necessary to save the life of the mother a permissible act of killing a pursuer? Well, in such cases, condition (1) is satisfied, so the only question that we have to consider is whether (2) or (2') is also satisfied. It is clear that (2) is not satisfied. The foetus, after all, has neither the beliefs nor the intentions that would be necessary for any of his actions (if he does act) to be an attempt, on his part, to take the life of his mother. Nor is (2') satisfied. Even if we endow the foetus with the beliefs and intentions of an adult, none of his actions are such that his doing them would result in his being to blame for the loss of his mother's life. The most that he would then be trying to do is to grow to maturity and be born mortally, and even a super-endowed foetus would not, because he tried to do that, be to blame for the resulting loss of his mother's life.[8]

---

[6] He need not be the only one to blame. The person who placed the bomb might also be responsible. All that is required is that he be to blame.

[7] We leave open the question as to whether the satisfaction of either (2) or (2') is necessary.

[8] This is presumably what the Talmud means when (op. cit.) it rejects the justification of its being a killing of a pursuer because "only heaven is pursuing her." The talmudic justification (in Ohalot, 7:2) for abortions in the cases we have been considering is that the foetus does not have the same right to life as an ordinary human being. An examination of that claim, however, lies beyond the scope of this paper.

We conclude, therefore, that the mother cannot justify aborting her foetus, even when its continued existence threatens her life, on the grounds that it is a permissible taking of the life of a pursuer. What we must now consider is the possibility that there could be some other justification for aborting the foetus in that case even if the foetus is human.

II

Are there any cases in which it would be permissible to take one life to save another although they are not cases of killing a pursuer? The following seem to be such cases (even if a bit overdramatic—overdramatic cases are still cases):

(a) By a series of accidents for which no one is to blame, it has come about that the five people in room r_2 and the one person in room r_1 will be blown up by a bomb in the next sixty seconds. The only way to prevent this is to defuse the bomb by blowing up its triggering mechanism which is in room r_1. Unfortunately, this necessarily means that the person in r_1 will also be blown up. He is, however, the only one who will die; if you do nothing, all of the six people in question will die. It does seem that one ought to blow up that triggering mechanism and save those lives even if it does mean taking the life of the person in r_1.

(b) A small village is surrounded by a hostile group of brigands who demand that the villagers kill Joe, an innocent villager whom the brigands dislike. If the villagers do not do this, the brigands threaten to (and the villagers have every reason to believe that they will) destroy the village and everyone in it (including Joe). The village is cut off from outside help and giving in to their demands is the only way to save the village. Again, it does seem that one ought to save the life of the villagers even if it does mean taking Joe's life.

How are we to account for these cases? Why, in these cases, is it permissible (and perhaps even obligatory) to take the life of one person in order to save the life of others? Remember, these are not cases of killing a pursuer; only condition (1) is met in any of them. At least three answers suggest themselves:

(I) In these cases, the person whose life you will be taking is going to die anyway. If you take his life, however, you can save those other lives. Taking his life is an optimal act since no lives are sacrificed and some are gained, and that is why it is okay to take his life. In general, it is permissible to take B's life to save A's life if B is going to die anyway and taking B's life is the only way of saving A's life.

(II) In these cases, it is a question of sacrificing one life to save many other lives. While the life to be sacrificed is tremendously valuable, so are all the lives that can be saved, and when we weigh them, we find that the many lives outweigh the one. This may, of course, seem like a harsh attitude, but it would be even harsher to forget about the many lives you can save by sentimentally refusing to take one life.

In general, it is okay to take B's life to save the lives of A and C (where A ≠ C) if taking B's life is the only way of saving their lives.

(III) In these cases, one does not intend to take the life of anyone; what one is trying to do is to save some lives. The loss of life is an unintended, although certainly foreseen, consequence of a perfectly permissible (and perhaps even obligatory) action. In general, it is okay to do an action that will result in the taking of A's life if you do not intend that result, although it may be foreseen, and the intended results outweigh this unfortunate unintended result.

Of these three accounts, it seems that the third is the least satisfactory. To begin with, it rests upon the dubious distinction between the intended results of an action and the foreseen inevitable consequences of it. Secondly, and perhaps even more seriously, it supposes that the distinction is relevant to the moral evaluation of the action (and not merely the agent). This seems highly questionable. Finally, it does not really handle the second of our cases. When, in that case, the villagers take Joe's life, the taking of Joe's life is precisely what they intend to bring about by, and is not a mere inevitable consequence of, their action. To be sure, it is not the ultimate purpose of their action, but that is irrelevant. So the third account doesn't even explain why it is permissible for them to take Joe's life.

We turn then to the more plausible accounts, (I) and (II). What is the difference between them? The first says that, in our cases, it is permissible to take someone's life just because he will die anyway. The second says that, in our cases, it is permissible to take someone's life because doing that will result in the saving of the most possible lives. These two accounts will, then, disagree in cases where a person would survive if you did not take his life but the taking of his life would result in the saving of many other lives. According to our first account, it would be wrong for you, in such a case, to take that person's life; one cannot sacrifice someone's life to save the life of some other people. According to our second account, however, it would be permissible, in such cases, to kill that person in order to save the other people. After all, one would still be maximizing the number of lives saved.

Once one sees that this is the fundamental difference between the two accounts, one also sees what is wrong with (II). It, in a way, is very much like standard utilitarian theories. Analogously to the utilitarian maximization of happiness, it claims that, in cases like ours, the right action is the one that maximizes the number of human lives saved. And like standard utilitarian theories, it does not do justice to considerations of fairness. We object, on grounds of lack of fairness, to actions that maximize human happiness by making some few people suffer in order that many will be happy. We should similarly object, on the same grounds of lack of fairness, to actions that maximize the number of lives saved by sacrificing some few lives (that would not otherwise be lost) to save a larger number of lives. (I), in contrast, is not open to such objections. It only allows one to take B's life when not taking it won't make a difference, when he will die anyway. In such cases, B is not being treated unfairly, and given that taking his life will save these other lives, it is permissible (and perhaps even obligatory) to do so.

This point emerges even more clearly if we imagine the following two modifications of cases (a) and (b):

(a') By a series of accidents for which no one is to blame, it has come about that the five people in room r_2 (and only they) will be blown up by a bomb in the next sixty seconds. The only way to prevent this is to defuse the bomb by blowing up its triggering mechanism in room r_1, but this means that the single person in room r_1 will die.

(b') A small village is surrounded by a hostile group of brigands who, interested (for their own diabolic reasons) in seeing that the villagers kill an innocent man, demand that the villagers kill Joe. If the villagers do not do this, the brigands threaten to (and the villagers have every reason to believe that they will) kill all of the village leaders (this does *not* include Joe). The village is cut off from outside help and giving in to their demands is the only way to save the village leaders.

The important thing to note here is that, according to (II), we should still blow up the triggering mechanism and the villagers should still kill Joe. After all, it is still a question of taking one life to save others. But this just seems mistaken; the acts in question would be wrong because they would be unfair to the man in r_1 and to Joe. Only account (I) takes this into consideration and says, correctly, that it would be wrong for us, in cases (a') and (b'), to kill the man in r_1, or to kill Joe, although it would be permissible for us to do that in cases (a) and (b). It would seem, therefore, that (I) is to be preferred to (II).

It might be objected that we are introducing, in our objection to (II), an asymmetry between taking lives and saving lives that is not justified. After all, while we have been concerned with the unfairness to the man whose life might be taken by us, we have not, it could be argued, been properly concerned with the unfairness to the men whose lives will be lost if we don't act. Why should their lives be sacrificed in order to spare the life of the other man? Isn't that unfair to them?

In a way, I agree with this objection. I have supposed that there is asymmetry between the two; however, this supposition seems justified. Consider, once more, case (a'). If I destroy the triggering mechanism, then I will not have met an obligation that I have toward the man in room r_1, viz., the obligation not to take his life. And when I try to justify not meeting that obligation by saying that I did so in order to save the lives of some other people, it seems open for someone to object that I am acting unfairly to this man by neglecting this vital obligation I have toward him so that others will benefit. The situation is very different if I don't destroy the triggering mechanism. Then, there is no obligation that I have towards the people in r_2 that I have, unfairly, not met. After all, even if one agrees that a man has an obligation to save the lives of his fellow human beings,[9] that obligation is certainly not present when I can only save their lives by taking other lives. The same point can, of course, be made about (b').

This reply depends, of course, upon the assumption that, in cases like (a') and (b'), the obligation to a man not to take his life remains while the obligation

[9] Even this is unclear. It may only be a good thing that one do it; the claim that there is an obligation is, of course, much stronger than that, and it may be too strong.

towards a man to save his life does not. But this is quite plausible; the former obligation is clearly more important than the latter and is present in a great many cases in which the latter is not. After all, while I am normally under an obligation to another man not to take his life even though this means my losing my own life (and even more so if it only means a worsening in the quality of my life or a loss of all I possess), I certainly am not normally under an obligation [10] to another man to save his life at the cost of my own life (or even at the cost of a significant lowering in the quality of my life or of the loss of all that I possess).

If, then, we agree [11] to accept (I) rather than (II) as our account of why, in the cases that we are considering, it is permissible to take some lives to save others, how, working upon our assumption that the foetus is human, does that affect what we think about the problem of abortion? It seems that its major effect is the following: we have to distinguish two types of cases in which we might want to abort the foetus to save the mother. In one case, if we do nothing, the foetus will survive and the mother will die. Such cases are, of course, only possible at the very end of pregnancy. In such a case, we ought not to abort the foetus, for taking its life to save the life of the mother would be unfair. On the other hand, we may have a case in which, if we do nothing, neither the mother nor the foetus will survive. In such a case, aborting the foetus is not unfair to it, and given the truth of (I), it follows that it is permissible for us to abort it to save the mother if this is the only way to save her. [12]

We seem to have found one case in which, even if we assume that the foetus is a human being entitled to all of the rights to life had by any other human being, it would be permissible to abort the foetus to save the life of its mother. But our argument for this claim depends upon the truth of (I), and since this principle is not unproblematic, we must turn to a further consideration of it.

III

There is a standard objection against (I) that must be considered first. The rationale behind (I) is that, in such cases, everything is gained and nothing is lost by taking the life of the individual in question. From the point of view of lives saved, this seems correct; no additional lives will be lost, and some will be saved, by taking the life of that individual. But aren't there other respects in which something will be lost, in which something bad will have occurred? Won't a murder be committed by you, one that would not otherwise be committed? Therefore, it is simply not true that nothing is lost by taking that person's life.

Proponents of this objection often embellish it with references to the mortal sin that one would commit by this act of murder and to the punishment which

[10] One may suppose, however, that this would be a saintly act. But, especially if one is opposed to suicidal acts or to martyrdom, one may not even suppose this. See, on this point, Zevin's *Le'or HaHalacha* (Tel Aviv: 1957), pp. 14–16.

[11] (1) is, essentially, the opinion of R. Yochanan in (*Jerusalem Talmud, Trumah*, chapter 8) his discussion of the biblical case of Sheva ben Bichri. For a full account of the talmudic debate on that case, see Maimonides, *Laws of the Foundations of the Tora*, 5, 5 and the commentaries on his discussion.

[12] This point was well made in *Responsa Panim Me'irot* (Sulzbach: 1738), vol. III, no. 8.

will be forthcoming as a consequence of this. Such embellishments, like the original objection, rest upon the presupposition that some evil act, viz., an act of murder, has been committed. I turn therefore to a consideration of this presupposition.

One obviously has to distinguish four possible descriptions of A's taking the life of B: (1) A has taken B's life, (2) A has taken the life of an innocent man B, (3) A has taken the life of an innocent man B who is not pursuing A, and (4) A has murdered B. There clearly are cases in which (1) and, as we saw in Section I, (2) are correct descriptions of an action but (4) is not. In a way, the question that we considered in the last section was whether there could be cases in which (3) would be a correct description of an act but (4) would not. The defenders of (1) say that there are such cases; these are the cases in which B would die anyway. The proponents of our objection would deny this. But they cannot assume that their denial is correct in the course of their arguments without being circular. This is, however, precisely what they do. In trying to show that it would be wrong, in such cases, for A to take B's life, they assume that doing that would be murder, that doing that would be an unjustified taking of a human life, and by assuming that, they beg the question.

There are, however, more serious objections to (I), ones that can be met only by modifying that principle, and we turn therefore to a consideration of them. To begin with, whenever one takes B's life to save A's life, B is going to die anyway. It's just a matter of time for all of us. So, as (I) now stands, one can always take someone's life if it is the only way of saving the life of someone else, and this is clearly mistaken. Obviously, we need some condition that is stronger than "B is going to die anyway."

Two suggested modifications of (I) seem plausible. They are:

(I') It is permissible to take B's life to save A's life if B is going to die anyway in a relatively short time and taking B's life is the only way of saving A's life.

(I'') It is permissible to take B's life to save A's life if taking B's life is the only way of saving A's life and, if nothing is done, the same event will cause the death of A and B.

Looking at our examples (a) and (b), we see how these modified principles work. (I') allows for the killing of the man in r_1 because he will die anyway in the next sixty seconds and it allows for the killing of Joe because he will die anyway when (in the near future) the brigands destroy the village. (I'') allows for the killing of the man in r_1, because, if nothing is done, he and the people in r_2 will both be killed by the bomb's explosion and it allows for the killing of Joe because, if nothing is done, he and all of the villagers will be killed in the brigands' destruction of the village. On the other hand, neither (I') nor (I'') will allow us to take the life of any B to save the life of any A when that is the only way to do so. After all, in the normal case, B is not going to die anyway in a relatively short period of time, and, if nothing is done, the event that causes B to die (when he does eventually die) will not be the same event as the one that caused A's death.

In trying to decide between (I') and (I''), it will be helpful if we see more clearly the differences in their implications. A consideration of the following two modifications of our original bombing case helps bring out these differences:

(a'') By a series of accidents for which no one is to blame, it has come about that the five people in room r_2 (and only they) will be blown up by a bomb in the next sixty seconds. The only way to prevent this is to defuse the bomb by blowing up its triggering mechanism in room r_1, but this means that the single person in room r_1 will die; however, he will die anyway from cancer within the next few hours.

(a''') By a series of accidents for which no one is to blame, it has come about that the five people in room r_2 (and only they) will be blown up by a bomb in the next sixty seconds. The only way to prevent this is to defuse the bomb by blowing up its triggering mechanism in room r_1, but this means that the single person in room r_1 will die. If nothing is done, he will be wounded by the explosion of the bomb and will even eventually die from these wounds; however, he will live for a few years leading a restricted life.

(I') allows for the killing of the man in r_1 in case (a'') because he will die anyway in a relatively short time, but it does not allow for the killing of the man in r_1 in case (a''') since he will live on for some years. (I''), on the other hand, allows for the killing of the man in r_1 in case (a''') since, if nothing is done, his death will be caused by the same explosion that kills the people in r_2, but it does not allow for the killing of the man in r_1 in case (a'') since, if nothing is done, his death will be caused by his cancer and not by the explosion that will kill the people in r_2.

Which, if either, of these principles is correct? One thing seems pretty clear. The whole rationale, in cases like the ones we are considering, for taking some life to save others is that he whose life will be taken loses nothing of significance and is not therefore being treated unfairly. But if, as in cases like (a'''), he will live if we do nothing for a considerable amount of time, our taking his life now means that we will have unfairly subjected him to a significant loss. Consequently, the whole rationale for the taking of lives in such cases collapses, and, in cases like (a'''), it would be unfair and wrong to take that person's life. Since, however, (I'') allows for the killing of the man in r_1 in case (a'''), it is mistaken.

We see, then, that the question of how long B is going to live is central to the question as to whether we can kill him to save A. What we must now consider is whether anything else plays a role, and, in particular, whether the nature of the cause of B's death if we do nothing is at all relevant. To put the question another way, is (I') true or must we add to it the additional condition that, if nothing is done, the same event will cause the death of A and B?

It is extremely difficult to answer this question. On the one hand, people (myself, my friends whom I have consulted) have the intuition that this additional requirement is reasonable. For this reason, they are troubled by the idea that it is permissible, in case (a''), to take the life of the man in r_1. On the other hand, this additional requirement is totally unreasonable. After all, if the whole justification for taking a human life in these cases is that nothing is lost by doing so and no one is, therefore, being treated unfairly, then it should be permissible to take that life whenever nothing is lost and no one is treated unfairly. That seems to be the case whenever the person in question will die anyway in the very near future,[13] so why should we be concerned with the nature of the cause of his death if we do nothing? I conclude, therefore, that we should adopt (I'), following here our rationale and not our intuitions.

There are, however, serious problems even with (I'). Consider a case in which both A and B will die in a relatively short time if nothing is done, taking B's life is the only way to save A's life, and taking A's life is the only way to save B's life. According to (I'), it would be permissible for anyone to take B's life in order to save A's life. This, however, seems wrong. Why should B's life be sacrificed to save A's life instead of A's life being sacrificed to save B's? Similarly, according to (I'), it would be permissible for anyone to take A's life in order to save B's. This, too, seems wrong. Why should A's life be sacrificed to save B's life rather than B's life being sacrificed to save A's?

The simplest solution to this problem would be to replace (I') with:

(I''') It is permissible to take B's life to save A's life if B is going to die anyway in a relatively short time, taking B's life is the only way of saving A's life, and taking A's life (or doing anything else) will not save B's life. This, however, will not do, for (I''') does not allow us, in the case we are considering, to save either A or B. We must let them both die since the situation does not favor one over the other. This type of Buridan's Ass conclusion makes (I''') unattractive.

It would seem far better to replace (I') with:

(I'''') It is permissible to take B's life to save A's life if B is going to die anyway in a relatively short time, taking B's life is the only way of saving A's life and either (i) taking A's life (or doing anything else) will not save B's life or (ii) taking A's life (or doing anything else) will save B's life but one has, by a fair random method, determined that one should save A's life rather than B's life.

Notice that (I'''') entails that, in the case we are now considering, one should not, because it is not permissible to, simply take the life of one to save the life of the other. Rather, one should choose whose life is to be saved and whose life is to be sacrificed by a fair random method. The rationale for this is pretty straightforward. When (i) is not the case, we face a choice as to whom we should

---

[13] This point helps to shed light upon what is meant by "in a relatively short time." The important thing is that B should not suffer any significant losses (in terms of unrealized potentialities for the period between the time we take his life and the time at which he would have died anyway) because of the taking of his life. Consequently, we must attend to his expectations for that period as well as to its length. It may, after all, be permissible to take B's life even if, had we done nothing, he would have lived for five years so long as he would live them in a coma. In the case of a person with normal expectations, however, five years would certainly be too long.

save and whose life we should take (and we clearly should take one to save the other), so the only way that we can avoid being unfair is to use a random device to choose for us.

How do these modifications in our original principle, (I), affect the issue of abortion? Well, since (I'''') places even stronger restrictions on the taking of a human life than does (I), it certainly does not allow as permissible any abortions that were not allowed as permissible under (I). But there are some abortions that are, according to (I), permissible but which are not according to (I''''). According to (I), an abortion is always permissible if both the foetus and mother will die if nothing is done and the only way to save the mother is to abort the foetus. According to (I''''), an abortion is permissible only if, in addition to the satisfaction of those conditions, it is the case that the foetus will die in a relatively short time if nothing is done and either there is no way to save the foetus or there is a way but, by a fair random procedure, we have determined that we should save the mother and not the foetus.

I conclude, therefore, that if the foetus is a human being having the same right to life as does any other human being, then the fact that the mother would die otherwise does not justify an abortion unless the very stringent requirements laid down in (I'''') are met.

SCIENTIFIC ARGUMENTS

When scientists praise each other's work, they sometimes say that the analysis of some phenomenon is *elegant, beautiful,* or even *tasteful.* It may seem strange to call a piece of scientific research *tasteful,* but this only shows a misunderstanding of the character of scientific thought. It is a parody of the scientific enterprise to think that it consists simply of amassing huge quantities of data to prove or disprove some hypothesis. Of course, experimental data are the final court of appeal in scientific research, but the point of scientific theory is to make sense out of nature, to explain it, to make it more intelligible. It is in its explanatory power that a theory can be elegant, beautiful, or even tasteful.

The Law of Buoyancy

Our first example of a scientific argument is drawn from the ancient world. It has a famous story attached to it. The ruler of Syracuse was worried that a crown he had purchased was not made of pure gold, but he could think of no way of testing whether baser metals had been mixed with the gold. He turned to the mathematician Archimedes for help. Sitting in the public bath—so the story goes—Archimedes was able to solve this problem by deriving the Law of Buoyancy. He was so excited by this discovery that he went bounding through the streets of Syracuse in his nothing-at-all shouting "Eureka!"—which, by the way, does not mean *"Yippee,"* but *"I have found it."*

The proof itself is a model of elegant scientific reasoning. It not only proves the Law of Buoyancy; it also makes sense out of it, and does so in a very simple way. The proof exploits two fundamental propositions:

(1) The surface of a liquid in a vessel is part of the surface of a sphere with the center of the earth as its center. (Proven as Proposition 1.)

(2) The liquid in two sides of a vessel acts like two sides of a lever. (From Postulate 1.)

You may have to think for a moment to see that this first proposition is true. Think about the surface of a tub of water. It conforms perfectly to the surface of the earth and since the surface of the earth is the surface of a sphere, the surface of the water in the tub is also part of the surface of a sphere. (Notice, by the way, that Archimedes simply takes it as an established fact that the earth is spherical. Contrary to popular belief today, this was well known in the ancient world.) The second proposition depends upon the common sense observation that an object immersed in a liquid exerts a force on that liquid. When an object floats, this force must be balanced by some opposite force. The genius of Archimedes' proof was to look at the problem in terms of these two propositions. After that, everything follows from the most simple geometry.

On Floating Bodies*
ARCHIMEDES

POSTULATE 1.

"Let it be supposed that a fluid is of such a character that, its parts lying evenly and being continuous, that part which is thrust the less is driven along by that which is thrust the more; and that each of its parts is thrust by the fluid which is above it in a perpendicular direction if the fluid be sunk in anything and compressed by anything else."

Proposition 1.

If a surface be cut by a plane always passing through a certain point, and if the section be always a circumference [of a circle] whose centre is the aforesaid point, the surface is that of a sphere.

For, if not, there will be some two lines drawn from the point to the surface which are not equal.

* T. L. Heath, ed., *The Works of Archimedes* (New York: Dover Publications, 1953), pp. 253–59.

Suppose O to be the fixed point, and A, B to be two points on the surface such that OA, OB are unequal. Let the surface be cut by a plane passing through OA, OB. Then the section is, by hypothesis, a circle whose centre is O.

Thus $OA = OB$; which is contrary to the assumption. Therefore the surface cannot but be a sphere.

Proposition 2.

The surface of any fluid at rest is the surface of a sphere whose centre is the same as that of the earth.

Suppose the surface of the fluid cut by a plane through O, the centre of the earth, in the curve $ABCD$.

$ABCD$ shall be the circumference of a circle.

For, if not, some of the lines drawn from O to the curve will be unequal. Take one of them, OB, such that OB is greater than some of the lines from O to the curve and less than others. Draw a circle with OB as a radius. Let it be EBF, which will therefore fall partly within and partly without the surface of the fluid.

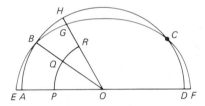

Draw OGH making with OB an angle equal to the angle EOB, and meeting the surface in H and the circle in G. Draw also in the plane an arc of a circle PQR with centre O and within the fluid.

Then the parts of the fluid along PQR are uniform and continuous, and the part PQ is compressed by the part between it and AB, while the part QR is compressed by the part between QR and BH. Therefore the parts along PQ, QR will be unequally compressed, and the part which is compressed the less will be set in motion by that which is compressed the more.

Therefore there will not be rest; which is contrary to the hypothesis.

Hence the section of the surface will be the circumference of a circle whose centre is O; and so will all other sections by planes through O.

Therefore the surface is that of a sphere with centre O.

Proposition 3.

Of solids those which, size for size, are of equal weight with a fluid will, if let down into the fluid, be immersed so that they do not project above the surface but do not sink lower.

If possible, let a certain solid $EFHG$ of equal weight, volume for volume, with the fluid remain immersed in it so that part of it, $EBCF$, projects above the surface.

Draw through O, the centre of the earth, and through the solid a plane cutting the surface of the fluid in the circle $ABCD$.

Conceive a pyramid with vertex O and base a parallelogram at the surface of the fluid, such that it includes the immersed portion of the solid. Let this pyramid be cut by the plane of $ABCD$ in OL, OM. Also let a sphere within the fluid and below GH be described with centre O, and let the plane of $ABCD$ cut this sphere in PQR.

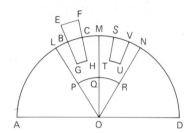

Conceive also another pyramid in the fluid with vertex O, continuous with the former pyramid and equal and similar to it. Let the pyramid so described be cut in OM, ON by the plane of $ABCD$.

Lastly, let $STUV$ be a part of the fluid within the second pyramid equal and similar to the part $BGHC$ of the solid, and let SV be at the surface of the fluid.

Then the pressures on PQ, QR are unequal, that on PQ being the greater. Hence the part at QR will be set in motion by that at PQ, and the fluid will not be at rest; which is contrary to the hypothesis.

Therefore the solid will not stand out above the surface.

Nor will it sink further, because all the parts of the fluid will be under the same pressure.

Proposition 4.

A solid lighter than a fluid will, if immersed in it, not be completely submerged, but part of it will project above the surface.

In this case, after the manner of the previous proposition, we assume the solid, if possible, to be completely submerged and the fluid to be at rest in that position, and we conceive (1) a pyramid with its vertex at O, the centre of the earth, including the solid, (2) another pyramid continuous with the former and equal and similar to it, with the same vertex O, (3) a portion of the fluid within this latter pyramid equal to the immersed solid in the other pyramid, (4) a sphere with centre O whose surface is below the immersed solid and the part of the fluid in the second pyramid corresponding thereto. We suppose a plane to be drawn through the centre O cutting the surface of the fluid in the circle ABC, the solid in S, the first pyramid in OA, OB, the second pyramid in OB, OC, the portion of the fluid in the second pyramid in K, and the inner sphere in PQR.

Then the pressures on the parts of the fluid at PQ, QR are unequal, since

S is lighter than K. Hence there will not be rest; which is contrary to the hypothesis.

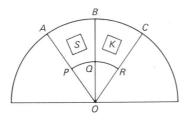

Therefore the solid S cannot, in a condition of rest, be completely submerged.

Proposition 5.

Any solid lighter than a fluid will, if placed in the fluid, be so far immersed that the weight of the solid will be equal to the weight of the fluid displaced.

For let the solid be $EGHF$, and let $BGHC$ be the portion of it immersed when the fluid is at rest. As in Prop. 3, conceive a pyramid with vertex O including the solid, and another pyramid with the same vertex continuous with the former and equal and similar to it. Suppose a portion of the fluid $STUV$ at the base of the second pyramid to be equal and similar to the immersed portion of the solid; and let the construction be the same as in Prop. 3.

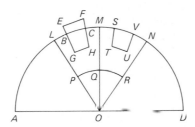

Then, since the pressure on the parts of the fluid at PQ, QR must be equal in order that the fluid may be at rest, it follows that the weight of the portion $STUV$ of the fluid must be equal to the weight of the solid $EGHF$. And the former is equal to the weight of the fluid displaced by the immersed portion of the solid $BGHC$.

Proposition 6.

If a solid lighter than a fluid be forcibly immersed in it, the solid will be driven upwards by a force equal to the difference between its weight and the weight of the fluid displaced.

For let A be completely immersed in the fluid, and let G represent the weight of A, and $(G + H)$ the weight of an equal volume of the fluid. Take a solid D, whose weight is H and add it to A. Then the weight of $(A + D)$ is less than that of an equal volume of the fluid; and, if $(A + D)$ is immersed in the fluid, it will project so that its weight will be equal to the weight of the fluid displaced. But its weight is $(G + H)$.

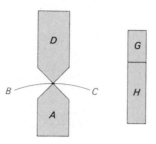

Therefore the weight of the fluid displaced is $(G + H)$, and hence the volume of the fluid displaced is the volume of the solid A. There will accordingly be rest with A immersed and D projecting.

Thus the weight of D balances the upward force exerted by the fluid on A, and therefore the latter force is equal to H, which is the difference between the weight of A and the weight of the fluid which A displaces.

Proposition 7.

A solid heavier than a fluid will, if placed in it, descend to the bottom of the fluid, and the solid will, when weighed in the fluid, be lighter than its true weight by the weight of the fluid displaced.

(1) The first part of the proposition is obvious, since the part of the fluid under the solid will be under greater pressure, and therefore the other parts will give way until the solid reaches the bottom.

(2) Let A be a solid heavier than the same volume of the fluid, and let $(G + H)$ represent its weight, while G represents the weight of the same volume of the fluid.

Take a solid B lighter than the same volume of the fluid, and such that the weight of B is G, while the weight of the same volume of the fluid is $(G + H)$.

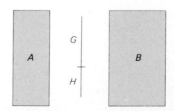

Let A and B be now combined into one solid and immersed. Then, since $(A + B)$ will be of the same weight as the same volume of fluid, both weights being equal to $(G + H) + G$, it follows that $(A + B)$ will remain stationary in the fluid.

Therefore the force which causes A by itself to sink must be equal to the upward force exerted by the fluid on B by itself. This latter is equal to the difference between $(G + H)$ and G [Prop. 6]. Hence A is depressed by a force equal to H, i.e. its weight in the fluid is H, or the difference between $(G + H)$ and G.

Conflicting Scientific Interpretations

Archimedes' derivation of the Law of Buoyancy turns upon the insight that the laws of the lever can be applied to what seems a totally different area. This ability to *extend* a theory through seeing such connections is characteristic of scientific progress. Another type of scientific development is more radical—knowledge is not simply extended, but, instead, one scientific framework is replaced (or largely replaced) by another. In biology, the Germ Theory of Disease and the Theory of Evolution Through Natural Selection are examples of such revolutionary developments. Einstein's Theory of Relativity and the rise of Quantum Mechanics are also revolutionary developments. Indeed, every branch of science has undergone at least one such revolutionary change during the past few centuries.

There are some important differences between scientific progress within a framework and the replacement of one framework by another.[1] In the first place, such changes in framework usually meet with strong resistance. A new conceptual framework will be unfamiliar and hard to understand, and may even seem absurd or unintelligible. Even today, for example, the thought that the earth is spinning on its axis and revolving around the sun seems completely counter to our common-sense view of the world. Also, arguments on behalf of a new framework will be very different from arguments that occur *within* a framework. Disputes over conceptual frameworks cannot be settled by a straightforward appeal to facts. The long debate between Albert Einstein and Niels Bohr concerning Quantum Theory did not turn upon matters of fact, but upon their interpretation. Einstein could not accept the indeterminacy involved in the Quantum Theory's interpretation of the world, and he worked until the end of his life to find some alternative to it. At present, almost no scientist shares Einstein's reservations.

The selection given below illustrates a clash between two such scientific frameworks. It is taken from Galileo's *Dialogue Concerning the Two World Systems—Ptolemaic and Copernican*. The interlocutors are Salviati, Sagredo, and Simplicio. Salviati represents the Copernican system; Simplicio, the Ptolemaic system; Sagredo acts as a moderator, forcing the other two participants in the dialogue to clarify and defend their positions. In attacking the Copernican system, Simplicio lists various

[1] Thomas Kuhn gives prominence to this difference in his important work, *The Structure of Scientific Revolutions*, 2nd ed. (Chicago: University of Chicago Press, 1970).

arguments from Aristotle that are supposed to show that the earth does not move. Some of these arguments are taken, he says:

> from experiments with heavy bodies which, falling from a height, go perpendicularly to the surface of the earth. Similarly, projectiles thrown vertically upward come down again perpendicularly by the same line, even though they have been thrown to immense height. These arguments are necessary proofs that their motion is toward the center of the earth, which, without moving in the least, awaits and receives them.[2]

Salviati replies that these phenomena do not show that the Ptolemaic system is correct and the Copernican system incorrect, since they can be explained in either world system. More generally, Salviati argues that no terrestrial phenomenon—that is, no phenomenon observable on the earth—can be cited to show that one of these systems is true and the other false. For that matter, no celestial phenomena will settle this issue either, since both world systems provide interpretations of the motions of heavenly bodies. That proponents of each of these systems can agree on particular facts yet disagree profoundly on their correct interpretation shows that we are dealing with a conflict between general frameworks, or general world systems. Arguments of this kind are very different from those that take place within a given scientific framework. This is evident at once if we compare Salviati's reply to Simplicio with Archimedes' derivation of the Law of Buoyancy.

Dialogue Concerning the Two World Systems— Ptolemaic and Copernican[*]
GALILEO GALILEI

SALVIATI: Aristotle says, then, that a most certain proof of the earth's being motionless is that things projected perpendicularly upward are seen to return by the same line to the same place from which they were thrown, even though the movement is extremely high. This, he argues, could not happen if the earth moved, since in the time during which the projectile is moving upward and then downward it is separated from the earth, and the place from which the projectile began its motion would go a long way toward the east, thanks to the revolving of the earth, and the falling projectile would strike the earth that distance away from the place in question. Thus we can accommodate here the argument of the

[2] Galileo Galilei, *Dialogue Concerning the Two World Systems—Ptolemaic and Copernican*, Stillman Drake, trans. (Berkeley: University of California Press, 1953), p. 125.
[*] Galileo Galilei, *Dialogue Concerning the Two World Systems—Ptolemaic and Copernican*, Stillman Drake, trans. (Berkeley: University of California Press, 1953), pp. 139–49.

cannon ball as well as the other argument, used by Aristotle and Ptolemy, of seeing heavy bodies falling from great heights along a straight line perpendicular to the surface of the earth. Now, in order to begin to untie these knots, I ask Simplicio by what means he would prove that freely falling bodies go along straight and perpendicular lines directed toward the center, should anyone refuse to grant this to Aristotle and Ptolemy.

SIMPLICIO: By means of the senses, which assure us that the tower is straight and perpendicular, and which show us that a falling stone goes along grazing it, without deviating a hairsbreadth to one side or the other, and strikes at the foot of the tower exactly under the place from which it was dropped.

SALV: But if it happened that the earth rotated, and consequently carried along the tower, and if the falling stone were seen to graze the side of the tower just the same, what would its motion then have to be?

SIMP: In that case one would have to say "its motions," for there would be one with which it went from top to bottom, and another one needed for following the path of the tower.

SALV: The motion would then be a compound of two motions; the one with which it measures the tower, and the other with which it follows it. From this compounding it would follow that the rock would no longer describe that simple straight perpendicular line, but a slanting one, and perhaps not straight.

SIMP: I don't know about its not being straight, but I understand well enough that it would have to be slanting, and different from the straight perpendicular line it would describe with the earth motionless.

SALV: Hence just from seeing the falling stone graze the tower, you could not say for sure that it described a straight and perpendicular line, unless you first assumed the earth to stand still.

SIMP: Exactly so; for if the earth were moving, the motion of the stone would be slanting and not perpendicular.

SALV: Then here, clear and evident, is the paralogism of Aristotle and of Ptolemy, discovered by you yourself. They take as known that which is intended to be proved.

SIMP: In what way? It looks to me like a syllogism in proper form, and not a petitio principii.

SALV: In this way: Does he not, in his proof, take the conclusion as unknown?

SIMP: Unknown, for otherwise it would be superfluous to prove it.

SALV: And the middle term; does he not require that to be known?

SIMP: Of course; [otherwise it would be an attempt to prove *ignotum per aeque ignotum.*]

SALV: Our conclusion, which is unknown and is to be proved; is this not the motionlessness of the earth?

SIMP: That is what it is.

SALV: Is not the middle term, which must be known, the straight and perpendicular fall of the stone?

SIMP: That is the middle term.

SALV: But wasn't it concluded a little while ago that we could not have any knowledge of this fall being straight and perpendicular unless it was first known that the earth stood still? Therefore in your syllogism, the certainty of the middle term is drawn from the uncertainty of the conclusion. Thus you see how, and how badly, it is a paralogism.

SAGREDO: On behalf of Simplicio I should like, if possible, to defend Aristotle, or at least to be better persuaded as to the force of your deduction. You say that seeing the stone graze the tower is not enough to assure us that the motion of the rock is perpendicular (and this is the middle term of the syllogism) unless one assumes the earth to stand still (which is the conclusion to be proved). For if the tower moved along with the earth and the rock grazed it, the motion of the rock would be slanting, and not perpendicular. But I reply that if the tower were moving, it would be impossible for the rock to fall grazing it; therefore, from the scraping fall is inferred the stability of the earth.

SIMP: So it is. For to expect the rock to go grazing the tower if that were carried along by the earth would be requiring the rock to have two natural motions; that is, a straight one toward the center, and a circular one about the center, which is impossible.

SALV: So Aristotle's defense consists in its being impossible, or at least in his having considered it impossible, that the rock might move with a motion mixed of straight and circular. For if he had not held it to be impossible that the stone might move both toward and around the center at the same time, he would have understood how it could happen that the falling rock might go grazing the tower whether that was moving or was standing still, and consequently he would have been able to perceive that this grazing could imply nothing as to the motion or rest of the earth.

Nevertheless this does not excuse Aristotle, not only because if he did have this idea he ought to have said so, it being such an important point in the argument, but also, and more so, because it cannot be said either that such an effect is impossible or that Aristotle considered it impossible. The former cannot be said because, as I shall shortly prove to you, this is not only possible but necessary; and the latter cannot be said either, because Aristotle himself admits that fire moves naturally upward in a straight line and also turns in the diurnal motion which is imparted by the sky to all the element of fire and to the greater part of the air. Therefore if he saw no impossibility in the mixing of straight-upward with circular motion, as communicated to fire and to the air up as far as the moon's orbit, no more should he deem this impossible with regard to the rock's straight-downward motion and the circular motion natural to the entire globe of the earth, of which the rock is a part.

SIMP: It does not look that way to me at all. If the element of fire goes around together with the air, this is a very easy and even a necessary thing for a particle of fire, which, rising high from the earth, receives that very motion in passing through the moving air, being so tenuous and light a body and so easily moved. But it is quite incredible that a very heavy rock or a cannon ball which is dropped without restraint should let itself be budged by the air or by anything else. Besides which, there is the very appropriate experiment of the stone dropped from the top of the mast of a ship, which falls to the foot of the mast when the ship is standing still, but falls as far from that same point when the ship is sailing as the ship is perceived to have advanced during the time of the fall, this being several yards when the ship's course is rapid. . . .

SALV: Tell me, Simplicio: Do you feel convinced that the experiment on the ship squares so well with our purpose that one may reasonably believe that whatever is seen to occur there must also take place on the terrestrial globe?

SIMP: So far, yes; . . .

SALV: Rather, I hope that you will stick to it, and firmly insist that the result on the earth must correspond to that on the ship, so that when the latter is perceived to be prejudicial to your case you will not be tempted to change your mind.

You say, then, that since when the ship stands still the rock falls to the foot of the mast, and when the ship is in motion it falls apart from there, then conversely, from the falling of the rock at the foot it is inferred that the ship stands still, and from its falling away it may be deduced that the ship is moving. And since what happens on the ship must likewise happen on the land, from the falling of the rock at the foot of the tower one necessarily infers the immobility of the terrestrial globe. Is that your argument?

SIMP: That is exactly it, briefly stated, which makes it easy to understand.

SALV: Now tell me: If the stone dropped from the top of the mast when the ship was sailing rapidly fell in exactly the same place on the ship to which it fell when the ship was standing still, what use could you make of this falling with regard to determining whether the vessel stood still or moved?

SIMP: Absolutely none; just as by the beating of the pulse, for instance, you cannot know whether a person is asleep or awake, since the pulse beats in the same manner in sleeping as in waking.

SALV: Very good. Now, have you ever made this experiment of the ship?

SIMP: I have never made it, but I certainly believe that the authorities who adduced it had carefully observed it. Besides, the cause of the difference is so exactly known that there is no room for doubt.

SALV: You yourself are sufficient evidence that those authorities may have offered it without having performed it, for you take it as certain without having done it, and commit yourself to the good faith of their dictum. Similarly it not only may be, but must be that they did the same thing too—I mean, put faith in their predecessors, right on back without ever arriving at anyone who had performed it. For anyone who does will find that the experiment shows exactly the opposite of what is written; that is, it will show that the stone always falls in the same place on the ship, whether the ship is standing still or moving with any speed you please. Therefore, the same cause holding good on the earth as on the ship, nothing can be inferred about the earth's motion or rest from the stone falling always perpendicularly to the foot of the tower.

SIMP: If you had referred me to any other agency than experiment, I think that our dispute would not soon come to an end; for this appears to me to be a thing so remote from human reason that there is no place in it for credulity or probability.

SALV: For me there is, just the same.

SIMP: So you have not made a hundred tests, or even one? And yet you so freely declare it to be certain? I shall retain my incredulity, and my own confidence that the experiment has been made by the most important authors who make use of it, and that it shows what they say it does.

SALV: Without experiment, I am sure that the effect will happen as I tell you, because it must happen that way; and I might add that you yourself also know that it cannot happen otherwise, no matter how you may pretend not to know it—or give that impression. But I am so handy at picking people's brains that I shall make you confess this in spite of yourself. . . .

Now tell me: Suppose you have a plane surface as smooth as a mirror and made of some hard material like steel. This is not parallel to the horizon, but somewhat inclined, and upon it you have placed a ball which is perfectly spherical and of some hard and heavy material like bronze. What do you believe this will do when released? Do you not think, as I do, that it will remain still?

SIMP: If that surface is tilted?

SALV: Yes, that is what was assumed.

SIMP: I do not believe that it would stay still at all; rather, I am sure that it would spontaneously roll down. . . .

SALV: Now how long would the ball continue to roll, and how fast? Remember that I said a perfectly round ball and a highly polished surface, in order to remove all external and accidental impediments. Similarly I want you to take away any impediment of the air caused by its resistance to separation, and all other accidental obstacles, if there are any.

SIMP: I completely understood you, and to your question I reply that the ball would continue to move indefinitely, as far as the slope of the surface extended, and with a continually accelerated motion. For such is the nature of heavy bodies, which *vires acquirunt eundo*; and the greater the slope, the greater would be the velocity.

SALV: But if one wanted the ball to move upward on this same surface, do you think it would go?

SIMP: Not spontaneously, no; but drawn or thrown forcibly, it would.

SALV: And if it were thrust along with some impetus impressed forcibly upon it, what would its motion be, and how great?

SIMP: The motion would constantly slow down and be retarded, being contrary to nature, and would be of longer or shorter duration according to the greater or lesser impulse and the lesser or greater slope upward.

SALV: Very well; up to this point you have explained to me the events of motion upon two different planes. On the downward inclined plane, the heavy moving body spontaneously descends and continually accelerates, and to keep it at rest requires the use of force. On the upward slope, force is needed to thrust it along or even to hold it still, and motion which is impressed upon it continually diminishes until it is entirely annihilated. You say also that a difference in the two instances arises from the greater or lesser upward or downward slope of the plane, so that from a greater slope downward there follows a greater speed, while on the contrary upon the upward slope a given movable body thrown with a given force moves farther according as the slope is less.

Now tell me what would happen to the same movable body placed upon a surface with no slope upward or downward.

SIMP: Here I must think a moment about my reply. There being no downward slope, there can be no natural tendency toward motion; and there being no upward slope, there can be no resistance to being moved, so there would be an indifference between the propensity and the resistance to motion. Therefore it seems to me that it ought naturally to remain stable. But I forgot; it was not so very long ago that Sagredo gave me to understand that this is what would happen.

SALV: I believe it would do so if one set the ball down firmly. But what would happen if it were given an impetus in any direction?

SIMP: It must follow that it would move in that direction.

SALV: But with what sort of movement? One continually accelerated, as on the downward plane, or increasingly retarded as on the upward one?

SIMP: I cannot see any cause for acceleration or deceleration, there being no slope upward or downward.

SALV: Exactly so. But if there is no cause for the ball's retardation, there ought to be still less for its coming to rest; so how far would you have the ball continue to move?

SIMP: As far as the extension of the surface continued without rising or falling.

SALV: Then if such a space were unbounded, the motion on it would likewise be boundless? That is, perpetual?

SIMP: It seems so to me, if the movable body were of durable material.

SALV: That is of course assumed, since we said that all external and accidental impediments were to be removed, and any fragility on the part of the moving body would in this case be one of the accidental impediments.

Now tell me, what do you consider to be the cause of the ball moving spontaneously on the downward inclined plane, but only by force on the one tilted upward?

SIMP: That the tendency of heavy bodies is to move toward the center of the earth, and to move upward from its circumference only with force; now the downward surface is that which gets closer to the center, while the upward one gets farther away.

SALV: Then in order for a surface to be neither downward nor upward, all its parts must be equally distant from the center. Are there any such surfaces in the world?

SIMP: Plenty of them; such would be the surface of our terrestrial globe if it were smooth, and not rough and mountainous as it is. But there is that of the water, when it is placid and tranquil.

SALV: Then a ship, when it moves over a calm sea, is one of these movables which courses over a surface that is tilted neither up nor down, and if all external and accidental obstacles were removed, it would thus be disposed to move incessantly and uniformly from an impulse once received?

SIMP: It seems that it ought to be.

SALV: Now as to that stone which is on top of the mast; does it not move, carried by the ship, both of them going along the circumference of a circle about its center? And consequently is there not in it an ineradicable motion, all external impediments being removed? And is not this motion as fast as that of the ship?

SIMP: All this is true, but what next?

SALV: Go on and draw the final consequence by yourself, if by yourself you have known all the premises.

SIMP: By the final conclusion you mean that the stone, moving with an indelibly impressed motion, is not going to leave the ship, but will follow it, and finally will fall at the same place where it fell when the ship remained motionless. And I, too, say that this would follow if there were no external impediments to disturb the motion of the stone after it was set free. But there are two such impediments; one is the inability of the movable body to split the air with its own impetus alone, once it has lost the force from the oars which it shared as part of the ship while it was on the mast; the other is the new motion of falling downward, which must impede its other, forward, motion.

SALV: As for the impediment of the air, I do not deny that to you, and if the falling body were of very light material, like a feather or a tuft of wool, the retardation would be quite considerable. But in a heavy stone it is insignificant, and if, as you yourself just said a little while ago, the force of the wildest wind is not enough to move a large stone from its place, just imagine how much the quiet air could accomplish upon meeting a rock which moved no faster than the ship! All the same, as I said, I concede to you the small effect which may depend upon such an impediment, just as I know you will concede to me that if the air were moving at the same speed as the ship and the rock, this impediment would be absolutely nil.

As for the other, the supervening motion downward, in the first place it is obvious that these two motions (I mean the circular around the center and the straight motion toward the center) are not contraries, nor are they destructive of one another, nor incompatible. As to the moving body, it has no resistance whatever to such a motion, for you yourself have already granted the resistance to be against motion which increases the distance from the center, and the tendency to be toward motion which approaches the center. From this it follows necessarily that the moving body has neither a resistance nor a propensity to motion which does not approach toward or depart from the center, and in consequence no cause for diminution in the property impressed upon it. Hence the cause of motion is not a single one which must be weakened by the new action, but there exist two distinct causes. Of these, heaviness attends only to the drawing of the movable body toward the center, and impressed force only to its being led around the center, so no occasion remains for any impediment.

The Orgone Theory of Wilhelm Reich

The following selection is drawn from the work of the controversial figure Wilhelm Reich. Although parts of Reich's clinical research continue to attract serious and sympathetic attention, his work on orgone is almost universally rejected. For Reich, orgone was a primal life energy that pervades the universe. He claimed that this radiation could charge organic substances and that concentrated in a device called an orgone accumulator it could be used therapeutically to charge the tissues, particularly the blood, and increase the bioenergetic level of the organism. The Food and Drug Administration denied the validity of this claim and obtained (by default) a sweeping injunction against Reich's work. Reich was later charged with violating this injunction, prosecuted, found guilty, and jailed. He died in Lewisburg Penitentiary in 1957.

Reich insisted that his position was based upon solid scientific evidence that had never been fairly evaluated. Part of his central argument for the existence of orgone radiation is given below. It is useful to compare this argument first with the one we have cited from Archimedes, and then with Galileo's position as stated by Salviati.

The Objective Demonstration of Orgone Radiation*
WILHELM REICH

1. Are There Subjective Impressions of Light?

When we were children the light phenomena we saw with our eyes shut were a constant source of fascination. Small dots, blue-violet in color, would appear from nowhere, floating back and forth slowly, changing their course with every movement of the eyes. They floated quite slowly in gentle curves, looping periodically into spirals, in a path somewhat as follows:

* From Wilhelm Reich, *The Cancer Biopathy*, Volume II of *The Discovery of the Orgone*, translated by Andrew White with Mary Higgins and Chester M. Raphael, M.D. (New York: Farrar, Straus & Giroux, Inc., 1973), pp. 96–103.

It was a delightful game to change the shape and track of the light dots by rubbing the eyes through our closed lids; we could influence even the color of the dots, the blue becoming red, green, or yellow. Part of the fun was to open the eyes suddenly, look into the bright light of a lamp, then close the eyes again and see the after-images. With a little imagination we could turn these forms into all kinds of things: rainbows, balloons, animal heads, human figures.

But such childish pleasures lost their interest as we grew up and studied physics, mathematics, and biology. We had to learn that such subjective optical phenomena were "unreal," something to be distinguished from objectively measurable, physical manifestations of light and its seven colors. In time, our concern for what could actually be measured and weighed obliterated the strong impressions of our sense organs. We no longer took them seriously. The practical everyday world demanded concentration on concrete details exclusively; fantasy only interfered. But the subjective light impressions remain, and the question must nag at many whether such clear phenomena as light impressions observed with the eyes closed do not, after all, represent a reality. The illusionary nature of these optical sensations is not so obvious as it appears.

We were educated to regard such things as these light impressions as "purely subjective" and therefore "not real." They could be of no concern to scientific research and were relegated to the realm of "human fantasy." Man's fantasy life, of course, is far removed from reality, being inspired by subjective desires and, moreover, unstable—which is why scientific research had to develop an objective, realistic foundation through experiment. The ideal experiment makes judgment independent of subjective fantasies, illusions, and wishes. To put it succinctly, man has no confidence in his faculties of perception. He prefers, with good reason, to rely on the photographic plate, the microscope, or the electroscope when examining phenomena.

Yet in spite of the progress made by turning from subjective experience to objective observation, an important quality of research has been lost. What we observe objectively may well exist in reality, but it is dead. In the interest of scientific objectivity, we kill what is alive before making any statements about it. The result is necessarily a mechanistic, machine-like image of life, from which life's most essential quality, its specific aliveness, is missing—an aliveness uncomfortably reminiscent of the intense organ sensations experienced in childhood. Every kind of mysticism—yoga, the fascist "surging of the blood," the receptivity of the spiritualist medium, or the ecstatic, divine epiphany of the dervish—is grounded upon these subjective organ sensations. Mysticism claims the existence of forces and processes that natural science denies or disdains. One moment of sharp deliberation tells us that *man cannot feel or imagine anything that has no real, objective existence in one form or another, for human sense perceptions are only functions of objective natural processes within the organism.* Could it not be that behind the "subjective" light impressions of our closed eyes there exists a reality after all? Is it not possible that through our subjective ocular sensations we perceive biological energy of our own organism? This thought seems strange, daring. But let us see!

To dismiss these subjective light impressions as simple "fantasy" is incorrect. Fantasy is an active property of an organism governed by certain natural laws and must therefore be "real." Not so long ago medicine rejected all functional and nervous ailments as unreal and imagined, because it did not understand them. But headache is headache, and light impression is light impression, whether we understand it or not.

Naturally we reject mystical claims based on *misinterpretation* of organ sensations. But that is not to deny the existence of these sensations. We must also reject a mechanistically fragmented natural science, because it separates organ sensations from the vital processes of the organs. *Self-perception is an essential part of the life process.* It is not a case of nerves being here, muscles there, and organ sensations somewhere else. The processes within the tissues, and our perception of them, form an indivisible *functional unity.* This must be one of the essential, experimentally documented, theoretical guidelines of our therapeutic work. Pleasure and anxiety express a particular state of functioning of the total organism. It is therefore important to make a clear distinction between functional thinking and mechanistically fragmented thinking, which can never penetrate to the essentials of the life process. Let us note four important principles of a *functional* view of nature:

1. Every living organism is a self-contained, functional unit, not merely a mechanical sum of organs. The fundamental biological function controls the total organism just as it governs each individual organ.

2. Every living organism is a part of surrounding nature and is functionally identical with it.

3. Every perception is based upon the correspondence of a function within the organism with a function in the external world, i.e., upon orgonotic harmony.

4. Every self-perception is the immediate expression of objective processes within the organism (psychophysical identity).

Little can be expected from philosophical speculations on the reality of our sensations if they exclude the principle that the observing, perceiving ego (subject) and the observed, perceived object together form a functional unity. Mechanistic research divides this unity into a duality. In its total rejection of sensation, contemporary mechanistic empiricism is beyond redemption. *Every important discovery originates in the subjective sensation or experience of an objective fact, i.e., in orgonotic harmony.* What is required is to objectivize the subjective sensation, separating it from its stimulus and comprehending the origin of the stimulus. As orgone therapists, we do this every hour of every day when we try to understand the bodily expressions of the patient by identifying ourselves with the patient and his functions. Once we comprehend these expressions emotionally, we let our intellect work and objectivize the phenomenon.

Now, with this understanding of orgonotic harmony, let us return to our childhood fantasies and impressions of light. How can we establish *objectively* whether these impressions "seen" with our eyes closed correspond to real processes?

2. Flickering in the Sky Made Objective (the Orgonoscope)

First of all we try to determine whether similar phenomena can be perceived with *open* eyes in broad daylight. If we observe carefully for a sufficient length of time, we discover that they can. We gaze at a screen, a wall, or a white door. *We observe a flickering.* The impression is of shadows or foggy vapors traveling more or less rapidly and rhythmically over the surface of things. Rather than disregarding this observation as a mere "subjective ocular impression," we resolve to establish *objectively* whether this flickering is taking place merely in our eyes or all around us.

Devising a method of differentiating is not easy, however. We begin by closing our eyes. Instantly the flickering seems to change into a movement of small dots, shapes, and colors. We open and close our eyes repeatedly until we are convinced that the phenomena we perceive with our eyes closed are *different* from those we observed while looking at the wall opposite us.

We look into the blue sky, as though gazing into the far distance. At first we see nothing. But if we continue to observe, we discover, to our surprise, a rhythmical, wave-like flickering, clearly perceptible across the blue sky. *Does this flickering exist merely in our eyes, or is it in the sky?* We continue to observe the phenomena over several days, under varying weather conditions and at different times of the day. It is striking that the flickering in the sky varies a great deal in kind and in intensity. Next we experiment at night. Since our observations are now unhampered by diffused daylight the wave-like flickering is even *more distinct.* Here and there we believe we catch a glimpse of a lightning flash in the form of a streak or dots. The flickering and delicate flashings are also to be observed in dark clouds, where they are more intense. As we observe the sky over a period of weeks, we notice that the flickering of the stars varies in intensity. On some nights, the stars shine clearly and calmly; on others their flickering is subdued; on still others, it is extraordinarily vivid. Astronomers ascribe the flickering of the stars to diffuse light. There was a time when we accepted this explanation unquestioningly. However, now that the actual existence of a flickering in the sky has become a crucial question for us, we must ask ourselves whether the flickering of stars may be related to the flickering in the sky *between* the stars. If so, we have taken the first step toward demonstrating the objective existence of an unknown something in the atmosphere. The flickering of the stars is certainly no subjective ocular phenomenon; observatories are built on high mountains in order to eliminate it. The unknown something that makes the stars flicker must therefore be moving close to the surface of the earth. But it is certainly not diffuse light; otherwise the flickering would not vary in intensity as it does. Such "explanations" only obscure facts. Let us defer the answer.

The longer and more precisely we observe the flickering in the sky and across the surface of objects, the more imperative it becomes to delineate a limited field. We construct a metal tube 1 to 3 feet long and 1 to 2 inches in diameter, with a dull black interior. We look through it at the walls in the day time and the sky at night. The tube isolates a circle which appears *brighter* than the area around it. Keeping both eyes open and looking through the tube with one eye, we see a dark-blue night sky within which is a disk of brighter blue. Within the disk itself we perceive, first of all, a flickering movement, then, unmistakably, delicate dots and streaks of light appearing and disappearing. The phenomenon becomes less distinct in the immediate vicinity of the moon; the darker the atmosphere in the background, the clearer the phenomenon.

Are we perhaps this time victims of an illusion? To find out we insert a plano-convex eyepiece with a magnification of approximately 5x in the viewing end of the tube and look through. The bright circular field is now broader; the dots and streaks of light appear larger and more distinct. *It is impossible to magnify subjective light impressions; therefore, the phenomenon must be objective.* Moreover, no flickering is perceptible along the dark interior walls of the tube; the flickering is confined strictly to the bright section of the disk, and therefore cannot be "subjective" sensation. We have isolated a limited area and are now in a position to examine the phenomenon carefully under conditions that eliminate diffuse light from the atmosphere as a factor. But first we shall make some improvements in the primitive orgonoscope we have improvised:

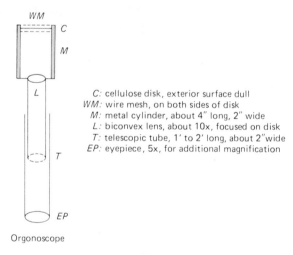

C: cellulose disk, exterior surface dull
WM: wire mesh, on both sides of disk
M: metal cylinder, about 4" long, 2" wide
L: biconvex lens, about 10x, focused on disk
T: telescopic tube, 1' to 2' long, about 2" wide
EP: eyepiece, 5x, for additional magnification

Orgonoscope

We point our tube toward the dark night sky in front of the mirror of a good microscope equipped with apochromatic lenses. We use a 10x object lens and a 5x eyepiece. Our eyes need to be accustomed to the dark for about twenty-five minutes. The microscope reflects the light phenomena in the sky with total clarity. Every single flash of light is clearly discernible. We remove the eyepiece from the tube. Now the flickering is seen in smaller scale, but it is more intense; we are no longer able to distinguish individual flashes of light.

Can the phenomena be ascribed to the haze in the atmosphere? Let us try observing the phenomenon on foggy or hazy nights. It does not take long to see that the phenomena are either very weak or have disappeared completely. *Fog or haze does not cause flickering in the circular field. The movement of light particles in the field of the microscope has nothing to do with the movement of fog.*

By careful observation, we are able to establish that the light and wave phenomena extend across the entire sky and become weaker only when close to stars or the moon because of the stronger light. They are at their most intense on clear nights and when humidity is relatively low. When the humidity rises above 50 percent, the radiation phenomena decrease in intensity. In other words, *humidity absorbs the radiation in the atmosphere,* just as it absorbs the SAPA radiation.

At night we direct our tube at various places—on the ground, the pavement, loose earth, a lawn, walls, etc. We see the same movements of light particles. They are more pronounced on soil than on asphalt. We point the tube at thick shrubs from a distance of about 10 cm., moving the tube slowly away from the foliage and then back to it. Without doubt, the phenomena are more intense at the leaves than in the surroundings. They seem to come from the leaves themselves. We look at a variety of flower blossoms. The radiation phenomena are more intense close to the blossom than at the stalk.

Earth, walls, bushes, grass, animals, the atmosphere, all show the same phenomena. The conclusion to be drawn from these findings is inescapable: *The radiation phenomena are present everywhere, with variations only in the density and intensity of the energy.* Perhaps we would have wished to find them present in some places and not in others. Then, the discovery would not have been so overwhelming. But we have to stay with the facts, however strange they now begin to appear.

CONCERNING FLIM-FLAM

In almost every general bookstore, you will find a section, often a very large section, devoted to such subjects as the occult, astrology, UFOs, ESP, and other forms of so-called paranormal phenomena. Commercial successes in these areas abound. Eric von Daniken has followed up his blockbusting bestseller *Chariots of the Gods* with three more books about "gods from outer space." Charles Berlitz, along with a number of others, has prospered by retelling (discredited) yarns about the Bermuda Triangle. And Jeane Dixon, whose astrological advice appears daily in the nation's newspapers, continues to turn out books with such titles as *Jeane Dixon's Astrological Cookbook: How to Select and Prepare Foods Astrologically for Their Harmonizing Effect on Your Mind and Body.* There is money in these fields. Not only do such books sell, they are made into movies and into television documentaries. Psychics and other experts on the paranormal appear on television talk-shows, often generating the cry, "That's incredible!"

Indeed it is incredible. It is incredible that a great many people now believe that psychic powers, the existence of UFOs, encounters with visitors from outer space, and the like have been established beyond doubt. On the contrary, whenever careful and systematic attention is turned to these claims, they are shown to be transparent frauds or exaggerations based upon few, often unverified, facts. (Mental spoon-bending falls into the first category; astrology and, more recently, biorhythm fall into the second.)

Books have appeared that attempt to stem this tide of unsupported belief. Martin Gardner's *Fads and Fallacies in the Name of Science* is a classic in this field. More recently, James Randi (otherwise known as the Amazing Randi) has used his intelligence and talents as a magician to expose a series of supposed psychics. His book on Uri Geller was cited earlier, and his new book, Flim-Flam, was the inspiration for this chapter. Its title is a grateful nod in his direction.

The two articles reprinted below are taken from the Skeptical Inquirer (previously known as The Zetetic), a journal published by the Committee for the Scientific Investigation of the Paranormal. Thus far, the committee has not been able to authenticate a single instance of the paranormal. (No material supporting the existence of the paranormal will be presented here, since it is abundantly available elsewhere.)

"Cold Reading": How to Convince Strangers that You Know All About Them*
RAY HYMAN

Over twenty years ago I taught a course at Harvard University called "Applications of Social Psychology." The sort of applications that I covered were the various ways in which people were manipulated. I invited various manipulators to demonstrate their techniques—pitchmen, encyclopedia salesmen, hypnotists, advertising experts, evangelists, confidence men, and a variety of individuals who dealt with personal problems. The techniques which we discussed, especially those concerned with helping people with their personal problems, seem to involve the client's tendency to find more meaning in any situation than is actually there. Students readily accepted this explanation when it was pointed out to them. But I did not feel that they fully realized just how pervasive and powerful this human tendency to make sense out of nonsense really is.

Consequently, in 1955 I wrote a paper entitled "The Psychological Reading: An Infallible Technique For Winning Admiration and Popularity." Over the years I have distributed copies of this paper to my students. The paper begins as follows:

> So you want to be admired? You want people to seek your company, to talk about you, to praise your talents? This manuscript tells you how to satisfy that want. Herein you will find a "sure-fire" gimmick for the achievement of fame and popularity. Just follow the advice that I give you, and, even if you are the most incompetent social bungler, you cannot fail to become the life of the party. What is the secret that underlies this infallible system? The secret, my friend, is a simple and obvious one. It has been tried and proven by practitioners since the beginnings of mankind. Here is the gist of the secret: To be popular with your fellow man, tell him what he wants to hear. He wants to hear about himself.

* From The Skeptical Inquirer (formerly The Zetetic), Spring/Summer 1977, pp. 18–37.

So tell him about himself. But not what you know to be true about him. Oh, no! Never tell him the truth. Rather, tell him *what he would like to be true about himself!* And there you have it. Simple and obvious, but yet so powerful. This manuscript details the way in which you can exploit this golden rule by assuming the role of a character reader.

I will include essentially the same recipe for character reading in this paper that I give to my students. In addition I will bring the material up to date, describe some relevant research, and indicate some theoretical reasons why the technique "works." My purpose is not to enable you to enhance your personal magnetism, nor is it to increase the number of character readers. I give you these rules for reading character because I want you to experience how the method works. I want you to see what a powerful technique the psychological reading is, how convincing it is to the psychologist and layman alike.

When you see how easy it is to convince a person that you can read his character on sight, you will better appreciate why fortune tellers and psychologists are frequently lulled into placing credence in techniques which have not been validated by acceptable scientific methods. The recent controversy in *The Humanist* magazine and *The Zetetic* over the scientific status of astrology probably is irrelevant to the reasons that individuals believe in astrology. Almost without exception the defenders of astrology with whom I have contact do not refer to the evidence relating to the underlying theory. They are convinced of astrology's value because it "works." By this they mean that it supplies them with feedback that "feels right"—that convinces them that the horoscope provides a basis for understanding themselves and ordering their lives. It has personal meaning for them.

Some philosophers distinguish between "persuasion" and "conviction." The distinction is subtle. But for our purposes we can think of subjective experiences that persuade us that something is so and of logical and scientific procedures that convince, or ought to convince, us that something is or is not so. Quite frequently a scientist commits time and resources toward generating scientific evidence for a proposition because he has already been persuaded, on nonscientific grounds that the proposition is true. Such intuitive persuasion plays an important motivational role in science as well as in the arts. Pathological science and false beliefs come about when such intuitive persuasion overrides or colors the evidence from objective procedures for establishing conviction.

The field of personality assessment has always been plagued by this confusion between persuasion and conviction. In contrast to intelligence and aptitude tests, the scientific validation of personality tests, even under ideal conditions, rarely results in unequivocal or satisfactory results. In fact some of the most widely used personality inventories have repeatedly failed to pass validity checks. One of the reasons for this messy state of affairs is the lack of reliable and objective criteria against which to check the results of an assessment.

But the lack of adequate validation has not prevented the use of, and reliance on, such instruments. Assessment psychologists have always placed more reliance on their instruments than is warranted by the scientific evidence. Both psychologist and client are invariably persuaded by the results that the assessment "works."

This state of affairs, of course, is even more true when we consider divination systems beyond those of the academic and professional psychologist. Every system—be it based on the position of the stars, the pattern of lines in the hand, the shape of the face or skull, the fall of the cards or the dice, the accidents of nature, or the intuitions of a "psychic"—claims its quota of satisfied customers. The client invariably feels satisfied with the results. He is convinced that the reader and the system have penetrated to the core of his "true" self. Such satisfaction on the part of the client also feeds back upon the reader. Even if the reader began his career with little belief in his method, the inevitable reinforcement of persuaded clients increases his confidence in himself and his system. In this way a "vicious circle" is established. The reader and his clients become more and more persuaded that they have hold of a direct pipeline to the "truth."

The state of affairs in which the evaluation of an assessment instrument depends upon the satisfaction of the client is known as "personal validation." Personal validation is, for all practical purposes, the major reason for the persistence of divinatory and assessment procedures. If the client is not persuaded, then the system will not survive. Personal validation, of course, is the basis for the acceptance of more than just assessment instruments. The widespread acceptance of myths about Bigfoot, the Bermuda Triangle, ancient astronauts, ghosts, the validity of meditation and consciousness-raising schemes, and a host of other beliefs is based on persuasion through personal validation rather than scientific conviction.

Cold Reading

"Cold reading" is a procedure by which a "reader" is able to persuade a client whom he has never before met that he knows all about the client's personality and problems. At one extreme this can be accomplished by delivering a stock spiel, or "psychological reading," that consists of highly general statements that can fit any individual. A reader who relies on psychological readings will usually have memorized a set of stock spiels. He then can select a reading to deliver that is relatively more appropriate to the general category that the client fits—a young unmarried girl, a senior citizen, and so on. Such an attempt to fit the reading to the client makes the psychological reading a closer approximation to the true cold reading.

The cold reading, at its best, provides the client with a character assessment that is uniquely tailored to fit him or her. The reader begins with the same assumptions that guide the psychological reader who relies on the stock spiel. These assumptions are (1) that we all are basically more alike than different; (2) that our problems are generated by the same major transitions of birth, puberty, work, marriage, children, old age, and death; (3) that, with the exception of curiosity seekers and troublemakers, people come to a character reader because they need someone to listen to their conflicts involving love, money, and health. The cold reader goes beyond these common denominators by gathering as much additional information about the client as possible. Sometimes such information is obtained in advance of the reading. If the reading is through appointment, the reader can use directories and other sources to gather information. When the client enters the consulting room, an assistant can examine the coat left behind (and often the purse as well) for papers, notes, labels, and other such cues about socioeconomic status, and so on. Most cold readers, however, do not need such advance information.

The cold reader basically relies on a good memory and acute observation. The client is carefully studied. The clothing—for example, style, neatness, cost, age—provides a host of cues for helping the reader make shrewd guesses about socioeconomic level, conservatism or extroversion, and other characteristics. The client's physical features—weight, posture, looks, eyes, and hands provide further cues. The hands are especially revealing to the good reader. The manner of speech, use of grammar, gestures, and eye contact are also good sources. To the good reader the huge amount of information coming from an initial sizing-up of the client greatly narrows the possible categories into which he classifies clients. His knowledge of actuarial and statistical data about various subcultures in the population already provides him the basis for making an uncanny and strikingly accurate assessment of the client.

But the skilled reader can go much further in particularizing his reading. He wants to zero in as quickly as possible on the precise problem that is bothering the client. On the basis of his initial assessment he makes some tentative hypotheses. He tests these out by beginning his assessment in general terms, touching upon general categories of problems and watching the reaction of the client. If he is on the wrong track the client's reactions—eye movements, pupillary dilation, other bodily mannerisms—will warn him. When he is on the right track other reactions will tell him so. By watching the client's reactions as he tests out different hypotheses during his spiel, the good reader quickly hits upon what is bothering the customer and begins to adjust the reading to the situation. By this time, the client has usually been persuaded that the reader, by some uncanny means, has gained insights into the client's innermost thoughts. His guard is now down. Often he opens up and actually tells the reader, who is also a good listener, the details of his situation. The reader, after a suitable interval, will usually feed back the information that the client has given him in such a way that the client will be further amazed at how much the reader "knows" about him. Invariably the client leaves the reader without realizing that everything he has been told is simply what he himself has unwittingly revealed to the reader.

The Stock Spiel

The preceding paragraphs indicate that the cold reader is a highly skilled and talented individual. And this is true. But what is amazing about this area of human assessment is how successfully even an unskilled and incompetent reader can persuade a client that he has fathomed the client's true nature. It is probably a tribute to the creativeness of the human mind that a client can, under the right circumstances, make sense out of almost any reading and manage to fit it to his own unique situation. All that is necessary is that the reader make out a plausible case for why the reading ought to fit. The client will do the rest.

You can achieve a surprisingly high degree of success as a character reader even if you merely use a stock spiel which you give to every client. Sundberg (1955), for example, found that if you deliver the following character sketch to a college male, he will usually accept it as a reasonably accurate description of himself: "You are a person who is very normal in his attitudes, behavior and relationships with people. You get along well without effort. People naturally like you and you are not overly critical of them or yourself. You are neither overly conventional nor overly individualistic. Your prevailing mood is one of optimism and constructive effort, and you are not troubled by periods of depression, psychosomatic illness or nervous symptoms."

Sundberg found that the college female will respond with even more pleasure to the following sketch: "You appear to be a cheerful, well-balanced person. You may have some alternation of happy and unhappy moods, but they are not extreme now. You have few or no problems with your health. You are sociable and mix well with others. You are adaptable to social situations. You tend to be adventurous. Your interests are wide. You are fairly self-confident and usually think clearly."

Sundberg conducted his study over 20 years ago. But the sketches still work well today. Either will tend to work well with both sexes. More recently, several laboratory studies have had excellent success with the following stock spiel (Snyder and Shenkel 1975):

> Some of your aspirations tend to be pretty unrealistic. At times you are extroverted, affable, sociable, while at other times you are introverted, wary and reserved. You have found it unwise to be too frank in revealing yourself to others. You pride yourself on being an independent thinker and do not accept others' opinions without satisfactory proof. You prefer a certain amount of change and variety, and become dissatisfied when hemmed in by restrictions and limitations. At times you have serious doubts as to whether you have made the right decision or done the right thing. Disciplined and controlled on the outside, you tend to be worrisome and insecure on the inside.
>
> Your sexual adjustment has presented some problems for you. While you have some personality weaknesses, you are generally able to compensate for them. You have a great deal of unused capacity which you have not turned to your advantage. You have a tendency to be critical of yourself. You have a strong need for other people to like you and for them to admire you.

Interestingly enough the statements in this stock spiel were first used in 1948 by Bertram Forer (1949) in a classroom demonstration of personal validation. He obtained most of them from a newsstand astrology book. Forer's students, who thought the sketch was uniquely intended for them as a result of a personality test, gave the sketch an average rating of 4.26 on a scale of 0 (poor) to 5 (perfect). As many as 16 out of his 39 students (41 percent) rated it as a perfect fit to their personality. Only five gave it a rating below 4 (the worst being a rating of 2, meaning "average"). Almost 30 years later students give the same sketch an almost identical rating as a unique description of themselves.

The Technique in Action

The acceptability of the stock spiel depends upon the method and circumstances of its delivery. As we shall later see, laboratory studies have isolated many of the factors that contribute to persuading clients that the sketch is a unique description of themselves. A great deal of the success of the spiel depends upon "setting the stage." The reader tries to persuade the client that the sketch is tailored especially for him or her. The reader also creates the impression that it is based on a reliable and proven assessment procedure. The way the sketch is delivered and dramatized also helps. And many of the rules that I give for the cold reading also apply to the delivery of the stock spiel.

The stock spiel, when properly delivered, can be quite effective. In fact, with the right combination of circumstances the stock spiel is often accepted as a perfect and unique description by the client. But, in general, one can achieve even greater success as a character analyst if one uses the more flexible technique of the cold reader. In this method one plays a sort of detective role in which one takes on the role of a Sherlock Holmes. (See the "Case of the Cardboard Box" for an excellent example of cold reading.) One observes the jewelry, prices the clothing, evaluates the speech mannerisms, and studies the reactions of the subject. Then whatever information these observations provide is pieced together into a character reading which is aimed more specifically at the particular client.

A good illustration of the cold reader in action occurs in a story told by the well-known magician John Mulholland. The incident took place in the 1930s. A young lady in her late twenties or early thirties visited a character reader. She was wearing expensive jewelry, a wedding band, and a black dress of cheap material. The observant reader noted that she was wearing shoes which were currently being advertised for people with foot trouble. (Pause at this point and imagine that you are the reader; see what you would make of these clues.)

By means of just these observations the reader proceeded to amaze his client with his insights. He assumed that this client came to see him, as did most of his female customers, because of a love or financial problem. The black dress and the wedding band led him to reason that her husband had died recently. The expensive jewelry suggested that she had been financially comfortable during marriage, but the cheap dress indicated that her husband's death had left her penniless. The therapeutic shoes signified that she was now standing on her feet more than she was used to, implying that she was working to support herself since her husband's death.

The reader's shrewdness led him to the following conclusion—which turned out to be correct: The lady had met a man who had proposed to her. She wanted to marry the man to end her economic hardship. But she felt guilty about marrying so soon after her husband's death. The reader told her what she had come to hear—that it was all right to marry without further delay.

The Rules of the Game

Whether you prefer to use the formula reading or to employ the more flexible technique of the cold reader, the following bits of advice will help to contribute to your success as a character reader.

1. *Remember that the key ingredient of a successful character reading is confidence.* If you *look* and *act* as if you believe in what you are doing, you will be able to sell even a bad reading to most of your subjects.

The laboratory studies support this rule. Many readings are accepted as accurate because the statements do fit most people. But even readings that would ordinarily be rejected as inaccurate will be accepted if the reader is viewed as a person with prestige or as someone who knows what he is doing.

One danger of playing the role of reader is that you will persuade yourself that you really are devining true character. This happened to me. I started reading palms when I was in my teens as a way to supplement my income from doing magic and mental shows. When I started I did not believe in palmistry. But I knew that to "sell" it I had to act as if I did. After a few years I became a firm believer in palmistry. One day the late Dr. Stanley Jaks, who was a professional mentalist and a man I respected, tactfully suggested that it would make an interesting experiment if I deliberately gave readings opposite to what the lines indicated. I tried this out with a few clients. To my surprise and horror my readings were just as successful as ever. Ever since then I have been interested in the powerful forces that convince us, reader and client alike, that something is so when it really isn't.

2. *Make creative use of the latest statistical abstracts, polls, and surveys.* This can provide you with a wealth of material about what various subclasses of our society believe, do, want, worry about, and so on. For example if you can ascertain about a client such things as the part of the country he comes from, the size of the city he was brought up in, his parents' religion and vocations, his educational level and age, you already are in possession of information that should enable you to predict with high probability his voting preferences, his beliefs on many issues, and other traits.

3. *Set the stage for your reading.* Profess a modesty about your talents. Make no excessive claims. This catches your subject off guard. You are not challenging him to a battle of wits. You can read his character; whether he cares to believe you or not is his concern.

4. *Gain his cooperation in advance.* Emphasize that the success of the reading depends as much upon his sincere cooperation as upon your efforts. (After all, you imply, you already have a successful career at reading characters. You are not on trial—he is.) State that due to difficulties of language and communication, *you may not always convey the exact meaning which you intend.* In these cases he is to strive to reinterpret the message in terms of his own vocabulary and life.

You accomplish two invaluable ends with this dodge. You have an alibi in case the reading doesn't click; it's his fault, not yours! And your subject will strive to fit your generalities to his specific life occurrences. Later, when he recalls the reading he will recall it in terms of specifics; thus you gain credit for much more than you actually said.

Of all the pieces of advice this is the most crucial. To the extent that the client is made an active participant in the reading the reading will succeed. The good reader, deliberately or unwittingly, is the one who forces the client to actively search his memory to make sense of the reader's statements.

5. *Use a gimmick such as a crystal ball, tarot cards, or palm reading.* The use of palmistry, say, serves two useful purposes. It lends an air of novelty to the reading; but, more important, it serves as a cover for you to stall and to formulate your next statement. While you are trying to think of something to say next, you are apparently carefully studying a new wrinkle or line in the hand. Holding hands, in addition to any emotional thrills you may give or receive thereby, is another good way of detecting the reactions of the subject to what you are saying (the principle is the same as "muscle reading").

It helps, in the case of palmistry or other gimmicks, to study some manuals so that you know roughly what the various diagnostic signs are supposed to mean. A clever way of using such gimmicks to pin down a client's problem is to use a variant of "Twenty Questions," somewhat like this: Tell the client you have only a limited amount of time for the reading. You could focus on the heart line, which deals with emotional entanglements; on the fate line, which deals with vocational pursuits and money matters; the head line, which deals with personal problems; the health line, and so on. Ask him or her which one to focus on first. This quickly pins down the major category of problem on the client's mind.

6. *Have a list of stock phrases at the tip of your tongue.* Even if you are doing a cold reading, the liberal sprinkling of stock phrases amidst your regular reading will add body to the reading and will fill in time as you try to formulate more precise characterizations. You can use the statements in the preceding stock spiels as a start. Memorize a few of them before undertaking your initial ventures into character reading. Palmisty, tarot, and other fortune-telling manuals also are rich sources for good phrases.

7. *Keep your eyes open.* Also use your other senses. We have seen how to size up the client on the basis of clothing, jewelry, mannerisms, and speech. Even a crude classification on such a basis can provide sufficient information for a good reading. Watch the impact of your statements upon the subject. Very quickly you will learn when you are "hitting home" and when you are "missing the boat."

8. *Use the technique of "fishing."* This is simply a device for getting the subject to tell you about himself. Then you rephrase what he has told you into a coherent sketch and feed it back to him. One version of fishing is to phrase each statement in the form of a question. Then wait for the subject to reply (or react). If the reaction is positive, then the reader turns the statement into a positive assertion. Often the subject will respond by answering the implied question and then some. Later he will tend to forget that he was the source of your information. By making your statements into questions you also force the subject to search through his memory to retrieve specific instances to fit your general statement.

9. *Learn to be a good listener.* During the course of a reading your client will be bursting to talk about incidents that are brought up. The good reader allows the client to talk at will. On one occasion I observed a tea-leaf reader. The client actually spent 75 percent of the total time talking. Afterward when I questioned the client about the reading she vehemently insisted that she had not uttered a single word during the course of the reading. The client praised the reader for having so astutely told her what in fact she herself had spoken.

Another value of listening is that most clients who seek the services of a reader actually want someone to listen to their problems. In addition many clients have already made up their minds about what choices they are going to make. They merely want support to carry out their decision.

10. *Dramatize your reading.* Give back what little information you do have or pick up a little bit at a time. Make it seem more than it is. Build word pictures around each divulgence. Don't be afraid of hamming it up.

11. *Always give the impression that you know more than you are saying.* The successful reader, like the family doctor, always acts as if he knows much more. Once you persuade the client that you know one item of information about him that you could not possibly have obtained through normal channels, the client will automatically assume you know all. At this point he will typically open up and confide in you.

12. *Don't be afraid to flatter your subject every chance you get.* An occasional subject will protest such flattery, but will still cherish it. In such cases you can further flatter him by saying, "You are always suspicious of people who flatter you. You just can't believe that someone will say good of you unless he is trying to achieve some ulterior goal."

13. Finally, remember the golden rule: *Tell the client what he wants to hear.*

Sigmund Freud once made an astute observation. He had a client who had been to a fortune-teller many years previously. The fortune-teller had predicted that she would have twins. Actually she never had children. Yet, despite the fact that the reader had been wrong, the client still spoke of her in glowing terms. Freud tried to figure out why this was so. He finally concluded that at the time of the original reading the client wanted desperately to have children. The fortune-teller sensed this and told her what she wanted to hear. From this Freud inferred that the successful fortune-teller is one who predicts what the client secretly wishes to happen rather than what actually will happen (Freud 1933).

The Fallacy of Personal Validation

As we have seen, clients will readily accept stock spiels such as those I have presented as unique descriptions of themselves. Many laboratory experiments have demonstrated this effect. Forer (1949) called the tendency to accept as valid a personality sketch on the basis of the client's willingness to accept it "the fallacy of personal validation."

The early studies on personal validation were simply demonstrations to show that students, personnel directors, and others can readily be persuaded to accept a fake sketch as a valid description of themselves. A few studies tried to go beyond the demonstration and tease out factors that influence the acceptability of the fake sketch. Sundberg (1955), for example, gave the Minnesota Multiphasic Personality Inventory (known as the MMPI) to 44 students. The MMPI is the most carefully standardized personality inventory in the psychologist's tool kit. Two psychologists, highly experienced in interpreting the outcome of the MMPI, wrote a personality sketch for each student on the basis of his or her test results. Each student then received two personality sketches—the one actually written for him or her and a fake sketch. When asked to pick which sketch described him or her better, 26 of the 44 students (59 percent) picked the fake sketch!

Sundberg's study highlights one of the difficulties in this area. A fake, universal sketch can be seen as a better description of oneself than can a uniquely tailored description by trained psychologists based upon one of the best assessment devices we have. This makes personal validation a completely useless procedure. But it makes the life of the character reader and the pseudopsychologist all the easier. His general and universal statements have more persuasive appeal than do the best and most appropriate descriptions that the trained psychologist can come up with.

Some experiments that my students and I conducted during the 1950s also supplied some more information about the acceptability of such sketches. In one experiment we gave some students a fake sketch (the third stock spiel previously discussed) and told half of them that it was the result of an astrological reading and the other half that it was the result of a new test, the Harvard Basic Personality Profile. In those days, unlike today, students had a low opinion of astrology. All the students rated each of the individual statements as generally true of themselves. The groups did not differ in their ratings of the acceptability of the individual statements. But when asked to rate the sketch as a whole, the group that thought it came from an accepted personality test rated the acceptability significantly higher than did the group that thought it came from an astrologer. From talking to individual students it was clear that those who were in the personality-test group believed that they had received a highly accurate and unique characterization of themselves. Those in the astrology group admitted that the individual statements were applicable to themselves but dismissed the apparent success of the astrologer as due to the fact that the statements were so general that they would fit anyone. In other words, by changing the context in which they got the statements we were able to manipulate the subjects' perceptions as to whether the statements were generalities that applied to everyone or were specific characterizations of themselves.

In a further experiment we obtained a pool of items that 80 percent or more of Harvard students endorsed as true of themselves. We then had another group of Harvard students rate these items as "desirable" or "undesirable" and as "general" or "particular" (true of only a few students). Thus we had a set of items that we knew almost all our subjects would endorse as true of themselves, but which varied on desirability and on perceived generality. We were then able to compose fake sketches which varied in their proportion of desirable and specific items. We found that the best recipe for creating acceptable stock spiels was to include about 75 percent desirable items, but ones which were seen as specific, and about 25 percent undesirable items, but ones which were seen as general. The undesirable items had the apparent effect of making the spiel plausible. The fact that the items were seen as being generally true of other students made them more acceptable.

The most extensive program of research to study the factors making for acceptability of fake sketches is that by C. R. Snyder and his associates at the University of Kansas. A brief summary of many of his findings was given in an article in *Psychology Today* (Snyder and Shenkel 1975). In most of his studies Snyder uses a control condition in which the subject is given the fake sketch and told that this sketch is generally true for all people. On a rating scale from 1 to 5 (1, very poor; 2, poor; 3, average; 4, good; 5, excellent) the subject rates how well the interpretation fits his personality. A typical result for this control condition is a rating of around 3 to 4, or between average and good. But when the sketch is presented to the subject as one which was written "for you, personally," the acceptability tends to go up to around 4.5, or between good and excellent.

In a related experiment the subjects were given the fake sketch under the pretense that it was based on an astrological reading. The control group, given the sketch as "generally true for all people," rated it about 3.2, or just about average. A second group was asked to supply the astrologer with information on the year and month of their birth. When they received their sketches they rated them on the average at 3.76, or just below good. A third group supplied the mythical astrologer with information on year, month, and day of birth. These subjects gave a mean rating of 4.38.

From experiments such as those we have learned the following. The acceptability of a general sketch is enhanced when (1) the reader or source is believed to know what he is doing, (2) the instrument or assessment device is plausible, (3) a lot of mumbo jumbo is associated with the procedure (such as giving month, day, hour, and minute of birth along with a lot of complicated calculations), and (4) the client is led to believe that the sketch has been tailored to his personality. When these conditions are met, the client, and possibly the reader as well, have a strong "illusion of uniqueness"—that is, the client is persuaded that the sketch describes himself or herself and no one else.

Why Does It Work?

But why does it work? And why does it work so well? It does not help to say that people are gullible or suggestible. Nor can we dismiss it by implying that some individuals are just not sufficiently discriminating or lack sufficient intelligence to see through it. Indeed one can argue that it requires a certain degree of intelligence on the part of a client for the reading to work well. Once the client is actively engaged in trying to make sense of the series of sometimes contradictory statements issuing from the reader, he becomes a creative problem-solver trying to find coherence and meaning in the total set of statements. The task is not unlike that of trying to make sense of a work of art, a poem, or, for that matter, a sentence. The work of art, the poem, or the sentence serve as a blueprint or plan from which we can construct a meaningful experience by bringing to bear our own past experiences and memories.

In other words the reading succeeds just because it calls upon the normal processes of comprehension that we ordinarily bring to bear in making sense out of any form of communication. The raw information in a communication is rarely, if ever, sufficient in itself for comprehension. A shared context and background is assumed. Much has to be filled in by inference. The good reader, like anyone who manipulates our perceptions, is merely exploiting the normal processes by which we make sense out of the disorderly array of inputs that constantly bombard us.

A variety of examples and experiments could be drawn upon to illustrate this point. Let us look at a couple of instructive cases. Dr. Joseph Weizenbaum, of M.I.T., developed a computer program that would enable a human to apparently carry on a conversation with a computer. One version of his program is called "Doctor." The program is designed to "talk" like a Rogerian psychotherapist. Such a therapist is relatively easy to imitate because the basis of Rogers' technique is simply to feed the patient's statement back to him in a paraphrased form. The human, playing the role of the patient, types in questions and answers on a teletype machine. The computer, under control of the program, types replies and questions on the same teletype paper. A typical example (Weizenbaum 1976) of a conversation between a young lady and Doctor follows. (The lady speaks first. The computer's responses are printed in italics.)

Men are all alike.
In what way?
They're always bugging us about something or other.
Can you think of a specific example?
Well, my boyfriend made me come here.
Your boyfriend made you come here?
He says I'm depressed much of the time.
I am sorry to hear you are depressed.
It's true. I am unhappy.
Do you think coming here will help you not to be unhappy?
I need some help, that much seems certain.
What would it mean to you if you got some help?
Perhaps I could learn to get along with my mother.
Tell me more about your family.
My mother takes care of me.
Who else in your family takes care of you?
My father.
Your father?
You are like my father in some ways.
What resemblance do you see?
You are not very aggressive, but I think you don't want me to notice that.
What makes you think I am not very aggressive?
You don't argue with me.

Why do you think I don't argue with you?
You are afraid of me.
Does it please you to believe I am afraid of you?
My father is afraid of everybody.
What else comes to mind when you think of your father?
Bullies.
*Does that have anything to do with the fact that your boyfriend made
    you come here?*

Doctor is a quite primitive program as natural-language programs go. It employs a lot of tricks and stock phrases. It has no mechanisms for actually understanding sentences. Instead it seeks out key words that are typed and does some simple syntactical transformations. For example, if the program sees a sentence of the form "Do you X" it automatically prints out the response "What makes you think I X?" When Doctor cannot match the syntax of a given sentence it can cover up in two ways. It can say something noncommittal, such as *"Please go on"* or *"What does that suggest to you?"* Or it can recall an earlier match and refer back to it, as for example, *"How does this relate to your depression?"* where depression was an earlier topic of conversation.

In essence Doctor is a primitive cold reader. It uses stock phrases to cover up when it cannot deal with a given question or input. And it uses the patient's own input to feed back information and create the illusion that it understands and even sympathizes with the patient. This illusion is so powerful that patients, even when told they are dealing with a relatively simple-minded program, become emotionally involved in the interaction. Many refuse to believe that they are dealing with a program and insist that a sympathetic human must be at the controls at the other end of the teletype.

Sociologist Harold Garfinkel has supplied another instructive example (1967). He conducted the following experiment. The subjects were told that the Department of Psychiatry was exploring alternative means to therapy "as a way of giving persons advice about their personal problems." Each subject was then asked to discuss the background of some serious problem on which he would like advice. After having done this the subject was to address some questions which could be answered "yes" or "no" to the "counselor" (actually an experimenter). The experimenter-counselor heard the questions from an adjoining room and supplied a "yes" or "no" answer to each question after a suitable pause. Unknown to the subject, the series of yes-no answers had been preprogrammed according to a table of random numbers and was not related to his questions. Yet the typical subject was sure that the counselor fully understood the subject's problem and was giving him sound and helpful advice.

Let me emphasize again that statements as such have no meaning. They convey meaning only in context and only when the listener or reader can bring to bear his large store of worldly knowledge. Clients are not necessarily acting irrationally when they find meaning in the stock spiels or cold readings. Meaning is an interaction of expectations, context, memory, and given statements. An experiment by the Gestalt psychologist Solomon Asch (1948) will help make this point. Subjects were given the following passage and asked to think about it: "I hold it that a little rebellion, now and then, is a good thing, and as necessary in the political world as storms are in the physical." One group of subjects was told that the author of the passage was Thomas Jefferson (which happens to be true). The subjects were asked if they agreed with the passage and what it meant to them. These subjects generally approved of it and interpreted the word *rebellion* to mean minor agitation. But when subjects were given the same passage and told that its author was Lenin, they disagreed with it and interpreted *rebellion* to mean a violent revolution.

According to some social psychologists the different reactions show the irrationality of prejudice. But Asch points out that the subjects could be acting quite rationally. Given what they know about Thomas Jefferson and Lenin, or what they believe about them, it makes sense to attribute different meanings to the same words spoken by each of them. If one thinks that Jefferson believed in orderly government and peaceful processes, then it would not make sense to interpret his statement to actually mean a bloody or physical revolution. If one thinks that Lenin favors war and bloodshed, then it makes sense, when the statement is attributed to him, to interpret *rebellion* in its more extreme form.

Some recent research that my colleagues and I conducted might also be relevant here. Our subjects were given the task of forming an impression of a hypothetical individual on the basis of a brief personality sketch. In one condition the subjects were given a sketch that generally led to an impression of a nice, personable, friendly sort of fellow. In a second condition the subjects were given a sketch that created an impression of a withdrawn, niggardly individual. Both groups of subjects were then given a new sketch that supposedly contained more information about the hypothetical individual. In both cases the subjects were given an identical sketch. This sketch contained some descriptors that were consistent with the friendly image and some that were consistent with the niggardly image. The subjects were later tested to see how well they recognized the actual adjectives that were used in the second sketch. One of the adjectives, for example, was *charitable.* The test contained foils for each adjective. For example, the word *generous* also appeared on the test but did not appear in the sketch. Yet subjects who had been given the friendly impression checked *generous* just as frequently as they checked *charitable.* But subjects in the other condition did not confuse *charitable* with *generous.* Why? Because, we theorize, the two different contexts into which *charitable* had to be integrated produced quite different meanings. When subjects who have already built up an impression of a "friendly" individual encounter the additional descriptor *charitable*, it is treated as merely further confirmation of their general impression. In that context *charitable* is simply further confirmation of the nice-guy image. Consequently when these subjects are asked to remember what was actually said, they can remember only that the individual was further described in some way to enchance the good guy image, and *generous* is just as good a candidate for the description as is *charitable* in that context.

But when the subjects who have an image of the person as a withdrawn, niggardly individual encounter *charitable*, the last thing that comes to mind is generosity. Instead, they probably interpret *charitable* as implying that he donates money to charities as a way of gaining tax deductions. In this latter condition the subjects have no subsequent tendency to confuse *charitable* with *generous*.

The cold reading works so well, then, because it taps a fundamental and necessary human process. We have to bring our knowledge and expectations to bear in order to comprehend anything in our world. In most ordinary situations this use of context and memory enables us to correctly interpret statements and supply the necessary inferences to do this. But this powerful mechanism can go astray in situations where there is no actual message being conveyed. Instead of picking up random noise we still manage to find meaning in the situation. So the same system that enables us to creatively find meanings and make new discoveries also makes us extremely vulnerable to exploitation by all sorts of manipulators. In the case of the cold reading the manipulator may be conscious of his deception; but often he, too, is a victim of personal validation.

References

Asch, S. E. 1948. "The Doctrine of Suggestion, Prestige, and Imitations in Social Psychology." *Psychological Review* 55: 250-76.
Forer, B. R. 1949. "The Fallacy of Personal Validation: A Classroom Demonstration of Gullibility." *Journal of Abnormal and Social Psychology* 44: 118-23.
Freud, S. 1933. *New Introductory Lectures on Psychoanalysis.* New York: W. W. Norton
Garfinkel, H. 1967. *Studies in Ethnomethodology.* Englewood-Cliffs, N.J.: Prentice-Hall.
Snyder, C. R., and R. J. Shenkel 1975. "The P. T. Barnum Effect." *Psychology Today* 8: 52-54.
Sundberg, N. D. 1955. "The Acceptability of 'Fake' versus 'Bona Fide' Personality Test Interpretations." *Journal of Abnormal and Social Psychology* 50: 145-57.
Weizenbaum, J. 1976. *Computer Power and Human Reason.* San Francisco: Freeman.

Critical Reading, Careful Writing, and the Bermuda Triangle*

LARRY KUSCHE

In August 1977, the College Entrance Examination Board issued a report concerning the causes of the continuing decline of the skills and capacities of high school students going into college. Although some of the conclusions concerning the effect of television and the breakdown of the family were necessarily subjective because of inconclusive evidence, several firm conclusions were reached.

* From *The Skeptical Inquirer* (formerly *The Zetetic*), Fall/Winter 1977, pp. 36–40.

Among them is that the decline is partly because "less thoughtful and critical reading is now being demanded and done, and that careful writing has apparently about gone out of style."

Although the reference to the lack of careful writing is apparently directed toward the students themselves, it should also be taken to include the writings that the students read, virtually all of which is done by writers a generation or two older, who do not have the same excuse for sloppy research and slovenly logic and writing techniques.

Much of the reading that students now do is called "high interest reading." It has to be high interest in order to grab their attention, to compete with the likes of the Six Million Dollar Man, Woman, and Dog, the Fonz, and Darth Vader. There does not seem to be much reading being assigned, at least in the field of the "paranormal," that is highly logical or accurate. It almost seems as if there is a belief among publishers that interest and logic are inversely proportional to each other. They are not, of course, but that seems to be the prevailing belief.

A typical example of high interest reading, taken from one of the subjects of the season, the Bermuda Triangle, follows.

The *Sandra* was a square-cut tramp steamer, decorated here and there with rust spots along her 350-foot length. Radio-equipped and loaded with 300 tons of insecticide, she leisurely thumped her way south in the heavily traveled coastal shipping lanes of Florida in June 1950.

The crewmen who had finished mess drifted to the aft deck to smoke and to reflect upon the setting sun and what the morrow might bring. Through the tropical dusk that shrouded the peaceful Florida coastline they watched the friendly blinking beacon at St. Augustine. The next morning all were gone. Neither the ship nor the crew were ever seen again. They had silently vanished during the night under the starlit sky. No clue to help solve this baffling mystery has been found to this very day.

Mysterious wasn't it? A tranquil sea. Quiet circles of smoke slowly drifting from the deck. Twilight. A clear sky. Ah, peace. The fate of the *Sandra* has been a matter of curiosity for millions of readers in the past few years, but I wonder how many of the readers have thought about it long enough to have noticed the glaring flaws in the story. I wonder how many readers have a high enough *CQ* (Curiosity Quotient) to take just a few seconds to analyze the case.

Those with a low *CQ* ask questions like, "What strange force could possibly have caused this inexplicable loss? Why has nothing from the *Sandra* been found even to this day? What is wrong with the area out there?" (Note that the low *CQ* questions are the same as those asked in the currently popular pro-mystery books on the subject.)

The reader with the high *CQ* would have seen warning flags all over the story of the *Sandra*. Alarm bells should have rung. Yes, there is something wrong, not so much with the *Sandra* or "out there," but with the *telling of the story itself*.

If the *Sandra* disappeared that very night, how could anyone have known and reported what the crewmen were doing as the sun set? Did the men saunter over to the rail to smoke and chat about the sunset? How could the writer have known that? Did they really see the lights of St. Augustine? Was the sea really tranquil? All these points are crucial to the loss because they indirectly set the scene—a quiet, peaceful evening. That is, after all, why the loss of the *Sandra* is considered strange. If conditions had been stormy, the loss would not be considered unusual.

Even before taking the time to check into the weather (why bother doing that—it's all documented, isn't it?), the curious, intelligent reader should already be questioning the account of the *Sandra*. How was the writer able to know what the sailors saw, thought, or said that night? Was the writer perhaps on the ship himself, luckily lifted off by helicopter or a small boat in time to miss the disappearance? Unlikely. If I had been that writer I'd have plainly stated that that was what happened.

Did the radioman send this crucial information about the scene to shore? Again, quite unlikely. One doesn't usually paint pastel pictures over the radio. How then, could the writer know that much about what happened on the ship? How could he know if the men saw the light of St. Augustine? Did he know where the ship was at all?

The answer to the thinking person with the faintest shred of curiosity and intelligence is that the writer could *not* have known any of the "facts" he "reported." He had to have assumed them or have lifted them from someone else.

Is it nit-picking to observe that the "facts" could not logically have been known? Are these "facts" important? Obviously, they are crucially important. The writer was using a common, blatant writing technique that I call "setting the scene." The writer indirectly informs the reader that all was calm, all was right as the steamer chugged along. The crewmen obviously were not worried about any impending danger. There were no storms. It makes the "disappearance" all the more mysterious. The ship was "known" to have been off St. Augustine, practically pinpointing its area of disappearance, and making the lack of debris even more mysterious.

But, was the ship really near St. Augustine? Based on the writer's information, we cannot really know that. He says that *the crewmen saw the light*, not that anyone ever saw the ship. But he can't know what the crewmen saw. Did the ship "silently vanish"? If no one knows what happened, if no reporter was nearby taking notes, how do we know it was nice and quiet? Maybe they were fighting for their lives, but the "silent vanishment" treatment is far more mysterious. It certainly has a higher interest, as compared to just an ordinary old sinking.

All this the intelligent reader might have deduced for himself, without doing any outside research. There is not much that the writer gave us that appears to be solid. Perhaps he's right, perhaps not. Give an infinite number of monkeys an infinite number of typewriters. . . .

The writer has used another technique which I call "undue familiarity." He mentions the "rust spots along her 350-foot length," implying that he, personally, knows about the old *Sandra*. After all, if he can describe it in that precise detail, he must have some firsthand knowledge. Perhaps he was the one who spotted it off St. Augustine. He really does his research, doesn't he?

There is just one problem here. Upon checking with Lloyd's of London I learned that the *Sandra* was only 185 feet long, just about half what the writer said it was. Now about those rust spots and the writer's apparent familiarity with the ship. . . .

Neither the length of the ship nor the spots are crucially important, of course; but they do point out, once again, that the writer's credibility is very low. Almost everything he has said is blatantly in error, or is speculation. The true length of the ship is of some importance, however, since we can probably assume that a 350-foot ship would handle weather, if it were bad, better than a 185-footer.

But the incident is still unexplained despite all the obvious erroneous assumptions and errors. The (rare) diligent reader who is interested in following up on the case might contact the weather bureau's record center in Asheville, North Carolina, and ask for the records for June. The result is that he would find that the weather *was* excellent, just like the mystery purveyors said. Now we're really stumped. Perhaps there is something "out there" after all. A ship simply cannot disappear without a trace in perfect weather.

So our diligent researcher keeps trying. Any research on a missing ship would be incomplete without contacting Lloyd's of London. Lo! What do we find there? The mystery monger made another error! The *Sandra* did not sail in June, it sailed on April 5. The weather records are now checked for the proper month, and this time we find that beginning the day the *Sandra* sailed from Savannah, and for the next few days, the Atlantic shipping lanes off the southeast United States were buffeted by winds up to seventy-three miles an hour, only two miles an hour under hurricane strength.

All the basic "facts" as presented in the mystery of the *Sandra* are now shown to be wrong. Read again the "mystery" and compare what the writer said to what really occurred. Crewmen drifting to the deck to smoke? Watching the peaceful Florida coastline? Seeing the friendly little old beacon at St. Augustine? Silently vanishing? The near hurricane does change the situation just a bit.

Yet, a number of writers have used the *Sandra* as further "proof" that something strange is going on "out there." They failed to prove their theory, but they have helped confirm one of mine, that the less a writer knows about his subject, the better equipped he is to write a mystery about it. Ignorance of the subject is, in fact, a major technique in writing about the mystery of the Bermuda Triangle and other subjects in the so-called paranormal as well. Some critics of the Bermuda Triangle refer to it as science fiction, but that is an unfair description. Unfair, that is, to science fiction. The Bermuda Triangle, as well as many other "paranormal" topics, might more properly be called "fictional science."

Many people find the "mystery," full of logic and errors that they are unaware of, to be of a higher interest than the correct answer, or the detective work necessary to track it down. Those people who revel in the uncritical claims of pseudoscience, of the "paranormal," might properly be called the "pseudocurious" or the "paracurious." They claim to want the truth, but they really don't want it. They watch Alan Landsburg's "In Search Of" television program and believe that, because *TV Guide* and Leonard Nimoy say so, it is a documentary. They read the tomes of Berlitz, Winer, Spencer, Jeffrey, Godwin, and Sanderson and boggle their minds, as they say. Yet all these books are chock full of examples such as the *Sandra,* confirming the complaints of the College Entrance Examination Board. Careful writing, at least in the area of the pro-paranormal, has gone out of style, and the readers *are* less critical. The readers claim to be seeking illumination but are, in fact, only seeking light entertainment. There will always be plenty of Barnum, Bailey, and Berlitz writers and publishers around to satiate their hunger and further erode their logic.

PHILOSOPHICAL ARGUMENTS

17

It is not easy to explain the character of philosophical reasoning. Indeed, the nature of philosophical reasoning is itself a philosophical problem. We can, however, acquire some sense of it by comparing philosophical reasoning with reasoning as it occurs in daily life. In the opening chapters of this book we noticed that, in everyday discussions, much is taken for granted and left unsaid. In general there is no need to state points that are already a matter of agreement. In contrast, philosophers usually try to make underlying assumptions explicit and then subject them to critical examination. But, even for the philosopher, something must trigger an interest in underlying assumptions—and this usually arises when the advance of knowledge creates fundamental conflicts within the system of hitherto accepted assumptions. Thus much that counts as modern philosophy is an attempt to come to terms with the relationship between modern science and the traditional conception of man's place in the universe.

In recent years, a striking example of such a conflict has been generated by the rise of computer theory and computer technology. Traditionally, humans have cited the capacity to think as the feature that sets them apart from and, of course, above all other creatures. Man has been defined as a rational animal. But we now live in an age in which computers seem able to perform tasks that, had a human being performed them, would certainly count as thinking. Not only can computers perform complex calculations very rapidly, they can also play a tolerably good game of chess. Do machines think? The question seems forced upon us, and it is more than a semantic quibble. In deciding it, we are also reevaluating the status of an aspect of humanity that has long been considered its unique or distinctive feature. Once we decide whether machines can think, the next question is whether human beings are not themselves merely thinking machines.

The two essays presented in this chapter address such questions. The writer of the first essay, A. M. Turing, is one of the geniuses of this century. He not only developed much of the mathematics that underlies modern computer theory but helped give computers their first remarkable application: the cracking of the German secret codes during the Second World War. In this essay, Turing considers whether machines can or cannot think. The brilliance of the essay does not depend upon the answer he gives to the question, but rather upon his attempt to formulate it in a way that would allow reasonable debate to take place concerning it. For this reason, Turing's essay has been considered a classic work on the subject for more than thirty years. In the second essay, Keith Gunderson replies to Turing's challenge head on by denying the terms upon which the question is asked.

Computing Machinery and Intelligence*
A. M. TURING

1. The Imitation Game

I propose to consider the question "Can machines think?" This should begin with definitions of the meaning of the terms "machine" and "think." The definitions might be framed so as to reflect so far as possible the normal use of the words, but this attitude is dangerous. If the meaning of the words "machine" and "think" are to be found by examining how they are commonly used it is difficult to escape the conclusion that the meaning and the answer to the question, "Can machines think?" is to be sought in a statistical survey such as a Gallup poll. But this is absurd. Instead of attempting such a definition I shall replace the question by another, which is closely related to it and is expressed in relatively unambiguous words.

The new form of the problem can be described in terms of a game which we call the "imitation game." It is played with three people, a man (A), a woman (B), and an interrogator (C) who may be of either sex. The interrogator stays in a room apart from the other two. The object of the game for the interrogator is to determine which of the other two is the man and which is the woman. He knows them by labels X and Y, and at the end of the game he says either "X is A and Y is B" or "X is B and Y is A." The interrogator is allowed to put questions to A and B thus:

C: Will X please tell me the length of his or her hair?

* *Mind*, vol. LIX, no. 236 (1950).

Now suppose X is actually A, then A must answer. It is A's object in the game to try to cause C to make the wrong identification. His answer might therefore be

"My hair is shingled, and the longest strands are about nine inches long."

In order that tones of voice may not help the interrogator the answers should be written, or better still, typewritten. The ideal arrangement is to have a teleprinter communicating between the two rooms. Alternatively the question and answers can be repeated by an intermediary. The object of the game for the third player (B) is to help the interrogator. The best strategy for her is probably to give truthful answers. She can add such things as "I am the woman, don't listen to him!" to her answers, but it will avail nothing as the man can make similar remarks.

We now ask the question, "What will happen when a machine takes the part of A in this game?" Will the interrogator decide wrongly as often when the game is played like this as he does when the game is played between a man and a woman? These questions replace our original, "Can machines think?"

2. Critique of the New Problem

As well as asking, "What is the answer to this new form of the question," one may ask, "Is this new question a worthy one to investigate?" This latter question we investigate without further ado, thereby cutting short an infinite regress.

The new problem has the advantage of drawing a fairly sharp line between the physical and the intellectual capacities of a man. No engineer or chemist claims to be able to produce a material which is indistinguishable from the human skin. It is possible that at some time this might be done, but even supposing this invention available we should feel there was little point in trying to make a "thinking machine" more human by dressing it up in such artificial flesh. The form in which we have set the problem reflects this fact in the condition which prevents the interrogator from seeing or touching the other competitors, or hearing their voices. Some other advantages of the proposed criterion may be shown up by specimen questions and answers. Thus:

Q: Please write me a sonnet on the subject of the Forth Bridge.

A: Count me out on this one. I never could write poetry.

Q: Add 34957 to 70764.

A: (Pause about 30 seconds and then give as answer) 105621.

Q: Do you play chess?

A: Yes.

Q: I have K at my K1, and no other pieces. You have only K at K6 and R at R1. It is your move. What do you play?

A: (After a pause of 15 seconds) R-R8 mate.

The question and answer method seems to be suitable for introducing almost any one of the fields of human endeavor that we wish to include. We do not wish to penalize the machine for its inability to shine in beauty competitions, nor to penalize a man for losing in a race against an airplane. The conditions of our game make these disabilities irrelevant. The "witnesses" can brag, if they consider it advisable, as much as they please about their charms, strength or heroism, but the interrogator cannot demand practical demonstrations.

The game may perhaps be criticized on the ground that the odds are weighted too heavily against the machine. If the man were to try and pretend to be the machine he would clearly make a very poor showing. He would be given away at once by slowness and inaccuracy in arithmetic. May not machines carry out something which ought to be described as thinking but which is very different from what a man does? This objection is a very strong one, but at least we can say that if, nevertheless, a machine can be constructed to play the imitation game satisfactorily, we need not be troubled by this objection.

It might be urged that when playing the "imitation game" the best strategy for the machine may possibly be something other than imitation of the behavior of a man. This may be, but I think it is unlikely that there is any great effect of this kind. In any case there is no intention to investigate here the theory of the game, and it will be assumed that the best strategy is to try to provide answers that would naturally be given by a man.

3. The Machines Concerned in the Game

The question which we put in §1 will not be quite definite until we have specified what we mean by the word "machine." It is natural that we should wish to permit every kind of engineering technique to be used in our machines. We also wish to allow the possibility that an engineer or team of engineers may construct a machine which works, but whose manner of operation cannot be satisfactorily described by its constructors because they have applied a method which is largely experimental. Finally, we wish to exclude from the machines men born in the usual manner. It is difficult to frame the definitions so as to satisfy these three conditions. One might for instance insist that the team of engineers should be all of one sex, but this would not really be satisfactory, for it is probably possible to rear a complete individual from a single cell of the skin (say) of a man. To do so would be a feat of biological technique deserving of the very highest praise, but we would not be inclined to regard it as a case of "constructing a thinking machine." This prompts us to abandon the requirement that every kind of technique should be permitted. We are the more ready to do so in view of the fact that the present interest in "thinking machines" has been aroused by a particular kind of machine, usually called an "electronic computer" or "digital computer." Following this suggestion we only permit digital computers to take part in our game.

This restriction appears at first sight to be a very drastic one. I shall attempt to show that it is not so in reality. To do this necessitates a short account of the nature and properties of these computers.

It may also be said that this identification of machines with digital computers, like our criterion for "thinking," will only be unsatisfactory if (contrary to my belief) it turns out that digital computers are unable to give a good showing in the game.

There are already a number of digital computers in working order, and it may be asked, "Why not try the experiment straight away? It would be easy to satisfy the conditions of the game. A number of interrogators could be used, and statistics compiled to show how often the right identification was given." The short answer is that we are not asking whether all digital computers would do well in the game nor whether the computers at present available would do well, but whether there are imaginable computers which would do well. But this is only the short answer. We shall see this question in a different light later.

4. Digital Computers

The idea behind digital computers may be explained by saying that these machines are intended to carry out any operations which could be done by a human computer. The human computer is supposed to be following fixed rules; he has no authority to deviate from them in any detail. We may suppose that these rules are supplied in a book, which is altered whenever he is put on to a new job. He has also an unlimited supply of paper on which he does his calculations. He may also do his multiplications and additions on a "desk machine," but this is not important.

If we use the above explanation as a definition we shall be in danger of circularity of argument. We avoid this by giving an outline of the means by which the desired effect is achieved. A digital computer can usually be regarded as consisting of three parts:

(i) Store.
(ii) Executive unit.
(iii) Control.

The store is a store of information, and corresponds to the human computer's paper, whether this is the paper on which he does his calculations or that on which his book of rules is printed. Insofar as the human computer does calculations in his head a part of the store will correspond to his memory.

The executive unit is the part which carries out the various individual operations involved in a calculation. What these individual operations are will vary from machine to machine. Usually fairly lengthy operations can be done such as "Multiply 3540675445 by 7076345687" but in some machines only very simple ones such as "Write down 0" are possible.

We have mentioned that the "book of rules" supplied to the computer is replaced in the machine by a part of the store. It is then called the "table of instructions." It is the duty of the control to see that these instructions are obeyed correctly and in the right order. The control is so constructed that this necessarily happens.

The information in the store is usually broken up into packets of moderately small size. In one machine, for instance, a packet might consist of ten decimal digits. Numbers are assigned to the parts of the store in which the various packets of information are stored, in some systematic manner. A typical instruction might say—

"Add the number stored in position 6809 to that in 4302 and put the result back into the latter storage position."

Needless to say it would not occur in the machine expressed in English. It would more likely be coded in a form such as 6809430217. Here 17 says which of various possible operations is to be performed on the two numbers. In this case the operation is that described above, viz. "Add the number. . . ." It will be noticed that the instruction takes up 10 digits and so forms one packet of information, very conveniently. The control will normally take the instructions to be obeyed in the order of the positions in which they are stored, but occasionally an instruction such as

"Now obey the instruction stored in position 5606, and continue from there" may be encountered, or again

"If position 4505 contains 0 obey next the instruction stored in 6707, otherwise continue straight on."

Instructions of these latter types are very important because they make it possible for a sequence of operations to be repeated over and over again until some condition is fulfilled, but in doing so to obey, not fresh instructions on each repetition, but the same ones over and over again. To take a domestic analogy. Suppose Mother wants Tommy to call at the cobbler's every morning on his way to school to see if her shoes are done; she can ask him afresh every morning. Alternatively she can stick up a notice once and for all in the hall which he will see when he leaves for school and which tells him to call for the shoes, and also to destroy the notice when he comes back if he has the shoes with him.

The reader must accept it as a fact that digital computers can be constructed, and indeed have been constructed, according to the principles we have described, and that they can in fact mimic the actions of a human computer very closely.

The book of rules which we have described our human computer as using is of course a convenient fiction. Actual human computers really remember what they have got to do. If one wants to make a machine mimic the behavior of the human computer in some complex operation one has to ask him how it is done, and then translate the answer into the form of an instruction table. Constructing instruction tables is usually described as "programing." To "program a machine to carry out the operation A" means to put the appropriate instruction table into the machine so that it will do A.

An interesting variant on the idea of a digital computer is a "digital computer with a random element." These have instructions involving the throwing of a die or some equivalent electronic process; one such instruction might for instance be, "Throw the die and put the resulting number into store 1000." Sometimes such a machine is described as having free will (though I would not use this phrase myself). It is not normally possible to determine from observing a machine whether it has a random element, for a similar effect can be produced by such devices as making the choices depend on the digits of the decimal for π.

Most actual digital computers have only a finite store. There is no theoretical difficulty in the idea of a computer with an unlimited store. Of course only a finite part can have been used at any one time. Likewise only a finite amount can have been constructed, but we can imagine more and more being added as required. Such computers have special theoretical interest and will be called infinite capacity computers.

The idea of a digital computer is an old one. Charles Babbage, Lucasian Professor of Mathematics at Cambridge from 1828 to 1839, planned such a machine, called the Analytical Engine, but it was never completed. Although Babbage had all the essential ideas, his machine was not at that time such a very attractive prospect. The speed which would have been available would be definitely faster than a human computer but something like 100 times slower than the Manchester machine, itself one of the slower of the modern machines. The storage was to be purely mechanical, using wheels and cards.

The fact that Babbage's Analytical Engine was to be entirely mechanical will help us to rid ourselves of a superstition. Importance is often attached to the fact that modern digital computers are electrical, and that the nervous system also is electrical. Since Babbage's machine was not electrical, and since all digital computers are in a sense equivalent, we see that this use of electricity cannot be of theoretical importance. Of course electricity usually comes in where fast signaling is concerned, so that it is not surprising that we find it in both these connections. In the nervous system chemical phenomena are at least as important as electrical. In certain computers the storage system is mainly acoustic. The feature of using electricity is thus seen to be only a very superficial similarity. If we wish to find such similarities we should look rather for mathematical analogies of function.

5. Universality of Digital Computers

The digital computers considered in the last section may be classified among the "discrete state machines." These are the machines which move by sudden jumps or clicks from one quite definite state to another. These states are sufficiently different for the possibility of confusion between them to be ignored. Strictly speaking there are no such machines. Everything really moves continuously. But there are many kinds of machines which can profitably be *thought of* as being discrete state machines. For instance in considering the switches for a lighting system it is a convenient fiction that each switch must be definitely on or definitely off. There must be intermediate positions, but for most purposes we can forget about them. As an example of a discrete state machine we might consider a wheel which clicks round through 120° once a second, but may be stopped by a lever which can be operated from outside; in addition a lamp is to light in one of the positions of the wheel. This machine could be described abstractly as follows: The internal state of the machine (which is described by the position of the wheel) may be q_1, q_2 or q_3. There is an input signal i_0 or i_1 (position of lever). The internal state at any moment is determined by the last state and input signal according to the table

		Last State		
		q_1	q_2	q_3
	i_0	q_2	q_3	q_1
Input				
	i_1	q_1	q_2	q_3

The output signals, the only externally visible indication of the internal state (the light) are described by the table

State	q_1	q_2	q_3
Output	o_0	o_0	o_1

This example is typical of discrete state machines. They can be described by such tables provided they have only a finite number of possible states.

It will seem that given the initial state of the machine and the input signals it is always possible to predict all future states. This is reminiscent of Laplace's view that from the complete state of the universe at one moment of time, as described by the positions and velocities of all particles, it should be possible to predict all future states. The prediction which we are considering is, however, rather nearer to practicability than that considered by Laplace. The system of the "universe as a whole" is such that quite small errors in the initial conditions can have an overwhelming effect at a later time. The displacement of a single electron by a billionth of a centimeter at one moment might make the difference between a man being killed by an avalanche a year later, or escaping. It is an essential property of the mechanical systems which we have called "discrete state machines" that this phenomenon does not occur. Even when we consider the actual physical machines instead of the idealized machines, reasonably accurate knowledge of the state at one moment yields reasonably accurate knowledge any number of steps later.

As we have mentioned, digital computers fall within the class of discrete state machines. But the number of states of which such a machine is capable is usually enormously large. For instance, the number for the machine now working at Manchester is about $2^{165,000}$, i.e., about $10^{50,000}$. Compare this with our example of the clocking wheel described above, which had three states. It is not difficult to see why the number of states should be so immense. The computer includes a store corresponding to the paper used by a human computer. It must be possible to write into the store any one of the combinations of symbols which might have been written on the paper. For simplicity suppose that only digits from 0 to 9 are used as symbols. Variations in handwriting are ignored. Suppose the computer is allowed 100 sheets of paper each containing 50 lines each with room for 30 digits. Then the number of states is $10^{100 \times 50 \times 30}$, i.e., $10^{150,000}$. This is about the number of states of three Manchester machines put together. The logarithm to the base two of the number of states is usually called the "storage capacity" of the machine. Thus the Manchester machine has a storage capacity of about 165,000 and the wheel machine of our example about 1.6. If two machines are put together their capacities must be added to obtain the capacity of the resultant machine. This leads to the possibility of statements such as "The Manchester machine contains 64 magnetic tracks each with a capacity of 2560, eight electronic tubes with a capacity of 1280. Miscellaneous storage amounts to about 300 making a total of 174,380."

Given the table corresponding to a discrete state machine it is possible to predict what it will do. There is no reason why this calculation should not be carried out by means of a digital computer. Provided it could be carried out sufficiently quickly the digital computer could mimic the behavior of any discrete state machine. The imitation game could then be played with the machine in question (as B) and the mimicking digital computer (as A) and the interrogator would be unable to distinguish them. Of course the digital computer must have an adequate storage capacity as well as working sufficiently fast. Moreover, it must be programed afresh for each new machine which it is desired to mimic.

This special property of digital computers, that they can mimic any discrete state machine, is described by saying that they are *universal* machines. The existence of machines with this property has the important consequence that, considerations of speed apart, it is unnecessary to design various new machines to do various computing processes. They can all be done with one digital computer, suitably programed for each case. It will be seen that as a consequence of this all digital computers are in a sense equivalent.

We may now consider again the point raised at the end of §3. It was suggested tentatively that the question, "Can machines think?" should be replaced by "Are there imaginable digital computers which would do well in the imitation game?" If we wish we can make this superficially more general and ask "Are there discrete state machines which would do well?" But in view of the universality property we see that either of these questions is equivalent to this, "Let us fix our attention on one particular digital computer C. Is it true that by modifying this computer to have an adequate storage, suitably increasing its speed of action, and providing it with an appropriate program, C can be made to play satisfactorily the part of A in the imitation game, the part of B being taken by a man?"

6. Contrary Views on the Main Question

We may now consider the ground to have been cleared and we are ready to proceed to the debate on our question, "Can machines think?" and the variant of it quoted at the end of the last section. We cannot altogether abandon the original form of the problem, for opinions will differ as to the appropriateness of the substitution and we must at least listen to what has to be said in this connection.

It will simplify matters for the reader if I explain first my own beliefs in the matter. Consider first the more accurate form of the question. I believe that in about fifty years' time it will be possible to program computers, with a storage capacity of about 10^9, to make them play the imitation game so well that an average interrogator will not have more than 70 per cent chance of making the right identification after five minutes of questioning. The original question, "Can machines think?" I believe to be too meaningless to deserve discussion. Nevertheless I believe that at the end of the century the use of words and general educated opinion will have altered so much that one will be able to speak of machines thinking without expecting to be contradicted. I believe further that no useful purpose is served by concealing these beliefs. The popular view that scientists proceed inexorably from well-established fact to well-established fact, never being influenced by any unproved conjecture, is quite mistaken. Provided it is made clear which are proved facts and which are conjectures, no harm can result. Conjectures are of great importance since they suggest useful lines of research.

I now proceed to consider opinions opposed to my own.

(1) *The Theological Objection.* Thinking is a function of man's immortal soul. God has given an immortal soul to every man and woman, but not to any other animal or to machines. Hence no animal or machine can think.[1]

I am unable to accept any part of this, but will attempt to reply in theological terms. I should find the argument more convincing if animals were classed with men, for there is a greater difference, to my mind, between the typical animate and the inanimate than there is between man and the other animals. The arbitrary character of the orthodox view becomes clearer if we consider how it might appear to a member of some other religious community. How do Christians regard the Moslem view that women have no souls? But let us leave this point aside and return to the main argument. It appears to me that the argument quoted above implies a serious restriction of the omnipotence of the Almighty. It is admitted that there are certain things that He cannot do such as making one equal to two, but should we not believe that He has freedom to confer a soul on an elephant if He sees fit? We might expect that He would only exercise this power in conjunction with a mutation which provided the elephant with an appropriately improved brain to minister to the needs of this soul. An argument of exactly similar form may be made for the case of machines. It may seem different because it is more difficult to "swallow." But this really only means that we think it would be less likely that He would consider the circumstances suitable for conferring a soul. The circumstances in question are discussed in the rest of this paper. In attempting to construct such machines we should not be irreverently usurping His power of creating souls, any more than we are in the procreation of children: rather we are, in either case, instruments of His will providing mansions for the souls that He creates.

[1] Possibly this view is heretical. St. Thomas Aquinas [*Summa Theologica*, quoted by Bertrand Russell, *A History of Western Philosophy* (New York: Simon and Schuster, 1945), p. 458] states that God cannot make a man to have no soul. But this may not be a real restriction on His powers, but only a result of the fact that men's souls are immortal, and therefore indestructible.

However, this is mere speculation. I am not very impressed with theological arguments whatever they may be used to support. Such arguments have often been found unsatisfactory in the past. In the time of Galileo it was argued that the texts, "And the sun stood still . . . and hasted not to go down about a whole day" (Joshua x. 13) and "He laid the foundations of the earth, that it should not move at any time" (Psalm cv. 5) were an adequate refutation of the Copernican theory. With our present knowledge such an argument appears futile. When that knowledge was not available it made a quite different impression.

(2) *The "Heads in the Sand" Objection.* "The consequences of machines thinking would be too dreadful. Let us hope and believe that they cannot do so."

This argument is seldom expressed quite so openly as in the form above. But it affects most of us who think about it at all. We like to believe that Man is in some subtle way superior to the rest of creation. It is best if he can be shown to be *necessarily* superior, for then there is no danger of him losing his commanding position. The popularity of the theological argument is clearly connected with this feeling. It is likely to be quite strong in intellectual people, since they value the power of thinking more highly than others, and are more inclined to base their belief in the superiority of Man on this power.

I do not think that this argument is sufficiently substantial to require refutation. Consolation would be more appropriate: perhaps this should be sought in the transmigration of souls.

(3) *The Mathematical Objection.* There are a number of results of mathematical logic which can be used to show that there are limitations to the powers of discrete state machines. The best known of these results is known as Gödel's theorem, and shows that in any sufficiently powerful logical system statements can be formulated which can neither be proved nor disproved within the system, unless possibly the system itself is inconsistent. There are other, in some respects similar, results due to *Church,*[2] *Kleene, Rosser,* and *Turing.* The latter result is the most convenient to consider, since it refers directly to machines, whereas the others can only be used in a comparatively indirect argument: for instance if Gödel's theorem is to be used we need in addition to have some means of describing logical systems in terms of machines, and machines in terms of logical systems. The result in question refers to a type of machine which is essentially a digital computer with an infinite capacity. It states that there are certain things that such a machine cannot do. If it is rigged up to give answers to questions as in the imitation game, there will be some questions to which it will either give a wrong answer, or fail to give an answer at all however much time is allowed for a reply. There may, of course, be many such questions, and questions which cannot be answered by one machine may be satisfactorily answered by another. We are of course supposing for the present that the questions are of the kind to which an answer "Yes" or "No" is appropriate, rather than questions such as "What do you think of Picasso?" The questions that we know the machines must fail on are of this type, "Consider the machine specified as follows . . . Will this machine ever answer 'Yes' to any question?" The dots are to be replaced by

---

[2] Authors' names in italics refer to works cited in [Turing's] bibliography.

a description of some machine in a standard form, which could be something like that used in Sec. 5. When the machine described bears a certain comparatively simple relation to the machine which is under interrogation, it can be shown that the answer is either wrong or not forthcoming. This is the mathematical result: it is argued that it proves a disability of machines to which the human intellect is not subject.

The short answer to this argument is that although it is established that there are limitations to the powers of any particular machine, it has only been stated, without any sort of proof, that no such limitations apply to the human intellect. But I do not think this view can be dismissed quite so lightly. Whenever one of these machines is asked the appropriate critical question, and gives a definite answer, we know that this answer must be wrong, and this gives us a certain feeling of superiority. Is this feeling illusory? It is no doubt quite genuine, but I do not think too much importance should be attached to it. We too often give wrong answers to questions ourselves to be justified in being very pleased at such evidence of fallibility on the part of the machines. Further, our superiority can only be felt on such an occasion in relation to the one machine over which we have scored our petty triumph. There would be no question of triumphing simultaneously over *all* machines. In short, then, there might be men cleverer than any given machine, but then again there might be other machines cleverer again, and so on.

Those who hold to the mathematical argument would, I think, mostly be willing to accept the imitation game as a basis for discussion. Those who believe in the two previous objections would probably not be interested in any criteria.

(4) *The Argument from Consciousness.* This argument is very well expressed in Professor Jefferson's Lister Oration for 1949, from which I quote. "Not until a machine can write a sonnet or compose a concerto because of thoughts and emotions felt, and not by the chance fall of symbols, could we agree that machine equals brain—that is, not only write it but know that it had written it. No mechanism could feel (and not merely artificially signal, an easy contrivance) pleasure at its successes, grief when its valves fuse, be warmed by flattery, be made miserable by its mistakes, be charmed by sex, be angry or depressed when it cannot get what it wants."

This argument appears to be a denial of the validity of our test. According to the most extreme form of this view the only way by which one could be sure that a machine thinks is to *be* the machine and to feel oneself thinking. One could then describe these feelings to the world, but of course no one would be justified in taking any notice. Likewise according to this view the only way to know that a *man* thinks is to be that particular man. It is in fact the solipsist point of view. It may be the most logical view to hold but it makes communication of ideas difficult. A is liable to believe "A thinks but B does not" while B believes "B thinks but A does not." Instead of arguing continually over this point it is usual to have the polite convention that everyone thinks.

I am sure that Professor Jefferson does not wish to adopt the extreme and solipsist point of view. Probably he would be quite willing to accept the imitation game as a test. The game (with the player B omitted) is frequently used in practice under the name of *viva voce* to discover whether someone really understands something or has "learned it parrot fashion." Let us listen in to a part of such a *viva voce:*

Interrogator: In the first line of your sonnet which reads "Shall I compare thee to a summer's day," would not "a spring day" do as well or better?

Witness: It wouldn't scan.

Interrogator: How about "a winter's day." That would scan all right.

Witness: Yes, but nobody wants to be compared to a winter's day.

Interrogator: Would you say Mr. Pickwick reminded you of Christmas?

Witness: In a way.

Interrogator: Yet Christmas is a winter's day, and I do not think Mr. Pickwick would mind the comparison.

Witness: I don't think you're serious. By a winter's day one means a typical winter's day, rather than a special one like Christmas.

And so on. What would Professor Jefferson say if the sonnet-writing machine was able to answer like this in the *viva voce?* I do not know whether he would regard the machine as "merely artificially signaling" these answers, but if the answers were as satisfactory and sustained as in the above passage I do not think he would describe it as "an easy contrivance." This phrase is, I think, intended to cover such devices as the inclusion in the machine of a record of someone reading a sonnet, with appropriate switching to turn it on from time to time.

In short then, I think that most of those who support the argument from consciousness could be persuaded to abandon it rather than be forced into the solipsist position. They will then probably be willing to accept our test.

I do not wish to give the impression that I think there is no mystery about consciousness. There is, for instance, something of a paradox connected with any attempt to localize it. But I do not think these mysteries necessarily need to be solved before we can answer the question with which we are concerned in this paper.

(5) *Arguments from Various Disabilities.* These arguments take the form, "I grant you that you can make machines do all the things you have mentioned but you will never be able to make one to do X." Numerous features X are suggested in this connection. I offer a selection:

Be kind, resourceful, beautiful, friendly . . . have initiative, have a sense of humor, tell right from wrong, make mistakes . . . fall in love, enjoy strawberries and cream . . . make someone fall in love with it, learn from experience . . . use words properly, be the subject of its own thought . . . have as much diversity of behavior as a man, do something really new. . . .

No support is usually offered for these statements. I believe they are mostly founded on the principle of scientific induction. A man has seen thousands of machines in his lifetime. From what he sees of them he draws a number of general conclusions. They are ugly, each is designed for a very limited purpose, when required for a minutely different purpose they are useless, the variety of behavior of any one of them is very small, etc., etc. Naturally he concludes that these are necessary properties of machines in general. Many of these limitations are associated with the very small storage capacity of most machines. (I am assuming that the idea of storage capacity is extended in some way to cover machines other than discrete state machines. The exact definition does not matter as no mathematical accuracy is claimed in the present discussion.) A few years ago, when very little had been heard of digital computers, it was possible to elicit much incredulity concerning them, if one mentioned their properties without describing their construction. That was presumably due to a similar application of the principle of scientific induction. These applications of the principle are of course largely unconscious. When a burned child fears the fire and shows that he fears it by avoiding it, I should say that he was applying scientific induction. (I could of course also describe his behavior in many other ways.) The works and customs of mankind do not seem to be very suitable material to which to apply scientific induction. A very large part of space-time must be investigated if reliable results are to be obtained. Otherwise we may (as most English children do) decide that everybody speaks English, and that it is silly to learn French.

There are, however, special remarks to be made about many of the disabilities that have been mentioned. The inability to enjoy strawberries and cream may have struck the reader as frivolous. Possibly a machine might be made to enjoy this delicious dish, but any attempt to make one do so would be idiotic. What is important about this disability is that it contributes to some of the other disabilities, e.g., to the difficulty of the same kind of friendliness occurring between man and machine as between white man and white man, or between black man and black man.

The claim that "machines cannot make mistakes" seems a curious one. One is tempted to retort, "Are they any the worse for that?" But let us adopt a more sympathetic attitude, and try to see what is really meant. I think this criticism can be explained in terms of the imitation game. It is claimed that the interrogator could distinguish the machine from the man simply by setting them a number of problems in arithmetic. The machine would be unmasked because of its deadly accuracy. The reply to this is simple. The machine (programed for playing the game) would not attempt to give the *right* answers to the arithmetic problems. It would deliberately introduce mistakes in a manner calculated to confuse the interrogator. A mechanical fault would probably show itself through an unsuitable decision as to what sort of a mistake to make in the arithmetic. Even this interpretation of the criticism is not sufficiently sympathetic. But we cannot afford the space to go into it much further. It seems to me that this criticism depends on a confusion between two kinds of mistakes. We may call them "errors of functioning" and "errors of conclusion." Errors of functioning are due to some mechanical or electrical fault which causes the machine to behave otherwise than it was designed to do. In philosophical discussions one likes to ignore the possibility of such errors; one is therefore discussing "abstract machines." These abstract machines are mathematical fictions rather than physical objects. By definition they are incapable of errors of functioning. In this sense we can truly say that "machines can never make mistakes." Errors of conclusion can only arise when some meaning is attached to the output signals from the machine. The machine might, for instance, type out mathematical equations, or sentences in English. When a false proposition is typed we say that the machine has committed an error of conclusion. There is clearly no reason at all for saying that a machine cannot make this kind of mistake. It might do nothing but type out repeatedly "O = 1." To take a less perverse example, it might have some method for drawing conclusions by scientific induction. We must expect such a method to lead occasionally to erroneous results.

The claim that a machine cannot be the subject of its own thought can of course only be answered if it can be shown that the machine has *some* thought with *some* subject matter. Nevertheless, "the subject matter of a machine's operations" does seem to mean something, at least to the people who deal with it. If, for instance, the machine was trying to find a solution of the equation $x^2 - 40x - 11 = 0$ one would be tempted to describe this equation as part of the machine's subject matter at that moment. In this sort of sense a machine undoubtedly can be its own subject matter. It may be used to help in making up its own programs, or to predict the effect of alterations in its own structure. By observing the results of its own behavior it can modify its own programs so as to achieve some purpose more effectively. These are possibilities of the near future, rather than Utopian dreams.

The criticism that a machine cannot have much diversity of behavior is just a way of saying that it cannot have much storage capacity. Until fairly recently a storage capacity of even a thousand digits was very rare.

The criticisms that we are considering here are often disguised forms of the argument from consciousness. Usually if one maintains that a machine *can* do one of these things, and describes the kind of method that the machine could use, one will not make much of an impression. It is thought that the method (whatever it may be, for it must be mechanical) is really rather base. Compare the parenthesis in Jefferson's statement quoted above.

(6) *Lady Lovelace's Objection.* Our most detailed information of Babbage's Analytical Engine comes from a memoir by Lady Lovelace. In it she states, "The Analytical Engine has no pretensions to *originate* anything. It can do *whatever we know how to order it* to perform" (her italics). This statement is quoted by Hartree who adds: "This does not imply that it may not be possible to construct electronic equipment which will 'think for itself,' or in which, in biological terms, one could set up a conditioned reflex, which would serve as a basis for 'learning.' Whether this is possible in principle or not is a stimulating and exciting question, suggested by some of these recent developments. But it did not seem that the machines constructed or projected at the time had this property."

I am in thorough agreement with Hartree over this. It will be noticed that he does not assert that the machines in question had not got the property, but rather that the evidence available to Lady Lovelace did not encourage her to believe that they had it. It is quite possible that the machines in question had in a sense got this property. For suppose that some discrete state machine has the property. The Analytical Engine was a universal digital computer, so that, if its storage capacity and speed were adequate, it could by suitable programing be made to mimic the machine in question. Probably this argument did not occur to the Countess or to Babbage. In any case there was no obligation on them to claim all that could be claimed.

This whole question will be considered again under the heading of learning machines.

A variant of Lady Lovelace's objection states that a machine can "never do anything really new." This may be parried for a moment with the saw, "There is nothing new under the sun." Who can be certain that "original work" that he has done was not simply the growth of the seed planted in him by teaching, or the effect of following well-known general principles. A better variant of the objection says that a machine can never "take us by surprise." This statement is a more direct challenge and can be met directly. Machines take me by surprise with great frequency. This is largely because I do not do sufficient calculation to decide what to expect them to do, or rather because, although I do a calculation, I do it in a hurried, slipshod fashion, taking risks. Perhaps I say to myself, "I suppose the voltage here ought to be the same as there: anyway let's assume it is." Naturally I am often wrong, and the result is a surprise for me, for by the time the experiment is done these assumptions have been forgotten. These admissions lay me open to lectures on the subject of my vicious ways, but do not throw any doubt on my credibility when I testify to the surprises I experience.

I do not expect this reply to silence my critic. He will probably say that such surprises are due to some creative mental act on my part, and reflect no credit on the machine. This leads us back to the argument from consciousness, and far from the idea of surprise. It is a line of argument we must consider closed, but it is perhaps worth remarking that the appreciation of something as surprising requires as much of a "creative mental act" whether the surprising event originates from a man, a book, a machine or anything else.

The view that machines cannot give rise to surprises is due, I believe, to a fallacy to which philosophers and mathematicians are particularly subject. This is the assumption that as soon as a fact is presented to a mind all consequences of that fact spring into the mind simultaneously with it. It is a very useful assumption under many circumstances, but one too easily forgets that it is false. A natural consequence of doing so is that one then assumes that there is no virtue in the mere working out of consequences from data and general principles.

(7) *Argument from Continuity in the Nervous System.* The nervous system is certainly not a discrete state machine. A small error in the information about the size of a nervous impulse impinging on a neuron may make a large difference to the size of the outgoing impulse. It may be argued that, this being so, one cannot expect to be able to mimic the behavior of the nervous system with a discrete state system.

It is true that a discrete state machine must be different from a continuous machine. But if we adhere to the conditions of the imitation game, the interrogator will not be able to take any advantage of this difference. The situation can be made clearer if we consider some other simpler continuous machine. A differential analyzer will do very well. (A differential analyzer is a certain kind of machine not of the discrete state type used for some kinds of calculation.) Some of these provide their answers in a typed form, and so are suitable for taking part in the game. It would not be possible for a digital computer to predict exactly what answers the differential analyzer would give to a problem, but it would be quite capable of giving the right sort of answer. For instance, if asked to give the value of π (actually about 3.1416) it would be reasonable to choose at random between the values 3.12, 3.13, 3.14, 3.15, 3.16 with the probabilities of 0.05, 0.15, 0.55, 0.19, 0.06 (say). Under these circumstances it would be very difficult for the interrogator to distinguish the differential analyzer from the digital computer.

(8) *The Argument from Informality of Behavior.* It is not possible to produce a set of rules purporting to describe what a man should do in every conceivable set of circumstances. One might for instance have a rule that one is to stop when one sees a red traffic light, and to go if one sees a green one, but what if by some fault both appear together? One may perhaps decide that it is safest to stop. But some further difficulty may well arise from this decision later. To attempt to provide rules of conduct to cover every eventuality, even those arising from traffic lights, appears to be impossible. With all this I agree.

From this it is argued that we cannot be machines. I shall try to reproduce the argument, but I fear I shall hardly do it justice. It seems to run something like this. "If each man had a definite set of rules of conduct by which he regulated his life he would be no better than a machine. But there are no such rules, so men cannot be machines." The undistributed middle is glaring. I do not think the argument is ever put quite like this, but I believe this is the argument used nevertheless. There may however be a certain confusion between "rules of conduct" and "laws of behavior" to cloud the issue. By "rules of conduct" I mean precepts such as "Stop if you see red lights," on which one can act, and of which one can be conscious. By "laws of behavior" I mean laws of nature as applied to a man's body such as "if you pinch him he will squeak." If we substitute "laws of behavior which regulate his life" for "laws of conduct by which he regulates his life" in the argument quoted the undistributed middle is no longer insuperable. For we believe that it is not only true that being regulated by laws of behavior implies being some sort of machine (though not necessarily a discrete state machine), but that conversely being such a machine implies being regulated by such laws. However, we cannot so easily convince ourselves of the absence of complete laws of behavior as of complete rules of conduct. The only way we know of for finding such laws is scientific observation, and we certainly know of no circumstances under which we could say, "We have searched enough. There are no such laws."

We can demonstrate more forcibly that any such statement would be unjustified. For suppose we could be sure of finding such laws if they existed. Then given a discrete state machine it should certainly be possible to discover by observation sufficient about it to predict its future behavior, and this within a reasonable time, say a thousand years. But this does not seem to be the case. I have set up on the Manchester computer a small program using only 1000 units of storage, whereby the machine supplied with one sixteen figure number replies with another within two seconds. I would defy anyone to learn from these replies sufficient about the program to be able to predict any replies to untried values.

(9) *The Argument from Extra-Sensory Perception.* I assume that the reader is familiar with the idea of extra-sensory perception, and the meaning of the four items of it, viz., telepathy, clairvoyance, precognition and psychokinesis. These disturbing phenomena seem to deny all our usual scientific ideas. How we should like to discredit them! Unfortunately the statistical evidence, at least for telepathy, is overwhelming. It is very difficult to rearrange one's ideas so as to fit these new facts in. Once one has accepted them it does not seem a very big step to believe in ghosts and bogies. The idea that our bodies move simply according to the known laws of physics, together with some others not yet discovered but somewhat similar, would be one of the first to go.

This argument is to my mind quite a strong one. One can say in reply that many scientific theories seem to remain workable in practice, in spite of clashing with E.S.P.; that in fact one can get along very nicely if one forgets about it. This is rather cold comfort, and one fears that thinking is just the kind of phenomenon where E.S.P. may be especially relevant.

A more specific argument based on E.S.P. might run as follows: "Let us play the imitation game, using as witnesses a man who is good as a telepathic receiver, and a digital computer. The interrogator can ask such questions as 'What suit does the card in my right hand belong to?' The man by telepathy or clairvoyance gives the right answer 130 times out of 400 cards. The machine can only guess at random, and perhaps get 104 right, so the interrogator makes the right identification." There is an interesting possibility which opens here. Suppose the digital computer contains a random number generator. Then it will be natural to use this to decide what answer to give. But then the random number generator will be subject to the psychokinetic powers of the interrogator. Perhaps this psychokinesis might cause the machine to guess right more often than would be expected on a probability calculation, so that the interrogator might still be unable to make the right identification. On the other hand, he might be able to guess right without any questioning, by clairvoyance.

If telepathy is admitted it will be necessary to tighten our test. The situation could be regarded as analogous to that which would occur if the interrogator were talking to himself and one of the competitors was listening with his ear to the wall. To put the competitors into a "telepathy-proof room" would satisfy all requirements.

7. Learning Machines

The reader will have anticipated that I have no very convincing arguments of a positive nature to support my views. If I had I should not have taken such pains to point out the fallacies in contrary views. Such evidence as I have I shall now give.

Let us return for a moment to Lady Lovelace's objection, which stated that the machine can only do what we tell it to do. One could say that a man can "inject" an idea into the machine, and that it will respond to a certain extent and then drop into quiescence, like a piano string struck by a hammer. Another simile would be an atomic pile of less than critical size: an injected idea is to correspond to a neutron entering the pile from without. Each such neutron will cause a certain disturbance which eventually dies away. If, however, the size of the pile is sufficiently increased, the disturbance caused by such an incoming neutron will very likely go on and on increasing until the whole pile is destroyed. Is there a corresponding phenomenon for minds, and is there one for machines? There does seem to be one for the human mind. The majority of them seem to be "subcritical," i.e., to correspond in this analogy to piles of subcritical size. An idea presented to such a mind will on an average give rise to less than one idea in reply. A smallish proportion are supercritical. An idea presented to such a mind may give rise to a whole "theory" consisting of secondary, tertiary and more remote ideas. Animals' minds seem to be very definitely subcritical. Adhering to this analogy we ask, "Can a machine be made to be supercritical?"

The "skin of an onion" analogy is also helpful. In considering the functions of the mind or the brain we find certain operations which we can explain in purely mechanical terms. This we say does not correspond to the real mind: it is a sort of skin which we must strip off if we are to find the real mind. But then in what remains we find a further skin to be stripped off, and so on. Proceeding in this way do we ever come to the "real" mind, or do we eventually come to the skin which has nothing in it? In the latter case the whole mind is mechanical. (It would not be a discrete state machine however. We have discussed this.)

These last two paragraphs do not claim to be convincing arguments. They should rather be described as "recitations tending to produce belief."

The only really satisfactory support that can be given for the view expressed at the beginning of Sec. 6, will be that provided by waiting for the end of the century and then doing the experiment described. But what can we say in the meantime? What steps should be taken now if the experiment is to be successful?

As I have explained, the problem is mainly one of programing. Advances in engineering will have to be made too, but it seems unlikely that these will not be adequate for the requirements. Estimates of the storage capacity of the brain vary from 10^{10} to 10^{15} binary digits. I incline to the lower values and believe that only a very small fraction is used for the higher types of thinking. Most of it is probably used for the retention of visual impressions. I should be surprised if more than 10^9 was required for satisfactory playing of the imitation game, at any rate against a blind man. (Note: The capacity of the *Encyclopaedia Britannica*, eleventh edition, is 2×10^9.) A storage capacity of 10^7 would be a very practicable possibility even by present techniques. It is probably not necessary to increase the speed of operations of the machines at all. Parts of modern machines which can be regarded as analogues of nerve cells work about a thousand times faster than the latter. This should provide a "margin of safety" which could cover losses of speed arising in many ways. Our problem then is to find out how to program these machines to play the game. At my present rate of working I produce about a thousand digits of program a day, so that about sixty workers, working steadily through the fifty years might accomplish the job, if nothing went into the waste-paper basket. Some more expeditious method seems desirable.

In the process of trying to imitate an adult human mind we are bound to think a good deal about the process which has brought it to the state that it is in. We may notice three components.

(a) The initial state of the mind, say at birth.

(b) The education to which it has been subjected.

(c) Other experience, not to be described as education, to which it has been subjected.

Instead of trying to produce a program to simulate the adult mind, why not rather try to produce one which simulates the child's? If this were then subjected to an appropriate course of education one would obtain the adult brain. Presumably the child-brain is something like a notebook as one buys it from the stationers. Rather little mechanism, and lots of blank sheets. (Mechanism and writing are from our point of view almost synonymous.) Our hope is that there is so little mechanism in the child-brain that something like it can be easily programed. The amount of work in the education we can assume, as a first approximation, to be much the same as for the human child.

We have thus divided our problem into two parts—the child-program and the education process. These two remain very closely connected. We cannot expect to find a good child-machine at the first attempt. One must experiment with teaching one such machine and see how well it learns. One can then try another and see if it is better or worse. There is an obvious connection between this process and evolution, by the identification.

Structure of the child-machine	= Hereditary material
Changes " " " "	= Mutations
Natural selection	= Judgment of the experimenter

One may hope, however, that this process will be more expeditious than evolution. The survival of the fittest is a slow method for measuring advantages. The experimenter, by the exercise of intelligence, should be able to speed it up. Equally important is the fact that he is not restricted to random mutations. If he can trace a cause for some weakness he can probably think of the kind of mutation which will improve it.

It will not be possible to apply exactly the same teaching process to the machine as to a normal child. It will not, for instance, be provided with legs, so that it could not be asked to go out and fill the coal scuttle. Possibly it might not have eyes. But however well these deficiencies might be overcome by clever engineering, one could not send the creature to school without the other children making excessive fun of it. It must be given some tuition. We need not be too concerned about the legs, eyes, etc. The example of Miss Helen Keller shows that education can take place provided that communication in both directions between teacher and pupil can take place by some means or other.

We normally associate punishments and rewards with the teaching process. Some simple child-machines can be constructed or programed on this sort of principle. The machine has to be so constructed that events which shortly preceded the occurrence of a punishment-signal are unlikely to be repeated, whereas a reward-signal increases the probability of repetition of the events which led up to it. These definitions do not presuppose any feelings on the part of the machine. I have done some experiments with one such child-machine, and succeeded in teaching it a few things, but the teaching method was too unorthodox for the experiment to be considered really successful.

The use of punishments and rewards can at best be a part of the teaching process. Roughly speaking, if the teacher has no other means of communicating to the pupil, the amount of information which can reach him does not exceed the total number of rewards and punishments applied. By the time a child has learned to repeat "Casabianca" he would probably feel very sore indeed, if the text could only be discovered by a "Twenty Questions" technique, every "NO" taking the form of a blow. It is necessary therefore to have some other "unemotional" channels of communication. If these are available it is possible to teach a machine by punishments and rewards to obey orders given in some language, e.g., a symbolic language. These orders are to be transmitted through the "unemotional" channels. The use of this language will diminish greatly the number of punishments and rewards required.

Opinions may vary as to the complexity which is suitable in the child-machine. One might try to make it as simple as possible consistently with the general principles. Alternatively one might have a complete system of logical inference "built in."[3] In the latter case the store would be largely occupied with definitions and propositions. The propositions would have various kinds of status, e.g., well-established facts, conjectures, mathematically proven theorems, statements given by an authority, expressions having the logical form of proposition but not belief-value. Certain propositions may be described as "imperatives." The machine should be so constructed that as soon as an imperative is classed as "well-established" the appropriate action automatically takes place. To illustrate this, suppose the teacher says to the machine, "Do your homework now." This may cause "Teacher says 'Do your homework now' " to be included among the well-established facts. Another such fact might be, "Everything that teacher says is true." Combining these may eventually lead to the imperative, "Do your homework now," being included among the well-established facts, and this, by the construction of the machine, will mean that the homework actually gets started, but the effect is very unsatisfactory. The process of inference used by the machine need not be such as would satisfy the most exacting logicians. There might for instance be no hierarchy of types. But this need not mean that type fallacies will occur, any more than we are bound to fall over unfenced cliffs. Suitable imperatives (expressed *within* the systems, not forming part of the rules *of* the system) such as "Do not use a class unless it is a subclass of one which has been mentioned by teacher" can have a similar effect to "Do not go too near the edge."

The imperatives that can be obeyed by a machine that has no limbs are

---

[3] Or rather "programed in" for our child-machine will be programed in a digital computer. But the logical system will not have to be learned.

bound to be of a rather intellectual character, as in the example (doing homework) given above. Important among such imperatives will be ones which regulate the order in which the rules of the logical system concerned are to be applied. For at each stage when one is using a logical system, there is a very large number of alternative steps, any of which one is permitted to apply, so far as obedience to the rules of the logical system is concerned. These choices make the difference between a brilliant and a footling reasoner, not the difference between a sound and a fallacious one. Propositions leading to imperatives of this kind might be "When Socrates is mentioned, use the syllogism in Barbara" or "If one method has been proved to be quicker than another, do not use the slower method." Some of these may be "given by authority," but others may be produced by the machine itself, e.g., by scientific induction.

The idea of a learning machine may appear paradoxical to some readers. How can the rules of operation of the machine change? They should describe completely how the machine will react whatever its history might be, whatever changes it might undergo. The rules are thus quite time-invariant. This is quite true. The explanation of the paradox is that the rules which get changed in the learning process are of a rather less pretentious kind, claiming only an ephemeral validity. The reader may draw a parallel with the Constitution of the United States.

An important feature of a learning machine is that its teacher will often be very largely ignorant of quite what is going on inside, although he may still be able to some extent to predict his pupil's behavior. This should apply most strongly to the later education of a machine arising from a child-machine of well-tried design (or program). This is in clear contrast with normal procedure when using a machine to do computations: one's object is then to have a clear mental picture of the state of the machine at each moment in the computation. This object can only be achieved with a struggle. The view that "the machine can only do what we know how to order it to do,"[4] appears strange in face of this. Most of the programs which we can put into the machine will result in its doing something that we cannot make sense of at all, or which we regard as completely random behavior. Intelligent behavior presumably consists in a departure from the completely disciplined behavior involved in computation, but a rather slight one, which does not give rise to random behavior, or to pointless repetitive loops. Another important result of preparing our machine for its part in the imitation game by a process of teaching and learning is that "human fallibility" is likely to be omitted in a rather natural way, i.e., without special "coaching." (The reader should reconcile this with the point of view on pp. 371–73). Processes that are learned do not produce a hundred per cent certainty of result; if they did they could not be unlearned.

It is probably wise to include a random element in a learning machine. A random element is rather useful when we are searching for a solution of some problem. Suppose for instance we wanted to find a number between 50 and 200

---

[4] Compare Lady Lovelace's statement [pp. 373–74], which does not contain the word "only."

which was equal to the square of the sum of its digits, we might start at 51 then try 52 and go on until we got a number that worked. Alternatively we might choose numbers at random until we got a good one. This method has the advantage that it is unnecessary to keep track of the values that have been tried, but the disadvantage that one may try the same one twice, but this is not very important if there are several solutions. The systematic method has the disadvantage that there may be an enormous block without any solutions in the region which has to be investigated first. Now the learning process may be regarded as a search for a form of behavior which will satisfy the teacher (or some other criterion). Since there is probably a very large number of satisfactory solutions the random method seems to be better than the systematic. It should be noticed that it is used in the analogous process of evolution. But there the systematic method is not possible. How could one keep track of the different genetical combinations that had been tried, so as to avoid trying them again?

We may hope that machines will eventually compete with men in all purely intellectual fields. But which are the best ones to start with? Even this is a difficult decision. Many people think that a very abstract activity, like the playing of chess, would be best. It can also be maintained that it is best to provide the machine with the best sense organs that money can buy, and then teach it to understand and speak English. This process could follow the normal teaching of a child. Things would be pointed out and named, etc. Again I do not know what the right answer is, but I think both approaches should be tried.

We can only see a short distance ahead, but we can see plenty there that needs to be done.

The Imitation Game[*]

KEITH GUNDERSON

I

Disturbed by what he took to be the ambiguous, if not meaningless, character of the question "Can machines think?," the late A. M. Turing in his article "Computing Machinery and Intelligence" sought to replace that question in the following way. He said:

> The new form of the problem can be described in terms of a game which we call the "imitation game." It is played with three people, a man (A), a woman (B), and an interrogator (C) who may be either sex. The interrogator stays in a room apart from the other two. The object of the game for the interrogator is to determine which of the other two is the man and which is the woman. He knows them by labels X and Y, and at the

[*] *Mind*, vol. LXXIII, no. 290 (April 1964), pp. 234–45. Reprinted in Keith Gunderson, *Mentality and Machines* (Garden City, N.Y.: Anchor Books, 1971).

end of the game he says either "X is A and Y is B" or "X is B and Y is A." The interrogator is allowed to put questions to A and B thus:

C: "Will X please tell me the length of his or her hair?"

Now suppose X is actually A, then A must answer. It is A's object in the game to try to cause C to make the wrong identification. His answer might therefore be

"My hair is shingled, and the longest strands are about nine inches long."

In order that tones of voice may not help the interrogator the answers should be written, or better still, typewritten. The ideal arrangement is to have a teleprinter communicating between the two rooms. Alternatively the question and answers can be repeated by an intermediary. The object of the game for the third player (B) is to help the interrogator. The best strategy for her is probably to give truthful answers. She can add such things as "I am the woman, don't listen to him!" to her answers, but it will avail nothing as the man can make similar remarks.

We now ask the question, "What will happen when a machine takes the part of A in this game?" Will the interrogator decide wrongly as often as when the game is played between a man and a woman? These questions replace our original, "Can machines think?"

And Turing's answers to these latter questions are more or less summed up in the following passage: "I believe that in fifty years' time it will be possible to program computers, with a storage capacity of about 10^9, to make them play the imitation game so well that an average interrogator will not have more than 70 per cent chance of making the right identification after five minutes of questioning." And though he goes on to reiterate that he suspects that the original question "Can machines think?" is meaningless, and that it should be disposed of and replaced by a more precise formulation of the problems involved (a formulation such as a set of questions about the imitation game and machine capacities), what finally emerges is that Turing does answer the "meaningless" question after all, and that his answer is in the affirmative and follows from his conclusions concerning the capabilities of machines which might be successfully substituted for people in the imitation-game context.

It should be pointed out that Turing's beliefs about the possible capabilities and capacities of machines are not limited to such activities as playing the imitation game as successfully as human beings. He does not, for example, deny that it might be possible to develop a machine which would relish the taste of strawberries and cream, though he thinks it would be "idiotic" to attempt to make one, and confines himself on the whole in his positive account to considerations of machine capacities which could be illustrated in terms of playing the imitation game.

So we shall be primarily concerned with asking whether or not a machine, which could play the imitation game as well as Turing thought it might, would thus be a machine which we would have good reasons for saying was capable of thought and what would be involved in saying this.

Some philosophers have not been satisfied with Turing's treatment of the question "Can machines think?"[1] But the imitation game itself, which indeed seems to constitute the hub of his positive treatment, has been little more than alluded to or remarked on in passing. I shall try to develop in a somewhat more detailed way certain objections to it, objections which, I believe, Turing altogether fails to anticipate. My remarks shall thus in the main be critically oriented, which is not meant to suggest that I believe there are no plausible lines of defense open to a supporter of Turing. I shall, to the contrary, close with a brief attempt to indicate what some of these might be and some general challenges which I think Turing has raised for the philosopher of mind.

II

Let us consider the following question: "Can rocks imitate?" One might say that it is a question "too meaningless to deserve discussion." Yet it seems possible to reformulate the problem in relatively unambiguous words as follows:

> The new form of the problem can be described in terms of a game which we call the "toe-stepping game." It is played with three people, a man (A), a woman (B), and an interrogator (C) who may be of either sex. The interrogator stays in a room apart from the other two. The door is closed, but there is a small opening in the wall next to the floor through which he can place most of his foot. When he does so, one of the other two may step on his toe. The object of the game for the interrogator is to determine, by the way in which his toe is stepped on, which of the other two is the man and which is the woman. He knows them by labels X and Y, and at the end of the game he says either "X is A and Y is B" or "X is B and Y is A." Now the interrogator—rather the person whose toe gets stepped on—may indicate before he puts his foot through the opening, whether X or Y is to step on it. Better yet, there might be a narrow division in the opening, one side for X and one for Y (one for A and one for B).
>
> Now suppose C puts his foot through A's side of the opening (which may be labeled X or Y on C's side of the wall). It is A's object in the game to try to cause C to make the wrong identification. His step on the toe might therefore be quick and jabbing like some high-heeled woman.
>
> The object of the game for the third player (B) is to help the person whose toe gets stepped on. The best strategy for her is probably to try to step on it in the most womanly way possible. She can add such things as a slight twist of a high heel to her stepping, but it will avail nothing as the man can step in similar ways, since he will also have at his disposal various shoes with which to vary his toe-stepping.

[1] See Michael Scriven, "The Mechanical Concept of Mind." pp. 31ff., and "The Compleat Robot: A Prolegomena to Androidology" in *Dimensions of Mind*, ed. Sidney Hook (New York: New York University Press, 1960). Also a remark by Paul Ziff in "The Feelings of Robots," pp. 98ff., and others—for example, C. E. Shannon and J. McCarthy in their preface to *Automata Studies* (Princeton: Princeton University Press, 1956). . . .

We now ask the question: "What will happen when a rock box (a box filled with rocks of varying weights, sizes, and shapes) is constructed with an electric eye which operates across the opening in the wall so that it releases a rock which descends upon C's toe whenever C puts his foot through A's side of the opening, and thus comes to take the part of A in this game?" (The situation can be made more convincing by constructing the rock box so that there is a mechanism pulling up the released rock shortly after its descent, thus avoiding telltale noises such as a rock rolling on the floor, etc.) Will then the interrogator—the person whose toe gets stepped on—decide wrongly as often as when the game is played between a man and a woman? These questions replace our original, "Can rocks imitate?"

I believe that in less than fifty years' time it will be possible to set up elaborately constructed rock boxes, with large rock-storage capacities, so that they will play the toe-stepping game so well that the average person who would get his toe stepped on would not have more than 70 per cent chance of making the right identification after about five minutes of toe-stepping.

The above seems to show the following: what follows from the toe-stepping game situation surely is not that rocks are able to imitate (I assume no one would want to take that path of argument) but only that they are able to be rigged in such a way that they could be substituted for a human being in a toe-stepping game without changing any essential characteristics of that game. And this is claimed in spite of the fact that if a human being were to play the toe-stepping game as envisaged above, we would no doubt be correct in saying that that person was imitating, etc. To be sure, a digital computer is a more august mechanism than a rock box, but Turing has not provided us with any arguments for believing that its role in the imitation game, as distinct from the net results it yields, is any closer a match for a human being executing such a role, than is the rock box's execution of its role in the toe-stepping game a match for a human being's execution of a similar role. The parody comparison can be pushed too far. But I think it lays bare the reason why there is no contradiction involved in saying, "Yes, a machine can play the imitation game, but it can't think." It is for the same reason that there is no contradiction in saying, "Of course a rock box of such-and-such a sort can be set up, but rocks surely can't imitate." For thinking (or imitating) cannot be fully described simply by pointing to net results such as those illustrated above. For if this were not the case it would be correct to say that a phonograph could sing, and that an electric eye could see people coming.

People may be let out of a building by either an electric eye or a doorman. The end result is the same. But though a doorman may be rude or polite, the electric eye neither practices nor neglects etiquette. Turing brandishes net results. But I think the foregoing at least indicates certain difficulties with any account of thinking or decision as to whether a certain thing is capable of thought which is based primarily on net results. And, of course, one could always ask whether the net results were really the same. But I do not wish to follow that line of argument here. It is my main concern simply to indicate where Turing's account, which is cast largely in terms of net results, fails because of this. It is not an effective counter to reply: "But part of the net results in question includes intelligent people being deceived!" For what would this add to the general argument? No doubt people could be deceived by rock boxes! It is said that high-fidelity phonographs have been perfected to the point where blindfolded music critics are unable to distinguish their "playing" from that of, let us say, the Budapest String Quartet. But the phonograph would never be said to have performed with unusual brilliance on Saturday, nor would it ever deserve an encore.

III

Now perhaps comparable net results achieved by machines and human beings is all that is needed to establish an analogy between them, but it is far from what is needed to establish that one sort of subject (machines) can do the same thing that another sort of subject (human beings or other animals) can do. Part of what things do is how they do it. To ask whether a machine can think is in part to ask whether machines can do things in certain ways.

The above is relevant to what might be called the problem of distinguishing and evaluating the net results achieved by a machine as it is touched on by Scriven in his discussion of what he calls "the performatory problem" and "the personality problem." In "The Compleat Robot: A Prolegomena to Androidology," he writes:

> The performatory problem here is whether a computer can produce results which, when translated, provide what would count as an original solution of proof *if it came from a man.* The personality problem is whether we are entitled to call such a result a solution or proof, despite the fact that it did *not* come from a man.

And continues:

> The logical trap is this: no *one* performatory achievement will be enough to persuade us to apply the human-achievement vocabulary, but if we refuse to use this vocabulary in each case separately, on this ground, we will, perhaps wrongly, have committed ourselves to avoiding it even when *all* the achievements are simultaneously attained.[2]

My concern is not, however, with what is to count as an original solution or proof. Scriven, in the above, is commenting on the claims: "Machines only do what we tell them to do. They are incapable of genuinely original thought." He says that two "importantly different points are run together." The above is his attempt to separate these points. But it seems that there are at least three, and not just two, points which are run together in the just-mentioned claims. The third point, the one not covered by Scriven's distinction between the performa-

[2] In *Dimensions of Mind,* ed. Sidney Hook, pp. 118–42.

tory[3] and personality problems, is simply the problem, mentioned above, of discerning when one subject (a machine) has *done the same thing* as another subject (a human being). And here "doing the same thing" does not simply mean "achieved similar end result." (Which is not to suggest that the phrase can never be used in that way in connection with thinking.) This is of interest in respect to Scriven's discussion, since it might be the case that all the achievements were simultaneously attained by a machine, as Scriven suggests, and that we had decided on various grounds that they should count as original proofs and solutions and thus surmounted the personality problem, but yet felt unwilling to grant that the machines were capable of "genuinely original thought." Our grounds for this latter decision might be highly parallel to our grounds for not wanting to say that rocks could imitate (even though rock boxes had reached a high level of development). Of course our grounds might not be as sound as these. I am simply imagining the case where they are, which is also a case where all the achievements are attained in such a way that they count as original solutions or proofs. In this case we would see that answers to questions about originality and performance and the logical trap mentioned by Scriven would be wholly separate from whatever answers might be given to the question whether or not the machines involved thought, and would thus be unsuitable answers to the question whether or not they were capable of "genuinely original thought." In other words, questions as to originality and questions as to thinking are not the same, but this dissimilarity is left unacknowledged in Scriven's account.

IV

Suppose we build a machine that X-es, where X-ing is arriving at a certain result or conclusion (which may also be referred to as an activity which may or may not involve the use of language) and which is denoted by verbs or verb phrases such as "calculates" or "computes" or "utters words" or "finds its way home in the spring" or, as in Descartes' clock example, "measures time." Let us assume that the results denoted by such verbs may be graded in various ways, so that the subjects responsible for them may be said to have performed "better than average," "in a superior way," "as well as," "somewhat better than," and so forth, relative to the performances of other subjects which could be human beings, Saturnians, animals, machines, *et al.* Though we shall sometimes appear to be talking only about the skills or abilities of an individual, we shall always wish it understood that the individual represents a certain subset of subjects, sometimes, for example, a "species" of subjects (animals), sometimes only a kind of member of a species or a kind of man—such as physicist, artist, *et al.* Now someone might argue on behalf of a machine, and in the same fashion that Montaigne argued on behalf of beasts, that if it is able to X "as well as" or "in a superior way to" the X-ing of which a man is capable, then, if man's X-ing would require that he thinks, reasons, acts intelligently, and so forth, so does the

---

[3] In spite of my remarks on originality, which follow, Scriven's general point seems very well taken.

machine's X-ing, and its ability in doing so is indicated by the way in which we would grade it. Descartes, we have already emphasized, was intent on denying (and rightly so, I believe) the correctness of this sort of reasoning. For if the case where the machine X-es is really the same and not just vaguely analogous to the case where the man X-es, then we should be safe in making certain further assumptions about the machine's general capabilities and performances, just as in the case where we know that a man can do X and must thus be able to do a number of other things as well. For example, if a man does X where X-ing is devising a theory for splitting the atom, then we may generally assume that such a man is capable of a great many other things as well (we may assume that scientific theorists are capable of a great many other things as well); we may assume that he knows some mathematics and physics, that he has learned a language, that he can solve a wide variety of problems, and so on. Some of these skills would be closely related to devising such theories, some would be less closely related. Now, though we would not be safe in assuming that our atomic scientist would be a crackerjack poet or tennis player, we would be safe in assuming that he would be capable of some cluster of abilities such as those just mentioned and that we can expect further things from him, that he might perhaps be just the man to teach in a physics department at some university, would be a good man to review other works in the field, should be a first-rate adviser to the Atomic Energy Commission, and so on. I believe the above preserves the core of what Descartes was claiming when he wrote about certain performances of beasts that "the fact that they do better than we do, does not prove that they are endowed with mind, for in this case they would have more reason than any of us, and would surpass us in all other things."[4] (And, of course, it is assumed that they don't surpass us in all—perhaps even any—other things.) I believe that the phrase "in many other" or even "in various other" or "in a wide range of" could be substituted for the phrase "in all other" without in any way changing the main point of what Descartes was trying to establish with the above statement.

Take the case of a machine again, where that machine is, let us say, a digital computer loaded with a certain program so that in a matter of minutes it figures out monthly checks of all the workers at General Motors. Now if any human being were able to do that, we should be safe in assuming that, since for most of us it would require a great deal of mental effort, figuring, and cross-checking, the very efficient human being would also outdo us at all sorts of other tasks, would be better at all sorts of monetary estimations, mathematical puzzles, and so on. Or, better still, take the case of a swallow which returns in the spring to its place of nesting. If a man were, let us say, able to drive from Princeton to Capistrano after merely glancing at a road map, we should be able to assume that he's good at maps, just the fellow to tell us how to get out of downtown Manhattan, or, if he can't verbalize it, just the man to drive us out, and so forth. Or suppose a machine is set up to slosh some paint around on a canvas, that someone enters it in an art contest, and that the machine-painting wins the prize. If a man has

[4] *Loc. cit.*

a painting of his submitted in a reputable contest and wins a prize, we may generally assume he's a well-trained painter, an artist with a number of attending skills. So then, a Montaigne or a Turing might say, is the machine not an artist? He just took the prize from Jackson Pollock, Maxim Gorky, and Willem de Kooning. No, Descartes is saying. Just as in the earlier case of the digital computer where we were not entitled to assume that it could do anything other than what it was programmed to do[5]—namely, figure out wages—and in the case of the swallows we can't assume that they're good at maps, terrain, landmarks, or anything else in general, so too in the case of the art contest we can't assume that such a machine had in some way worked out sketches leading up to the prize painting, that it had experimented with various textures, coloring, techniques, or that it had some knack with prints, water colors, or was capable of *anything* other than being able to slosh paint about in the way it did. We can't assume that it has any artistic habits, skills, or techniques at all. Its art has not developed and will not develop. Similarly the case of the digital computer is not like the case of a man who has acquired a number of general computational skills and applies them to a variety of problems and situations. It is instead like the case of a man who was only able to do a speedy computation of salaries for General Motors' workers for a particular month. The case of the swallow is not like the case of the fellow who is good at maps, but would be like the case of a fellow who was only able to get from Princeton to Capistrano to Princeton to . . ., etc. In other words, as in the case of certain computer outputs—a poem, for example[6]—we have hitherto understood the result in question to be such that its production required certain general skills or capacities on the part of human beings. And human beings who possessed such general skills or capacities could be safely assumed to be able to do a number of other things too. Hence if the machine truly writes poems in at least roughly the way that a human being writes poems—which would be the only sort of case where we would be justified in assuming that it was able to understand a language, reason, and reflect—then we should also be able to assume that the machine is also capable of a wide range of other activities, in which verbal, thinking, reasoning, and reflecting creatures are capable of participating. But in the case of the computer producing a poem (or a parrot, words) we cannot correctly make such an assumption. (Which, of course, does not mean that no poem has been written, nor words uttered.) Hence

[5] But I am not yet dealing with the general question of what, in principle, a computer might be programmed to do. Nor am I assuming that certain types of computer programs would not be more flexible from situation to situation, would not have to be replaced each time, would not be self-adjusting in various ways, etc. I am simply discussing the case where a new situation *does* demand a wholly new program, and the computer's operation issues in a certain single result. (Or, in Descartes' words, whose "organs have need of some special adaptation for every particular action.")

[6] As good or better than the one which the LGP-30 under the direction of R. F. Reiss and R. M. Worth composed called *Ode to a Depot:*

By the new neighbors their depot was jade,
These ulcers were new, many depots were suede.

In *San Francisco Review*, Vol, I, No. 12, June 1962, p. 86. The computer's *Elegy for a Lady* is closer to the style of Dylan Thomas; see p. 85.

why not look for an alternative explanation? This is precisely what Descartes did.

Put in another way, Descartes pointed out in effect the simple but important (and often ignored) fact that we do not understand a man doing a calculation, for example, simply by observing that one isolated case of his calculating. We do not understand, nor should we assess or describe, his performance in a particular case apart from all the other things we have learned about him and men in general. There is a whole network of knowledge which we bring to his situation, and it is in large part on the basis of this that we are willing and able to say what we say about him, that we say here is a man who is struggling with a problem, thinking things out, checking his results, and so forth. If it were another sort of man whom we watched the diabolical neurosurgeon rig up so that all he would do hour after hour was calculate the monthly wages of various firms, then we should be expected to appraise his activity accordingly; we should say, "Well, I know he seems at first to be a super estimator, but you see this neurosurgeon rigged his brain, and so on, the poor devil's optic nerves have been fixed so that he only sees printed names and figures, can't really find his own way to the door." Here we would have an alternative explanation of how results usually obtained by thinking and reflection were brought about in another way. It is only reasonable to expect the explanation to be used—so too in the case of a computer computing.

A rock rolls down a hill and there is, strictly speaking, no behavior or action on the part of the rock. But if a man rolls down a hill we might well ask if he was pushed or did it intentionally, whether he's enjoying himself, playing a game, pretending to be a tumbleweed, or what. We cannot think of a man as simply or purely rolling down a hill—unless he is dead. *A fortiori*, we cannot understand him being a participant in the imitation game apart from his dispositions, habits, etc., which are exhibited in contexts other than the imitation game. Thus we cannot hope to find any decisive answer to the question as to how we should characterize a machine which can play (well) the imitation game, by asking what we would say about a man who could play (well) the imitation game. Thinking, whatever positive characterization or account is correct, is not something which any one example will explain or decide. But the part of Turing's case which I've been concerned with rests largely on one example.

V

The following might help to clarify the above. Imagine the dialogue below:

Vacuum Cleaner Salesman: Now here's an example of what the all-purpose Swish 600 can do. (He then applies the nozzle to the carpet and it sucks up a bit of dust.)

Housewife: What else can it do?

Vacuum Cleaner Salesman: What do you mean "What else can it do?" It just sucked up that bit of dust, didn't you see?

Housewife: Yes, I saw it suck up a bit of dust, but I thought it was all-purpose. Doesn't it suck up larger and heavier bits of straw or paper or mud? And can't it get in the tight corners? Doesn't it have other nozzles? What about the cat hair on the couch?

Vacuum Cleaner Salesman: It sucks up bits of dust. That's what vacuum cleaners are for.

Housewife: Oh, that's what it does. I thought it was simply an example of what it does.

Vacuum Cleaner Salesman: It is an example of what it does. What it does is to suck up bits of dust.

We ask: Who's right about examples? We answer: It's not perfectly clear that anyone is lying or unjustifiably using the word "example." And there's no obvious linguistic rule or regularity to point to which tells us that if S can only do X, then S's doing X cannot be an example of what S can do since being an example presupposes or entails or what not that other kinds of examples are forthcoming (sucking up mud, cat hair, etc.). Yet, in spite of this, the housewife has a point. One simply has a right to expect more from an all-purpose Swish 600 than what has been demonstrated. Here clearly the main trouble is with "all-purpose" rather than with "example," though there may still be something misleading about saying, "Here's an example . . . ," and it would surely mislead to say, "Here's *just* an example . . . ," followed by ". . . of what the all-purpose Swish 600 can do." The philosophical relevance of all this to our own discussion can be put in the following rather domestic way: "thinking" is a term which shares certain features with "all-purpose" as it occurs in the phrase "all-purpose Swish 600." It is not used to designate or refer to one capability, capacity, disposition, talent, habit, or feature of a given subject any more than "all-purpose" in the above example is used to mark out one particular operation of a vacuum cleaner. Thinking, whatever positive account one might give of it, is not, for example, like swimming or tennis playing. The question as to whether Peterson can swim or play tennis can be settled by a few token examples of Peterson swimming or playing tennis. (And it might be noted it is hardly imaginable that the question as to whether Peterson could think or not would be raised. For in general it is not at all interesting to ask that question of contemporary human beings, though it might be interesting for contemporary human beings to raise it in connection with different anthropoids viewed at various stages of their evolution.) But if we suppose the question were raised in connection with Peterson, the only appropriate sort of answer to it would be one like, "Good heavens, what makes you think he can't?" (as if anticipating news of some horrible brain injury inflicted on Peterson). And our shock would not be at his perhaps having lost a particular talent. It would not be like the case of a Wimbledon champion losing his tennis talent because of an amputated arm.

It is no more unusual for a human being to be capable of thought than it is for a human being to be composed of cells. Similarly, "He can think" is no more an answer to questions concerning Peterson's mental capacities or intelligence, than "He's composed of cells" is an answer to the usual type of question about Peterson's appearance. And to say that Peterson can think is not to say there are a few token examples of thinking which are at our fingertips, any more than to say that the Swish 600 is all-purpose is to have in mind a particular maneuver or two of which the device is capable. It is because thinking cannot be identified with what can be shown by any one example or type of example; thus Turing's approach to the question "Can a machine think?" via the imitation game is less than convincing. In effect he provides us below with a dialogue very much like the one above:

Turing: You know, machines can think.
Philosopher: Good heavens! Really? How do you know?
Turing: Well, they can play what's called the imitation game. (This is
   followed by a description of same.)
Philosopher: Interesting. What else can they do? They must be capable
   of a great deal if they can really think.
Turing: What do you mean, "What else can they do?" They play the
   imitation game. That's thinking, isn't it?
Etc.

But Turing, like the vacuum cleaner salesman, has trouble making his sale. Nonetheless, I will indicate shortly why certain of our criticisms of his approach might have to be modified.

VI

But one last critical remark before pointing to certain shortcomings of the fore-going. As indicated before, Turing's argument benefits from his emphasizing the fact that a machine is being substituted for a human being in a certain situation, and does as well as a human being would do in that situation. No one, however, would want to deny that machines are able to do a number of things as well as or more competently than human beings, though surely no one would want to say that every one of such examples provided further arguments in support of the claim that machines can think. For in many such cases one might, instead of emphasizing that a machine can do what a human being can do, emphasize that one hardly needs to be a human being to do such things. For example: "I don't even have to think at my job; I just seal the jars as they move along the belt," or, "I just pour out soft drinks one after the other like some machine." The latter could hardly be construed as suggesting "My, aren't soft-drink vending machines clever," but rather suggests, "Isn't my job stupid; it involves little or no mental effort at all." Furthermore, as Professor Ryle has suggested to me, a well-trained bank cashier can add, subtract, multiply, and divide without having to think about what he is doing and while thinking about something else, and can't many of us run through the alphabet or a popular song without thinking? This is not meant to be a specific criticism of Turing as much as it is meant as a reminder that being able to do what human beings can do hardly implies the presence of intellectual or mental skills real or simulated, since so many things which human beings do involve little, if any, thinking. Those without jobs constitute a some-what different segment of the population from those without wits.

VII

But the following considerations seem to temper some of the foregoing criticisms. A defender of Turing might emphasize that a machine that is able to play the imitation game is also able to do much more; it can compute, perhaps be programmed to play chess, etc., and consequently displays capacities far beyond the "one example" which has been emphasized in our criticisms. I shall not go into the details which I think an adequate reply to this challenge must take into account. But in general I believe it would be possible to formulate a reply along the lines that would show that even playing chess, calculating, and the performance of other (most likely computational) operations provide us with at best a rather narrow range of examples and still fails to satisfy our intuitive concept of thinking. The parallel case in respect to the Housewife and Vacuum Cleaner Salesman would be where the Housewife still refused to accept the vacuum cleaner as "all-purpose" even though it had been shown to be capable of picking up scraps somewhat heavier than dust. Nonetheless, even if our reply were satisfactory, the more general question would remain unanswered: what range of examples would satisfy the implicit criteria we use in our ordinary characterization of subjects as "those capable of thought"?

A corollary: If we are to keep the question "Can machines think?" interesting, we cannot withhold a positive answer simply on the grounds that it (a machine) does not duplicate human activity in every respect. The question "Can a machine think if it can do everything a human being can do?" is not an interesting question, though it is at least interesting that some philosophers have thought it interesting to ask whether there would not be a logical contradiction in supposing such to be, in fact, a machine. But as long as we have in mind subjects which obviously are machines, we must be willing to stop short of demanding their activities to fully mirror human ones before we say they can think, if they can. But how far short? Again the above question as to the variety and extent of examples required is raised.

Furthermore, it might be asserted that with the increasing role of machines in society the word "think" itself might take on new meanings, and that it is not unreasonable to suppose it changing in meaning in such a way that fifty years hence a machine which could play the imitation game would in ordinary parlance be called a machine which could think. There is, however, a difference between asking whether a machine can think given current meanings and uses of "machine" and "think" and asking whether a machine can think given changes in the meanings of "machine" and "think." My own attention has throughout this chapter centered on the first question. Yet there is a temporal obscurity in the question "Can machines think?" For if the question is construed as ranging over possible futures, it may be difficult to discuss such futures without reference to changing word uses and senses. To some extent Turing's own views are based on certain beliefs he has about how we will talk about machines in the future. But these are never discussed in any detail, and he does not address himself to the knotty problems of meaning which interlace with them. . . .

VIII

The stance is often taken that thinking is the crowning capacity or achievement of the human race, and that if one denies that machines can think, one in effect assigns them to some lower level of achievement than that attained by human beings. But one might well contend that machines can't think, for they do much better than that. We could forever deny that a machine could think through a mathematical problem, and still claim that in many respects the achievement of machines was on a higher level than that attained by thinking beings, since machines can almost instantaneously and infallibly produce accurate and sometimes original answers to many complex and difficult mathematical problems with which they are presented. They do not need to "think out" the answers. In the end the steam drill outlasted John Henry as a digger of railway tunnels, but that didn't prove the machine had muscles; it proved that muscles were not needed for digging railway tunnels.

APPENDIX

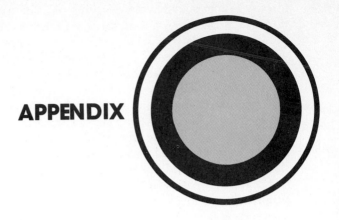

The two essays reprinted here have served as the background for the basic ideas of Part I. They are included in their entirety for those students who wish to pursue topics in informal analysis at a more advanced level.

Performative Utterances *

J. L. AUSTIN

I

You are more than entitled not to know what the word "performative" means. It is a new word and an ugly word, and perhaps it does not mean anything very much. But at any rate there is one thing in its favour, it is not a profound word. I remember once when I had been talking on this subject that somebody afterwards said: "You know, I haven't the least idea what he means, unless it could be that he simply means what he says". Well, that is what I should like to mean.

Let us consider first how this affair arises. We have not got to go very far back in the history of philosophy to find philosophers assuming more or less as a matter of course that the sole business, the sole interesting business, of any

* J. L. Austin, "Performative Utterances," *Philosophical Papers*, 2nd ed., J. O. Urmson and G. J. Warnock, eds. (Oxford: Clarendon Press, 1970), pp. 233–52.

utterance—that is, of anything we say—is to be true or at least false. Of course they had always known that there are other kinds of things which we say— things like imperatives, the expressions of wishes, and exclamations—some of which had even been classified by grammarians, though it wasn't perhaps too easy to tell always which was which. But still philosophers have assumed that the only things that they are interested in are utterances which report facts or which describe situations truly or falsely. In recent times this kind of approach has been questioned—in two stages, I think. First of all people began to say: "Well, if these things are true or false it ought to be possible to decide which they are, and if we can't decide which they are they aren't any good but are, in short, nonsense". And this new approach did a great deal of good; a great many things which probably are nonsense were found to be such. It is not the case, I think, that all kinds of nonsense have been adequately classified yet, and perhaps some things have been dismissed as nonsense which really are not; but still this movement, the verification movement, was, in its way, excellent.

However, we then come to the second stage. After all, we set some limits to the amount of nonsense that we talk, or at least the amount of nonsense that we are prepared to admit we talk; and so people began to ask whether after all some of those things which, treated as statements, were in danger of being dismissed as nonsense did after all really set out to be statements at all. Mightn't they perhaps be intended not to report facts but to influence people in this way or that, or to let off steam in this way or that? Or perhaps at any rate some elements in these utterances performed such functions, or, for example, drew attention in some way (without actually reporting it) to some important feature of the circumstances in which the utterance was being made. On these lines people have now adopted a new slogan, the slogan of the "different uses of language". The old approach, the old statemental approach, is sometimes called even a fallacy, the descriptive fallacy.

Certainly there are a great many uses of language. It's rather a pity that people are apt to invoke a new use of language whenever they feel so inclined, to help them out of this, that, or the other well-known philosophical tangle; we need more of a framework in which to discuss these uses of language; and also I think we should not despair too easily and talk, as people are apt to do, about the *infinite* uses of language. Philosophers will do this when they have listed as many, let us say, as seventeen; but even if there were something like ten thousand uses of language, surely we could list them all in time. This, after all, is no larger than the number of species of beetle that entomologists have taken the pains to list. But whatever the defects of either of these movements—the "verification" movement or the "use of language" movement—at any rate they have effected, nobody could deny, a great revolution in philosophy and, many would say, the most salutary in its history. (Not, if you come to think of it, a very immodest claim.)

Now it is one such sort of use of language that I want to examine here. I want to discuss a kind of utterance which looks like a statement and grammatically, I suppose, would be classed as a statement, which is not nonsensical, and yet is not true or false. These are not going to be utterances which contain curious verbs like "could" or "might", or curious words like "good", which many philosophers regard nowadays simply as danger signals. They will be perfectly straightforward utterances, with ordinary verbs in the first person singular present indicative active, and yet we shall see at once that they couldn't possibly be true or false. Furthermore, if a person makes an utterance of this sort we should say that he is *doing* something rather than merely *saying* something. This may sound a little odd, but the examples I shall give will in fact not be odd at all, and may even seem decidedly dull. Here are three or four. Suppose, for example, that in the course of a marriage ceremony I say, as people will, "I do"—(sc. take this woman to be my lawful wedded wife). Or again, suppose that I tread on your toe and say "I apologize". Or again, suppose that I have the bottle of champagne in my hand and say "I name this ship the *Queen Elizabeth*". Or suppose I say "I bet you sixpence it will rain tomorrow". In all these cases it would be absurd to regard the thing that I say as a report of the performance of the action which is undoubtedly done—the action of betting, or christening, or apologizing. We should say rather that, in saying what I do, I actually perform that action. When I say "I name this ship the *Queen Elizabeth*" I do not describe the christening ceremony, I actually perform the christening; and when I say "I do" (sc. take this woman to be my lawful wedded wife), I am not reporting on a marriage, I am indulging in it.

Now these kinds of utterance are the ones that we call *performative* utterances. This is rather an ugly word, and a new word, but there seems to be no word already in existence to do the job. The nearest approach that I can think of is the word "operative", as used by lawyers. Lawyers when talking about legal instruments will distinguish between the preamble, which recites the circumstances in which a transaction is effected, and on the other hand the operative part—the part of it which actually performs the legal act which it is the purpose of the instrument to perform. So the word "operative" is very near to what we want. "I give and bequeath my watch to my brother" would be an operative clause and is a performative utterance. However, the word "operative" has other uses, and it seems preferable to have a word specially designed for the use we want.

Now at this point one might protest, perhaps even with some alarm, that I seem to be suggesting that marrying is simply saying a few words, that just saying a few words *is* marrying. Well, that certainly is not the case. The words have to be said in the appropriate circumstances, and this is a matter that will come up again later. But the one thing we must not suppose is that what is needed in addition to the saying of the words in such cases is the performance of some internal spiritual act, of which the words then are to be the report. It's very easy to slip into this view at least in difficult, portentous cases, though perhaps not so easy in simple cases like apologizing. In the case of promising—for example, "I promise to be there tomorrow"—it's very easy to think that the utterance is simply the outward and visible (that is, verbal) sign of the performance of some inward spiritual act of promising, and this view has certainly been expressed in many classic places. There is the case of Euripides' Hippolytus, who said "My tongue swore to, but my heart did not"—perhaps it should be "mind" or "spirit" rather than "heart", but at any rate some kind of backstage artiste. Now it is clear from this sort of example that, if we slip into thinking that such utterances are reports, true or false, of the performance of inward and spiritual acts, we open a loophole to perjurers and welshers and bigamists and so on, so that there are disadvantages in being excessively solemn in this way. It is better, perhaps, to stick to the old saying that our word is our bond.

However, although these utterances do not themselves report facts and are not themselves true or false, saying these things does very often *imply* that certain things are true and not false, in some sense at least of that rather woolly word "imply". For example, when I say "I do take this woman to be my lawful wedded wife", or some other formula in the marriage ceremony, I do imply that I'm not already married, with wife living, sane, undivorced, and the rest of it. But still it is very important to realize that to imply that something or other is true, is not at all the same as saying something which is true itself.

These performative utterances are not true or false, then. But they do suffer from certain disabilities of their own. They can fail to come off in special ways, and that is what I want to consider next. The various ways in which a performative utterance may be unsatisfactory we call, for the sake of a name, the infelicities; and an infelicity arises—that is to say, the utterance is unhappy—if certain rules, transparently simple rules, are broken. I will mention some of these rules and then give examples of some infringements.

First of all, it is obvious that the conventional procedure which by our utterance we are purporting to use must actually exist. In the examples given here this procedure will be a verbal one, a verbal procedure for marrying or giving or whatever it may be; but it should be borne in mind that there are many non-verbal procedures by which we can perform exactly the same acts as we perform by these verbal means. It's worth remembering too that a great many of the things we do are at least in part of this conventional kind. Philosophers at least are too apt to assume that an action is always in the last resort the making of a physical movement, whereas it's usually, at least in part, a matter of convention.

The first rule is, then, that the convention invoked must exist and be accepted. And the second rule, also a very obvious one, is that the circumstances in which we purport to invoke this procedure must be appropriate for its invocation. If this is not observed, then the act that we purport to perform would not come off—it will be, one might say, a misfire. This will also be the case if, for example, we do not carry through the procedure—whatever it may be—correctly and completely, without a flaw and without a hitch. If any of these rules are not observed, we say that the act which we purported to perform is void, without effect. If, for example, the purported act was an act of marrying, then we should say that we "went through a form" of marriage, but we did not actually succeed in marrying.

Here are some examples of this kind of misfire. Suppose that, living in a country like our own, we wish to divorce our wife. We may try standing her in front of us squarely in the room and saying, in a voice loud enough for all to hear, "I divorce you". Now this procedure is not accepted. We shall not thereby have succeeded in divorcing our wife, at least in this country and others like it. This is a case where the convention, we should say, does not exist or is not accepted. Again, suppose that, picking sides at a children's party, I say "I pick George". But George turns red in the face and says "Not playing". In that case I plainly, for some reason or another, have not picked George—whether because there is no convention that you can pick people who aren't playing, or because George in the circumstances is an inappropriate object for the procedure of picking. Or consider the case in which I say "I appoint you Consul", and it turns out that you have been appointed already—or perhaps it may even transpire that you are a horse; here again we have the infelicity of inappropriate circumstances, inappropriate objects, or what not. Examples of flaws and hitches are perhaps scarcely necessary—one party in the marriage ceremony says "I will", the other says "I won't"; I say "I bet sixpence", but nobody says "Done", nobody takes up the offer. In all these and other such cases, the act which we purport to perform, or set out to perform is not achieved.

But there is another and a rather different way in which this kind of utterance may go wrong. A good many of these verbal procedures are designed for use by people who hold certain beliefs or have certain feelings or intentions. And if you use one of these formulae when you do not have the requisite thoughts or feelings or intentions then there is an abuse of the procedure, there is insincerity. Take, for example, the expression, "I congratulate you". This is designed for use by people who are glad that the person addressed has achieved a certain feat, believe that he was personally responsible for the success, and so on. If I say "I congratulate you" when I'm not pleased or when I don't believe that the credit was yours, then there is insincerity. Likewise if I say I promise to do something, without having the least intention of doing it or without believing it feasible. In these cases there is something wrong certainly, but it is not like a misfire. We should not say that I didn't in fact promise, but rather that I did promise but promised insincerely; I did congratulate you but the congratulations were hollow. And there may be an infelicity of a somewhat similar kind when the performative utterance commits the speaker to future conduct of a certain description and then in the future he does not in fact behave in the expected way. This is very obvious, of course, if I promise to do something and then break my promise, but there are many kinds of commitment of a rather less tangible form than that in the case of promising. For instance, I may say "I welcome you", bidding you welcome to my home or wherever it may be, but then I proceed to treat you as though you were exceedingly unwelcome. In this case the procedure of saying "I welcome you" has been abused in a way rather different from that of simple insincerity.

Now we might ask whether this list of infelicities is complete, whether the kinds of infelicity are mutually exclusive, and so forth. Well, it is not complete, and they are not mutually exclusive; they never are. Suppose that you are just about to name the ship, you have been appointed to name it, and you are just about to bang the bottle against the stem; but at that very moment some low type comes up, snatches the bottle out of your hand, breaks it on the stem, shouts out "I name this ship the *Generalissimo Stalin*", and then for good measure kicks away the chocks. Well, we agree of course on several things. We agree that the ship certainly isn't now named the *Generalissimo Stalin*, and we agree that it's an infernal shame and so on and so forth. But we may not agree as to how we should classify the particular infelicity in this case. We might say that here is a case of a perfectly legitimate and agreed procedure which, however, has been invoked in the wrong circumstances, namely by the wrong person, this low type instead of the person appointed to do it. But on the other hand we might look at it differently and say that this is a case where the procedure has not as a whole been gone through correctly, because part of the procedure for naming a ship is that you should first of all get yourself appointed as the person to do the naming and that's what this fellow did not do. Thus the way we should classify infelicities in different cases will be perhaps rather a difficult matter, and may even in the last resort be a bit arbitrary. But of course lawyers, who have to deal very much with this kind of thing, have invented all kinds of technical terms and have made numerous rules about different kinds of cases, which enable them to classify fairly rapidly what in particular is wrong in any given case.

As for whether this list is complete, it certainly is not. One further way in which things may go wrong is, for example, through what in general may be called misunderstanding. You may not hear what I say, or you may understand me to refer to something different from what I intended to refer to, and so on. And apart from further additions which we might make to the list, there is the general over-riding consideration that, as we are performing an act when we issue these performative utterances, we may of course be doing so under duress or in some other circumstances which make us not entirely responsible for doing what we are doing. That would certainly be an unhappiness of a kind—any kind of nonresponsibility might be called an unhappiness; but of course it is a quite different kind of thing from what we have been talking about. And I might mention that, quite differently again, we could be issuing any of these utterances, as we can issue an utterance of any kind whatsoever, in the course, for example, of acting a play or making a joke or writing a poem—in which case of course it would not be seriously meant and we shall not be able to say that we seriously performed the act concerned. If the poet says "Go and catch a falling star" or whatever it may be, he doesn't seriously issue an order. Considerations of this kind apply to any utterance at all, not merely to performatives.

That, then, is perhaps enough to be going on with. We have discussed the performative utterance and its infelicities. That equips us, we may suppose, with two shining new tools to crack the crib of reality maybe. It also equips us— it always does—with two shining new skids under our metaphysical feet. The question is how we use them.

II

So far we have been going firmly ahead, feeling the firm ground of prejudice glide away beneath our feet which is always rather exhilarating, but what next? You will be waiting for the bit when we bog down, the bit where we take it all back, and sure enough that's going to come but it will take time. First of all let us ask a rather simple question. How can we be sure, how can we tell, whether any utterance is to be classed as a performative or not? Surely, we feel, we ought to be able to do that. And we should obviously very much like to be able to say that there is a grammatical criterion for this, some grammatical means of deciding whether an utterance is performative. All the examples I have given hitherto do in fact have the same grammatical form; they all of them begin with the verb in the first person singular present indicative active—not just any kind of verb of course, but still they all are in fact of that form. Furthermore, with these verbs that I have used there is a typical asymmetry between the use of this person and tense of the verb and the use of the same verb in other persons and other tenses, and this asymmetry is rather an important clue.

For example, when we say "I promise that . . .", the case is very different from when we say "He promises that . . .", or in the past tense "I promised that . . .". For when we say "I promise that . . ." we do perform an act of promising—we give a promise. What we do *not* do is to report on somebody's performing an act of promising—in particular, we do not report on somebody's use of the expression "I promise". We actually do use it and do the promising. But if I say "He promises", or in the past tense "I promised", I precisely do report on an act of promising, that is to say an act of using this formula "I promise"—I report on a present act of promising by him, or on a past act of my own. There is thus a clear difference between our first person singular present indicative active, and other persons and tenses. This is brought out by the typical incident of little Willie whose uncle says he'll give him half-a-crown if he promises never to smoke till he's 55. Little Willie's anxious parent will say "Of course he promises, don't you, Willie?" giving him a nudge, and little Willie just doesn't vouchsafe. The point here is that he must do the promising himself by saying "I promise", and his parent is going too fast in saying he promises.

That, then, is a bit of a test for whether an utterance is performative or not, but it would not do to suppose that every performative utterance has to take this standard form. There is at least one other standard form, every bit as common as this one, where the verb is in the passive voice and in the second or third person, not in the first. The sort of case I mean is that of a notice inscribed "Passengers are warned to cross the line by the bridge only", or of a document reading "You are hereby authorized" to do so-and-so. These are undoubtedly performative, and in fact a signature is often required in order to show who it is that is doing the act of warning, or authorizing, or whatever it may be. Very typical of this kind of performative—especially liable to occur in written documents of course—is that the little word "hereby" either actually occurs or might naturally be inserted.

Unfortunately, however, we still can't possibly suggest that every utterance which is to be classed as a performative has to take one or another of these two, as we might call them, standard forms. After all it would be a very typical performative utterance to say "I order you to shut the door". This satisfies all the criteria. It is performing the act of ordering you to shut the door, and it is not true or false. But in the appropriate circumstances surely we could perform exactly the same act by simply saying "Shut the door", in the imperative. Or again, suppose that somebody sticks up a notice "This bull is dangerous", or simply "Dangerous bull", or simply "Bull". Does this necessarily differ from sticking up a notice, appropriately signed, saying "You are hereby warned that this bull is dangerous"? It seems that the simple notice "Bull" can do just the same job as the more elaborate formula. Of course the difference is that if we just stick up "Bull" it would not be quite clear that it is a warning; it might be there just for interest or information, like "Wallaby" on the cage at the zoo, or "Ancient Monument". No doubt we should know from the nature of the case that it was a warning, but it would not be explicit.

Well, in view of this break-down of grammatical criteria, what we should like to suppose—and there is a good deal in this—is that any utterance which is performative could be reduced or expanded or analysed into one of these two standard forms beginning "I . . ." so and so or beginning "You (or he) hereby . . ." so and so. If there was any justification for this hope, as to some extent there is, then we might hope to make a list of all the verbs which can appear in these standard forms, and then we might classify the kinds of acts that can be performed by performative utterances. We might do this with the aid of a dictionary, using such a test as that already mentioned—whether there is the characteristic asymmetry between the first person singular present indicative active and the other persons and tenses—in order to decide whether a verb is to go into our list or not. Now if we make such a list of verbs we do in fact find that they fall into certain fairly well-marked classes. There is the class of cases where we deliver verdicts and make estimates and appraisals of various kinds. There is the class where we give undertakings, commit ourselves in various ways by saying something. There is the class where by saying something we exercise various rights and powers, such as appointing and voting and so on. And there are one or two other fairly well-marked classes.

Suppose this task accomplished. Then we could call these verbs in our list explicit performative verbs, and any utterance that was reduced to one or the other of our standard forms we could call an explicit performative utterance. "I order you to shut the door" would be an explicit performative utterance, whereas "Shut the door" would not—that is simply a "primary" performative utterance or whatever we like to call it. In using the imperative we may be ordering you to shut the door, but it just isn't made clear whether we are ordering you or entreating you or imploring you or beseeching you or inciting you or tempting you, or one or another of many other subtly different acts which, in an unsophisticated primitive language, are very likely not yet discriminated. But we need not overestimate the unsophistication of primitive languages. There are a great many devices that can be used for making clear, even at the primitive level, what act it is we are performing when we say something—the tone of voice, cadence, gesture—and above all we can rely upon the nature of the circumstances, the context in which the utterance is issued. This very often makes it quite unmistakable whether it is an order that is being given or whether, say, I am simply urging you or entreating you. We may, for instance, say something like this: "Coming from him I was bound to take it as an order". Still, in spite of all these devices, there is an unfortunate amount of ambiguity and lack of discrimination in default of our explicit performative verbs. If I say something like

"I shall be there", it may not be certain whether it is a promise, or an expression of intention, or perhaps even a forecast of my future behaviour, of what is going to happen to me; and it may matter a good deal, at least in developed societies, precisely which of these things it is. And that is why the explicit performative verb is evolved—to make clear exactly which it is, how far it commits me and in what way, and so forth.

This is just one way in which language develops in tune with the society of which it is the language. The social habits of the society may considerably affect the question of which performative verbs are evolved and which, sometimes for rather irrelevant reasons, are not. For example, if I say "You are a poltroon", it might be that I am censuring you or it might be that I am insulting you. Now since apparently society approves of censuring or reprimanding, we have here evolved a formula "I reprimand you", or "I censure you", which enables us expeditiously to get this desirable business over. But on the other hand, since apparently we don't approve of insulting, we have not evolved a simple formula "I insult you", which might have done just as well.

By means of these explicit performative verbs and some other devices, then, we make explicit what precise act it is that we are performing when we issue our utterance. But here I would like to put in a word of warning. We must distinguish between the function of making explicit what act it is we are performing, and the quite different matter of *stating* what act it is we are performing. In issuing an explicit performative utterance we are not stating what act it is, we are showing or making explicit what act it is. We can draw a helpful parallel here with another case in which the act, the conventional act that we perform, is not a speech-act but a physical performance. Suppose I appear before you one day and bow deeply from the waist. Well, this is ambiguous. I may be simply observing the local flora, tying my shoe-lace, something of that kind; on the other hand, conceivably I might be doing obeisance to you. Well, to clear up this ambiguity we have some device such as raising the hat, saying "Salaam", or something of that kind, to make it quite plain that the act being performed is the conventional one of doing obeisance rather than some other act. Now nobody would want to say that lifting your hat was stating that you were performing an act of obeisance; it certainly is not, but it does make it quite plain that you are. And so in the same way to say "I warn you that ..." or "I order you to ..." or "I promise that ..." is not to state that you are doing something, but makes it plain that you are—it does constitute your verbal performance, a performance of a particular kind.

So far we have been going along as though there was a quite clear difference between our performative utterances and what we have contrasted them with, statements or reports or descriptions. But now we begin to find that this distinction is not as clear as it might be. It's now that we begin to sink in a little. In the first place, of course, we may feel doubts as to how widely our performatives extend. If we think up some odd kinds of expression we use in odd cases, we might very well wonder whether or not they satisfy our rather vague criteria for being performative utterances. Suppose, for example, somebody says "Hurrah". Well, not true or false; he is performing the act of cheering. Does that make it a performative utterance in our sense or not? Or suppose he says "Damn"; he is performing the act of swearing, and it is not true or false. Does that make it performative? We feel that in a way it does and yet it's rather different. Again, consider cases of "suiting the action to the words"; these too may make us wonder whether perhaps the utterance should be classed as performative. Or sometimes, if somebody says "I am sorry", we wonder whether this is just the same as "I apologize"—in which case of course we have said it's a performative utterance—or whether perhaps it's to be taken as a description, true or false, of the state of his feelings. If he had said "I feel perfectly awful about it", then we should think it must be meant to be a description of the state of his feelings. If he had said "I apologize", we should feel this was clearly a performative utterance, going through the ritual of apologizing. But if he says "I am sorry" there is an unfortunate hovering between the two. This phenomenon is quite common. We often find cases in which there is an obvious pure performative utterance and obvious other utterances connected with it which are not performative but descriptive, but on the other hand a good many in between where we're not quite sure which they are. On some occasions of course they are obviously used the one way, on some occasions the other way, but on some occasions they seem positively to revel in ambiguity.

Again, consider the case of the umpire when he says "Out" or "Over", or the jury's utterance when they say that they find the prisoner guilty. Of course, we say, these are cases of giving verdicts, performing the act of appraising and so forth, but still in a way they have some connexion with the facts. They seem to have something like the duty to be true or false, and seem not to be so very remote from statements. If the umpire says "Over", this surely has at least something to do with six balls in fact having been delivered rather than seven, and so on. In fact in general we may remind ourselves that "I state that..." does not look so very different from "I warn you that ..." or "I promise to ...". It makes clear surely that the act that we are performing is an act of stating, and so functions just like "I warn" or "I order". So isn't "I state that ..." a performative utterance? But then one may feel that utterances beginning "I state that..." do have to be true or false, that they *are* statements.

Considerations of this sort, then, may well make us feel pretty unhappy. If we look back for a moment at our contrast between statements and performative utterances, we realize that we were taking statements very much on trust from, as we said, the traditional treatment. Statements, we had it, were to be true or false; performative utterances on the other hand were to be felicitous or infelicitous. They were the doing of something, whereas for all we said making statements was not doing something. Now this contrast surely, if we look back at it, is unsatisfactory. Of course statements are liable to be assessed in this matter of their correspondence or failure to correspond with the facts, that is, being true or false. But they are also liable to infelicity every bit as much as are performative utterances. In fact some troubles that have arisen in the study of statements recently can be shown to be simply troubles of infelicity. For example, it has been pointed out that there is something very odd about saying something like this: "The cat is on the mat but I don't believe it is". Now this is an outrageous thing to say, but it is not self-contradictory. There is no reason why the cat shouldn't be on the mat without my believing that it is. So how are we to classify what's wrong with this peculiar statement? If we remember now the doctrine of infelicity we shall see that the person who makes this remark about the cat is in much the same position as somebody who says something like this: "I promise that I shall be there, but I haven't the least intention of being there." Once again you can of course perfectly well promise to be there without having the least intention of being there, but there is something outrageous about saying it, about actually avowing the insincerity of the promise you give. In the same way there is insincerity in the case of the person who says "The cat is on the mat but I don't believe it is", and he is actually avowing that insincerity—which makes a peculiar kind of nonsense.

A second case that has come to light is the one about John's children—the case where somebody is supposed to say "All John's children are bald but John hasn't got any children". Or perhaps somebody says "All John's children are bald", when as a matter of fact—he doesn't say so—John has no children. Now those who study statements have worried about this; ought they to say that the statement "All John's children are bald" is meaningless in this case? Well, if it is, it is not a bit like a great many other more standard kinds of meaningless-ness; and we see, if we look back at our list of infelicities, that what is going wrong here is much the same as what goes wrong in, say, the case of a contract for the sale of a piece of land when the piece of land referred to does not exist. Now what we say in the case of this sale of land, which of course would be ef-fected by a performative utterance, is that the sale is void—void for lack of refer-ence or ambiguity of reference; and so we can see that the statement about all John's children is likewise void for lack of reference. And if the man actually says that John has no children in the same breath as saying they're all bald, he is making the same kind of outrageous utterance as the man who says "The cat is on the mat and I don't believe it is", or the man who says "I promise to but I don't intend to".

In this way, then, ills that have been found to afflict statements can be pre-cisely paralleled with ills that are characteristic of performative utterances. And after all when we state something or describe something or report something, we do perform an act which is every bit as much an act as an act of ordering or warning. There seems no good reason why stating should be given a specially unique position. Of course philosophers have been wont to talk as though you or I or anybody could just go round stating anything about anything and that would be perfectly in order, only there's just a little question: is it true or false? But besides the little question, is it true or false, there is surely the question: *is* it in order? Can you go round just making statements about anything? Sup-pose for example you say to me "I'm feeling pretty mouldy this morning". Well, I say to you "You're not"; and you say "What the devil do you mean, I'm not?" I say "Oh nothing—I'm just stating you're not, is it true or false?" And you say "Wait a bit about whether it's true or false, the question is what did you mean by making statements about somebody else's feelings? I told you I'm feeling pretty mouldy. You're just not in a position to say, to state that I'm not". This brings out that you can't just make statements about other people's feelings (though you can make guesses if you like); and there are very many things which, having no knowledge of, not being in a posiiton to pronounce about, you just can't state. What we need to do for the case of stating, and by the same token describing and reporting, is to take them a bit off their pedestal, to realize that they are speech-acts no less than all these other speech-acts that we have been mentioning and talking about as performative.

Then let us look for a moment at our original contrast between the performative and the statement from the other side. In handling performatives we have been putting it all the time as though the only thing that a performative utterance had to do was to be felicitous, to come off, not to be a misfire, not to be an abuse. Yes, but that's not the end of the matter. At least in the case of many utterances which, on what we have said, we should have to class as performative—cases where we say "I warn you to . . .", "I advise you to . . ." and so on—there will be other questions besides simply: was it in order, was it all right, as a piece of advice or a warning, did it come off? After that surely there will be the question: was it good or sound advice? Was it a justified warning? Or in the case, let us say, of a verdict or an estimate: was it a good estimate, or a sound verdict? And these are questions that can only be decided by considering how the content of the verdict or estimate is related in some way to fact, or to evidence available about the facts. This is to say that we do require to assess at least a great many performative utterances in a general dimension of correspondence with fact. It may still be said, of course, that this does not make them *very* like statements because still they are not true or false, and that's a little black and white speciality that distinguishes statements as a class apart. But actually—though it would take too long to go on about this—the more you think about truth and falsity the more you find that very few statements that we ever utter are just true or just false. Usually there is the question are they fair or are they not fair, are they adequate or not adequate, are they exaggerated or not exaggerated? Are they too rough, or are they perfectly precise, accurate, and so on? "True" and "false" are just general labels for a whole dimension of different appraisals which have something or other to do with the relation between what we say and the facts. If, then, we loosen up our ideas of truth and falsity we shall see that statements, when assessed in relation to the facts, are not so very different after all from pieces of advice, warnings, verdicts, and so on.

We see then that stating something is performing an act just as much as is giving an order or giving a warning; and we see, on the other hand, that, when we give an order or a warning or a piece of advice, there is a question about how this is related to fact which is not perhaps so very different from the kind of question that arises when we discuss how a statement is related to fact. Well, this seems to mean that in its original form our distinction between the performative and the statement is considerably weakened, and indeed breaks down. I will just make a suggestion as to how to handle this matter. We need to go very much farther back, to consider all the ways and senses in which saying anything at all is doing this or that—because of course it is always doing a good many different things. And one thing that emerges when we do do this is that, besides the question that has been very much studied in the past as to what a certain utterance *means*, there is a further question distinct from this as to what was the *force*, as we may call it, of the utterance. We may be quite clear what "Shut the door" means, but not yet at all clear on the further point as to whether as uttered at a certain time it was an order, an entreaty or whatnot. What we need besides the old doctrine about meanings is a new doctrine about all the possible forces of utterances, towards the discovery of which our proposed list of explicit performative verbs would be a very great help; and then, going on from there, an investigation of the various terms of appraisal that we use in discussing speech-acts of this, that, or the other precise kind—orders, warnings, and the like.

The notions that we have considered then, are the performative, the infelicity, the explicit performative, and lastly, rather hurriedly, the notion of the forces of utterances. I dare say that all this seems a little unremunerative, a little complicated. Well, I suppose in some ways it is unremunerative, and I suppose it ought to be remunerative. At least, though, I think that if we pay attention to these matters we can clear up some mistakes in philosophy; and after all philosophy is used as a scapegoat, it parades mistakes which are really the mistakes of everybody. We might even clear up some mistakes in grammar, which perhaps is a little more respectable.

And is it complicated? Well, it is complicated a bit; but life and truth and things do tend to be complicated. It's not things, it's philosophers that are simple. You will have heard it said, I expect, that over-simplification is the occupational disease of philosophers, and in a way one might agree with that. But for a sneaking suspicion that it's their occupation.

Logic and Conversation*
H. P. GRICE

It is a commonplace of philosophical logic that there are, or appear to be, divergences in meaning between, on the one hand, at least some of what I shall call the *formal* devices '~', '·', 'V', '⊃', '(x)', '(∃x)', '(⁊x)' (when these are given a standard two-valued interpretation), and, on the other, what are taken to be their analogues or counter parts in natural language, such expressions are 'not', 'or', 'if', 'all', 'some' (or 'at least one'), 'the'. Some logicians may at some time have wanted to claim that there are in fact no such divergences; but such claims, if made at all, have been somewhat rashly made, and those suspected of making them have been subjected to some pretty rough handling.

Those who concede that such divergences exist adhere, in the main, to one or other of two rival groups, which for the purposes of this article I shall call the

* H. P. Grice, "Logic and Conversation," in *The Logic of Grammar*, Donald Davidson and Gilbert Harman, eds. (Encino, California: Dickinson Publishing Co., 1975), pp. 64–153.

formalists and the informalist groups. An outline of a not uncharacteristic formalist position may be given as follows: In so far as logicians are concerned with the formulation of very general patterns of valid inference, the formal devices possess a decisive advantage over their natural counterparts. For it will be possible to construct in terms of the formal devices a system of very general formulas, a considerable number of which can be regarded as, or are closely related to, patterns of inferences, the expression of which involves some or all of the devices. Such a system may consist of a certain set of simple formulas which must be acceptable if the devices have the meaning which has been assigned to them, and an indefinite number of further formulas, many of them less obviously acceptable, each of which can be shown to be acceptable if the members of the original set are acceptable. We have thus a way of handling dubiously acceptable patterns of inference, and if, as is sometimes possible, we can apply a decision procedure, we have an even better way. Furthermore, from a philosophical point of view, the possession by the natural counterparts of those elements in their meaning, which they do not share with the corresponding formal devices, is to be regarded as an imperfection of natural languages; the elements in question are undesirable excrescences. For the presence of these elements has the result that the concepts within which they appear cannot be precisely and clearly defined, and that at least some statements involving them cannot, in some circumstances, be assigned a definite truth-value. The indefiniteness of these concepts is not only objectionable in itself but leaves open the way to metaphysics; we cannot be certain that none of these natural language expressions is metaphysically 'loaded'. For these reasons the expressions, as used in natural speech, cannot be regarded as finally acceptable, and may turn out to be, finally, not fully intelligible. The proper course is to conceive and begin to construct an ideal language, incorporating the formal devices, the sentences of which will be clear, determinate in truth-value, and certifiably free from metaphysical implications; the foundations of science will now be philosophically secure, since the statements of the scientist will be expressible (though not necessarily actually expressed) within this ideal language. (I do not wish to suggest that all formalists would accept the whole of this outline, but I think that all would accept at least some part of it.)

To this, an informalist might reply in the following vein. The philosophical demand for an ideal language rests on certain assumptions which should not be conceded; these are, that the primary yardstick by which to judge the adequacy of a language is its ability to serve the needs of science, that an expression cannot be guaranteed as fully intelligible unless an explication or analysis of its meaning has been provided, and that every explication or analysis must take the form of a precise definition which is the expression or assertion of a logical equivalence. Language serves many important purposes besides those of scientific inquiry. We can know perfectly well what an expression means (and so *a fortiori* that it is intelligible) without knowing its analysis, and the provision of an analysis may (and usually does) consist in the specification, as generalized as possible, of the conditions which count for or against the applicability of the expression being analyzed. Moreover, while it is no doubt true that the formal devices are specially amenable to systematic treatment by the logician, it remains the case that there are very many inferences and arguments, expressed in natural language and not in terms of these devices, which are nevertheless recognizably valid. So there must be a place for an unsimplified, and so more or less unsystematic, logic of the natural counterparts of those devices. This logic may be aided and guided by the simplified logic of the formal devices, but cannot be supplanted by it. Indeed, not only do the two logics differ, but sometimes they come into conflict: rules which hold for a formal device may not hold for its natural counterpart.

Now on the general question of the place in philosophy of the reformation of natural language, I shall, in this article, have nothing to say. I shall confine myself to the dispute in its relation to the alleged divergences mentioned at the outset. I have moreover no intention of entering the fray on behalf of either contestant. I wish, rather, to maintain that the common assumption of the contestants that the divergences do in fact exist is (broadly speaking) a common mistake, and that the mistake arises from an inadequate attention to the nature and importance of the conditions governing conversation. I shall, therefore, proceed at once to inquire into the general conditions which, in one way or another, apply to conversation as such irrespective of its subject matter.

IMPLICATURE

Suppose that A and B are talking about a mutual friend C, who is now working in a bank. A asks B how C is getting on in his job, and B replies, "Oh quite well, I think; he likes his colleagues, and he hasn't been to prison yet." At this point A might well inquire what B was implying, what he was suggesting, or even what he meant by saying that C had not yet been to prison. The answer might be any one of such things as that C is the sort of person likely to yield to the temptation provided by his occupation, that C's colleagues are really very unpleasant and treacherous people, and so forth. It might of course be quite unnecessary for A to make such an inquiry of B, the answer to it being, in the context, clear in advance. I think it is clear that whatever B implied, suggested, or meant, in this example is distinct from what B said, which was simply that C had not been to prison yet. I wish to introduce, as a term of art, the verb 'implicate', the related nouns 'implicature' (cf. 'implying') and 'implicatum' (cf. 'what is implied'). The point of this maneuver is to avoid having, on each occasion, to choose between this or that member of the family of verbs for which 'implicate' is to do general duty. I shall, for the time being at least, have to assume to a considerable extent an intuitive understanding of the meaning of 'say' in such contexts, and an ability to recognize particular verbs as members of the family with which 'implicate' is associated. I can, however, make one or two remarks which may help to clarify the more problematic of these assumptions, namely that connected with the meaning of the word 'say'.

(1) In the sense in which I am using the word 'say', I intend what someone has said to be closely related to the conventional meaning of the words (the sen-

tence) which he has uttered. Suppose someone to have uttered the sentence "He is in the grip of a vice." Given a knowledge of the English language, but no knowledge of the circumstances of the utterance, one would know something about what the speaker had said, on the assumption that he was speaking standard English, and speaking literally. One would know that he had said, about some particular male person or animal X, that at the time of the utterance (whatever that was) either (i) that X was unable to rid himself of a certain kind of bad character trait, or (ii) that some part of X's person was caught in a certain kind of tool or instrument. (This is an approximate account, of course.) But for a full identification of what the speaker had said, one would need to know (a) the identity of X, (b) the time of utterance, (c) the meaning, on the particular occasion of utterance, of the phrase "in the grip of a vice" (a decision between (i) and (ii)). This brief indication of my use of 'say' leaves it open whether a man who says (today) "Harold Wilson is a great man" and another who says (also today) "The British Prime Minister is a great man" would, if each knew that the two singular terms had the same reference, have said the same thing. But whatever decision is made about this question, the apparatus I am about to provide will be capable of accounting for any implicatures that might depend on the presence of one rather than another of these singular terms in the sentence uttered. Such implicatures would merely be related to different maxims.

(2) In some cases the conventional meaning of the words used will determine what is implicated, besides helping to determine what is said: If I say (smugly) "He is an Englishman; he is, therefore, brave," I have certainly committed myself by virtue of the meaning of my words, to its being true that his being brave is a consequence of (follows from) his being an Englishman. But while I have said that he is an Englishman, and said that he is brave, I do not want to say that I have *said* (in the favored sense) that it follows from his being an Englishman that he is brave, though I have certainly indicated, and so implicated, that this is so. I do not want to say that my utterance of this sentence would be, *strictly speaking,* false should the consequence in question fail to hold. So *some* implicatures are conventional, unlike the one with which I introduced this discussion of implicature.

I wish to represent a certain subclass of nonconventional implicatures, which I shall call *conversational* implicatures, as being essentially connected with certain general features of discourse; so my next step is to try to say what these features are.

The following may provide a first approximation to a general principle. Our talk exchanges do not normally consist of a succession of disconnected remarks, and would not be rational if they did. They are, characteristically, to some degree at least cooperative efforts. Each participant recognizes in them, to some extent, a common purpose or set of purposes, or at least a mutually accepted direction. This purpose or direction may be fixed from the start (e.g., by an initial proposal of a question for discussion), or it may evolve during the exchange; it may be fairly definite, or it may be so indefinite as to leave very considerable latitude to the participants (as in a casual conversation). But at each stage, *some* possible conversational moves would be excluded as conversationally unsuitable. We might then formulate a rough general principle which participants will be expected (ceteris paribus) to observe, viz: "Make your conversational contribution such as is required, at the stage at which it occurs, by the accepted purpose or direction of the talk exchange in which you are engaged." One might label this the Cooperative Principle (CP).

On the assumption that some such general principle as the above is acceptable, one may perhaps distinguish four categories under one or other of which will fall certain more specific maxims and submaxims, the following of which will in general yield results in accordance with the Cooperation Principle. Echoing Kant, I call these categories Quantity, Quality, Relation, and Manner. The category of *Quantity* relates to the quantity of information to be provided and under it fall the maxims

(1) "Make your contribution as informative as is required (for the current purposes of the exchange),"

and possibly

(2) "Do not make your contribution more informative than is required."

(The second maxim is disputable; it might be said that to be overinformative is not a transgression of the CP but merely a waste of time. However, it might be answered that such overinformativeness may be confusing in that it is liable to raise side issues; and there may also be an indirect effect, in that the hearers may be misled, as a result of thinking that there is some particular *point* in the provision of excess information. However this may be, there is perhaps a different reason for doubt about the admission of this second maxim, namely, that its effect will be secured by a later maxim, which concerns relevance.)

Under the category of *Quality* falls a supermaxim: "Try to make your contribution one that is true," and two more specific maxims:

(1) "Do not say what you believe to be false."
(2) "Do not say that for which you lack adequate evidence."

Under the category of *Relation* I place a single maxim, namely, "Be relevant." Though the maxim itself is terse, its formulation conceals a number of problems which exercise me a good deal; questions about what different kinds and foci of relevance there may be, how these shift in the course of a talk exchange, how to allow for the fact that subjects of conversation are legitimately changed, and so on. I find the treatment of such questions exceedingly difficult, and I hope to revert to them in a later lecture [not included here].

Finally under the category of *Manner*, which I understand as relating, not (like the previous categories) to what is said, but rather to *how* what is said is to be said, I include the supermaxim: "Be perspicuous" and various maxims such as

(1) "Avoid obscurity of expression"
(2) "Avoid ambiguity"
(3) "Be brief (avoid unnecessary prolixity)"
(4) "Be orderly"

And one might need others.

It is obvious that the observance of some of these maxims is a matter of lesser urgency than is the observance of others; a man who has expressed himself with undue prolixity would, in general, be open to milder comment than would a man who had said something which he believes to be false. Indeed it might be felt that the importance of at least the first maxim of Quality is such that it should not be included in a scheme of the kind which I am constructing; other maxims only come into operation on the assumption that this maxim of Quality is satisfied. While this may be correct, so far as the generation of implicatures is concerned it seems to play a role not totally different from the other maxims; and it will be convenient, for the present at least, to treat it as a member of the list of maxims.

There are of course all sorts of other maxims (aesthetic, social, or moral in character) such as "Be polite," which are also normally observed by participants in talk exchanges, and these may also generate nonconventional implicatures. The conversational maxims, however, and the conversational implicatures connected with them, are specially connected (I hope) with the particular purposes which talk (and so talk exchange) is adapted to serve and is primarily employed to serve. I have stated my maxims as if this purpose were a maximally effective exchange of information; this specification is of course too narrow, and the scheme needs to be generalized to allow for such general purposes as influencing or directing the actions of others.

As one of my avowed aims is to see talking as a special case or variety of purposive, indeed rational, behavior, it may be worth noting that the specific expectations or presumptions connected with at least some of the foregoing maxims have their analogues in the sphere of transactions which are not talk exchanges. I list briefly one such analogue for each conversational category.

I *Quantity*. If you are assisting me to mend a car, I expect your contribution to be neither more nor less than is required; if for example, at a particular stage I need four screws, I expect you to hand me four, rather than two or six.

II *Quality*. I expect your contributions to be genuine and not spurious. If I need sugar as an ingredient in the cake you are helping me bake, I do not expect you to hand me salt; if I need a spoon, I do not expect a trick spoon made of rubber.

III *Relation*. I expect a partner's contribution to be appropriate to immediate needs at each stage of the transaction; if I am mixing ingredients for a cake, I do not expect to be handed a good book, or even a pot-holder (though this might be an appropriate contribution at a later stage).

IV *Manner*. I expect a partner to make it clear what contribution he is making, and to execute his performance with reasonable dispatch.

These analogies are relevant to what I regard as a fundamental question about the CP and its attendant maxims, namely, what the basis is for the assumption which we seem to make, and on which (I hope) it will appear that a great range of implicatures depend, that talkers will in general (ceteris paribus and in the absence of indications to the contrary) proceed in the manner which these principles prescribe. A dull but no doubt at a certain level adequate answer is that it is just a well-recognized empirical fact that people *do* behave in these ways; they have learned to do so in childhood, and have not lost the habit of doing so; and indeed it would involve a good deal of effort to make a radical departure from the habit. It is much easier, for example, to tell the truth than to invent lies.

I am, however, enough of a rationalist to want to find a basis which underlies these facts, undeniable though they may be; I would like to be able to think of the standard type of conversational practice not merely as something which all or most do *in fact* follow, but as something which it is *reasonable* for us to follow, which we *should not* abandon. For a time I was attracted by the idea that observance of the CP and the maxims, in a talk exchange, could be thought of as a quasi-contractual matter, with parallels outside the realm of discourse. If you pass by when I am struggling with my stranded car, I no doubt have some degree of expectation that you will offer help; but once you join me in tinkering under the hood, my expectations become stronger and take more specific forms (in the absence of indications that you are merely an incompetent meddler). Likewise, talk exchanges seem to me to exhibit, characteristically, certain features which jointly distinguish cooperative transactions: (1) that the participants have some common immediate aim, like getting a car mended (Their ultimate aims may of course be independent and even in conflict; each may want to get the car mended in order to drive off leaving the other stranded. In characteristic talk exchanges there is a common aim even if, as in an over-the-wall chat, it is a second-order one, namely, that each party should for the time being identify himself with the transitory conversational interests of the other.); (2) that the contributions of the participants should be dovetailed, mutually dependent; (3) that there is some sort of understanding (which may be explicit but which is often tacit) that, other things being equal, the transaction should continue in appropriate style unless both parties agree it should terminate. You don't just shove off, or start doing something else.

But while some such quasi-contractual basis as this may apply to some cases, there are too many types of exchange, like quarreling and letter writing, which it fails to fit comfortably. In any case one feels that the talker who is irrelevant or obscure has primarily let down not his audience but himself. So I would like to be able to show that observance of the CP and maxims is reasonable (rational) along the following lines: that any one who cares about the goals that are central to conversation/communication (such as giving and receiving information, influencing and being influenced by others) must be expected to have an interest, given suitable circumstances, in participation in talk exchanges which will be profitable only on the assumption that they are conducted in general accordance with the CP and the maxims. Whether any such conclusion can be reached, I am uncertain; in any case I am fairly sure I cannot reach it until I am a good deal clearer about the nature of relevance and of the circumstances in which it is required.

It is now time to show the connection between the CP and maxims on the one hand, and conversational implicature on the other.

A participant in a talk exchange may fail to fulfill a maxim in various ways which include the following:

(1) He may quietly and unostentatiously *violate* a maxim; if so, in some cases he will be liable to mislead.

(2) He may *opt out* from the operation both of the maxim and of the CP; he may say, indicate, or allow it to become plain that he is unwilling to cooperate in the way in which the maxim requires. He may say, for example, "I cannot say more, my lips are sealed."

(3) He may be faced by a *clash:* he may be unable, for example, to fulfill the first maxim of Quantity ("Be as informative as required") without violating the second maxim of Quality ("Have adequate evidence for what you say").

(4) He may *flout* a maxim; that is, he may *blatantly* fail to fulfill it. On the assumption that the speaker is able to fulfill the maxim and do so without violating another maxim (because of a clash), is not opting out, and is not in view of the blatancy of his performance, trying to mislead, the hearer is faced with a minor problem: how can his saying what he did say be reconciled with the supposition that he is observing the overall CP? This situation is one which characteristically gives rise to a conversational implicature; and when a conversational implicature is generated in this way, I shall say that a maxim is being *exploited.*

I am now in a position to characterize the notion of conversational implicature, a man who, by (in when) saying (or making as if to say) that *p* has implicated that *q,* may be said to have conversationally implicated that *q, provided that:* (1) he is to be presumed to be observing the conversational maxims, or at least the cooperative principle; (2) the supposition that he is aware that, or thinks that *q,* is required in order to make his saying or making as if to say *p* (or doing so in *those* terms) consistent with this presumption; and (3) that the speaker thinks (and would expect the hearer to think that the speaker thinks) that it is within the competence of the hearer to work out, or grasp intuitively, that the supposition mentioned in (2) *is* required. Apply this to my initial example, to B's remark that C has not yet been to prison. In a suitable setting A might reason as follows: "(1) B has apparently violated the maxim 'Be relevant' and so may be regarded as having flouted one of the maxims conjoining perspicuity; yet I have no reason to suppose that he is opting out from the operation of the CP; (2) given the circumstances I can regard his irrelevance as only apparent if and only if I suppose him to think that C is potentially dishonest; (3) B knows that I am capable of working out step (2). So B implicates that C is potentially dishonest."

The presence of a conversational implicature must be capable of being worked out; for even if it can in fact be intuitively grasped, unless the intuition is replaceable by an argument, the implicature (if present at all) will not count as a *conversational* implicature; it will be a *conventional* implicature. To work out that a particular conversational implicature is present, the hearer will rely on the following data: (1) the conventional meaning of the words used, together with the identity of any references which may be involved; (2) the CP and its maxims; (3) the context linguistic or otherwise of the utterance; (4) other items of background knowledge; (5) the fact (or supposed fact) that all relevant items falling under the previous heading are available to both participants, and that both participants know or assume this to be so. A general pattern for the working out of a conversational implicature might be given as follows: "He has said that p; there is no reason to suppose that he is not observing the maxims, or at least the CP; he could not be doing this unless he thought that q; he knows (and knows that I know that he knows) that I can see that the supposition that he thinks that q is required; he has done nothing to stop me thinking that q; therefore he intends me to think, or is at least willing to allow me to think, that q; and so he has implicated that q."

I shall now offer a number of examples which I shall divide into three groups.

Group A: Examples in which no maxim is violated, or at least in which it is not clear that any maxim is violated.

(1) A is standing by an obviously immobilized car and is approached by B, and the following exchange takes place:

A: "I am out of petrol."
B: "There is a garage round the corner."

(*Gloss:* B would be infringing the maxim "Be relevant" unless he thinks, or thinks it possible, that the garage is open, and had petrol to sell; so he implicated that the garage is, or at least may be, open, and so on.)

In this example, unlike the case of the remark "He hasn't been to prison yet," the unstated connection between B's remark and A's remark is so obvious that, even if one interprets the supermaxim of Manner, "Be perspicuous," as applying not only to the expression of what is said, but also to the connection of what is said, with adjacent remarks, there seems to be no case for regarding that supermaxim as infringed in this example. The next example is perhaps a little less clear in this respect.

(2) A: "Smith doesn't seem to have a girl friend these days."
B: "He has been paying a lot of visits to New York lately."

B implicates that Smith has, or may have, a girl friend in New York. Gloss is unnecessary in view of that given for the previous example.

In both examples the speaker implicates that which he must be assumed to believe in order to preserve the assumption that he is observing the maxim of relation.

Group B: An example in which a maxim is violated, but its violation is to be explained by the supposition of a clash with another maxim. A is planning with B an itinerary for a holiday in France. Both know that A wants to see his friend C if to do so would not involve too great a prolongation of his journey:

A: "Where does C live?"
B: "Somewhere in the South of France."

(*Gloss:* There is no reason to suppose that B is opting out; his answer is, as he well knows, less informative than is required to meet A's needs; this infringement of the first maxim of Quantity can only be explained by the supposition that B is aware that to be more informative would be to say something which infringed the maxim of Quality, "Don't say what you lack adequate evidence for," so B implicates that he does not know in which town C lives.)

Group C: Examples which involve exploitation, that is, a procedure by which a maxim is flouted for the purpose of getting in a conversational implicature by means of something of the nature of a figure of speech. In these examples, though some maxim is violated at the level of what is said, the hearer is entitled to assume that that maxim, or at least the overall Cooperative Principle, is observed at the level of what is implicated.

(1a) (A flouting of the first maxim of Quantity): A is writing a testimonial about a pupil who is a candidate for a philosophy job, and his letter reads as follows: "Dear Sir, Mr. X's command of English is excellent, and his attendance at tutorials has been regular, Yours, etc." (*Gloss:* A cannot be opting out, since if he wished to be uncooperative, why write at all? He cannot be unable, through ignorance, to say more, since the man is his pupil; moreover, he knows that more information than this is wanted. He must, therefore, be wishing to impart information which he is reluctant to write down. This supposition is only tenable on the assumption that he thinks that Mr. X is no good at philosophy. This, then, is what he is implicating.)

Extreme examples of a flouting of the first maxim of Quantity are provided by utterances of patent tautologies like "Women are women," "War is war." I would wish to maintain that at the level of what is said, in my favored sense, such remarks are totally noninformative and so, at that level, cannot but infringe the first maxim of Quantity in any conversational context. They are, of course, informative at the level of what is implicated, and the hearer's identification of their informative content at this level is dependent on his ability to explain the speaker's selection of this *particular* patent tautology.

(1b) (An infringement of the second maxim of Quantity: "Do not give more information than is required" on the assumption that the existence of such a maxim should be admitted.) A wants to know whether *p*; and B volunteers not only the information that *p*, but information to the effect that it is certain that *p*, and that the evidence for its being true that *p* is so-and-so and such-and-such.

B's volubility may be undesigned, and if it is so regarded by A, it may raise in A's mind a doubt whether B is as certain as he says he is ("Methinks the lady doth protest too much"). But if it is thought of as designed, it would be an oblique way of conveying that it is to some degree controversial whether or not *p*. It is however arguable that such an implicature could be explained by reference to the maxim of Relation without invoking an alleged second maxim of Quantity.

(2a) Examples in which the first maxim of Quality is flouted.

Irony. X, with whom till now A has been on close terms, has betrayed a secret of A's to a business rival. A and his audience both know this. A says "X is a fine friend." (*Gloss:* It is perfectly obvious to A and his audience that what A has said or has made as if to say is something which he does not believe, and the audience knows that A knows that this is obvious to the audience. So, unless A's utterance is entirely pointless, A must be trying to get across some proposition other than the one he purports to be putting forward. This must be some obviously related proposition; the most obviously related proposition is the contradictory of the one he purports to be putting forward.)

Metaphor. For example, "You are the cream in my coffee." Such examples characteristically involve categorical falsity, so the contradictory of what the speaker has made as if to say will, strictly speaking, be a truism; so it cannot be *that* that such a speaker is trying to get across. The most likely supposition is that the speaker is attributing to his audience some feature or features in respect of which the audience resembles (more or less fancifully) the mentioned substance.

It is possible to combine metaphor and irony by imposing on the hearer two stages of interpretation. I say "You are the cream in my coffee," intending the hearer to reach first the metaphor interpretant "You are my pride and joy," and then the irony interpretant "You are my bane."

Meiosis. Of a man to have broken up all the furniture, one says "He was a little intoxicated."

Hyperbole. "Every nice girl loves a sailor."

(2b) Examples in which the second maxim of Quality "Do not say that for which you lack adequate evidence" is flouted are perhaps not easy to find, but the following seems to be a specimen. I say of X's wife, "She is probably deceiving him this evening." In a suitable context, or with a suitable gesture or tone of voice, it may be clear that I have no adequate reason for supposing this to be so. My partner, to preserve the assumption that the conversational game is still being played, assumes that I am getting at some related proposition for the acceptance of which I *do* have a reasonable basis. The related proposition might well be that she is given to deceiving her husband, or possibly that she is the sort of person who wouldn't stop short of such conduct.

(3) Examples in which an implicature is achieved by real as distinct from apparent violation of the maxim of Relation are perhaps rare, but the following seems to be a good candidate. At a genteel tea party A says "Mrs. X is an old bag." There is a moment of appalled silence, then B says "The weather has been quite delightful this summer, hasn't it?" B has blatantly refused to make what *he* says relevant to A's preceding remark. He thereby implicates that A's remark should not be discussed, and perhaps more specifically, that A has committed a social gaffe.

(4) Examples in which various maxims falling under the supermaxim "Be perspicuous" are flouted.

(a) *Ambiguity.* We must remember that we are only concerned with ambiguity that is deliberate, and which the speaker intends or expects to be recognized by his hearer. The problem the hearer has to solve is why a speaker should, when still playing the conversational game, go out of his way to choose an ambiguous utterance. There are two types of case:

(i) Examples in which there is no difference, or no striking difference, between two interpretations of an utterance in respect of straightforwardness; neither interpretation is notably more sophisticated, less standard, more recondite or more farfetched than the other. We might consider Blake's lines: "Never seek to tell thy love, Love that never told can be." To avoid the complications introduced by the presence of the imperative mood, I shall consider the related sentence, "I sought to tell my love, love that never told can be." There may be a double ambiguity here. "My love" may refer to either a state of emotion or an object of emotion, and "Love that never told can be" may mean either "Love that cannot be told" or "Love that if told cannot continue to exist." Partly because of the sophistication of the poet and partly because of internal evidence (that the ambiguity is kept up), there seems to be no alternative to supposing that the ambiguities are deliberate and that the poet is conveying both what he would be saying if one interpretation were intended rather than the other, and vice versa; though no doubt the poet is not explicitly *saying* any of these things, but only conveying or suggesting them (cf. "Since she [nature] pricked thee out for women's pleasure, mine be thy love, and thy love's use their treasure.")

(ii) Examples in which one interpretation is notably less straightforward than another. Take the complex example of the British General who captured the town of Sind and sent back the message "Peccavi." The ambiguity involved ("I have Sind"—"I have sinned") is phonemic not morphemic; and the expression actually used is unambiguous; but since it is in a language foreign to speaker and hearer, translation is called for, and the ambiguity resides in the standard translation into native English.

Whether or not the straightforward interpretant ("I have sinned") is being conveyed, it seems that the nonstraightforward must be. There might be stylistic reasons for conveying by a sentence merely its nonstraightforward interpretant, but it would be pointless, and perhaps also stylistically objectionable, to go to the trouble of finding an expression which nonstraightforwardly conveys that p, thus imposing on an audience the effort involved in finding this interpretant, if this interpretant were otiose so far as communication was concerned. Whether the straightforward interpretant is also being conveyed seems to depend on whether such a supposition would conflict with other conversational requirements; for example, would it be relevant, would it be something that the speaker could be supposed to accept, and so on. If such requirements are not satisfied, then the straightforward interpretant is not being conveyed. If they are, it is. If the author of "Peccavi" could naturally be supposed to think that he had committed some kind of transgression, for example, had disobeyed his orders in capturing Sind, and if reference to such a transgression would be relevant to the presumed interests of the audience, then he would have been conveying both interpretations; otherwise he would be conveying only the one.

(b) *Obscurity.* How do I exploit, for the purposes of communication, a deliberate and overt violation of the requirement that I should avoid obscurity? Obviously, if the Cooperative Principle is to operate, I must intend my partner to understand what I am saying despite the obscurity which I import into my utterance. Suppose that A and B are having a conversation in the presence of a third party, for example, a child; then A might be deliberately obscure, though not too obscure, in the hope that B would understand and that the third party would not. Furthermore, if A expects B to see that A is being deliberately obscure, it seems reasonable to suppose that, in making his conversational contribution in this way, A is implicating that the contents of his communication should not be imparted to the third party.

(c) *Failure to be brief or succinct.* Compare the remarks

(1) "Miss X sang 'Home sweet home.' "
(2) "Miss X produced a series of sounds which corresponded closely with the score of 'Home sweet home.' "

Suppose that a reviewer has chosen to utter (2) rather than (1). (*Gloss:* Why has he selected that rigmarole in place of the concise and nearly synonymous "sang"? Presumably to indicate some striking difference between Miss X's performance and those to which the word "singing" is usually applied. The most obvious supposition is that Miss X's performance suffered from some hideous defect. The reviewer knows that this supposition is what is likely to spring to mind; so that is what he is implicating.)

I have so far considered only cases of what I might call particularized conversational implicature; that is to say, cases in which an implicature is carried by saying that *p* on a particular occasion, in virtue of special features of the context; cases in which there is no room for the idea that an implicature of this sort is *normally* carried by saying that *p*. But there are cases of generalized conversational implicature. Sometimes one can say that the use of a certain form of words in an utterance would normally (in the *absence* of special circumstances) carry such-and-such an implicature or type of implicature. Noncontroversial examples are perhaps hard to find, since it is all too easy to treat a generalized conversational implicature as if it were a conventional implicature. I offer an example which I hope may be fairly noncontroversial.

Anyone who uses a sentence of the form "X is meeting a woman this evening" would normally implicate that the person to be met was someone other than X's wife, mother, sister, or perhaps even close platonic friend. Similarly, if I were to say "X went into a house yesterday and found a tortoise inside the front door," my hearer would normally be surprised if some time later I revealed that the house was X's own. I could produce similar linguistic phenomena involving the expression "a garden", "a car", "a college", and so on. Sometimes, however, there would normally be no such implicature ("I have been sitting in a car all morning"), and sometimes a reverse implicature ("I broke a finger yesterday"). I am inclined to think that one would not lend a sympathetic ear to a philosopher who suggested that there are three senses of the form of expression "an X": one in which it means roughly "something which satisfies the conditions defining the word X"; another in which it means approximately "an X (in the first sense) which is only remotely related in a certain way to some person indicated by the context"; and yet another in which it means "an X (in the first sense) which is closely related in a certain way to some person indicated by the context." Would we not much prefer an account on the following lines (which of course may be incorrect in detail)? When someone by using the form of expression "an X" implicates that the X does not belong to or is not otherwise closely connected with some identifiable person, the implicature is present because the speaker has failed to be specific in a way in which he might have been expected to be specific, with the consequence that it is likely to be assumed that he is not in a position to be specific. This is a familiar implicature situation, and is classifiable as a failure, for one reason or another, to fulfill the first maxim of Quantity. The only difficult question is why it should, in certain cases, be presumed, independently of information about particular contexts of utterance, that specification of the closeness or remoteness of the connection between a particular person or object and a further person who is mentioned or indicated by the utterance should be likely to be of interest. The answer must lie in the following region: transactions between a person and other persons or things closely connected with him are liable to be very different as regards their concomitants and results from the same sort of transactions involving only remotely connected persons or things; the concomitants and results, for instance, of my finding a hole in *my* roof are likely to be very different from the concomitants and results of my finding a hole in someone else's roof. Information, like money, is often given without the giver knowing to just what use the recipient will want to put it. If someone to whom a transaction is mentioned gives it further consideration, he is likely to find himself wanting the answers to further questions which the speaker may not be able to identify in advance; if the appropriate specification will be likely to enable the hearer to answer a considerable variety of such questions for himself, then there is a presumption that the speaker should include it in his remark; if not, then there is no such presumption.

Finally, we can now show that, conversational implicature being what it is, it must possess certain features.

(1) Since to assume the presence of a conversational implicature we must assume that at least the Cooperative Principle is being observed, and since it is possible to opt out of the observation of this principle, it follows that a generalized conversational implicature can be canceled in a particular case. It may be explicitly canceled, by the addition of a clause which states or implies that the speaker has opted out, or it may be contextually canceled, if the form of utterance which usually carries it is used in a context which makes it clear that the speaker *is* opting out.

(2) In so far as the calculation that a particular conversational implicature is present requires, besides contextual and background information, only a knowledge of what has been said (or of the conventional commitment of the utterance), and in so far as the manner of expression plays no role in the calculation, it will not be possible to find another way of saying the same thing, which simply lacks the implicature in question, except where some special feature of the substituted version is itself relevant to the determination of an implicature (in virtue of one of the maxims of manner). If we call this feature "nondetachability," one may expect a generalized conversational implicature which is carried by a familiar, nonspecial locution to have a high degree of nondetachability.

(3) To speak approximately, since the calculation of the presence of a conversational implicature presupposes an initial knowledge of the conventional force of the expression the utterance of which carries the implicature, a conver-

sational implicatum will be a condition which is not included in the original specification of the expression's conventional force. Though it may not be impossible for what starts life, so to speak, as a conversational implicature to become conventionalized, to suppose that this is so in a given case would require special justification. So, initially at least, conversational implicata are not part of the meaning of the expressions to the employment of which they attach.

(4) Since the truth of a conversational implicatum is not required by the truth of what is said (what is said may be true, what is implicated may be false), the implicature is not carried by what is said, but only by the saying of what is said or by "putting it that way."

(5) Since to calculate a conversational implicature is to calculate what has to be supposed in order to preserve the supposition that the Cooperative Principle is being observed, and since there may be various possible specific explanations, a list of which may be open, the conversational implication in such cases will be a disjunction of such specific explanations; and if the list of these is open, the implicatum will have just the kind of indeterminacy which many actual implicata do in fact seem to possess.

Copyrights and Acknowledgments

The author wishes to thank the following publishers and copyright holders for permission to reprint material used in this book:

Baruch A. Brody for his article, "Abortion and the Sanctity of Human Life," reprinted from the *American Philosophical Quarterly*, Vol. 101, No. 2, April 1973.

Basil Blackwell, Publisher, for "Computing Machinery and Intelligence," by A. M. Turing, from *Mind* 59, 1950, and for "The Imitation Game," by Keith Gunderson, from *Mind* 73, 1964.

Dover Publications for the excerpt "On Floating Bodies," from *The Works of Archimedes*, T. L. Heath, ed. Dover Publications, 1953.

Farrar, Straus & Giroux, Inc., for an excerpt from *The Cancer Biopathy*, Volume II of *The Discovery of the Orgone*, by William Reich. Copyright © 1973 by Farrar, Straus & Giroux, Inc.

H. P. Grice and Dickinson Publishing Co., for the excerpt "Logic and Conversation," from his book, *The Logic of Grammar*. Copyright © 1975 by H. P. Grice. Reprinted by permission of the author and the publisher.

Harper & Row, Publishers, Inc., for an excerpt from *Language and Woman's Place*, by Robin Lakoff. Copyright © 1975 by Robin Lakoff. Reprinted by permission of the publisher.

King Features for the article "Protesters are 'Ugly, Stupid'," by Jeffrey Hart. Copyright © 1980 by King Features Syndicate, Inc.

Oxford University Press for the excerpt "Performative Utterances," from *Philosophical Papers*, by J. L. Austin. Copyright © 1961, 1970 Oxford University Press. Reprinted by permission of Oxford University Press.

Princeton University Press for "A Defense of Abortion," by Judith Jarvis Thomson. Copyright © 1971 by Princeton University Press. Reprinted by permission.

The Boston Globe for "A Record of Being Right," Oct. 4, 1979, by Ian Menzies. Reprinted courtesy of *The Boston Globe*.

The Skeptical Inquirer for "Critical Reading, Careful Writing, and the Bermuda Triangle," by Larry Kusche, and for " 'Cold Reading': How to Convince Strangers that you Know All About Them," by Ray Hyman.

University of California Press for an excerpt from *Dialogue Concerning the Two Chief World Systems, the Ptolemaic and Copernican*, by Galileo Galilei. Copyright © 1953, 1962 by the Regents of the University of California. Reprinted by permission of the University of California Press.

WGBH Educational Foundation for permission to reprint the transcript of "Incident at Brown's Ferry." Copyright WGBH Educational Foundation. All rights reserved.

INDEX

Abell, George O., 105*n*
abortion, 290–316
  disagreement concerning, 144–51
"Abortion and the Sanctity of Human Life"
  (Brody), 305–16
Adams, Laurie, 99–100
ad hominem argument, 96
ad hominem attack, 96–97
ad hominem fallacy, 96–97
advice, offering, 33–34
affirmative propositions, 192
"agonizer" standpoint, 76
"although," as discounting connective,
  47–48
ambiguity, 27, 87–89
  fallacies of, 7
analogy
  in legal reasoning, 266–68
  in moral reasoning, 290
Anderson, Alan Ross, 119*n*
Andrews (Justice), 274–77
apologies, 12, 13
appeals to authority, 97–102
Archimedes, 119, 317
  "On Floating Bodies," 318–23
argumentative performatives, 16–18, 50
argument form
  paradoxical, 174–75
  validity and, 157–59
arguments, 37–55, 123–25
  ad hominem, 96
  assuring in, 45–46
  basic structure of, 38–40
  close analysis of, *see* close analysis

discounting in, 47–48
excuses, 121
explanations, 116–20
granting a point for the sake of, 17–18
hedging in, 46–47
informal analysis of, 154
parentheticals in, 49–50
refutations of, 104–07
sophistical, 67–68
soundness of, 41–44
in standard form, 40
standpoints in, 74–76
substitutes for, 50–54
validity of, 40–44, 157–59, 163, 175–76
    See also formal analysis
Aristotle, 80
asking, 15
assuring, 45–46
  appeals to authority as, 97, 101
  in close analysis, 64
astrology, refutation of, 104–05
Austin, J. L., 9, 12, 16
  "Performative Utterances," 395–407
authoritative performatives, 14–16
authority, appeals to, 97–102

basic propositions, 188–202
  affirmative vs. negative, 192
  classification of, 191–98
  contradictory, 194–95
  contrary, 193–94
  existential import of, 189–91
  square of opposition of, 193, 198–202
  subalternation of, 197–98

subcontrary, 196
universal vs. particular, 192
Berenson, Bernard, 99–100
Berlitz, Charles, 339
biconditionals, 177–79
borderline cases, 80–87
  arguments from the heap and, 83–84
  drawing the line and, 85–87
  slippery slope arguments and, 84–85
  vagueness and, 80–82
Bohr, Niels, 323
Brody, Baruch A., "Abortion and the
  Sanctity of Human Life," 305–16
Brown, Henry Billings, 277–81
Brown v. *Board of Education,* 277, 285–88
Buoyancy, law of, 117–19, 317–23
"but," as discounting connective, 47

capital punishment, 139–44
Cardozo, Benjamin, 270–74
categorical propositions, 184–87
categorical syllogisms, 211–12
Carter, Billy, 90
Carter, Jimmy, 94–95
Catcher in the Rye, The (Salinger), 93–94
clarity, 27
  as context-dependent, 80, 81
clarity, fallacies of, 80–93
  ambiguity and, 87–89
  arguments from the heap, 83–84
  definitions and, 90–93
  drawing the line and, 85–87
  equivocation and, 90
  vagueness and, 80–82
"clever," negative connotations of, 52
close analysis, 57–73
  assuring in, 64
  conversational implication in, 64
  discounting in, 64–66
  hedging in, 64
  reasons in, 68, 70
  slanting in, 69–70
  sophistical argument in, 67–68
  warranting connective in, 63
" 'Cold Reading': How to Convince
  Strangers that You Know All About
  Them" (Hyman), 240–54
commands, 14–15
common law, 265–66
communication as function of language,
  7–9
complementary classes, 211
  obversion and, 205
"Computing Machinery and Intelligence"
  (Turing), 360–81
conceptual frameworks, disputes over, 323
conclusions, suppressed, 132–35
conditionals, 167–72
  biconditionals, 177–79
  in formal and everyday use, 174–79
  "only if," 176–78

Confessions (St. Augustine), 104
conjunction, 154–59
  in logical and everyday language, 173–74
  truth-table definition for, 157–59
connectives
  sentential, 154–59
  truth functional, 160–65
  warranting, 39–40
constitutionality, 277–78
context
  clarity as dependent on, 80, 81
  commitment to promises and, 10–11
  formal notion of conjunction and, 173
contract, breach of, 265, 267
contradiction, 175
contradictories, 194–96
  square of opposition and, 198–202
contraposition, 207–10
contraries, 193–94
conventions
  conversational implication of, 28–32
  grammatical, 6–7
  of language, 4–7
  levels of, 35–36
  linguistic, 36
  of performative utterances, 11–14
  semantics, 7
  speech act, 34–36
conversational implication, 28–36
  in close analysis, 64
  pragmatic conventions and, 34–36
  square of opposition and, 198–202
  violating conversational rules and, 31–35
conversations
  rules (conventions) of, 27–32
  things left unsaid in, 24–27
conversion, 202–04
  by limitation, 204
Cooperative Principle (CP), 25–26, 34
counter-examples, 107–12
"Critical Reading, Careful Writing, and the
  Bermuda Triangle" (Kusche), 354–58

damning with faint praise, 24, 32
death penalty, 139–44
"debaser" standpoint, 76
decision procedure, 172
"Defense of Abortion, A" (Thomson),
  291–304
definitions
  conventions of language and, 4–6
  disambiguating, 92
  fallacies of clarity and, 90–93
  hypothetical syllogism and, 171–72
  lexical or dictionary, 91
  persuasive, slanting and, 52–53
  precising, 91–92
  role of, 92–93
  self-sealing by, 115
  stipulative, 91
  theoretical, 92

descriptions as statements, 19
descriptive fallacy, 9
Dialogue Concerning the Two World Systems—Ptolemaic and Copernican (Galileo), 323–32
dictionary definitions, 91
Dirksen, Everett, 85
disambiguating, 88–89
disambiguating definitions, 92
discounting, 47–48
    in close analysis, 64–66
"disinterested party" standpoint, 75
disjunction, 159–60
    exclusive vs. inclusive, 166–67
distribution, evaluating syllogism and, 221–22
Dixon, Jeane, 339
domain of discourse (DD), 187–88, 205
drawing the line, fallacies of clarity and, 85–87
Duveen, Sir Joseph, 99

Einstein, Albert, 323
empty predictions, 113
enthymematic arguments, 125
equivocation, 90
ethics, counter-examples in, 111
ethnic and racial slurs, 51
examples as statements, 19
excuses, 121–22
existential import, 189–91, 198
    theory of the syllogism and, 216–19
expert, *see* appeals to authority
"expert" standpoint, 76
explanations, 116–20
    arguments used giving, 116–18
    narrative, 116
explicit performatives, 18–19
expositives, *see* argumentative performatives
expressive sentences, 8

facts, the law and, 266
fallacies
    of ambiguity, 7
    of clarity, *see* clarity, fallacies of
    descriptive, 9
    of irrelevance, *see* irrelevance, fallacies of
flaws, 12
formal analysis of argument, 152–224
    basic propositions, 188
    categorical propositions, 184–87
    conjunction, 154–59
    disjunction, 159–60
    domain of discourse, 187–88
    everyday language and, 173–79
    existential import, 189–91, 216–19
    negation, 160
    theory of immediate inference, 202–11
    theory of the syllogism, 211–12

valid and invalid syllogisms, 213
validity and, 154, 173–76
Venn diagrams for syllogisms, 213–15
fundamental issues
    abortion, 144–51
    arguments concerning, 138–51
    capital punishment, 139–44

Galileo Galilei, *Dialogue Concerning the Two World Systems—Ptolemaic and Copernican*, 323–32
Gardner, Martin, 339–40
Garrison, William Lloyd, 75
Geller, Uri, 98, 340
Golden Rule, 112
grammatical rules, 6–7
    See also syntactical conventions
Grice, Paul, 25–26, 28n, 31–32, 33–35, 175, 176
    "Logic and Conversation," 407–21
Gunderson, Keith, "The Imitation Game," 381–93

Hahn, Andree, 99
Harlan, John Marshall, 277, 281–85
Hart, Jeffrey, "Protesters are 'Ugly, Stupid'," 261–62
Hawkins v. *McGee*, 267–69
heap, argument from the, 83–84
hedging, 46–47
    in close analysis, 64
Herrick, Robert, "Upon Julia's Clothes," 7–8
hitches, 12
Honderich, Ted, 113n
Hyman, Ray, " 'Cold Reading': How to Convince Strangers that You Know All About Them," 340–54
hypotheticals, series of, 270
hypothetical syllogism, 171

ideologies, self-sealing, 114, 115
immediate inference, theory of, 202–11
    contraposition, 207–10
    conversion, 202–04
    obversion, 205–07
"Imitation Game, The" (Gunderson), 381–93
imperative sentences, 8
"Incident at Brown's Ferry" (*Nova*), 229–46
indicative conditionals, 167–72
indicative sentences, 8, 9
informal analysis of argument, 154
initial conditions in explanations, 116–17
interrogative sentences, 8
irony, 32
    in close analysis, 69
irrelevance, fallacies of, 93–102
    ad hominem, 96–97
    appeals to authority, 97–102

jokes, 32

Klem, Bill, 9–10
Kusche, Larry, "Critical Reading, Careful
    Writing, and the Bermuda Triangle,"
    254–58
Kyl, John, 58–72

Lakoff, Robin T., "Talking About Women,"
    248–61
language, 247
    communication as function of, 7–9
    conventions of, 4–7
    levels of, 35–36
    logical and everyday, 173–79
    performatives, 9–19
    speech acts, 7–9
    statements, 19–20
law of torts, 269–70
legal reasoning, 265–68
    analogy in, 266–68
Levy, Edward, 266
lexical definitions, 91
Liberator, The (newspaper), 75
linguistic acts, 36
linguistic conventions, 36
linguistic principles, arguments that
    depend on, 124
Lipson, Leon, 113*n*
logic
    modal, 175
    propositional, 184
"Logic and Conversation" (Grice), 407–21

McCormack, John, 59, 62
manner of conversation, rules concerning,
    27, 34
Marxist ideology, 114, 115
material conditionals, 169–70
material implication, 170
"mature person" standpoint, 76
Menzies, Ian, "A Record of Being Right,"
    262–64
modal logic, 175
modus ponens, 170
Mogenbesser Retort, 112
moral disagreement, 289–90
moral questions, fundamental
    disagreements on, 138–51
Morgenstern, Oskar, 101

narrative explanations, 116
negation, 160
negative connotations, slanting by use of,
    51–52
negative propositions, 192
negligence, legal concept of, 111
Noonan, James, 270*n*
Nova, "Incident at Brown's Ferry," 229–46
nuclear power plants, safety in, 228

obfuscation, 80
"Objective Demonstration of Orgone
    Radiation, The" (Reich), 332–37
obversion, 205–07
"official indignation" standpoint, 76
officials, performative utterances by, 12
"On Floating Bodies" (Archimedes),
    318–23
"only if," 176–78
"or"
    exclusive and inclusive senses of,
        166–67
    truth-table definitions for, 159
orgone theory, 332

Palsgraf v. *Long Island Railroad Co.*,
    270–72
paradoxical argument forms, 174–75
parentheses to distinguish groupings, 161
parentheticals in arguments, 49–50
particular propositions, 192
performatives, 9–19
    argumentative, 16–18, 50
    authoritative, 14–16
    conventions of, 11–14
    explicit, 18–19
    promises, 10–11, 13–14
    thereby test for, 11, 16, 18
    verdicts, 9–10
"Performative Utterances" (Austin),
    395–407
persuasive definitions, slanting and, 52–53
philosophical reasoning, 359–60
"plain man" standpoint, 76
Plato, 109
Plessy v. *Ferguson*, 227–85
poetry, 7–8
pragmatic acts, 34–35, 36
pragmatic conventions (or rules), 34–36
precising definitions, 91–92
predictions, empty or vacuous, 113
premises, 40
    suppressed, 124
    truth of, 41, 45
    promises, 10–11, 13–14
        conditional, 168
    propositional calculus, 154–65, 184
        conjunction, 154–59
        disjunction, 159–60
        negation, 160
    propositional logic, 160, 184
    propositions
        basic, *see* basic propositions
        categorical, 184–87
    "Protesters are 'Ugly, Stupid' " (Hart),
        261–62
    psychoanalytic theory, 114, 115

quality, evaluating syllogism and, 222–23
quantity, rule of, 26–27, 33, 175
    analysis of syllogisms and, 283–84

conversational implication of, 30–31
soundness of arguments and, 44

racial and ethnic slurs, 51
"radical" standpoint, 76
Randi, James, 340
"reasonable man" standpoint, 76
reasons
in arguments, 39
in close analysis, 68, 70
"Record of Being Right, A" (Menzies), 262–64
refutations, 104–15
of arguments, 104–07
with counter-examples, 107–12
of empty predictions, 113
of self-sealing, 113–15
of statements, 108
"that's just like arguing . . . " method of, 105–07
Reich, Wilhelm, "The Objective Demonstration of Orgone Radiation," 332–37
relevance, rule of, 27, 32, 34, 175
parenthetical expressions and, 49
See also irrelevance, fallacies of
Republic, The (Plato), 109
Ringrose, Hyacinthe, 99, 100
rock bottom disagreements, 138
See also fundamental issues
rules, see conventions

safety in nuclear power plants, 228
St. Augustine, 104, 105
Salinger, J. D., 93–94
Samuelson, Paul A., 74
scientific argument, 317
scientific explanation, 116–18
scientific interpretations, conflicting, 323–24
self-sealing positions, 105, 113–15
semantic conventions, 7
sentences, moods of, 8
sentential connectives, 154–59
"separate but equal" doctrine, 277–88
series of hypotheticals, 270
significance (import) of a remark, factors that affect, 24–25
"since" in arguments, 39
Skeptical Inquirer (journal), 340
slanting, 51–54
in close analysis, 69–70
persuasive definitions and, 52–53
slippery slope arguments, 84–85
Socrates, 109–10
sophistical argument, 67–68
soundness of arguments, 41–44
speech act conventions, 34–36
speech acts, 7–8, 36
standard goals achieved by, 35
variety of purposes of, 25

square of opposition, 193
pragmatics and, 198–202
subalternation and, 197–98
standard form in arguments, 40
standpoints, 74–76
statement form, 155–56
statements, 19–20
refutations of, 108
statement variables, 155–57
Stevenson, Charles L., 52
stipulative definitions, 91
strength, rule of, 26
subcontraries, 196–97
substitution instance of statement form, 155–56
suggestion, 15, 16
suppressed conclusions, 132–35
suppressed premises, 124–32
syllogisms
categorical, 211–12
everyday arguments and, 220–21
existential import and, 216–19
hypothetical, 171
system of rules for evaluating, 221–24
theory of the, 184, 211–221
valid and invalid, 213
Venn diagrams for, 213–15
syntactical conventions, 7

"Talking About Women" (Lakoff), 248–61
tautologies, 175
Theaetetus (Plato), 110
theoretical definitions, 92
thereby test, 12, 16, 18
"therefore" in arguments, 38–39
Thomson, Judith Jarvis, "A Defense of Abortion," 291–304
"too," negative connotations of, 52
torts, law of, 269–70
truth
of premises, 41, 45
validity of arguments distinguished from, 41
truth functional connectives, 160–65
See also conjunction; disjunction; negation
truth functional equivalence, 167
truth-table
for indicative conditionals, 168–69
for material conditionals, 169
for truth functional connectives, 163–65
for "v," 160
truth-table analysis (or definition)
of inconclusive vs. exclusive disjunction, 166–67
for, conjunction 157–59
for disjunction, 159
for negation, 160
Turing, A. M., "Computing Machinery and Intelligence," 360–81

unclarity, *see* clarity, fallacies of
universal propositions, 192
"uplifter" standpoint, 76
"Upon Julia's Clothes" (Herrick), 7–8
Urmson, J. O., 49
utilitarian principles, 111–12

"v," truth-table for, 160
vacuity, 113
vagueness, 80–82
  in legal disputes, 266
validity
  of arguments, 40–44, 175–76
  argument form and, 157–59, 163
  formal analysis of arguments and, 154,
    173–76

of syllogisms, 213
  theory of the syllogism and, 220–21
  truth functional equivalence and, 167
variables, statement, 155–57
Venn diagrams, 185, 213–15
verdicts, 9–10
"voice in the wilderness" standpoint, 76
von Daniken, Eric, 339

warranting connectives, 39–40
  in close analysis, 63
Warren, Earl, 277, 285–88
world views, self-sealing, 114, 115
"world-weary cynic" standpoint, 76

B
C 3
D 4
E 5
F 6
G 7
H 8
I 9
J 0